# MAVERICK PUBLISHER:

## J. PATRICK O'CALLAGHAN

### A Life in Newspapers

# MAVERICK PUBLISHER:

# J. PATRICK O'CALLAGHAN

## A Life in Newspapers

Edited by Ed Piwowarczyk

Published with the consent
and collaboration of
E. Joan O'Callaghan

# Maverick Publisher:
# J. Patrick O'Callaghan
## A Life in Newspapers
## 1925 – 1996


Print Edition ISBN: 978-1-77242-029-6
Kindle Edition ISBN: 978-1-77242-027-2
Smashwords ISBN: 978-1-77242-028-9
Editor: Ed Piwowarczyk
Cover Photo: Edmonton Journal
Cover Design: Sara Carrick

Carrick Publishing 2015
Published with the consent and collaboration
of E. Joan O'Callaghan
The original manuscript derives from the
University of Alberta Archives Accession # 2012-20

Patrick O'Callaghan was among the best-loved Canadian newspapermen of his generation. He was famous for being fearless and fiercely independent. As publisher of some of Canada's leading newspapers, he ran them as if he owned them himself. He fought relentlessly for free speech and freedom of the press. He loathed bullies and pretension. Best of all, he believed that newspapers had a vital role to play in Canada's democracy. In his nearly half a century in journalism, he saw enormous changes in the business, but his principles never changed. They still inspire journalists today. This richly anecdotal memoir of his long career, and of the era, is like the man himself — opinionated, bracing and refreshingly frank.

*— Margaret Wente, columnist, The Globe and Mail*

Working for him as I did at the *Windsor Star* and the *Calgary Herald*, I was well aware that Pat O'Callaghan was a brilliant writer. He had an eye and an ear for a great story, and a witty and engaging way of telling it. His impassioned columns were frequently the talk of the newsroom — and far beyond it. So I'm not in the least surprised that his account of his newspaper career, which started in England and culminated at the helm of the *Calgary Herald*, is a terrific read. He brings his cast of characters — Pierre Elliot Trudeau, Peter Lougheed, Brian Mulroney, Ted Byfield, Doug Creighton and Peter Worthington, to name just a few — to life with a few choice words, not always flattering, but colourful and right on the mark. He gives a media insider's view of Canadian history in the 1970s and 1980s — Alberta's battles with Ottawa over oil pricing, the patriation of the Constitution, the turmoil within the newspaper industry — and makes it a page-turner.

*— Rosemary McCracken, freelance journalist and author of the Pat Tierney mystery series.*

# Dedication:

In loving memory of Pat O'Callaghan, newspaper publisher, husband, best friend.

Tread softly because you tread on my dreams.
~ *W. B. Yeats*

# FOREWORD

## By Catherine Ford

*Each of us … constructs and lives a "narrative" and is defined by this narrative.*

— Oliver Sacks, *On the Move: A Life*

What follows in this book is the narrative as constructed and lived by J. Patrick O'Callaghan, newspaperman.

Not for him the fancy word *journalist* so many of us used and are still using. It was, I suppose for women like myself, an attempt to get away from words that ended in "man" but what, then, would one make of the men who use this $10 word?

I suspect when the men and women of the newspaper world were able to attach more than "high-school graduate" or "school of hard knocks" after their names, when the days did not end with a lingering visit to the beer parlour but to the gym, and when women became a common fixture in newsrooms, then *journalism* and *journalist* replaced *news* and *reporter.* (It also helped that the business attained a certain respectability, salaries and benefits attracted college and university graduates, and a decent living and a career were promised, although nobody went into newspaper work to get rich.)

Some of us mourn the loss of straight talk, but those who lived through such changes accepted them reluctantly but thoroughly.

Pat O'Callaghan accepted little at face value. In him burned the heart and soul of an Irishman who was always up for a fight, whether it be with a premier, a prime minister or his God.

And, even more importantly, he was one of the last publishers of major newspapers to have risen to the top job from the newsroom without the aid of family ownership, connections or money. It was my great good fortune to have worked for two such publishers at the *Calgary Herald*, O'Callaghan and his successor, also a veteran of the newsroom, Kevin Peterson.

They both made their staff feel as if it was the journalism that was important, it was the stories told and the debates launched that made the newspaper business worthwhile and made it important to its community. They believed when one went home at the end of the day, the community should be a better place. While those words are Kevin Peterson's, the sentiments are Pat O'Callaghan's, albeit Pat believed his newspaper should be willing to fight in print for what was right and what the proper course of action for any business was. In particular, Pat believed any newspaper he ran had a responsibility to keep an eye and a sharp pencil pointed at municipal, provincial and federal governments, and all of their politics and policies. He never shied from a fight.

Of course, as publishers, both men had to contend with all the employees at the *Calgary Herald* — about 1,200 of them at the peak of its prosperity — from the pressroom and the back shop to the cafeteria and the staff nurse. And both of them had to worry about advertising sales, circulation and all the other responsibilities that come with the top job. But worries notwithstanding, there was always time to walk through the newsroom and talk to their employees. They were generous with their time, their friendship and opportunities. Today, no one would have paid for me to travel to Moscow or to China; no one would approve the nearly unlimited expense account; and it is equally certain that no modern publisher would ever stand up to a valuable advertising client who threatened to pull his accounts unless That Woman was reined in. That was Pat O'Callaghan who, when I wrote a column that offended a large advertiser, said simply: "They need us more than we need them."

The advertiser did pull his ads from the paper — for a week.

Those were heady and exciting days to work for a profitable and thriving newspaper. It was, in a word, fun. We all felt we were doing worthwhile work, making a difference. Few newspapers have that soul left intact. Most today are pale remnants of a once-thriving business that used to be considered a necessary part of daily life. I probably belong to the last generation who regularly subscribes to a daily paper. (We get three in our house, given that I am married to a newspaper junkie.)

The demise of the newspaper business had been a growing chorus in my ears for as long as I worked. Until now, I never thought such would happen. Some will survive, I'd like to think, although increasingly newspapers are becoming victims of a digital age when one can choose what news to read. It has always been my contention that the physical act of holding, folding and browsing through a newspaper delivers the small surprises that liven your day — the small fillers and bits that catch one's eye and you read something you would never otherwise read, just because you fancy it. The digital business does not deliver those surprises. It delivers reams of information, yes, but only in those links one chooses to follow. I believe we are a more ignorant world for it.

There is some hope, though. As Margaret Sullivan, the public editor of the *New York Times*, wrote in a column: "The money spent on journalism … is worth it." She quotes the newspaper's publisher, Arthur Sulzberger, Jr.: "The most precious thing we have is the quality of the news report and the range of opinion." Pat O'Callaghan would have agreed whole-heartedly.

It was Pat O'Callaghan who offered me a position as head of the editorial board at the *Herald*, with the bland and inaccurate title of "associate editor." As there was, at the time, no editor-in-chief of the paper, it was an amusing oxymoron. Anyone who knew O'Callaghan would attest to the fact that he did not want anyone between him and his editorial staff. He reported with some glee to Southam's head office that putting the opinionated Ms. Ford in charge of the *Herald*'s editorials and its editorial board was akin to putting the fox in charge of the henhouse.

Much of Pat's persona was rooted in words, in the beauty of language and its powerful force when unleashed. He embodied Czech writer Milan Kundera's belief: "Everyone is pained by the thought of disappearing, unheard and unseen, into an indifferent universe, and because of that, everyone wants, while there is still time, to turn himself into a universe of words."

Words soared in Pat's universe and when written, were always in peacock-blue ink in his fountain pen, a reminder that style does not always mean most modern. We cherished those personal notes.

Pat was a courtly man, given to singing Irish songs at the drop of a hat (and at the drop of strong liquor) and he was impish, an unusual word for a man who topped six feet.

When I married the first time and returned to work after the honeymoon, he left a tearsheet of the editorial page on my desk with the notation: "You forgot to change this; I did it for you." He had asked the back shop to change my last name on the masthead and print a single sheet as a joke. He well knew that I would never change my last name and he roared with laughter when I blanched at the change.

Pat "inherited" me; I was already working as an editorial writer when he arrived to replace the retiring publisher, Frank Swanson. We weren't strangers. While he was at the *Red Deer Advocate*, he and his family belonged to the same parish as my parents. He had once, in the middle 1960s, offered me the job of women's editor at the *Advocate*. I politely declined, not really wanting to try to forge a career in the same small city in which my parents and younger sister and brother lived

On his first day at the *Herald*, we met by accident outside the elevators. I was unsure, seeing that he would be the new publisher, whether I should call him by his first name or Mr. O'Callaghan. He looked at me as if I had suddenly become deranged. And he allowed that "Pat" was what everyone called him, from the janitor to the prime minister.

Make that almost everyone. In 1996, when Ted Byfield wrote an obituary for Pat in the *Globe and Mail*, I was horrified. Byfield, his old nemesis, referred to him throughout as Paddy, a derogatory term that no one at the *Globe* caught, changed or understood. It is the equivalent of the N-word. I believe Byfield — another newspaperman who took a different faith-based path through a writing career — enjoyed that immensely. He didn't often get the last word. This was, I suspect, the sole occasion between Byfield and O'Callaghan when the former got the final say.

One may not defame the dead, but we living Irish left behind were scalded at the insult. (As far as Pat was concerned, I was almost as Irish as he, my County Mayo-born mother having married a Canadian serviceman in London during the war, and I was "excused" for having the temerity to be born on British soil.)

If there is, indeed, a vengeful God, so channelled by the fire-and-brimstone types, a particular punishment awaits Ted Byfield. So much for the much vaunted acts of Christian charity and good works that a man such as Byfield is presumed to follow because of his evangelical beliefs. Were Byfield a Catholic, I'd remind him of the fate of sinners and the fires of purgatory, but as he is not, I'd remind him of Dante's fifth circle of hell, designed for the vengeful and the sullen.

Once, being the moderator of a debate between O'Callaghan and Byfield, I had the distinct pleasure of being able to say that I was the least opinionated person on stage. Both had the courtesy to laugh. It was true.

I'm not sure how well Pat understood in what regard his employees, not only in the newsroom, but also throughout the plant, held him. (Newspapers are essentially factories churning out a daily product.) He knew everyone's name, and he treated everyone with grace and courtesy.

The only time I ever heard him swear in my presence was on his last day at the *Herald.* He wanted no fuss made, no speeches, no ceremony. He did allow that at his last editorial board meeting, a bottle of Scotch could be produced for a ceremonial tot. Those of us around the table said goodbye and good luck, offered him a *slainte* (the Irish version of cheers) and downed our glasses.

What Pat did not know is that while we were purposefully lingering, the entire staff of the *Herald* was gathering in the foyer of the building, which is dominated by a circular staircase. It took a bit of fumbling around (Pat was the kind of man who would always let a woman go first) but I managed to get him to the first step down, alone on the staircase, when the applause from below broke out. Wave after wave. Thunderously. He turned and looked at me and uttered "bitch" under his breath. It didn't matter; no one at the *Herald* believed he should leave silently or quietly. We would not let him.

As his parting words to his recollections of a life in newspapers, Pat quotes the epitaph on William Butler Yeats' gravestone — the final lines of Yeats' poem, *Under Ben Bulben*. It is thus fitting to remember there is an entire poem that precedes those lines. Part of that poem is appropriate to remember Pat by:

*Many times man lives and dies*
*Between his two eternities,*
*That of race and that of soul,*
*And ancient Ireland knew it all.*
*Whether man die in his bed*
*Or the rifle knocks him dead,*
*A brief parting from those dear*
*Is the worst man has to fear.*

Calgary, Alta.
August 2015

*Catherine Ford is a former Calgary Herald columnist and associate editor.*

# INTRODUCTION

The family is now gone from the front offices, the company disbanded and its properties snapped up by other media enterprises, but the impact of the Southams on more than a century of Canadian newspaper ownership cannot be ignored.

To put that impact in the context of the times, Southam Inc. needs to be judged against its contemporaries and former rivals.

News that the family had finally relinquished control of the company was an occasion for reminiscence as well as melancholy, according to Pierre Berton. In a column in the *Toronto Star* on Feb. 22, 1992, Berton wrote: "The five legendary sons of William Southam Sr.[1] were without doubt the most colourful and eccentric publishers in what was once a colourful and eccentric profession. They just don't make them like that anymore."

One look at William Ardell, the choice of the board as the first non-family president and chief executive of the company, would confirm Berton's judgment. Ardell had no background in newspapers. He came to Southam in 1982 after a career in sporting goods and commercial printing. He earned the employee designation of "hatchet man" during the eight years he ran Coles bookstores for Southam. Asked to take over Southam Business Communications less than a year before being elevated to the company presidency, Ardell slashed more than 400 jobs from Southam's worst-performing division.

Dark-haired, handsome, well-groomed, voluble and hard-driving, Ardell, then aged 47, told the *Globe and Mail* soon after his appointment as Southam president: "I hate like hell being anything less than No. 1."

Ardell had a commerce degree from Concordia University in Montreal. The Fisher brothers — Gordon and John — who preceded him as presidents of Southam, held engineering degrees, and neither one of them had worked on a newspaper. But the Fishers had one built-in advantage over Ardell — they were Southams, great-grandsons of the founder, and steeped in family tradition.

When John Fisher, nearing his 65th birthday, finally tired of the boardroom infighting and stepped aside before the 1992 annual meeting, Ardell was cast in the role of the hired gun called in to restore law and order; the era of the "colourful and eccentric publishers" with Southam blood in their veins was already well past. The last publisher from the family to head the company was St. Clair Balfour, who apprenticed for the top job at the *Hamilton Spectator* before going to head office to work under Philip Fisher, the father of Gordon and John. Philip was not a Southam — but he was married to one. No one, not even Berton, would dare to call Balfour either eccentric or colourful. He was the latter-day patriarch, the man who kept the family flame alive, but in a more sedate Establishment way than the earlier generation, the sons of William Southam.

The last Southam actually to run a newspaper was Jim Thomson, himself a bit of a character, but far removed from the likes of Berton's "five legendary sons of William Southam." Thomson retired from the publisher's chair at the *Windsor Star* at the end of 1993.

As the newspaper business in general faces its own death-defying leap into the bottomless pit relentlessly being dug for it by the electronic media and the illiterate morons that television spawns, those who run newspapers are certainly different from earlier generations. Southam proved to be no exception.

The days of "apprenticing" for publishers' jobs through journalistic experience are gone. The occasional journalist will still make it to the top rank, but given the boardroom urge for a healthy bottom line rather than reporting and writing perfection, the brilliant journalist will have to fight his or her way past accountants, consultants and Harvard-educated, pinstriped yuppies more comfortable with survey-driven methodology than gut-instinct excellence in professional journalism.

Today's news industry is full of cardboard and sawdust characters. The vitality has gone out of it. Imperfection is a blemish that makes us all human, but the newspaper industry, in the most agonizing period of its existence, has chosen to replace visionary flashes of intuition and imagination with bafflegab that is bland and often boring.

Leadership seminars and "core purpose" meetings that have all the earnest appeal of fundamentalist missionary revivals are all the rage. Today's newspaper executives are great on conceptual thinking but totally lacking in imaginative perception or execution. Individualism is frowned on as a form of deviant behaviour.

In this pseudo-intellectual pursuit of cliché management, the smell of decay lingers where once the acrid scent of gunpowder alerted the nostrils to the quivering appeal of journalistic danger and excitement. A newspaper plant today might just as well be another factory run by Ford offering the reader any colour he wants, just so long as it is black. Berton's nostalgia for colour and eccentricity are gone for good, it seems.

The financial analysts loved Ardell when he said: "In the past, our tradition of editorial autonomy has been misinterpreted as local operational autonomy and has been taken to an extreme by our publishers."

I, for one, plead guilty to that, as charged. I published three dailies for Southam over 17 years, and I was often accused of running the *Windsor Star*, the *Edmonton Journal* and the *Calgary Herald* as if they were my own papers.

Nevertheless, today's newspaper, for all its faults, remains an important medium of record, a gatherer and summarizer of news, still capable on its best days of giving responsible guidance and leadership to those who trust it. However, it is also a commercial enterprise, and to that end it must make money to satisfy its owners and to survive.

When the ancient British humour magazine *Punch* was at death's door in the spring of 1992, Ian Hislop, the editor of *Private Eye*, commented: "It had to die; it was diagnosed as terminally unfunny years ago."

Whatever ails the modern newspaper, it is too early to claim the diagnosis is terminal. But newspapers are certainly in need of some form of resuscitation.

When David Jolley was publisher of the *Toronto Star*, he warned the 1992 annual meeting of the *Star* that it would take years for Canada's largest-circulation daily to recover from the deep wounds of a three-year recession. Ardell, speaking on behalf of Southam, agreed: "I don't see anything that's just going to rocket us right back to where we were in the 1980s, if ever."

Pessimism abounded in the newspaper industry that year. George Bain, a respected journalist of the old school, wrote in a Media Watch column in *Maclean*'s magazine that "the trend line of the competition between print and television is relentlessly downhill."

And right on Bain's heels came Tony Westell, former dean of the school of journalism at Carleton University. "We've seen every newspaper tightening and trimming and cutting back," he told the *Globe and Mail*'s Harvey Enchin. "The question is to what extent it is a product of the recession and to what extent it is a permanent decline in the newspaper business."

Enchin himself insisted that newspaper companies would never again see the profits they had enjoyed in the past.

But Conrad Black was not paying much attention to all these pallbearers for the newspaper industry. In November 1992, Black's Hollinger Inc. paid $259 million for Torstar's 22.6 per cent stake in Southam.

Southam, with the family influence shredded by five years of downturn, did not exactly demonstrate uncontrollable joy over the prospect of Black and Hollinger bringing their money-making enterprise into the Southam boardroom. There was even less enthusiasm when Paul Desmarais matched Black dollar for dollar from Power Corporation of Canada's treasure chest.

Southam chairman Ron Cliff hired Bay Street brokers to try to find a white knight to save the company, but there was no one out there willing to mount a steed and gallop to the rescue. Black and Desmarais more or less appointed themselves co-chairmen.

The decline of Southam Inc. and the snuffing out of the family connection after more than a century demonstrated that 1992 was a year in which reality overtook a lot of newspaper companies. Not least among them was the *Toronto Sun* chain and its sensational rift with its gregarious founding father, Doug Creighton.

The end for Creighton came without any public warning, just a few days before Black's successful raid on Southam. After more than 21 years of tweaking the nose of the Establishment, Creighton suffered a totally unexpected brush with journalistic mortality. After a furious three-hour meeting with the *Toronto Sun* board executive, headed by Maclean Hunter Limited's president and CEO, Ron Osborne, Creighton cleaned out his own desk and took off for the golf courses of Florida.

Adored and fawned over by his employees, Creighton had irritated and frustrated Maclean Hunter, which held more than 60 per cent of *Sun* shares. His joyful extravagances and his unabashed zest for high living at a time when the whole newspaper industry was battening down the hatches apparently did him in. Osborne described Creighton as "the heart and soul and the ethic" of the *Sun*, but that did not make Creighton any less expendable.

The irony of all that was that while Osborne and Maclean Hunter won the pitched battle with Creighton, two years later Maclean Hunter — *Sun* and all — lost a blitzkrieg to Rogers Communications, which never seemed to know what to do with the *Sun*.

Clearly the old order was changing, but nobody appeared willing to clarify where the newspaper business should be going.

In a sad sense, I was happy to be out of it, although I never regretted a second of the close to half a century that I played the newspaper game. I spent 22 years with Southam. It was, to some extent, almost a love-hate relationship, and what follows in later chapters in an insider's view of my upstart tenure with Southam, rather than a post-mortem on its exhumed body. Beyond Southam, it is an account of the rare ould times, in what may have been the heyday of the newspaper as a public institution. As a newspaperman, I watched Canadian history in the making, and it was always a stimulating experience.

Perhaps William Butler Yeats, the Irish poet and patriot, provides the most fitting epitaph for a newspaperman of my generation: "When all the story's finished, what's the news? In luck or out, the toll has left its mark — the day's vanity, the night's remorse."

The vanity I freely acknowledge, but there is little remorse.

# CHAPTER 1

Early Canadian papers were usually written by and for the elite. Government advertising and printing contracts were often life and death to newspapers. When the *Hamilton Spectator* was founded in 1846, it was a Tory supporter. For that reason, it had hit the skids when Sir John A. Macdonald's Conservatives were swept out of office.

With the Liberals in power in 1877, the *Spectator* was fading fast when William Southam, plant superintendent at the *London* (Ontario) *Free Press*, and his partner, William Carey, came to the rescue, $4,000 in hand. Up to then, payrolls were often missed, and staff traded advertising space for shoes and clothing. One employee, according to a company publication, *A Century of Southam*, even made a deal with an undertaker to bury his father in exchange for advertising space in the *Spectator*.

William Southam did more than just bide his time and wait for a change of government. He began printing lists of Grits allegedly tainted by political corruption. On election night, Sept. 17, 1878, the *Spectator* stayed open late to post bulletins for the crowds in the street. Macdonald's Conservatives, as well as winning both seats in Hamilton, were returned to power federally and Southam's Tory investment began to pay off.

Ironically, it was a Tory defeat in 1896 that led to Southam's purchase of the *Ottawa Citizen*. Dismayed that it would lose government revenues because it had backed the wrong party, the *Citizen* looked around for a buyer. William Southam, who had already added commercial printing operations in Toronto and Montreal to his ownership of the

*Spectator*, entered the newspaper field in the nation's capital in 1897.

William's sons, Wilson and Harry, took over the *Citizen* and also began to show the eccentric streak that has marked the family. They became Christian Scientists. They gave up alcohol. They angered other members of the family by running editorials critical of some buyers of Southam printing. In 1912, their father grew so outraged by what he regarded as their editorial trespasses and excesses that he cancelled his own home subscription. (In more recent times, Hamilton Southam did the same thing when he was at odds with the direction the *Citizen* was taking under publisher William Newbigging.)

The Southam tradition of editorial autonomy was forged by Wilson and Harry Southam, so there never was an official Southam editorial position on any issue during my tenure.

The *Citizen* campaigned for public ownership of the Ottawa Electric Railway, although Harry's father-in-law, Thomas Ahearn, was the founder. Harry's brother-in-law, Frank Ahearn, owner of the old Ottawa Senators hockey team, once sued the *Citizen* for libel — and won. Then he ran for office as a Liberal, and to show there were no hard feelings, the *Citizen* endorsed him editorially.

On Sept. 10, 1935, Harry and Wilson, along with their editor, Charles Bowman, had lunch with William Aberhart, the new premier of Alberta. The next day, Harry wrote to his sister, Ethel (mother of St. Clair Balfour): "I have a feeling that the economic salvation of the world is going to be staged in Alberta and I feel that a large number of Social Credit candidates from the West will be elected to Parliament next month. Events are in the saddle."

Putting the spurs to that Social Credit steed, the Southam brothers were still running enthusiastic editorials praising the new movement in 1936, while another Southam newspaper, the *Edmonton Journal*, was winning a special Pulitzer Prize citation for leading the fight against Aberhart's infamous press-gag bill[2]. No one has ever been able to accuse Southam newspapers of speaking with one voice on anything!

Canada's early newspapers were hardly incipient gold mines. The *Province* was founded in Victoria, B.C., in 1894 and by 1909, after its move to Vancouver on the mainland, it became one of only three or four papers in all of Canada with earnings in excess of $100,000. It was vision, more than dollars, that sparked the early newspaper founders, especially in the West.

The population of Calgary in 1883 was about 200 white settlers and 400 Sarcee. The first edition of the *Calgary Herald Mining and Ranche Advocate and Advertiser* rolled off a tiny Washington press, in a tent serving as a modest print shop on the banks of the Elbow River, in 1883. That press had been carried from Upper Canada on the first CPR train to visit that little huddle of tents and wooden buildings that dared to call itself a settlement. It didn't quite make it intact: the CPR dropped it while unloading it.

In their first edition, the founders, Andrew W. Armour and Thomas B. Braden, announced: "Having always the courage of its convictions, the *Herald* will not be found afraid to speak out its mind freely when there are wrongs to be addressed or manifest abuses to be remedied. We are content, in representing our commitments to the inhabitants of Calgary and vicinity in particular and the whole North West generally, to leave the result of that enterprise in their hands."

In their first editorial, Armour and Braden said: "The *Herald* will always lend its influence against the introduction of intoxicating liquors as a beverage in the NWT, believing that liquor traffic engenders vice, immorality and crime."

That was not the last *Herald* editorial to fall on deaf ears. Many of mine suffered the same fate in the seven years I was its publisher.

The editor of the earliest *Herald* was Hugh St. Quentin Cayley, a lawyer. In 1885, Cayley bought out Braden and Armour and made the *Herald* into a daily for a while. Armour moved to Medicine Hat to edit the *Medicine Hat News*, which was produced from one end of a disused boxcar donated by the CPR. Braden resurfaced in Calgary to start the *Tribune*, which the *Herald* immediately denounced as "a venal sheet ... run by a shameless libeller." The *Tribune* closed almost as soon as it opened.

Cayley was an extravagantly vivid writer. He once described a rival editor as a "childish egotist ... a vampire ... and a Lilliput (sic) from nowhere." By early 1886, his expressive extravagance had him in jail for contempt. That did nothing to hinder Cayley's career. After selling the *Herald* to two Winnipeg proprietors, who pursued a staunchly Tory line, he went on to Vancouver and eventually became a judge.

It was not uncommon for pioneer newspapermen to switch from publishing into active politics. Two who did so — William Alexander Smith and John Robson — became premiers of British Columbia.

Smith took part in the California Gold Rush and he prospected for a while along the Fraser River on the B.C. mainland. Smith always said he started the *British Colonist* in Victoria for amusement during the winter months, but he had clearly defined goals and he achieved the major ones: He saw the colonies of Vancouver Island and British Columbia united and later become part of Canada. Somewhere along the way to becoming premier, he changed his name to Amor De

Cosmos — Lover of the Universe. He died a madman, mocked and ridiculed.

John Robson founded the *New Westminster Times*. It became the *British Columbian* and finally the *Columbian*. Maintaining the political alignment, the next owner of the *Columbian* was James David Taylor, an MP who later became a senator. The paper remained in the Taylor family until Rick Taylor, the last of the line, folded it in 1988 on behalf of himself and his aunts. The unions, with exorbitant wage claims based on *Pacific Press* rates and working conditions, did him in.

Strong ties between newspapers and politics persisted long beyond the turn of the century. As late as the 1930s, Bert Wemp doubled as mayor of Toronto and city editor of the *Telegram*, without any personal sense of possible conflict of interest. By then, it had become a Toronto tradition. James Beaty, who owned the *Toronto Leader* and also the *Patriot and Colonist* at times, was also a director of the Grand Trunk Railroad and used the *Leader* shamelessly to further his railway schemes. Meanwhile, in Montreal, Hugh Graham, the future Lord Atholstan, capitalized on his ownership of the *Montreal Star* in the early 1920s to pursue his own railroad interests.

The *Toronto Daily Star* began as the *Evening Star* in 1892. It was the strike sheet of printers locked out of the *Toronto Daily News*. Its founder, E.E. Sheppard from the *News*, was soon eclipsed by Joseph E. (Holy Joe) Atkinson, who took over the paper in 1899. Holy Joe was a prohibitionist, a pacifist and a Liberal. Those who came after him, especially his son-in-law, Harry C. Hindmarsh, and Beland Honderich, carried on that deep Liberal tradition. The *Telegram*, which for the most part was run by somewhat more colourful characters such as John R. (Black Jack) Robertson and John Bassett, used to refer to the *Star* as the *Red Star* or the *Toronto Daily Pravda.*

Another newspaper with a long history of political connections is the *Winnipeg Free Press.* The man who wielded much of that early clout on behalf of the Liberals was John Dafoe, the long-time editor. But it was the Sifton family who directed the newspaper's fortunes. The paper became the *Manitoba Free Press* for a time after its purchase in 1898 by the Hon. J.W. Sifton. In turn, he passed it on to his son, Sir Clifford Sifton, who became equally famous as a federal Liberal cabinet minister whose immigration policies did much to open up the West by encouraging thousands of Ukrainians to settle the Prairies. That Ukrainian connection was one of the major factors in the ultimate success of the *Winnipeg Free Press* in its long circulation and advertising war with Southam's *Winnipeg Tribune.*

After an acrimonious family split, Clifford Sifton's branch acquired the *Star-Phoenix* (starting in the 1980s, spelled as *StarPhoenix*) in Saskatoon and the *Leader-Post* in Regina while the Winnipeg Siftons clung to the *Free Press.* The *Free Press* remained in Sifton hands until the merger with Calgary millionaire Max Bell and the founding of the FP Publications group. When, in turn, FP collapsed, the *Free Press* became one of Thomson's major revenue producers, second only to the *Globe and Mail.* When Thomson started to back away from newspaper ownership in the middle 1990s in its desire to become the world's biggest information company, the *Free Press* was saved the ignominy of being listed along with the 14 Canadian dailies offered for sale in 1995.

Meanwhile, the Saskatchewan Siftons branched out into more than newspapers. It was Michael Sifton's love of flying that led the company, through Armadale, its Ontario-based holding company, to acquire Buttonville Airport, the second-busiest airport in Ontario. Michael Sifton's other love was polo, and this was underscored by his ownership of Canada's only indoor polo arena. Michael Sifton died in the spring of 1995.

Southam, bitter rival of Sifton in Winnipeg after its purchase of the *Winnipeg Tribune* in 1920, was already well on its way by then to becoming a major national chain despite its never-ending problems with the *Tribune*. After its purchase of the *Hamilton Spectator* and the *Ottawa Citizen*, Southam acquired the *Calgary Herald* (1908) and the *Edmonton Journal* (1912) before moving into Winnipeg. Then, in 1923, Southam bought the *Province*. After that, it added, at various times, the *Medicine Hat News*, the *Montreal Gazette*, the *Windsor Star*, the *Kitchener-Waterloo Record*, the *Owen Sound Sun-Times*, the *Brantford Expositor*, the *Kamloops Daily News*, the *Prince George Citizen*, the *Sault Star*, the *North Bay Nugget* and *the Kingston Whig-Standard*. (Ironically, its purchase of the Kingston paper made Michael Davies a larger shareholder in the Southam company than any member of the Southam family, but it did nothing to further his feverish ambitions to be elected a Southam director.)

Southam folded the *Tribune* in 1980. It also had owned 49 per cent of the *Brandon Sun*, but sold its interest back to Lewis Whitehead, owner of the other 51 per cent. Whitehead moved swiftly to sell the paper to Thomson, then in its acquisitive mood. After Thomson acquired the remnants of the FP group and killed the *Ottawa Journal* on the day the *Tribune* died, it sold FP's interest in the *Vancouver Sun* to Southam. In 1985, in a deal designed to discourage takeover bids on the death of Southam chairman Gordon Fisher, Southam obtained 30 per cent of Torstar in return for giving up 22 per cent of its own company to Torstar. Ardell's 1992 sale of 3.5 million non-voting Torstar shares reduced

Southam's holding in Torstar to 22 per cent and Southam finally disposed of all its Torstar stock. Not to be outdone, Torstar then sold out its Southam investment to Conrad Black.

Southam, for all its stable of hay-burning thoroughbreds, never had a Toronto daily, but it sold more newspapers than any other company in Canada. The sheer weight of numbers of newspaper titles — not to mention profits — seemed to favour Thomson. Until it got its hands on the *Globe and Mail* and the *Winnipeg Free Press*, Thomson had concentrated on small markets. When Roy Thomson bought his first newspaper (the *Timmins Daily Press*) for some $6,000 in 1934, it was not because he wanted to be a press baron. His career interests to that point had been in radio. When asked why he bought the *Daily Press*, he replied with typical Roy Thomson logic: "There happened to be a newspaper in the same building as my broadcast station, so I bought it."

Over the next 60 years or so, the Thomson company built on the solid foundation laid for it by Roy Thomson. By 1995, it owned more than 40 of Canada's 110 dailies and outside of Toronto, its main competition was provided by giveaway weeklies with their full-market penetration. Torstar, building a protective suburban shield around the *Toronto Star*, hedged its bets by building the Metroland chain in the mushrooming dormitory areas outside Metropolitan Toronto.

From Roy Thomson's Canadian roots, in addition to its 40 Canadian dailies and a raft of weeklies, Thomson had dailies in Great Britain, the United States, Zimbabwe, Trinidad, Liberia, Nigeria, South Africa, Thailand, Australia and New Zealand. In May 1995, Thomson stunned the newspaper world with its announcement that it was willing to sell off 14 of its dailies. Roy Thomson, who had built one of the western world's biggest fortunes on small daily papers, must have been spinning in his grave.

Such papers, as John Saunders pointed out in the *Globe and Mail*, had been "cash boxes in the cost-conscious hands of Roy Thomson, yielding profits he parlayed into an international news empire, North Sea oil wealth and a British title, Lord Thomson of Fleet."

Offering virtually no explanation for its sale other than that "they don't fit ... there's no single element or commonality that I would assign to it — they just don't fit," Samuel Hindman, the head of Thomson's Canadian newspaper operations made it clear that newspapers had slipped down the list of profit-earners for Thomson. While Thomson's annual sales were estimated at US$6.4 billion in 1994, less than one-sixth came from its North American papers. Small dailies, competing with direct-mail companies and metropolitan dailies, are a lot of trouble to manage, according to some media analysts.

Michael Brown, president of Thomson, later expanded on the company's long-range plans. "I believe we are on track. We're gaining on competitors," he said after the May 1995 annual meeting of the company in Toronto. "I believe there's a good chance within the next century we'll be the biggest information company in the world."

By then, Thomson had three divisions — information-publishing, newspapers and British travel. Since the beginning of 1994, Thomson had added almost $1 billion in acquisitions to make its information-publishing division more than half the worth of the company. The future acquisition profile, said Brown, would be toward electronic applications.

In the early days of television, Southam and other companies then dominant in the media field were being shunted by government away from ownership of television outlets. Most gave up the fight, but by 1994 a new element was added to the media mix when Ted Rogers, who had launched Canada's first commercial FM station in the 1950s, approached the newspaper business by the back door. As his cable company swept all before it, in the vanguard of his multi-channel universe, he swooped on Maclean Hunter. In addition to its burgeoning holdings in the electronic highway, Maclean Hunter had many printing and publishing assets, including the *Toronto Sun* chain of dailies, in its corporate bag. Thus, with little resistance from Ottawa, a new press baron emerged on the scene, with little or no clear idea of what he wanted to do in the newspaper business. Ron Osborne, who had engineered the purchase of the *Sun* newspapers for Maclean Hunter, was an early casualty of the Rogers takeover. In a sense, the embittered Doug Creighton, who had been so ignominiously shown the door by Maclean Hunter when he lost control of the *Sun*, must have felt justice was finally done to him.

Nothing, it appears, is ever static in the newspaper business. Apart from government, which suffers the vicissitudes of having to face the electorate every few years, no business experiences more crisis management than the newspaper industry. For a while, excluding the *Toronto Star*, which is basically a Toronto newspaper, three companies dominated the national scene — Southam, Thomson and FP. Then, because of terribly inappropriate decisions on how to deal with a strike at the *Montreal Star*, FP sank without a trace. The company originally put together by Max Bell virtually vanished from sight, parts of it swallowed up by Thomson and Southam. One by one, the independents began slipping into the grasp of the wealthy chains, until a new boy on the block, the *Toronto Sun*, was salvaged from the old *Toronto Telegram*. The era of the colourful tabloid appeared to have arrived and Creighton, Don Hunt and Peter Worthington, founders of an outrageous "rag" with more life than most of the mainstream broadsheets, opened other "branch plants" in Edmonton, Calgary and Ottawa.

But the pickings were not as appetizing as once imagined, and a majority interest in the *Sun* went to Maclean Hunter when the *Sun* decided to hedge its bets in growing hard times. There was a "hands-off" agreement that supposedly allowed the Creighton faction and the developer-dominated *Sun* board to run its own show at least for a 10-year period. This agreement came in the form of a voluntary offer made by Maclean Hunter at a Canadian Radio-television and Telecommunications (CRTC) hearing in Calgary. Maclean Hunter made the pledge to support its application to retain a television station in Calgary, a city in which it now also owned a majority interest in the *Calgary Sun*. Maclean Hunter wanted to have its cake and eat it in violation of a government regulation that forbade the ownership of both a newspaper and television station in the same city. Pledge or not, it is almost certain that a metaphorical shake of the head from Maclean Hunter was sufficient more than once to prevent Creighton from pursuing his own Holy Grail of a tabloid to challenge the mighty *Washington Post*. The nearest Creighton ever came to that dream was when the *Sun* bought the *Houston Post*. It soon found itself badly out of its depth and could never catch up with the *Houston Chronicle*. Eventually, it was forced to pull out, but the sale went sour when the *Sun* was faced with a major writedown and diminished returns in American dollars. It got out of Texas, dragging its upstart tail, and was probably relieved to be gone from the scene by the time the *Houston Post* folded in 1995.

It is interesting to recall that when the *Sun* opened its Edmonton tabloid on April 2, 1978, it did so over the objections of Worthington. Nor did Worthington support the next move to Calgary. While Worthington pocketed the millions of dollars the *Sun* had earned for him, he became less and less of an influence on the organization. The most pragmatic of the *Sun*'s three founders, Don Hunt, severed his ties with the *Sun* when the Houston venture foundered.

Thus, Creighton was more or less on his own when Maclean Hunter flexed its muscles in 1992 to oust him. The glamour had gone from the *Sun*. However, wearing the scalp of the *Sun* on its belt proved to be a relatively short-lived battle honour for Maclean Hunter when Ted Rogers proved more than willing to take over the *Sun* group in order to get at Maclean Hunter's multimedia assets.

The kaleidoscopic nature of the newspaper business clearly has been undergoing more bewildering changes of colour since the Second World War. The withdrawal of Thomson from small-market newspaper ownership and changes in the *Sun*'s masters should have put Southam in the unchallenged leadership of the print medium, but who owned Southam? Conrad Black and Paul Desmarais clearly controlled the board with more than 40 per cent of company shares between them. By May 1995, Black held about 19.4 per cent of Southam and Desmarais another 21.4 per cent. Both had been restricted from going much beyond that ownership until April 1995, when shareholders voted to end its poison-pill scheme set up in 1990 to make a hostile bid for the company virtually impossible. By disposing of the corporate poison, the way was clearly open for Black or Desmarais — or anyone else — to seek total control of Southam. That held its own difficulties, because both Black and Desmarais owned other newspaper groups that were in no way connected with Southam.

So what did that leave? Instead of the Southam family, the FP alliance, the *Sun*'s own little empire, the inheritors of newspaper power were for the moment, Southam — whoever Southam was at any given moment — Ted Rogers and Torstar. But by far the key players emerging from the ranks were Conrad Black and Paul Desmarais, with or without the Southam dailies in tow.

Desmarais, despite ownership of *La Presse* (Montreal), was not a man who had actively involved himself in newspapers. Black, who started out with other things on his corporate plate, was now concentrating on print. Obviously, given his association with Southam, and his own opinionated personality, this ownership raised some editorial questions for a company whose principle of autonomy flowed directly from Wilson and Harry Southam. Black was certainly erudite enough and egotistically bold enough to believe there might be an audience waiting for the word from him. However, despite his occasional outbursts decrying the perils of socialism, he appeared to be resisting the temptations to use newspapers he controlled in most of Canada's major markets as his personal political platform, an opportunity Max Aitken[3], Lord Beaverbrook, would certainly not have passed up.

Southam's newspapers had never demonstrated united political clout; they had always set their standards at the whim of their individual publishers. Indeed, when I became publisher of the *Windsor Star* in 1968, it was just three days after it had declared its editorial support for the New Democratic Party (NDP) in a federal election — the first Canadian daily newspaper ever to do so. One can imagine the horror with which Black would have greeted such action, had he been a major shareholder in Southam at that time.

The *Sun* group, in its Creighton-Hunt-Worthington heyday, unabashedly used its newspapers as political platforms. Beland Honderich certainly used the *Toronto Star* for his secular theological polemics of liberal socialism, but he was always one of a kind, perhaps the last of the great press barons who believed a newspaper was his exclusive soapbox. While insisting that a newspaper "should engage in the full and frank dissemination of news and opinion from the perspective of its values and particular view of society," Honderich made no bones about a newspaper playing an activist role in society and not being content with simply reporting events.

Perhaps the rip-roaring fervour of an Amor de Cosmos, or the eccentricities of William Southam's sons, have been eradicated permanently from the Canadian newspaper psyche. The early newspapermen had the wit to cheerfully acknowledge their own incipient "imperfections" in the most imperfect of all media. Personality and individuality rarely survive cold business perceptions, but when creativity and passion wither, the smugness becomes far too stifling. Something has been lost and is gone forever.

# CHAPTER 2

When Alfred Harmsworth, Lord Northcliffe, founder of Britain's *Daily Mail* and the *Daily Mirror*, was diagnosed in the early 1920s as having an incurable mental disease, he went back to his office and phoned his city editor. "They tell me I am going mad," he said. "Put your best reporter on the story."

I don't know why he needed a doctor to tell him he was out of his mind. I have known all my life that you have to be born crazy to work in the newspaper business. But I would not change the disposition of my mind even if some tempestuous thunderbolt were to cause all the darkness to fall.

My mother wanted me to be a priest, but God, in His infinite wisdom, would have none of that. So the reality is that I am, and always have been, what I always wanted to be: a journalist, a reporter, an editor, a writer. And, in my time, by accident of circumstances perhaps, publisher of three Canadian daily newspapers.

I was born in Mallow, County Cork, in the south of Ireland, but it was in England, at the age of 16, that I was inflicted on the newspaper business as a junior reporter on the *Malvern Gazette*, in Worcestershire. The *Gazette* paid me a weekly wage of 30 shillings, plus an extra 10 shillings for the use of my bicycle.

I covered my first rape case in magistrate's court when I was still trying to puzzle out the reason God made women physically different from men. I have since figured it all out, but it was hard as a junior reporter trying to cover a rape case when you don't even understand the mechanics of those distinct differences. The old police chief gave me invaluable advice as we walked out of court one day. "Son," he said, "just remember: you'll never get into trouble if you always keep it between your own legs."

The tide of victory turned dramatically in favor of the Allies on Boxing Day, 1943: I joined the Royal Air Force (RAF) just after my 18th birthday. In truth, I had a "good" war, both sides escaping my wrath. I never fired a shot, nor heard one fired, in anger.

By the time I came along, the RAF was concentrating on chanelling all air crew volunteers into putative wireless/operator air gunners or "straight" AGs (tail-end Charlies). As a wireless operator/air gunner, all that was required was six weeks of initial training and three months at a radio school, with a little air gunnery thrown in. I was perhaps the only would-be air gunner who failed aircraft recognition — I couldn't tell "ours" from "theirs." However, I was a bit of a whiz at taking a Browning .303 aircraft machine-gun apart, but I never really had any success at putting it together again.

As a special treat in wartime England, aircrew were allotted a fried egg for breakfast every Sunday. Some treat! I hate eggs.

The RAF gave me entrée to more public houses than I care to remember, but that was the extent of my cultural development in uniform. Nevertheless, to show its gratitude, when I became a civilian again at the age of 21, the armed forces gave me demobilization pay of less than £50, along with the regulation Queen's issue of a new brown suit, shirt, socks, shoes, a snappy hat and a very modest set of underwear.

My first job after the air force was as sub-editor (deskman) on the *Northern Echo* in Darlington. That lasted all of three weeks, mainly because I was about to be married in Church Fenton in Yorkshire to Lorna Nattriss and wanted a job closer to home. Lorna had been born in Church Fenton and would probably have been content to spend the rest of her life there. However, being ambitious, I wanted something more out of life than a job on one of Britain's papers, still slimmed down by wartime newsprint rationing to no more than six or eight pages a day. In my spare time, I was the backup fast bowler on the village's cricket team but even that was not enough to compensate me for the otherwise sleepy existence of Church Fenton.

After Darlington, I moved to York and Lord Kemsley's *Yorkshire Evening Press.* The main attraction of York was that it was only a half-hour train ride from Church Fenton. My gypsy lifestyle as a newspaperman thus began early. The *Yorkshire Evening Press* had a rather sedate reputation, and once pictorially emasculated a prize bull at the whim of Lady Kemsley, who felt it was too crude in its natural state to be inflicted on the somewhat gentle readers of the *Evening Press.*

Thus, I started married life at the age of 21 with an income of about £5 a week. I had always wanted to be a sportswriter, but there was little scope for that as all that York had to offer for newspaper coverage was York City, a third-division soccer team, and Wilf Meek, the assistant editor of the *Evening Press*, had squatter's rights on that for the Saturday afternoon sports final. After a year at the *Yorkshire Evening Press* in York, I was offered a job in the sports department of the *Yorkshire Evening Post* in Leeds, some 24 kilometres away. The editor of the *Yorkshire Evening Press* tried to bribe me to stay by handing me a pile of books sent to the paper for review. He couldn't offer me any more money, so he tried to do the best he could with what he had. By then, I had become the "splash sub," the deskman who handles the main front-page story every day, amongst other things. Being splash sub at that early age demonstrated no great talent on my part; this was 1947, and a lot of good journalists had gone off to the war and not come back, so that most newsrooms were soldiering on with old and tired retreads from another generation, most of them waiting for retirement.

I had always wanted to be a sports columnist. I got my wish, but you won't find my name in the sports writers' hall of fame. I floundered abysmally as a sports writer in my five years in Leeds, although I did get an extra two guineas a week to write a column on pigeon racing. I may well be the only failed pigeon racing columnist to become a Canadian daily newspaper publisher.

The *Yorkshire Evening Post* was then owned by the Yorkshire Conservative Newspaper Company. The company had been dominated by Edward Wood, Lord Halifax, Neville Chamberlain's foreign minister in the dark days before Winston Churchill was called out of self-imposed political exile to lead wartime Britain. I was once bounding up the stairs in the old *Post* building and nearly bowled over the slower moving Richard Wood, son of Lord Halifax. In acknowledgement of my youthful nimbleness, he stepped aside and waved me on cheerily, this man with two tin legs — he had left his own legs in the blown-up wreckage of a tank he had commanded in the Western Desert campaign against Rommel.

While I was serving my time in the sports department of the *Yorkshire Evening Post* I got my one and only scoop. I was sent to Harrogate to cover the pre-season golfing get-together of the Yorkshire County Cricket Club. I had been tipped off that Norman Yardley, then the captain not only of Yorkshire's cricket team but also of England's, would not be there because of some mysterious illness, and I was to get the full facts.

The chairman of the Yorkshire Club and England's selection committee was Brian Sellars, a blunt ex-army officer, a rather forbidding figure to be addressed by a callow young sports reporter.

In a quavering voice, I asked him to unlock the riddle of Yardley's illness for our eager readers.

"I'll tell you what's wrong with Yardley, young man, but you won't print it in that family newspaper of yours," Sellars bellowed at me in full range of all the grinning cricketeers waiting on the first tee. "He's had surgery to remove a pimple from his arsehole."

Sellars was right. The *Evening Post* never did print my scoop. And it was about then that I decided that pimples and pigeons were hardly the combination to fuel the dreams and desires of an ambitious young journalist.

It was at the *Yorkshire Evening Post* that I first met Paddy Sherman, in later years publisher of the *Vancouver Province* and the *Ottawa Citizen*, and finally president of the Southam Newspaper Group. I'm not sure that long acquaintance worked to the advantage of either one of us, although I always had the highest regard for his journalistic talents. Sherman was the *Evening Post*'s Bradford correspondent in those days, and he and Maureen Sherman moved to Canada a few years before I did. Sherman was a diminutive dynamo, always knowing exactly where he was going, equally adept at scaling mountaintops and the peaks of the Canadian newspaper industry.

Howard Channon, an intense and moody ex-Navy type from Derbyshire, moved from Leeds to Merseyside to become chief sub-editor of the *Liverpool Daily Post*, and it was not long before he asked me to join him there. Before being hired, I had to undergo a disconcerting interview featuring communication by grunt from a father-and-son combination. Allen Jeans was then nominally head of the company that also put out the *Liverpool Echo* and the *Evening Express*. "Young" Alexander (Alick) Jeans was just starting to edge out his father. When I was summoned into their presence, they were sitting on either side of a huge, old-fashioned desk. I was given a chair just off to the side, so that I was always under double scrutiny. Young Alick, perhaps then in his 50s, conducted the interview, his Adam's apple bobbing up and down above one of the stiff collars he always wore. The older Jeans never spoke, but each of my answers to young Alick drew a certain type of grunt from the father. I never fathomed the code, but Alick clearly understood. I guess I passed the test: they hired me.

I arrived in Liverpool just in time for a double national celebration: the 1953 coronation of Queen Elizabeth and the conquest of Mount Everest by the Hunt-Hillary team of mountaineers. (Sir John Hunt, who commanded the expedition, was a Merseysider.) The *Daily Post*'s headline on the Everest climb: The Crowning Glory.

Liverpool was the base from which the Battle of the Atlantic between the Allied convoys and Hitler's U-boats had been fought. Because of its strategic importance, it had been a favourite target of the Luftwaffe. Even 10 years after the war, when I saw it first, this once-great cosmopolitan seaport was already in decline, although all the Cunard Line steamships — except the Queen liners — were still sailing from Pier Head. Liverpool had once been the heart of the blackbird fleet, the slave ships from Africa with their human cargoes bound for the cotton fields of the American South.

Alick Jeans, beginning to act like an embryonic newspaper mogul, went to a Commonwealth Press Union conference in Vancouver in 1957 and was struck by the contrast between the two seaports — dying, dingy Liverpool and the beautiful west coast harbour where the mountains rise out of the Pacific.

Having by then displaced his father as head of the company, he wanted to make his own imprint on it. He talked to Charlie Peters, then the owner of the *Montreal Gazette*, and asked his advice about investing in Canadian newspapers. Peters told him to concentrate on weeklies ripe for conversion to dailies in fast-growing areas of Canada. He put Jeans in touch with Philip Galbraith, who owned the *Red Deer Advocate* in Alberta. Galbraith was in his early 60s, but his daughter and son were still at school and would not be ready to succeed him for several years. He felt it was too late in life for him to undertake the financial burden of the sort of expenditures he thought the *Advocate* would need in the years ahead. He was open to offers.

In 1958, Jeans bought the *Advocate* for $300,000. He asked Galbraith to stay on as publisher, and room was found for Galbraith's former partner, Fred Turnbull. Galbraith later told me he made more money in his first year of running the paper for Liverpool than he had made in any year since he had taken over the *Advocate* from his father.

Jeans had found himself a little gold mine in the *Advocate*, but he offset that smart move by buying the *Estevan Mercury* in Saskatchewan. (Liverpool later sold the *Mercury* as it shopped around for the right mix of small properties.)

One day, Jeans came into the newsroom at the *Liverpool Echo*, to which I had been transferred a couple of years earlier. I was taken a little off guard, because I couldn't ever recall having seen him there before. In any case, I was in the middle of an important game of soccer with the copy boys, the ball being a rolled-up newspaper.

Without batting an eyelid at this unseemly behaviour, Jeans said to me: "How would you like to go to Canada for us?"

"To Canada?" I asked, having only sketchy knowledge of the company's purchase of the two western Canadian weeklies. "Whereabouts in Canada?"

"Alberta," he said.

That made me no wiser, because I was totally ignorant of the geography of Canada.

"To Red Deer," he went on.

"There can't be a place called Red Deer!" I said, in a slightly incredulous tone.

"There is," he replied patiently, "and we own the weekly there. We want you to go there as managing editor to turn it into a daily paper."

I was proud of myself when I negotiated a salary of $7,500 a year, instead of the $6,500 Jeans at first offered me.

In January 1959, I arrived in Canada, to spend the next six months in Peterborough, learning "Canadian" ways. This spell on the *Examiner*, then being run by Robertson Davies, was arranged between Robertson's father, Sen. Rupert Davies, and Allen Jeans. The senator owned a hall (mansion) in North Wales, and he and Allen Jeans had become close friends over the years. Liverpool paid my salary, so Peterborough got my services for nothing. To this day, I'm not sure the *Examiner* got value for its money.

When I finally arrived in Red Deer — having been forced to leave my pregnant wife and our three sons, Patrick, Michael and Sean, behind in Liverpool for my first nine months in a new country — the city came as something of a pleasant surprise after dirty old Liverpool. It was still pioneer country and Galbraith and Turnbull had grown up with it, but it still came as something of a mild shock to find history repeating itself — the first time I saw them they were seated at the same desk, to show their joint authority, just like father and son Jeans back in Liverpool. But there were no grunts between them.

By then, Turnbull was already in his middle 70s. When he reached 65, he had decided to retire from the newspaper business. So he went to Galbraith and asked him to buy out his shares of the *Advocate*. Being a shy, gentle man, Turnbull didn't want any fuss made about the retirement.

"We'll complete the deal quietly," he told Galbraith. "Then I'll go off to California for the rest of this winter and that will be that."

So Galbraith became the sole owner of the *Advocate*, with its twice-a-week circulation of about 6,000, and Turnbull went south for the winter. When he returned in the spring, he had had enough of retirement. Without a word to anyone, he simply walked into the old office he used to share with Galbraith, took off his coat as he had always done, hung it on the same old hook and sat at his desk as though nothing had changed. There he stayed for another 20 years until he died in 1979 at the age of 95. He outlived Galbraith, and his name was still on the masthead as honorary chairman of the *Advocate*.

Having come out from Galt (now Cambridge), Ont., soon after the turn of the century with Phil's father, Turnbull had been with the *Advocate* in the lean years when bills were sometimes paid with sacks of coal from the village of Delburne instead of cash. His partnership with Galbraith was a compatible blending of two totally different personalities. Turnbull was the quiet one, the printer who preferred poking about in the back shop amid the Linotypes, leaving the social side of small-city newspaper life to Galbraith. Turnbull was small and dapper. Galbraith was tall and dignified, as befitting the man who was the last chancellor of the University of Alberta before the Calgary campus of the U of A became a university in its own right.

Turnbull had once been mayor of Red Deer. If he had any political leanings, he was careful not to proselytize about them. Galbraith, on the other hand, never concealed the fact that he was an ardent supporter of the old CCF (Co-operative Commonwealth Federation) party — later reborn as the NDP. For all that he tried, Galbraith could never get himself elected mayor.

When Turnbull had sold his shares to Galbraith in 1950, Red Deer was in one of its periods of expansion. Poised on the edge of the Joffre oilfield and strategically placed midway between Edmonton and Calgary, it gave every appearance of bursting at the seams with oil-related secondary industry. It was that bubble of promising growth that put Galbraith under pressure to turn the *Advocate* into a daily. It wasn't a prospect he relished, for after eight years of paying off his loans to buy out Turnbull, the investment required for a switch to daily was somewhat daunting for a man already in his 60s. A rotary press would be needed to replace the old flatbed that was barely adequate for twice-weekly production. A new building was long overdue.

When word leaked out that he might be interested in selling, the Thomson company showed interest. But Galbraith told me he didn't have the highest regard for that organization. His own inclination was for a deal with Southam, but Southam already owned the *Edmonton Journal*, the *Calgary Herald* and the *Medicine Hat News*. Already commanding more than 80 per cent of total daily readership in Alberta — this was in the days before the branch plants of the *Toronto Sun* set up shop in Edmonton and Calgary — Southam did not want to be in a position where further acquisitions might raise the eyebrows of those who looked askance at provincial saturation of readership by one company. So Southam bowed out and Liverpool came on stage, Alick Jeans having decided that Canada was the country of the future and the place to invest eager capital.

Alick, emerging from the stultifying shadow of his father, dreamed of the *Advocate* becoming the flagship of a fleet of small Canadian dailies destined to be swept up in the postwar Canadian boom. In quick order, Liverpool bought the *Midland* (Ontario) *Free Press* and reached out to the Fraser Valley in British Columbia, seeing it as the dormitory for bustling Vancouver. Jeans grabbed up weeklies in Abbotsford, Chilliwack and Mission City.

In Liverpool, I had been assistant editor of the *Echo*, an afternoon paper that sold 450,000 copies and was the largest daily outside of London. By contrast, the *Advocate* had a news staff of four when we went daily in 1960. When we became a daily, the *Advocate* started with a circulation of 6,500. I had the title of managing editor, but I was in charge of the whole operation. Every department reported to me, which sounds terribly important until it is remembered that the entire staff of the *Advocate* was less than 50. I edited all the copy, wrote all the headlines, designed the page layouts, wound the teletypesetter tape and matched it with Canadian Press hard copy. I repaired the Klischograph photo platemaker and negotiated contracts with the International Typographical Union. For eight years, I wrote every editorial five days a week and, for a change of pace, produced a Saturday column, Onlooker's Diary. Once, when I took a vacation, I had to write 40 editorials in advance. On the side, I coached the fastball team; we had a perpetual losing record, but nobody could fire the coach!

Red Deer was a hotbed of the Social Credit Party in those days, and Robert N. Thompson was not only the member of Parliament for the city, but the national leader of the party. That was a somewhat empty title, because Réal Caouette appointed himself joint leader, the 25 Social Credit seats in Quebec outnumbering the pitiful handful of four westerners Thompson commanded in the Commons. Thompson later became an instant Tory, snatching a nomination from under the nose of Gordon Towers. Biding his time, Towers eventually won the riding as a Tory and had a long run as representative for the city, before retiring to become lieutenant-governor of Alberta.

Thompson had a colourful past, and some of it was true. He had been an *éminence grise* to Haile Selassie, the "Lion of Judah" and last emperor of Ethiopia. He had also tutored the emperor's children and headed the Ethiopian Air Force.

During one federal election, in Thompson's Social Credit days, I suggested editorially that Red Deer voters not waste their time casting a ballot for Thompson and his outdated party. A little old right-wing rancher, complete with string tie and big-brimmed hat, walked into the *Advocate* with a copy of the paper tucked under his arm, demanding to see the person who had written the editorial. I explained that it was against journalistic principle to disclose such information concerning what was the official stance of the newspaper itself and not an individual's viewpoint. However, as managing editor, I would be happy to discuss it with him.

"I don't want to discuss the fucking editorial," he said, handing me his copy of the *Advocate*. "I just want to tell you where to stuff it." Which he proceeded to do, in great anatomical detail.

The sad-eyed Thompson had a hopeless task trying to achieve federal recognition and credibility, although his Red

Deer supporters were legion. Included in his little band of four was Bud Olson from Medicine Hat, who later became a Liberal agriculture minister and then a senator. The rabble-rousing Caouette even had Thompson — an obscurant of high degree on his own — scratching his head in bewildered dismay whenever Caouette gave his public chalk-and-blackboard explanation of the Social Credit theorem.

I once asked Thompson why he did not give up the lost cause in pursuit of respectability federally when Caouette's knife was never far from his back.

"Why don't you go provincial?" I asked him. "Then when Ernest Manning steps down, you might become premier."

He countered my question with one of his own. "Would you want to succeed Ernest Manning?"

Come to think of it, he had a point. Too bad he never borrowed Caouette's blackboard and chalk to spell that out for Harry Strom, a southern Alberta farmer, who became Manning's short-lived successor. Strom might then have been spared the humiliation of being driven from office by the young Peter Lougheed, when there was not a single Tory in the Alberta legislature. He had taken over leadership of the party after stabs at it by flamboyant Milt Harradence — a cousin of Jack Horner[4] — and Cam Kirby, a Red Deer lawyer. Both Harradence, who flew around the province in an old wartime fighter, and Kirby survived political failure to become judges.

Red Deer was fun while it lasted, but in 1965, Finance Minister Walter Gordon and the Liberal government of Lester Pearson chilled our boyish laughter. Gordon introduced a tax measure, the effect of which would be to make foreign ownership of a Canadian daily newspaper virtually untenable. An outsider would not arbitrarily be prevented from buying a Canadian daily, but potential advertisers would lose taxation exemptions that would obviously discourage them from buying space in newspapers acquired by non-Canadians.

The legislation sprang from a genuine fear of some parliamentarians that our dailies were fair game being stalked for political reasons, rather than their commercial potential. The fear had surfaced most noticeably during the vicious pipeline debate of the late 1950s. At a time when the massive cost of the pipeline from Alberta to Ontario could mean hundreds of millions of dollars of government funding and future profits for those who might win the contract, rumours surfaced of a bid by one American oil company to take over the *Globe and Mail* with the obvious intent of using Canada's best-known newspaper as its private propaganda platform. And French President Charles de Gaulle did nothing to lower this tension when he shocked his host country in 1967 with the "Vive le Québec libre" cry from the balcony of Montreal's city hall. What if Paris interests were to take over Montreal's *La Presse* as France's instrument to push a pro-*indépendantiste* line in Canada?

Gordon and Pearson listened gravely to powerful lobbying by the heavy hitters of the Canadian newspaper industry, particularly Southam's St Clair. Balfour. Representing the view of the century-old company dominated by his family (on his mother's side), Balfour had a certain amount of vested interest. He was not willing to test the stimulus of competitive courtship from outside swains in the event of any newspapers in Canada being offered for sale. However, Balfour was also an innately decent man, and he recognized there was a certain imbalance in such an arrangement that might annoy Washington to the anguish of Ottawa, so he voluntarily pledged to the government that

Southam, in return for legislation keeping the Americans outside of Canadian newsrooms, would not attempt to fish in American waters. Southam kept its pledge faithfully for many years until the late 1980s, when it announced it would no longer stay within its own territorial waters if the right American property became available at a price it could afford.

The Balfour pledge came to be seen as more of a hindrance to Southam's growth than as an honourable trade-off for government assistance. While scrupulously keeping Balfour's word to Ottawa, Southam squirmed as Conrad Black snapped up dozens of small papers in the United States, following in the footsteps of Thomson. And the *Toronto Sun* took the biggest single plunge of all with its purchase of the *Houston Post*.

In unshackling the chains of the Balfour pledge, Southam discovered that time had passed it by in the American market. It looked at the Louisville (Kentucky) papers when it was hinted they were on the auction block, but then tiptoed away holding its breath, aghast at the asking price. It stayed home instead and contented itself by picking off the Kingston and Kitchener dailies. One major problem of the Kingston purchase was finding a buyer for Michael Davies' yacht. Who said there was no money in the newspaper business?

The Walter Gordon legislation was announced in the 1965 budget. At the time, I was flying to Toronto for the annual meetings of The Canadian Press and the Canadian Daily Newspaper Publishers Association (CDNPA). It was a hot topic for debate next day at CDNPA and it quickly became evident that the major publishers were prepared to bestow laurels on Gordon for barring the door to foreign buyers. In the vanguard of those welcoming government intervention, of course, was Balfour, as I quickly discovered when I scribbled a few hasty notes on the back of some of the endless reams of paper with which CDNPA constantly showered its members.

When I got up to speak, nobody knew who the hell I was.

I don't think I had ever uttered a word to that stuffy organization before. I think it was only my second meeting and nobody wants to listen to brassy newcomers from the backwoods of Alberta. For me, it was a highly emotional moment as I tried to explain what it felt like to run the only foreign-owned daily newspaper in Canada. This was the paper that Southam did not want to buy in the first place and still would not buy even if Liverpool were forced to sell. Liverpool, I said, had been a good corporate citizen in Canada. It had had the courage to risk turning a profitable weekly into a daily in the high-stakes poker game already dominated by the Calgary and Edmonton dailies of Southam in central Alberta.

As I sat down, feeling like an outcast, Balfour was kind enough to compliment me for speaking up against all the odds, but it was obviously a lost cause into which I was trying to breathe life. Later, the government decided that its legislation would not be retroactive. What Liverpool had it could hold, but there could be no further purchases of dailies and it could not turn any of its remaining weeklies into dailies.

Liverpool was under threat again in 1975 when another Liberal government set out to catch the whales of *Time* and *Reader's Digest*, and came up with the sprat from Red Deer instead. *Reader's Digest* had been a resident corporation, active in Canada since 1943. But, along with *Time*, it had been taking millions of dollars out of Canada, to the detriment of the struggling Canadian consumer magazine industry. Canadian content in both *Time* and *Reader's Digest* was minimal at best.

It was powerful lobbying by Canadian publishers, especially *Maclean*'s magazine, that led to new legislation. Secretary of State Hugh Faulkner's Bill C-58, introduced in 1975, killed *Time*'s Canadian edition altogether. The toughest provision of C-58 was that limiting foreign ownership of both Canadian dailies and magazines to 25 per cent. The Faulkner bill almost ended Liverpool's ownership of the *Red Deer Advocate.* The dream of a colonial empire seemed to be fading as Jeans sold Midland to Thomson. Then Estevan was dumped onto a local buyer. But Jeans summoned up all his Scottish stubborn ancestry to cling to both Red Deer and the Fraser Valley weeklies. It always tickled his fancy, he told me, to have in his stable a newspaper with the grand title of the *Abbotsford, Sumas and Matsqui Times.* It made a great conversation piece for him at the Liverpool Racquets Club. Eventually, Ottawa discreetly let it be known that it might look the other way if Liverpool went through some legal machinations ostensibly to transfer management and decision-making authority to Canada. This was done, through Hacker Press in the Fraser Valley, and Red Deer lived on as the only foreign-owned daily in Canada.[5] But Alick Jeans died of cancer before the reprieve was granted.

I started to consider my future once the Gordon legislation surfaced in 1965, but I didn't want to act hastily. My options were clear: I could stay on in Red Deer, a pleasant city in which to bring up children, but unlike Fred Turnbull, I had no desire to spend 72 years with one newspaper. I could go back to Liverpool, a thought immediately aborted. Or I could start a new career at a bigger newspaper. My ambition and energy told me that the last option made the most sense. So I started to look around and, on the basis of the old saw "If you can't beat 'em, join 'em," I made a pitch to Southam.

And that is how, late in the summer of 1967, I arrived poolside at Jasper Park Lodge where the Canadian publishers were holding their fall meetings. I was there for an interview with St. Clair Balfour and Gordon Fraser. While my first encounter with Southam in the Gordon affair had not been a happy one, I was prepared to forgive and forget. I was in my only decent suit, complete with shirt and tie. Balfour came out of the pool to greet me. He was impeccably dressed in a pair of natty swimming trunks, and he managed to convey the impression he was sartorially right for the occasion and I was not. There was something about that imperious but somewhat shy man that I could never fathom, and through all my subsequent years at Southam I was never comfortable in his presence.

It was agreed that Basil Dean, then the bright light of Southam's publisher corps, would follow up on our meeting. Dean was publisher of the *Edmonton Journal* and a member of the Southam board. If anyone were ever to be considered as the first non-family head of the company, Dean would have had the inside track. An affable, charming man, whose greatest delight seemed to be the weekly wine column he wrote for the *Journal*, Dean quickly set out the terms for me to join the paper as assistant to the publisher.

Dean hired me, but I never worked for him. One week before Christmas and two weeks before I was to go to the *Journal*, they found him dead in his bed in the Royal York Hotel in Toronto, a book open beside him. He had gone to Toronto for a Southam executive meeting. A heart attack killed him at the age of 53.

Southam quickly assured me it would honour the job commitment made to me by Dean, but first it would have to decide who was going to succeed him at the *Journal* and ascertain whether the new publisher was willing to take me on as "assistant to the publisher." In the meantime, under the guidance of John Muir, then general manager of the *Hamilton Spectator*, H.O. Thomasson and I were dispatched to do a study of suburban daily newspapers in the United States.

My biggest coup on that trip was to obtain tickets for a Chicago Blackhawks-Boston Bruins hockey game in the old six-team National Hockey League (NHL). Bobby Hull was then the major force for Chicago, before defecting to the World Hockey Association's (WHA) Winnipeg Jets. A new kid named Bobby Orr was in his first season with Boston. The game was in Boston and when I asked the head bellman at our hotel where we could get tickets, he laughed at me. Impossible, he said. But he took my name, anyway, knowing that action alone was worth a tip. When I said my name was O'Callaghan, he blinked and then smiled before calling over a number of his bellmen. "This gentleman," he said, "is Mr. O'Callaghan from County Cork. And my name, sir, is O'Brien. And this is Sheehan. And this is O'Donnell. And this is McCarthy. And this is Quinn. Tickets is it, you want?" And tickets, it was, we got. Sometimes it pays to be Irish. Especially in Boston.

If the suburban newspaper tour was a make-work project for me, Tommy Thomasson and I still managed a blockbuster of a report. I wonder what dusty shelf it rested on in the Southam archives, or if anybody ever read it.

Southam soon appointed Ross Munro as publisher of the *Journal.* He phoned me to say he would be delighted to have me as assistant to the publisher, so in the spring of 1968 I finally saw the rosewood-panelled office Dean had built for me.

In my last Onlooker's Diary for the *Advocate* on Dec. 30, 1967, I had quoted Jerome K. Jerome[6]: "Leave-takings are but wasted sadness; let me pass out quietly." I always liked it that way. Nevertheless, Red Deer had contributed immensely to my maturity and knowledge of small-city journalism. And, if nothing else, it gave me the opportunity to find a newspaper in which I could indulge myself with acerbic commentaries on life in general. Give or take some literary polishing, I doubt if I would want to retract a single word I have written since. Omnipotence, I suppose, is the curse of the Irish.

Letters to the editor of various newspapers on which I have worked since have labelled me at one time or another as being Communist, Social Credit, Tory, Liberal, Socialist, Marxist. However, I have never belonged to any political party or movement, not even Sinn Fein or the Irish Republican Army (IRA), although I have been accused of that as well.

But in all that time, including the 16 years I spent as publisher of three Southam dailies, I have always been struck by the morbid fear politicians have of the power of the press, a power that I found more myth than reality. The Gordon legislation, because it hit so close to home at the *Advocate*, convinced me that various Liberal governments will always feel the need to curb both the power and independence of the press.

Liberal Sen. Keith Davey ran the first Senate committee inquiry into concentration of newspaper ownership. And Pierre Trudeau, the man who did his finest Liberal thinking in a snowstorm, set up the Kent commission on the heels of the closing of the *Ottawa Journal* and the *Winnipeg Tribune*.

It was a Liberal government that took court action to try to break up the Irving newspaper chain in New Brunswick. And it was on the orders of a Liberal cabinet minister that my office at the *Edmonton Journal* was raided by the Combines people, the reason for which was never explained to me. The government lost that case, but the *Journal* had to go all the way to the Supreme Court of Canada to get a ruling that prevents any more blanket raids of that sort.

When we cited the then newly signed Charter of Rights and Freedoms as our basis for court action to stop the Combines raiders, Jean Chrétien, minister of justice of the day, phoned me to say: "I couldn't resist calling my good friend Patrick O'Callaghan, to get a chuckle out of the fact that after all the unkind things he had said about my Charter he was the first person to make use of Section 8 through the courts." I told him we were about to find out if his precious Charter was worth a damn! (Section 8 states: Everyone has the right to be secure against unreasonable search and seizure.)

Justice Brian Dickson, in writing the Supreme Court judgment, said the order to raid the *Journal* "has a breathtaking sweep; it is tantamount to a licence to roam at large on the premises of Southam Inc. at the stated address and elsewhere in Canada." (Dickson retired as chief justice in 1990.)

After the Supreme Court upheld our rights under Section 8, I wrote to Chrétien and told him perhaps his beloved Charter was, indeed, worth a damn after all. And in gracious reply, he wrote to me: "I am, indeed, gratified that our Charter of Rights is proving to be such a living and practical part of Canadian life which defends the things we both hold so dear."

All my professional life involved defending the freedom of the press, and I don't think any newspaperman should ever give up that struggle or allow such a basic freedom to be diluted by the self-righteous pomposity of politicians. Going all the way back to my Red Deer days, that has been the stimulation that made the newspaper business so exciting, provocative and stirring for me.

I remember one discussion I had with Chrétien when he was trying to persuade me why it was so imperative to enshrine in the Constitution language rights that recognized the historic significance of the two founding races. In demonstrating his own magnanimity toward the beleaguered Anglos of Westmount, Chrétien said: "You know, I grew up hating the British and the Protestants."

"So did I," I responded, "but I don't need a new Constitution to convince me of the uncharitable error of my ways."

# CHAPTER 3

I am the senior graduate of what might well have been the Ross Munro Charm School for Junior Executives.

Indeed, I was Munro's first trainee in the year I spent at the *Edmonton Journal* after arriving there in 1968 following my jaunt around the United States with Tommy Thomasson.

Bill Wheatley was the first to follow me. He actually became a publisher before I did, going to Brantford (Ontario) when Southam bought the *Expositor* from the Preston family. Wheatley later succeeded me as publisher of the *Windsor Star*, before moving on to Winnipeg for the last rites for the *Tribune*. He wound up his long Southam career in 1989 as president of Pacific Press — another of those wasted on the bloody battlefield of Vancouver's unforgiving newspaper trenches. Bill Newbigging, who became publisher of both the *Ottawa Citizen* and the *Edmonton Journal*, was another "assistant to," and so was Dona Harvey, who became editor of the *Winnipeg Tribune* and of the *Vancouver Province*.

"Assistant to the publisher" is really a glorified description of a hopeful nobody without power. It is the circumstance without the pomp, a being who casts no shadow of his own, while sitting in the glare created by the publisher's sun. It is just a step up the ladder from emptying the ashtrays of the mighty. Robert R. (Colonel) McCormick, the doughty *Chicago Tribune* publisher and champion of American isolationism, used to have his desk elevated several feet above the level of the rest of his office so that the common herd was forced to look up to him when in his presence.

Ross Munro was much too modest to want, or need, that sort of artificial aid to self-esteem. His reputation and character created their own aura of greatness. Watching Munro at work was an experience in itself, this shirt-sleeved, angular man puffing great clouds of blue smoke out of his pipe and making decisions with all the calm air of someone who has survived every possible crisis, physical and mental, and is prepared to endure still more.

Munro established his reputation as a war correspondent in the ill-fated Dieppe landings. He went ashore with the first wave of Canadians and he was one of the last plucked off that blood-soaked beach. One of the most touching moments in his life in the aftermath of that Dieppe slaughter was appearing at an open-air meeting in Jackson Park in Windsor to tell a hushed gathering of 15,000 relatives of the Essex Scottish how their men had taken the brunt of the fighting and suffered heavy casualties.

As a war correspondent, Munro had been under the military wing of Brig. Dick Malone. When Southam later sent Munro to Winnipeg as one of a long line of publishers supposed to breathe new life into the always ailing *Tribune*, Munro had a tough time doing battle with the insufferably tunnel-visioned Malone, who was then running the highly successful *Winnipeg Free Press.* Malone angered Winnipeg society in a rather messy divorce action by revealing that he had kept a complete diary of his wife's alleged infidelities — names, times, places.

After seven years in the barren fields of Winnipeg, Munro was whisked off to Toronto to start *The Canadian*, a magazine that was a joint venture of Southam and the *Toronto Star.* It ran as a Saturday insert in most of the Southam papers, finally edging out *Weekend* magazine, the former dominant publication in this field. Three years later, Basil

Dean and Munro moved to Edmonton, just in time to inherit me.

Bill Wheatley was already in Edmonton when I arrived. He was the spitting image, pound for pound, no less, of Raymond Burr, the actor from New Westminster who played lawyer Perry Mason, who never lost a case. Wheatley, by contrast, was the advertising director who never lost an account.

One crisis that even the normally imperturbable Munro failed to cope with arose from a golf game he arranged at the Derrick Golf and Winter Club in Edmonton, with Wheatley and myself completing the threesome. Munro was a serious golfer, striking the ball confidently with that left-hander's smooth arcing touch. Munro showed us the way off the first tee, driving straight down the middle as he always did. That was the last we saw of him that afternoon. Wheatley followed his own star down among the trees on the right-hand side. I made my usual hacking progress, through the trees on the left-hand side. That afternoon almost blighted the Southam careers of Wheatley and myself. Munro was so ashamed of our performance that he switched his golf membership from Don Getty's[7] favourite Edmonton course to the Mayfair. Neither one of us ever played golf with Munro again.

My first spell in Edmonton was relatively uneventful, but after the hectic one-man-band days in Red Deer I chafed at not having a hands-on role at the *Journal*. However, in May of 1968, I went on a bird-dog trip for Southam, disguised as a travelling reporter. Southam had been offered a group of newspapers, including the small dailies at Prince Rupert and Prince George in northern B.C., and it wanted some impression of growth prospects for the area.

It was not hard then to be enthusiastic about Prince George. In case anyone had any doubts about its reason for being, it had engraved around the base of its centennial foundation: "They sought fur and the far Pacific, but found their future in the waiting forests." The city, at the confluence of the Fraser and Nechako rivers at the geographic centre of British Columbia, had staked out a pretty impressive future for itself in the waiting forests of white spruce. It had spent $223 million in the previous five years in harvesting some of that forest wealth.

When I got there, the population was estimated at 27,000. Seven years earlier, only13,800 lived there. While the growth curve had levelled off, the city's boosters were convinced it was ready to advance from that stable base once Highway 16, via the Yellowhead Pass route from Jasper and McBride, was complete. This would then give the North a paved passage from the Prairies to meet the Pacific at Prince Rupert.

The Chamber of Commerce general manager, Ralph M. Williamson, could hardly contain his eagerness to spread the good word about his city. Once the link to Edmonton, via Highway 16, was fully operating, he told me, "Prince George is going to be a really hot spot." Prince George, he said, would then stand at the crossroads of the continent, with Highway 97 running virtually from Mexico to Fairbanks, Alaska, with Highway 16 crossing it at Prince George.

However, this "gateway to the continent" was still more of a swinging loggers' city than a sophisticated tourist attraction when I saw it first in 1968. To cater to the tastes of the rough-hewn roisterers, Prince George had the Tartan Brewery, then owned by a fabulous character named Ben Ginter. His special brew was Uncle Ben's. When I arrived in Prince George, he was feuding with the B.C. Liquor Control Board. He had pioneered canned beer in British Columbia and Alaska, and when the major brewers got into the act, they persuaded the liquor board to raise the price of a dozen cans from $2.63 to $2.73. Ginter wanted to remain competitive by rejecting the price increase, but when told he had to follow the liquor board regulations, he said he would put the extra dime in with each dozen cans. When that gimmick failed, he offered to give a dime to every customer who brought back a dozen of his empty cans.

But the brewery was little more than a sideline to the multimillion-dollar road-building firm, Ben Ginter Construction Ltd. The crewcut millionaire, who looked like a king-sized George Gobel[8], had acquired the bankrupt Tartan Brewery at an auction sale. Ginter had dropped out of school at Grade 7 when his father died in Swan River, Man., and he made the bulk of one of his many fortunes — all of which he lost at one time or another — building roads for former B.C. highways minister "Flying Phil" Gagliardi.

"My rivals complained that the roads were built by the three G's — Gagliardi, Ginter and God," he told me, "but it's quite untrue. I have no partner but God." And he didn't bat an eyelid as he said it.

Ginter had his own finance company in Prince George, ran a charter air service and took over the weekly paper, the *Prince George Progress*, in competition with the daily *Prince George Citizen.* He had a share in a copper mine at McConnell Lake, 322 kilometres north of Prince George. His ranch-style home, complete with indoor swimming pool and worth millions by today's standards in Vancouver, sat on 600 acres of his own private hillside. When he took me through the house, empty beer bottles — Uncle Ben's, of course — were scattered throughout. His wife had left him and he was living alone. In those days, *Time* magazine estimated his total worth at $30 million. When asked if this was an accurate estimate, he said: "Why should I count it? If I did, I might have the damn taxman down here telling me he has missed a nickel of my money somewhere." That was Ben Ginter, the epitome of brawling, hustling Prince George.

However, there wasn't the same atmosphere of pioneering wealth or explosive growth potential in the other towns I visited in my scouting trip for Southam. Kitimat ("the people of the snows") had been put on the map by Alcan in 1951, when the aluminum company built a huge power dam at nearby Kemano. Japex (the Japan Petroleum Exploration Co.) looked long and hard at Kitimat's natural deepwater port as a possible starting point for the quickest route to the Orient. Japex wanted to put a massive refinery in Kitimat to hold crude carried by pipeline from a treatment plant it was planning in Fort McMurray, where Japex had a permit for 49,500 acres of the tar sands. Alberta Mines and Minerals Minister Russ Patrick talked in extravagant terms of Japex extracting more than 200,000 barrels of oil a day from its acreage in the sands. But Kitimat was more a backwoods outpost of dreamers than anything else.

Prince Rupert had visions of itself as the northern counterpart of the port of Vancouver. One of the rainiest cities in Canada, it had wonderful sunsets, but you can't sell newspapers to sunsets, and my impression of Prince Rupert's potential for a Southam newspaper was not all that inspiring.

I dashed off several stories for the *Journal* on that northern trek as my "cover" for my main mission and, through Ross Munro, I recommended to Southam that it separate the *Prince George Citizen* from the rest of the package on offer and forget Prince Rupert and the others. This was one of the rare occasions when Southam took my advice: it bought only the *Citizen*!

In addition to being publisher of the *Journal*, Munro was chairman of the publishers' committee responsible for

Southam News Service. There was some dissatisfaction with the performance of what one publisher called the "high wire artists" in Ottawa and a somewhat delicate problem arose because Charlie Lynch[9], chief of Southam News, was so busy being an entertainer and political columnist, along with his many radio and TV broadcasts, that he wasn't able to give the news service the attention the papers demanded of it. Charlie's profile was higher than any note he ever produced from his beloved harmonica, but maintaining his position as Canada's best-read political columnist meant he had little time for a news service that looked as if it was being run out of his back pocket. It was, and Charlie was never great on detail!

Munro called me into his office one day and asked if I would be willing to go to Ottawa, to take charge of Southam News Service, to try to give it some direction and leadership. To save face, Charlie Lynch would keep the title of chief of Southam News. I would be the executive editor and direct all the Southam News bureaus and correspondents while Charlie got more time to sharpen his pool skills in his daily luncheon sessions at the old Rideau Club.

I wasn't sure I wanted to go to Ottawa, and finally it was decided it would be for two years only. After that, Southam would decide what to do with me next; after all, "assistants to" have only brief lifespans.

The Ottawa of 1969 was not the Ottawa of today. It was a shabby, neglected backwater. In any case, having told St. Clair Balfour when I joined Southam that I would prefer to be located in the West, I wasn't terribly keen about Central Canada in general. Nobody put out any streamers to welcome me to Southam News. Mary Liz Lynch thought I was an interloper and the whole thing was an insult to her husband, a wartime colleague of Munro's. She wouldn't even talk to me. John Walker felt he should have had the job. He certainly had all the right credentials and was a first-class reporter, although his prose was a little stilted. When I arrived, he stayed home for weeks to contemplate his future. Bruce Phillips, later Brian Mulroney's main press secretary and later still Canada's privacy commissioner, was mulling over an offer to become CTV's parliamentary equivalent of the CBC's Ottawa correspondent, Ron Collister, so his byline was not appearing on the news file. The "juniors," breezy Bob Cohen and the elongated Bob Hill, first full-time *Edmonton Journal* correspondent in Yellowknife, were pretty well the sole performers for a while and I was more or less pitched in to sink or swim by myself.

One of my happiest memories of Ottawa was the birth of my daughter, Fiona, in 1970. She was born 22 years after her oldest brother, Patrick, and was the only one of my five children born in Canada. Michael, Sean and Brendan make up the rest of the O'Callaghan brood.

I went to interview Bryce Mackasey[10], the exuberant minister of labour in the Pierre Trudeau government. When I mentioned to him that my time for the interview was limited as I had to see the parish priest to make christening arrangements for Fiona, he opened the bottom drawer of his desk, pulled out a bottle of gin, and poured us both a stiff shot so we could drink her health. Then we did it again. And again. Mackasey, who was very vocal on the subject of his Irish ancestry, was just back from a trip to Dublin.

"Let me know when you are going over there again," he told me, "and I'll give you an introduction to two fine fellows I met in Dublin." One was Charles Haughey, later Ireland's *an taioseach* (prime minister). But Haughey wasn't in such high estate in 1970 — he and the other "fine fellow"[11] were charged a few weeks later with running guns into Northern

Ireland for the Irish Republican Army. (They were eventually acquitted.)

# CHAPTER 4

Being executive assistant to the managing director of Southam was an even grander title than assistant to the publisher of the *Edmonton Journal*, but it still had the ring of impermanence to it. After two years in Ottawa, I had now become a head office man and, like all small and inquisitive creatures, it was my lot to be seen but not often heard.

To add to the suspense, Gordon Fisher was also in training, but for a higher calling. He was waiting patiently to succeed St. Clair Balfour, but Balfour was in no hurry to step down from the presidency. In that regard, Balfour was simply following the path pioneered by Gordon's father, Philip Fisher, who had stepped down from the presidency when he reached age 65 to take on the role of chairman. At that, Philip Fisher had had to persuade the board to bend a retirement rule so that chairmen in future could hold rank until they reached the age of 75 — starting with himself. Balfour had spent his first 10 years as president with Philip Fisher looking benignly over his shoulder, and he was determined to appoint himself Gordon's guardian angel in similar fashion.

As executive assistant to Gordon Fisher, I had no paper to write for and under Fisher's guidance I occupied some of my time rewriting a statement of corporate policy that went through many drafts before going to all officers of the company at the end of 1972 — by which time I was in Windsor.

We defined the company's business as "communications." And we made it clear, in the light of Balfour's assurances to Lester Pearson and Walter Gordon, that Southam "accepts the desirability of Canadian mass media being controlled by Canadian owners. As a corollary, the company will not acquire control of any mass medium outside Canada."

Perhaps anticipating the Kent Commission, we also declared: "The company recognizes that public concern with concentration of mass ownership is legitimate. As a result, the company will not acquire control of more than one medium of mass communication within a single community, nor will it acquire control of any group of media that might represent or seem to represent a regional concentration."

Our "publishing credo" was a masterpiece of noble intentions. "There is no 'Southam' editorial policy," we stated. "There are no rigid rules for producing a 'Southam' newspaper. Editorial autonomy rests with the individual publisher. All editorial opinion is formed at the local level." Ah, those were the good old days. In later years, the Southam newspapers had a rash of "national" columnists and "national" sports writers imposed on them. The relevance of local autonomy was eroding.

Winding up the Southam credo with a bang, Fisher and I wrote: "Freedom of the press is a right of all Canadians, and one that publishers should preserve and defend. It is not a special privilege of the press, but a simple extension of the concept of freedom of speech. The company charges its publishers with the responsibility to ensure that the trust and power inherent in publishing not be abused."

For an engineer, Fisher had the instincts of a genuine newspaperman, but he was sensitive about his lack of hands-on newspaper experience, as I discovered in one of the free-wheeling debates that Gordon enjoyed. Balfour had had editorial experience at the *Winnipeg Tribune* and was publisher for a time at the *Hamilton Spectator*. When Fisher asked me how I saw the head office structure developing in future years, I suggested he would need a distinguished editorial presence on his head office staff as his advisor when he succeeded Balfour as president of Southam Inc. I proposed Ross Munro, mainly because Munro was looked upon with respect by his fellow publishers. Because he was only a few years away from retirement, they would not feel threatened by having to answer to one of their own at head office.

Fisher looked at me and said very quietly: "Patrick, my family has been in the newspaper business for over 100 years. Don't you feel after all that time some of it would have rubbed off on me?"

I changed the subject.

At another of our blue-sky sessions, I told him: "I think we should kill the *Financial Times*. It costs us too much money. It's not like a daily newspaper — it doesn't have specific local community to cover. If the audience we are trying to reach doesn't want to buy it, we owe them no loyalty. Let's get out now, and save ourselves a lot of cash and a lot of grief."

That wasn't my day, either.

"We can't kill the *Financial Times*," he said, between clenched teeth. "Do you know why? Because it was on my recommendation to the board that we bought it. No matter how much it costs, we going to make it work."

Southam never did make it work. More than four years after Fisher died in 1985, after numerous brave tries and format changes, and faced with a new challenge because of the switch from weekly to daily by the *Financial Post*, the crippled *Times*, with its obscenely yellow front page, was sold to Thomson as a plaything for the *Globe and Mail*'s Roy Megarry. Eventually, the *Globe* gave up on it to and put it out of its misery. Most of the best talent on the *Financial Times* found its way to the *Globe's* Report on Business (ROB) section. The *Times* was ill-fated from the start and the advent of the *Financial Post* made one victor in the competition for the business reader virtually certain — the *Globe*'s ROB.

As a 49 per cent owner of the *Brandon Sun*, Southam had two directors on the Manitoba daily's board. One was John Ward, the venerable Southam marketing director, and the other was Fisher. It was decided I should take Fisher's place. Ward and I flew out to Winnipeg and rented a car to drive to Brandon for my first board meeting. On the way, Ward warned me that board meetings of the *Brandon Sun* were not like any other newspaper board meeting. He gave me no further details. Lew Whitehead was 51 per cent owner of the *Sun* and president of the company. His mother was chair and one of his aunts was also a director. It was the only board meeting I have ever attended at which two directors totally ignored talk of circulation losses, declining advertising linage and possible new press equipment while occupying themselves with their knitting.

Some years after my first board meeting, Whitehead was stabbed by two brothers who tried to rob him while he was walking the dog. He came perilously close to dying and he was left slower of speech and memory. The brothers were jailed. A confirmed bachelor, who looked after his mother until she was well into her 90s, Whitehead never again felt comfortable in his home town of Brandon.

It came as no surprise when he decided to sell the paper that his grandfather had founded with funds accumulated while helping to build the railway across the Prairies. Southam declined to exercise its option to buy Whitehead's 51 per cent. Instead it sold its 49 per cent to Whitehead and, in turn, he sold the paper to Thomson.

However, it wasn't the smaller dailies like Brandon that exercised the concentrated brain trust of Southam head office in my year there. Instead, it was the *Montreal Star*. Owned by the McConnell family, it was run — somewhat reluctantly — by Derek Price, who was married to a daughter of the late John McConnell. Price, a member of the affluent newsprint family and a millionaire in his own right, tipped Southam that the *Star* might be for sale. It was then Montreal's dominant English-language daily, far ahead of Southam's struggling *Gazette*. Southam, already on the record as acknowledging the legitimate concerns of the public over concentration of mass media, could not contemplate with equanimity the prospect of attempting to control both English-language dailies in Montreal. Nevertheless, it realized that the opportunity to grab the money-making *Montreal Star* was too rare to pass up.

Some thought was given to the possibility of buying the *Star* and offering the *Gazette* for sale. Then an ingenious proposal that would have had Southam owning the *Star* as well as the *Gazette*, but in a less direct way, got the think-tank humming. This would involve hands-off ownership of the *Star* through some form of trust to be run by Hugh Hallward. Married to Gordon Fisher's sister, Martha, Hallward was the owner of Argo Construction and a descendant of Lord Atholstan, a former owner of the *Star*. This pedigree was considered an impeccable asset in the strategic play then unfolding.

In a way, history seemed to be providing its own echo, because in 1923, F.N. Southam had talked to Atholstan about the possibility of his selling the *Star* to Southam, after Southam had made three abortive attempts — in 1899, 1902, and 1907 — to buy the *Gazette* from the White family. Unable to make a deal with Atholstan, Southam went off to Vancouver to purchase the *Province*. Atholstan sold the *Star* to J.W. McConnell in 1925 for $4 million while retaining the option of keeping possession of it until his death or retirement.

The idea of Hallward following in the Atholstan footsteps was explored at some length, but discussions between Price and Fisher bogged down on the question of how much Southam was willing to pay for the *Star*. Finally, exasperated by the waiting game, Price sold the *Star* to FP Publications and, in the process, became a major shareholder in FP. The deal caused some bad blood between Fisher and Price, former long-time friends from their Montreal days, and may well have contributed eventually to the collapse of FP, brought about by a long strike at the *Montreal Star*. The *Star*'s stubborn refusal to settle with its unions sprang from a position of initial strength and an understanding that the *Gazette* could not afford the same demands. The *Gazette* gambled on the obduracy of the *Star* and reaped the benefit of massive circulation and advertising gains while the presses at the *Star* remained silent. The *Star* finally caved in to the unions, but it had lost too much ground and was forced to close, leaving the *Gazette* all alone in the market.

Poor Art Wood — who had taken over the *Star* in its dying days after Bill Goodson, the architect of the flawed strike strategy, retired to Stowe, Vt. — was parachuted into Ottawa to try and prop up another FP loser, the *Ottawa Journal*, but that rescue attempt was also in vain. Forever after that, Wood was known as The Albatross in newspaper circles.

Southam's apparent dilly-dallying over the *Montreal Star* was not out of character. Under traditional management from within the family ranks, Southam had the reputation of being impeccably honest and straightforward, but not very venturesome, in its business dealings. It was always afraid of bidding too high on any available newspaper, and it was standard thinking at head office that Thomson, for instance, didn't know the value of money and spent far too much on certain acquisitions.

Another paper that got away from Southam for the same reason was the *Peterborough Examiner*, the first paper I worked for in Canada — on "loan" from Liverpool in 1959. The *Examiner*'s owner, Robertson Davies, the cerebral novelist and academic, had approached the three leading newspaper groups of the day — Thomson, Southam and FP — and told them he would entertain one bid from each, the *Examiner* to go to the highest bidder. Southam, it is believed, fell short of Thomson by $100,000. About a year after the sale, I talked to Robertson Davies at a cocktail party at St. Clair Balfour's Toronto home, in the shadow of Casa Loma. I asked Davies how he felt now that Thomson had owned his paper for a year. "To explain how I feel," he replied, "let me tell you I have even refused my free subscription to that paper."

Southam always felt its century-old reputation was its calling card and could never understand why it was being outhustled by vulgar carpetbaggers like Thomson. Nor did it want to soil its dignified hands with the likes of Doug Creighton, Don Hunt and Peter Worthington when that unholy trio burst on to the Toronto scene in November of 1971. When John Bassett finally pulled the plug on the *Toronto Telegram*, the establishment shunned Creighton, who had the look of a startled ferret and the soul of a buccaneer. No one recognized in him then the characteristics that were to make him the most influential figure in the Canadian newspaper industry over the next 20 years. To some, he was William Randolph Hearst, the American newspaper tycoon, reborn in a Canadian setting.

When Creighton's bagmen went looking for start-up funds for the outrageous new daily, the *Toronto Sun*, the

Southam door was shut in their faces. Although it had moved its head office from Montreal to Toronto in 1955, Southam had never had a Toronto daily, but it was not for lack of trying. It had once been outbid for the *Globe and Mail* by Howard Webster. While Southam sniffed haughtily at the prospect of a saucy tabloid, it was also aware of the struggles of the *Telegram* over the years. This convinced Southam the Toronto market was already overcrowded for the sort of broadsheet it was used to running.

Creighton's scrappy *Sun* not only outlived any expectations Southam might have had for it, but it went on to become a thorn in Southam's side in three of its major cash-box cities — Edmonton, Calgary and Ottawa. I was in the trenches for the Alberta battles.

When John Bassett put the *Telegram* to its final rest in 1971, it is ironic that it was son Johnny Bassett's discarded mockup for a *Telegram* tabloid that became the model for Creighton's new journalism. Lacking the funds to set up a major home distribution system along the lines of the *Toronto Star* and the *Globe*, Creighton and his tireless, sleeves-up general manager, Don Hunt, seized on the fact that Toronto, a major subway city for almost 40 years, was spreading out in all directions. Hundreds of thousands of people had to take long rides on public transportation to get to and from work every day. Rush-hour commuters were packed into the subway, bus and streetcar system. The tabloid was made-to-measure for this sardine crowd to read on the way to work every morning.

The *Sun* avoided the *Telegram* mistake of a futile head-to-head battle with the *Star* in the afternoon, leaving the mornings to the *Globe*. The target audiences for the *Sun* and the *Globe* were deemed to be totally different. By turning up its nose at the bread-and-butter boundaries of Toronto parochialism, the *Globe* had resigned itself to having the lowest Metropolitan Toronto readership of the three Toronto dailies. Instead, it sought a coast-to coast audience to justify its smug claim to being Canada's "national newspaper" — an arrogant assumption it has never really succeeded in advancing beyond the glorified myth stage.

In the early days of the *Sun*, while I was still at Southam's head office, the *Sun* operated out of a decrepit warehouse next door to a car wash[12]. From the start, it tried to convey to its readers that it was a fun paper, poking its finger in the eye of the oh-so-serious *Star*. Its readers came to believe that the *Sun* was produced daily by some sort of Keystone Kops co-operative. Nobody respected it, but everybody loved it for its brash ability to laugh at its own stumbles while sharing the joke with its readers.

Throwing perfume on its own dung heap, the *Sun* was forgiven its excesses in its early days mainly because of a columnist named Paul Rimstead, whose erratic extravagances of taste fitted the *Sun*'s own self-image. Rimstead was right for the times, demonstrating in his own flawed character the idea that the *Sun* was not so much a newspaper, but a perpetual party carousing endlessly as the Establishment reacted in horror to the *Sun*'s unprofessional behaviour, its inaccurate and unbalanced reporting and its quixotic promotion of offbeat causes without any sense of intelligent analysis. The *Sun* endeared itself to its readers because of its unpredictability. It was never dull or pompous, and Rimstead was its heart and soul. His antics would have graced a whole Damon Runyon[13] cast of characters. His columns — when he was sober enough to produce them — made him Toronto's best-loved low-life columnist of his day. His drinking habits eventually killed him, but long before that he had become an embarrassment to Creighton.

While Rimstead's end was a sad epitaph to an otherwise spectacular success story for the *Sun*, he was not the only columnist to make his mark in those early days. If Rimstead was wild and undisciplined, Peter Worthington was the pattern of total predictability. He was a dour writer, a somewhat odd character, almost a caricature in whom a conjunction of aggressive idealism and wayward thoughts were constantly at war. One of the *Sun*'s founding trinity, he was prone to see communist spies under every bush. In person, he was polite, quietly spoken, with the sad Rasputin eyes of a misunderstood Messiah. In print — and more certainly in those early days — he made Genghis Khan look like a milksop who had mislaid his rosary beads.

Worthington was firmly convinced Pierre Trudeau was somewhere out there worshipping, in turn, at the shrines of Lenin, Trotsky, Marx and Stalin. His anti-Trudeau obsession set the tone for the brawling tabloid's editorial stance. His suspicions always bordered on the hysterical when it came to the preservation of the Canada he loved.

For all that, he was a man of high principle, whose idealism and patriotism tended occasionally to lead him in some strange journalistic directions. He was accused of acting as an informer for the FBI in identifying Vietnam War protesters, and once wrote, narrated and promoted, a video extolling the virtues of South Africa under apartheid.

As the *Sun* struggled to find its niche, I was simply an observer in my year at Southam head office. The "little paper that grew" found the money it needed to establish itself, thanks to the contacts and energy of people like Eddie Goodman, the Tory lawyer and political bagman.

I knew when I arrived in Toronto that my time there was limited, and my office space was already earmarked for Bill Carradine, one-time crown prince at the *London Free Press.*

Bereft of a male heir following the suicide of his only son, Walter Blackburn had brought in Carradine as general manager of the *Free Press.* Carradine was a former manager for Procter and Gamble in Switzerland. As Bill Heine, editor of the *Free Press* for 17 years, described him, Carradine was a "slim, good-looking, energetic man, who knew a lot about soap and, at the time, damn all about the newspaper business." It was a description that I found accurate.

Carradine's progress at the *Free Press* had run into roadblocks when Peter White, then husband of Martha Blackburn, Walter's daughter, began to demonstrate strong tendencies of management interest, if not potential, and Walter decided it would be nice to keep the *Free Press* all in the family. Dear Walter, in his old-fashioned male chauvinist thinking, had never considered either of his daughters worthy of succeeding him. But a son-in-law, that was the next best thing!

When Carradine started looking around for other career avenues to explore, he and Southam looked like a natural fit. Gordon Fisher and Carradine were on the same wavelength philosophically and in Establishment terms, and I was no more than the company's token maverick. I did not have the head office logo indelibly stamped on my rear end.

One day, St. Clair Balfour marched briskly into my office — soon to be Carradine's — and said with a smile: "Pat, when you joined this company, you indicated you wanted to go to a newspaper out west. Well, Windsor is west of Toronto, so how would you like to be publisher of the *Windsor Star*?"

# CHAPTER 5

In the late 1960s, Richard Graybiel, one of the bright, young, independent newspaper owners, suffered a major heart attack on a visit to Leningrad. He came home on a stretcher, his days already numbered. When he died — within a week of his father — the *Windsor Star* passed into the hands of his widow, Tisha. It is said Roy Thomson wasted no time popping the question to Mrs. Graybiel at Richard's funeral: "How much do you want for your paper?"

She wanted to hold on to the paper until her two children were of an age and a maturity to decide for themselves if they wished to carry on the newspaper tradition of their father and grandfather, so she called on Mark Farrell, an old family friend, to become a stopgap publisher. Farrell, a sixth-generation Canadian with all the old-world courtesy and charm of a Victorian — albeit a Victorian with a salty tongue on occasion — had founded *Weekend* magazine for the *Montreal Standard*, a subsidiary of John McConnell's *Montreal Star*. Farrell had fallen out of favour with Derek Price and was willing to help Mrs. Graybiel, although he hated the city of Windsor. In his three years or so there, he seemed to spend more days skiing the slopes of the Alps each year than parking his flower-decal-festooned old Volkswagen in the publisher's parking spot on Ferry Street.

Farrell had the dubious distinction of having to cope with what may well have been the first sleep-in strike at a newspaper. Instead of hitting the bricks, the pressmen, printers and stereotypers had smuggled in sleeping bags on their last day at work. Families and sympathizers provided food for them in baskets that were hoisted up the sides of the old building to the composing room floor. However, Farrell was never the sort of man to go quietly into the twilight of union discontent. On the first day of the sleep-in, he called a pep rally for loyal supporters who were prepared to carry on working. Farrell was proud of his athleticism, and although he was then in his early 60s, Farrell leaped on to the counter top in the old-fashioned reception area on the ground floor, determined to command his troops for battle. In the process, he banged his head against an overhead beam. The whole effect of his stirring rally was spoiled somewhat by the blood trickling down his face.

In 1971, six months after that strike, Southam bought the *Star* from Mrs. Graybiel when it was clear her children had no interest in newspaper careers. A few months later, Southam sent Farrell back to Montreal to publish the *Gazette* and in 1972, I became the first "real" Southam publisher in Windsor. Even after my move had been promulgated by head office, Farrell wouldn't let me into the plant. He said it would upset the morale of his staff if they knew he was about to become a lame duck en route to Montreal. To compound my problem, my takeover date was to be a day or two after a November federal election. Farrell's last hurrah was to throw the *Star*'s editorial support behind the New Democrats. So, in the hometown of such leading Liberals and cabinet ministers as Paul Martin Sr., Herb Gray and Mark MacGuigan, I was handed the first ever Canadian daily to back a socialist party in a federal election.

Such political endorsement was not out of character for Farrell. On his office wall, he kept a framed diploma he had received from Leningrad University. To be fair, he said, he had balanced that off by throwing snowballs at Lenin's statue during a visit to Russia.

Farrell had me over for dinner at his home, where I met a few of his managers. He finally let me into the *Star* building on election night, with orders not to get in the way. He told me would allow me into his office the next morning to show me some of his secret files. This he duly did, before rushing off to the airport, leaving me alone in his office — now technically mine. Not once having toured the building and knowing virtually nobody on staff, I was totally scared. I went into his (my) private washroom to try and gather my thoughts and opened the decrepit medicine cabinet above the wash basin just to see what he might have left behind. It was totally stocked, not with patent medicines or toothpaste and the like, but with gin. I liked his style already!

Six months after Farrell had left Windsor, I had my own strike. It had been brewing since the sleep-in and was rooted in a resentment of the loss of the independence and benevolent paternalism of the Graybiel days. Windsor, geographically south of Detroit, had always felt insecure in its relationship to Canada. The strike was further based on fear of changing technology and the right to decide who would control new computer-driven equipment that the *Star* intended to pioneer. There had always been a touch of the Luddite in the International Typographical Union (ITU).

The signal that the strike was on in earnest came when I was called to the stereo department. Ron Dupuis was a prominent practitioner of another dying trade, stereotyping, and his union was part of the strike coalition. He told me he had ordered his members to disobey the directive of the foreman to cast stereotype plates from the few pages the composing room had prepared before walking off the job. He demanded that I fire him, making him a sacrificial lamb. This I did, while surrounded by his fellow workers. Then, in accordance with what was expected of both of us, I escorted

Dupuis off the promises to the applause of the members of the ITU, who were congregated outside the doors of the building with their picket signs at the ready.

Dupuis and I chatted amiably; there was no rancour on either part, which was just as well for my sake as Dupuis was a reformed ex-president of the Windsor branch of Hell's Angels.

The strike lasted two weeks, and we published the paper without pressmen, stereotypers or compositors. We employed no outsiders. Finally, Alan Heritage, the ITU's top man in Canada and also a member of the international board of the union, called me to see if we could find a way to end the stoppage. We went off to a hotel room, just the two of us, and I gave him my written list of terms that would ensure full management control over the optical character readers and video display terminals we were planning to install for newsroom and classified advertising use. He went through the motions of tinkering with my language, but he gave me everything I wanted. The management rights that sprang from that hotel meeting were to set a precedent throughout the industry, speeding the installation of the new technology.

There had been only one bad incident during the strike. One of our drivers, fresh from several hours in the beer parlour, had slugged the circulation manager as he crossed the picket line. We laid assault charges against the driver and fired him. On the morning after the last long night of negotiations with the strike leaders on the final words on the contract, I was yawning in my office waiting for the official vote on terms when my phone rang. It was Ron Dupuis. He wanted me to drop charges against the driver and to reinstate him because of his long service and advancing years. Being in a magnanimous frame of mind, I agreed. "Come on over," I told Dupuis, "and I'll give you a letter to that effect."

"I can't," he replied. "When you fired me, you also barred me from the premises,"

So I had to walk across the street with my letter, the listless pickets eyeing me curiously. Dupuis and I had a coffee in the restaurant from which the strike had been run. And when it was all over, I reinstated Dupuis as well.

Soon after the strike, Southam decided to hold a quarterly meeting of directors and publishers in Prince George, B.C. Southam wanted to show the flag to one of its newest publication cities, the one I had scouted for head office. The main topic on the board's agenda, however, was not the *Prince George Citizen*, but the future of the *Winnipeg Tribune*.

For years, the *Tribune* had played second fiddle to the *Winnipeg Free Press*. The papers were both afternoon broadsheets, with little to choose between them in quality or content, but the *Free Press* had one tremendous advantage in this city of Ukrainians — it had been a Sifton paper, and it was a Sifton whose federal initiative had brought Ukrainian immigrants to Western Canada at the beginning of the 20th century. Given a choice between a Sifton and a Southam paper — all other things being equal — the Ukrainians would choose Sifton. In one of my heart-to-heart talks with Gordon Fisher, I had once expressed the opinion that the *Tribune* could not survive unless it became dramatically different from the *Free Press*.

"Turn it into a tabloid," I said.

"Once you've done that, there's nothing left to try," he relied. "That's the last resort."

I thought we had already reached that point but I was wrong, as I discovered when the board at the Prince George meetings decided to accept a half-baked strategy for saving the *Tribune* that was the brainchild of Martin Goldfarb. The engagingly articulate pollster and newspaper consultant had studied the two Winnipeg dailies for Southam. He was struck by the fact that the *Free Press* bulged with classified advertising while the *Tribune*'s classified section was virtually bare. This made the *Free Press* better value for money than the *Tribune*, he argued, so why not give away personal classified to bolster the *Tribune*'s cover price of a dime?

The thought of giving away advertising space under any circumstances appalled me, so when those publishers, like me, who were not members of the board, were allowed to vote with the board on the Goldfarb strategy, I voted against the harebrained scheme. I wasn't just part of the minority — I was the total minority!

The company duly implemented the Goldfarb strategy, only to discover that the *Free Press* was prepared to match it, and with deeper pockets than the *Tribune*, to support the giveaway war. Would the *Tribune* have survived as a tabloid? Who knows? If it had made the effort, perhaps there would have been no Kent Commission.

On my way to that legendary meeting in Prince George, John Muir, publisher of the *Hamilton Spectator*, wandered down the plane to talk to me. The crusty Muir was always one of my favourite publishers, although I hardly knew him then. Muir took great delight in tweaking the noses of the mighty, not excluding the Southam board, and there were times when he clearly exasperated Balfour, who had once been his publisher. Muir had the same flying-wing eyebrows as Balfour and was just as adept as Balfour in stroking them until they bristled off the side of his forehead. At times, across the boardroom table, Balfour and Muir seemed to be in a confrontational competition in this hair-raising act of vanity.

On that flight to Prince George, Muir invited me to dinner that night with him and his wife, Pat. However, when I kept our rendezvous that evening, I discovered he had also invited every other publisher and director on the plane, plus assorted spouses, to be his guests. We took over the entire dining room at the Inn of the North, where we were all staying. Muir, in his courteous but gently imperious way, demanded the wine list. He picked the most expensive wines, and the bottles started arriving at each table. And they kept on coming. We cleaned out much of the Inn's wine cellar that night, and Balfour's face got blacker and blacker. With a final flourish, Muir charged the entire tab for dinner and wines to Southam rather than the *Hamilton Spectator*.

Balfour, tight-fisted at the best of times, a millionaire who travelled the Toronto subway using his senior citizen tickets, had some rather harsh words with Muir about his grandiose bill-paying, but Muir was unrepentant. The discussion between head office and Hamilton went on for weeks, but Bloor Street[14] was eventually shamed into paying the bill. It was Muir's way of making a point — if head office wanted to drag all its senior officers to a backwoods location on company business, it should at least take care of the troops and see they were properly fed and "watered."

One of the privileges of being a publisher in those gentler times was the right to disagree with those in the ivory tower of his own paper, who fill the editorial page with polished prose and reasoned rhetoric (some of the time, anyway). I found myself under pressure at *Windsor Star* editorial conferences, being reminded that even a transplanted Albertan must "think Canadian." However, I could never accept the *Star*'s stance on Ottawa's two-price oil policy.

Put forward by Energy Minister Donald Macdonald[15], this policy amounted to Ottawa putting still another tax on top of Alberta's taxes on its own natural resources. The money went to the federal treasury to subsidize Central

Canada with a lower price than the world market rate. Ottawa also forced Alberta to swallow the pipeline costs. This meant a double subsidy for Central Canada on Alberta's resource. The federal government, by keeping a false price for domestic energy, took the money right out of Alberta's pockets, the most major intrusion into provincial affairs since Canada became a Confederation.

Nothing ever changes, does it, when the power of Central Canada and Ottawa combines to turn the western provinces into colonial outposts? And yet nobody seemed to understand in the 1990s why Alberta was so insistent on a reformed Senate to try to find some means of preventing another massive takeaway of Alberta's rights in order to keep Quebec and Ontario happy. Alberta was signalling that it could never again trust a Parliament stacked with Quebec and Ontario MPs.

In other matters, while I was in Windsor, the old order was changing. After 33 years as an MP and Senate leader, Paul Martin Sr., in late 1974, walked away from the parliamentary institution he had loved and served so faithfully in his own dogged way. Within a few days, he was appointed high commissioner to Britain.

In his political life, Martin had prided himself on knowing everyone in Windsor. He didn't just mainstreet at election time; he did it all the time. Once, I walked with him to the Windsor Club, then in the old telephone building. It was a stately procession, Martin stopping every few seconds to shake somebody's hand. He asked one man his name and when the man told him, Martin said: "I know your father well. Please give him my best." The man replied: "He's been dead for 10 years." At the Windsor Club, he struck up a conversation with the waitress. "How's your husband?" he asked. She replied: "I've never been married." Striking out twice in one day was unheard of for Martin, although his biggest failure at the plate, politically speaking, was when he dyed his hair and ran for the leadership of the Liberal party. He was rejected as one of yesterday's men. When Martin became a senator, his former law partner, Sen. Keith Laird, used to refer to him as the "junior senator from Windsor." Martin was not amused.

In June 1975, the *Star* took another step into the future. We phased out the last remnants of hot metal. The traditional stereo department, producer of those monstrous 40-pound plates, gave way to lightweight Napp plates and the hernia rate for pressmen and stereotypers must have diminished. The old Linotypes had been silenced a year earlier with the advent of full photo-typesetting in the composing room. Surprisingly, there was no wake when the Linotypes went.

At the top of the unions' priority list for length of service at the time was Ted Tyrrell, who had come to the *Star* in 1926. He had worked for five years on the night shift and one thing he liked about it, he told me, was that he could leave the job in the morning and go to the bootlegger's across the street. "And sometimes there was a visit to the bootlegger's during the night," he confessed. Of the technological innovations, Tyrrell said: "Like any other business, the newspaper has to change. I have few regrets."

All of this was made possible through the agreement reached after the 1973 strike, but our guarantee of lifetime job security meant that none of our displaced production people became the victims of progress. It was a painless transition.

On July 5, 1974, I switched the *Star*'s support from the NDP to the Liberals in a federal general election. That may have been the only time in my life I ever advised anyone to vote Liberal. The reason for this switch hinged on one major factor (other than the concern that 20 months of minority government had left the country rudderless). What I feared, in the event of a Tory victory, was the "disaster that would ensue if Robert Stanfield's prices-and-incomes freeze were ever imposed." Having campaigned vigorously against Stanfield's policy on inflation ("Zap, you're dead!"), Pierre Trudeau could hardly wait to implement it as soon as the votes had been counted in his favour. That was political deceit of the highest order. But even while offering the *Star*'s backing for the Liberals, with reservations, my distaste for their leader was not concealed. "His arrogance is insufferable," I wrote in a signed article in the *Star*. "He is thin-skinned and abrasive. He can be aloof. He will never be a man of the people now that the charisma has gone."

However, I had hoped that Trudeau was somewhat chastened by the 20 months he had spent "having to sip tea and eat cookies at the bedside of the New Democrats every time he wanted to get a piece of legislation through the last Parliament."

In the fall of 1975, Gordon Fisher came to Windsor on a presidential visit. Knowing I was getting a little bored in Windsor after three years, now that things were settled down and morale restored at the *Star*, he offered me two options: I could go to Montreal and succeed Mark Farrell when he retired at the start of 1976, or I could wait two years and take over the *Journal* in Edmonton when Ross Munro retired. I said I would wait for the *Journal*.

Two weeks later, Fisher phoned me: Munro had agreed to go to Montreal, providing the company extended his retirement date by one year. The *Journal* was now mine!

# CHAPTER 6

A plaque used to hang on the wall behind the publisher's chair at the *Edmonton Journal* that served as a constant reminder of the fragility of freedom of the press.

The plaque signified the only Pulitzer Prize ever to be awarded outside the United States. The annual Pulitzers honour the best in American journalism.

The *Journal*, published at the time by John Imrie, won its citation for the stirring battle it led to fend off government control and censorship of the press in 1937. I was humbled and honoured to sit in the shadow of that plaque from January 1976 until August 1982.

In 1937, Alberta had the world's first Social Credit government. The party had only a vague concept of social justice. Premier William Aberhart had promised a $25-a-month basic dividend to every Albertan. But the government got so far away from the roots of its own Bible Belt fundamentalism and philosophical and political theory that when John Hargrave, the leader of the political wing of England's Social Credit, arrived in Edmonton to examine how the new-wave movement would perform as a government, he was somewhat astonished to find the implacable hostility of Aberhart toward the newspapers of Alberta. Wondering what brought about this situation, Hargrave remarked: "The newspaper files showed that the attacks made by the press were, on the whole, very mild indeed."

Hargrave's astonishment grew when Aberhart introduced an 11-point Social Credit program that included the issue of debt-free money negotiable within the province, the setting up of a central credit house to function in some respects like a chartered bank, a retail price-discount system and the $25 monthly dividends to be paid in Alberta scrip.

Hargrave severed his ties with the Alberta government when Solon Low's more conventional budget was suspended by Social Credit backbenchers and the legislature passed the Alberta Social Credit Act as not only an attempt to take "power to deal with public credit" but also to control the rebellious press of Alberta. Before it was all over, there was a flock of court judgments and appeals, imprisonment of two ranking Social Crediters and a reporter threatened with jail.

When the federal government disallowed the Social Credit Act, the Alberta government responded with the Accurate News and Information Act. When this press gag bill was introduced in the legislature, Peter Galbraith, publisher of the *Albertan* — the paper that used to carry the masthead line "A Publicly Owned Newspaper Supporting Social Credit Principles" — broke with Aberhart. He joined Imrie, Cliff Wallace (the *Journal*'s managing editor) and O. Leigh Spencer, publisher of the *Calgary Herald*, to work out a counter campaign.

In an editorial attacking the gag bill, the *Journal* said: "The Alberta government would turn back more than 200 years the clock of liberty and progress....The machinery of dictatorship and censorship is outlined clearly in the bill." If enacted, said the *Journal*, the bill "would place in the hands of a few men such power ... as no British monarch or government has presumed to assume for the past two centuries."

The Supreme Court of Canada had similar misgivings. It ruled it was beyond provincial powers to enact such a bill. And the Privy Council in London later referred to the measure as "no longer practical in any sense at all."

The newspapers of Alberta won that fight, although Alfie Hooke, a survivor of the Aberhart cabinet, told me in later years: "Patrick, the newspapers never really understood what we wanted. We didn't want to censor the press. We only wanted them to tell the truth accurately." As Social Credit judged the truth, of course.

I arrived in Edmonton in January 1976, and was immediately plunged into the upcoming Tory convention to find a leader to replace Robert Stanfield. As a kingmaker, I proved to be an abject failure.

Only a few days after settling under the Pulitzer plaque in the publisher's office, I was phoned by Walter Blackburn, owner and publisher of the *London Free Press*. Speaking on behalf of a group of high-level Tories, including John White, former Ontario treasurer, he urged me to do whatever I could to persuade Peter Lougheed to run for the federal party's leadership. Blackburn's group was not impressed with the declared list of candidates, and neither was I.

When I discussed the proposition with Lougheed, he gave me the standard politician's response — he had a job as premier, and Alberta was facing some "interesting" times; he wanted to be a part of that action.

Undeterred, I went public on Jan. 14, just 10 days after succeeding Ross Munro as publisher. And I did it in a front-page editorial. I ruled out the likes of Joe Clark, Claude Wagner, Jack Horner, Paul Hellyer, Sinclair Stevens, Jim Gillies and Flora MacDonald.

The editorial went on: "It is being made abundantly clear to him (Lougheed), in a swelling tide of anguish, that a federal party without his leadership is disintegrating to a point where its convention next month could be a disaster." Despite some Central Canadian dissatisfaction with Lougheed's "Alberta-first" stance on energy, I concluded that he "is the only candidate capable of erasing the scars of factionalism and regionalism within the party."

The editorial never mentioned one other candidate in the race: Brian Mulroney. However, after Joe Clark won that first battle with Mulroney on Feb. 22, I at least noted Mulroney was a "gifted amateur ... the young outsider cast in the Robert Redford mould."

With Lougheed ignoring my blandishments and holding fast as premier, Clark won the federal leadership, despite seeing his fellow Alberta caucus member, Jack Horner, attempt to take his western followers into Wagner's camp. He won despite seeing John Diefenbaker, the long time champion of the West, also opt for Wagner. Clark had only about three members of the Tory caucus at his side in the initial stages of the leadership convention and began as party leader having to deal with a rebellious caucus that did not want him. Worse than that, he had the cross of Diefenbaker to bear. To the crotchety former prime minister, Clark was always a joke, a boy sent on a man's errand.

Having drawn a blank with Lougheed, the next target for my front-page editorial treatment was Dr. Charles Allard, then the owner of the Edmonton Oilers. The peg for the editorial was a flaming row between Allard and the *Journal*'s sports department. The Oilers were then playing in the World Hockey Association, in their first season in the new Northlands Coliseum. They were playing badly, partly because the team was stocked with wonky-kneed NHL rejects and retreads, partly because Wild Bill Hunter was their coach and general manager, and partly because Wayne Gretzky had not yet been "invented."

Allard smarted at the *Journal*'s carping criticism, particularly that of a caustic columnist named Wayne Overland. Finally, Allard personally threw Overland out of the Oilers dressing room after yet another loss on the ice. In response, I wrote an editorial full of stirring words on preserving the independence of the paper and embellished it with a passionate defence of freedom of speech. Whether these words worked a full conversion based on the searing revelation that freedom of the press was being endangered by a two-bit hockey team, or whether Charlie Allard simply cooled off, is debatable, but Allard phoned me the day after the editorial appeared. Usually, his tongue had an edge as sharp as his surgeon's scalpel, but on this day he dripped honey into my ear.

"My mother told me there are two reasons I should not get mad at the *Journal*," Allard said. "First, you gave me my first job (as a carrier) and, second, she said I should never get into a pissing contest with a skunk." Having gotten that off his chest, Allard laughed and said: "Call off your dogs. Overland can come back into the dressing room for the next home game."

Allard was an Albertan-born Francophone. One day, as we were walking into the Chateau Lacombe, across the street from the *Journal*, he told me he had grown up in a rented house that once stood on the hotel site. His mother was offered the house for $3,000, but couldn't afford it. When Allard wanted to build the Chateau Lacombe, it cost him more than $2 million for the land on which the mother's $3,000 house had once stood.

Allard had been the chief of surgery at Misericordia Hospital. Finding he needed an office for his own practice, he bought some land and built his own office block. From that, he branched out into development on a massive scale as Edmonton began to shed its frontier-town image. He held the largest Chrysler dealership in Edmonton at one time and built a multimillion-dollar petrochemical industry based in

Medicine Hat — and just as shrewdly sold it at top price before the Alberta energy boom went bust. He was partner in a steak house. He dabbled in weekly newspaper ownership, but his real impact in the communications field came through his ownership of an Edmonton television station affiliated with the Independent TV network. Allard dominated ITV, as he did most things he got involved in. One battle he did not win was with the CBC over an all-news TV channel. But that was touch and go, given the mood of disgruntled Tory MPs in their ongoing belief that the people's network was run by card-carrying Marxists. Allard quickly tired of the Oilers and sold the team before it made it to the NHL, but his TV station held exclusive broadcast rights to Oiler games throughout the Gretzky era in Edmonton.

As for Gretzky, I saw his first game with the WHA team and I saw him dominate the last game ever played under WHA colours — the all-star finale[16]. He was the starting centre and his wingers were Mark Howe, later a heady defenceman with the Philadelphia Flyers, and Mark's father, the venerable Gordie Howe. Gretzky had always been in awe of the sharp-elbowed elder Howe and, at one point — the Coliseum being more than half-empty — you could hear this polite 17-year-old shouting to his 50-year-old winger: "Pass the puck, Mr. Howe!"

To test the waters for the *Journal*, I hired Goldfarb Consultants of Toronto to find out what sort of a newspaper our readers wanted the *Journal* to be. The consultants talked to some 600 people, selected at random, and interviews generally lasted upwards of an hour. By the middle of March, we were pondering the results of all that research.

The responses were instructive, humbling, confusing, belligerent, outraged, destructive, edifying, devastating, passionate, indifferent, angry, kind, cynical, bemused, predictable and even flattering. Some 25 per cent reported they were "very satisfied" with the new-style *Journal*. Another 64 per cent were "satisfied", and eight per cent were not satisfied at all. As for the remaining three per cent, their opinions were either incomprehensible or unprintable in a good family newspaper.

At the time, the *Journal* had 172,000 subscribers and close to 500,000 actual readers, and we were faced with the age-old dilemma — how to produce a newspaper that suited all their varied tastes.

Some readers told us to concentrate more on local news. Others said there was too much local news. Some wanted more international news ("I have a friend that takes the *New York Times* ... and the news coverage in that is terrific."). However, before attempting to turn the *Journal* into the *New York Times* of the Prairies, consideration would have to be given to those who wanted less international news. ("I can't improve my status in life by reading stuff that simply makes me unhappy or upsets me. There's a million people starving to death in India. It used to be that that bothered me. Today, if a million people starve to death in India, I couldn't care less.") Another reader said: "I think the people who write the paper are literary snobs. They won't write low enough."

Some readers wondered why we bothered to carry advertising, which accounts for more than 80 per cent of every dollar that comes into any newspaper's cash register. However, the Goldfarb survey also showed that advertising was a major motivation for buying the *Journal*. The price of the paper was too high, some readers complained. It was then 15 cents a copy. For that small sum, according to figures released by the Canadian Daily Newspaper Publishers Association, the reader got more pages in the *Journal* in 1975 than in any other newspaper in Canada, and that included the

*Toronto Star.* In that year, some 26,000 pages were printed by the *Journal.* How many *Gone With the Winds* did that add up to?

Commenting on the survey in a Chamber of Commerce speech, I noted that the *Journal* had undergone substantial technological change and even the newspaper's nameplate, in use in one form or another for more than half a century, was going to be replaced by something more colourful and exciting. I gave the first public hint of a new plant and offset presses, something I had been agitating for with the Southam board since coming to Edmonton. The urgency was real, but trying to convey this message to the board was another matter. The board was more than content with the money flowing over the transom and saw no reason for change.

The pitched battle I had to wage with Gordon Fisher and John Rothwell, Southam's vice-president of production, over that plant was one of the bitterest episodes of my often stormy career with Southam. Because of it, I came perilously close to quitting — or being fired. For more than two years, I seemed to be only one step away from either course. My bitterness grew even deeper in retrospect, because if we had had offset presses with colour capability when the *Sun* put its first branch plant into Edmonton, the tabloid might never have got beyond a tentative foothold. Southam still insisted on moving cautiously at a measured pace even when faced with the breathlessness of Doug Creighton's seat-of-the-pants intuition. Even without the *Sun* breathing down its neck, the *Journal* was having to make do with two clapped-out presses. And it was coining money!

In the fall, we announced that the *Journal* had a bold new nameplate, but it wasn't the one we had set our sights on. We had tinkered with a number of possibilities from a range provided by various designers, art houses, typographical experts, academics, consultants and our own staff. Then, confident of our choice, we picked a group of readers and asked them to judge it for us. We fully expected a vote of confidence as a mere formality. We didn't get it. The readers' panel said that the nameplate we liked suggested a newspaper that was simple, light and youth-oriented. It connoted a newspaper that was more for glancers than thorough readers. Its lasting impression, they said, was that of a shallow newspaper.

So it was back to the drawing board and the services of newspaper designer Peter Palazzo of New York City. We wanted something that would indicate that the city founded by the fur traders had long since passed into history and in its place was a booming, sprawling, metropolis of ever-increasing importance on the national scene. How you conveyed that to a New Yorker who had never set foot in the place was something else again, but Palazzo responded to the challenge by producing more than 40 different samples for us. From these, we selected a short list of six and, along with the old nameplate, these were pre-tested by still another group of readers. The old nameplate, beloved by *Journal* diehards, came fifth out of the seven tested. The one I liked best was dead last.

# CHAPTER 7

*Alberta Report*[17] is the mischievous changeling of legitimate journalism, seemingly left on the doorstep of Ted Byfield by renegade fairies of Puck[18] beyond puckish passion. He and his magazine have had an impact on Alberta beyond all reason, given the fringe elements of reactionary stubbornness that made up the bulk of their audience.

I spent nearly two decades trying to penetrate his off-the-wall logic on any given subject. He spent the same time trying to psychoanalyze me in his pages.

Byfield is a man riddled with obsessions and prejudices, a permanent and perverse professional odd man out. He has a prodigious talent, often misapplied to suit his mood and thesis of the moment. He is the most engaging of enemies, a delightful man, witty, charming, entertaining, stimulating, articulate, soul-disturbing. I could never dislike him.

There has always been in him a barely concealed desire to harpoon the mainstream of society with malice lurking just below the surface of his complicated personality. His swashbuckling challenge to the established Central Canadian order sprang from the outrage of the times, Alberta's revolt against the crushing tyranny of Pierre Trudeau's Quebec "pipsqueaks" — the label the Liberal prime minister pinned on his own political lieutenants.

I first ran into Byfield in my early days as publisher of the *Journal.* He was an itinerant journalist who really yearned to be a reincarnation of the old-fashioned tub-thumping pamphleteers. Over the ensuing years, he got his opinionated wish, using his magazine as a showcase for his often wildly distorted view of the world.

Byfield sacrificed credibility with every acid paragraph, but he was adored by the fanatical, redneck, always outraged and mostly paranoid audience that he pandered to in Alberta in the years of its anger against centrist government. By doing so, he paved the way for Preston Manning's Reform movement. He was a belligerent Christian, muscular in beliefs that tended to the charismatic Anglican. He was a fervent anti-abortionist, a firm believer in corporal and capital punishment.

Byfield had ended his active newspaper career in Winnipeg (at the *Free Press*) when he became interested in a school movement that combined Christian principles with a hearty, outdoors approach to acquiring values of sturdy independence along with the traditional three Rs. He moved to Edmonton to open a St. John's School there, but the journalistic fires had not quite gone out. He persuaded the Anglican Order of St. John of the Cross to back a magazine that was designed to provide funding for the St. John's School. Thus, to give it its original title, the *Saint John's Edmonton Report* was born. He got his early editorial help by talking adult students of the St. John's Order into accepting payment of $1 a day as part of their "missionary" work.

Byfield was the driving force, the unremitting taskmaster. He wrote and rewrote much of the copy himself, in the style of Henry Luce in the early days of *Time* magazine. He stole shamelessly from the daily papers of Alberta, but seasoned each with a spicy aroma of his own prejudice.

The Order of St. John wriggled out of its commitment as quickly as it could, a little worried that what it thought was to have been a magazine with a solid Anglican base was shifting away from religion toward more secular themes.

When the $1-a-day "missionary" journalist stream dried up and real wages had to be paid to their replacements, Byfield got financial assistance from a number of corporate angels who sympathized with the views of the magazine and its feisty proprietor. Eventually, with help from a wealthy dentist brother in San Diego, Byfield turned the magazine into a family enterprise. At one time or another, his wife, Virginia, and various sons, a daughter and assorted in-laws all worked for the magazine. It changed its name to *Edmonton Report*. At one time, there was a *Calgary Report* as well, but it could not sustain itself and *Alberta Report* emerged as the offspring of that odd couple.

However, it was still *Saint John's Edmonton Report* when I was finding my feet at the *Journal* and, after giving me one or two harmless shots across the bow, it did me the dubious honor of making me its cover subject on Nov. 8, 1976. Donned in one of my green suits and staring intently at an issue of the *Journal*, I was posed awkwardly in front of one of the old presses at 101 Street as papers snaked their way up from the folder on their way to the mailroom. The headline superimposed on the cover read: Renaissance at the *Journal*. Inside a feature spread over three pages tried to answer the question of its heading: Can the *Journal*'s Fervid Irish Chieftain Cure its Three-year Circulation Malaise?

According to that story, the Southam company "had always betrayed a regrettable inclination to fret — about editorial policy, about responsibility to readers, about the embarrassing size of the *Journal*'s profits, about its ungainly bulk as Canada's fattest newspaper and finally about the inevitability of its eventual decline. Surely its enemies must someday weaken it." With all this weight of tribulation on its mind, Southam —according to *Edmonton Report* — had turned to good old Superman. The man to check the downward slide of the *Journal* "is a six-foot-one, 51-year-old Irish Catholic named J. Patrick O'Callaghan. His efforts to do so have injected a new vigour and enthusiasm into the city's old and (its critics would say) overweight daily paper."

Critics and enemies the *Journal* certainly had, and high on that list would be a maverick alderman, Ed Leger. A small motel owner, a man who had achieved his own brief hour of local glory by initiating an inquiry that led to the downfall of popular Mayor Bill Hawrelak, he could spot alleged corruption and graft at 50 paces. He claimed to have a suitcase full of evidence that would send dozens of city officials to jail, but he never got around to opening it. Depending on whose version you believed, he was either a former RCMP officer or an immigration clerk. Nobody knew much about him, nobody liked him very much, but he kept on getting himself re-elected alderman as a self-proclaimed crusader against alleged corruption, the outsider fighting the Establishment. And he knew the easiest way to spread that self-image was by getting himself quoted in the *Journal*, generally by taking the newspaper's name in vain in some outrageous and totally unwarranted charges against its character.

Once he had come to see me and, after an hour or so, he told me, as he was leaving: "By God, Patrick, I like your style. We're two of a kind." Assuming an air of shocked indignation, I said: "Don't say that publicly or you'll ruin us both!"

On Jan. 26, 1977, city council approved a motion by Leger instructing the city's business development office and the city commissioners to gather all relevant marketing information to approach publishers across the country in the hope of establishing a second newspaper in Edmonton.

Carrot-topped Ald. Ron Hayter, once fired by the *Journal* for attempting to start a union and for allegedly importing strippers into the newsroom for a stag party, maintained that his old paper was not responsible for its monopoly position and had generally handled that delicate circumstance well. "I can just see it now," Hayter said. "The *City of Edmonton Reporter*. Editorial conferences would be so long and so extensive we would never get around to putting out a newspaper ... and that's probably the best thing you could say about it."

Ald. Laurence Decore, later mayor of Edmonton and leader of the Alberta Liberal Party, dismissed the Leger proposal as "a complete and totally contrived political issue."

In all likelihood, Leger maintained, one of the major newspaper chains, particularly FP Publications, was already interested in coming to Edmonton. But Brig. Richard Malone, publisher of the *Globe and Mail* and the man then running FP, shot down that line. "We took a look at the Edmonton market six years ago, but found it would not be economically feasible to start another newspaper there," he told a *Journal* reporter. Malone said that several other newspaper interests had researched the Edmonton market in recent years, but none of them had concluded that the *Journal* was "a bad newspaper ripe for the plucking," as Leger contended.

At that time, there were only seven cities in Canada with competing dailies, but the *Journal*'s runaway success in a one-paper city was an open invitation to anyone with even a minimal knowledge of newspaper economics. The *Journal* was vulnerable despite the off-putting start-up costs that a newcomer would face. What made me more concerned was the fact that my pitch for a new plant for the *Journal*, with greater press capacity and colour printing potential, was getting only half-hearted response at head office. We had got as far as agreement in principle from the board for a production plant that would cost about $35 million. We intended to keep our editorial, advertising, circulation and business functions downtown, proposing to join the Royal Bank of Canada in a major development, along with the rest of the block that the bank owned, all the way to Jasper Avenue.

We had bought the land at Eastgate for a production plant, but everything then bogged down at head office in Toronto as John Rothwell got into the act. He came up with a different press configuration almost daily while we remained consistent: we wanted three 10-unit presses, because we needed utmost page capacity. We had to print more than 180,000 copies for five days a week, with another 200,000 on Saturdays. We were averaging more than 100 pages each day. Our fallback position, which we never disclosed to head office as long as Rothwell continued to have the ear of Gordon Fisher at the Royal Canadian Yacht Club, was for three nine-unit Goss Metros. There were times when Rothwell wanted us to experiment with four six-unit presses, or six four-unit presses. This would have meant running the presses almost all day, with the paper going through endless preprint operations. In fairness to Rothwell, such a configuration would have saved $3 million in initial installation costs, but putting out the paper thereafter would have been a daily nightmare. Rothwell's final proposal — "final" in his sense, being a day-to-day thing at best — was for three seven-unit presses. In the end, we got our three nine-unit Goss Metros, ideal for the *Journal*'s needs, and when the *Calgary Herald* built its own integrated plant two years after the *Journal*, it got exactly the same press configuration without so much as a murmur from Rothwell.

Things got so bad during the *Journal*'s running feud with Rothwell — known as Lord John because of his patrician bearing, his very English accent and supercilious attitude, and his trick of keeping a clean, white handkerchief conspicuously on display tucked into his sleeve — that Fisher had to keep rushing to the battlements in hopes of stopping the war.

In one letter, dated Feb. 11, 1977, Fisher had this to say to me: "I think part of the problem is your mind works twice as fast as anyone else's and your body works twice the hours. You are capable of arriving rapidly at judgments that others will only plod toward more slowly. The result for you, I am sure, is a high degree of frustration. The result for others has been and will continue to be, unless you are very careful at disguising it, a sense of nervousness at your instant shoot-from-the-hip, straight-for-the-target sort of approach. In short, Pat, you are a touchy customer. It is not so much a question of whether you are right or wrong on any given issue. From my own experience, I know that 99 per cent of the time you will end up at the right decision substantially ahead of most of those people with whom you have to do business. The touchiness appears when others question your conclusions and your reasons, only to be confronted with your impatience to get on to the next problem."

In that same letter, Fisher explained that "as publisher of the company's largest and substantially the most profitable newspaper, you are in a perfect position to become our senior publisher although, as you know, we never designate such a position formally." That was before he got down to the serious business of burying his hobnailed boots in my ribs. But he hastened to add: "Finally, let me assure you that this letter is not in any way, shape, or form to be construed as a request for your resignation."

Picking up on this barely concealed iron fist in the velvet glove in my Feb. 15 reply, I wrote: "As to your reference to a possible request for my resignation, that is your privilege. If you are dissatisfied with my performance, then it is a decision for you, and you alone, to make. It is only fair to say that the question of resignation has crossed my mind and still exercises my thoughts to some extent." I went on to say I was totally disillusioned with Southam.

What I didn't tell Fisher was that my resignation had already been written. It was never sent because I was determined to see the Eastgate plant built before lighting the fuse to that bomb. It was not until September that the contract with Goss for the nine-unit Metros was signed, and Fisher and I were still exchanging acid-tipped darts because I flatly refused to deal with Rothwell or even allow him in any of the *Journal* buildings.

Although I was always living on borrowed time with Southam, Fisher was not by nature a confrontational person. Indeed, he made a special trip to Edmonton to soothe my ruffled feathers. In the course of that meeting, in that convoluted way of his, he said that "in the fullness of time, it is not beyond reason to see you as a director of the Southam company." It may not have been beyond the bounds of reason, but it never happened, although — like all the other publishers of the larger Southam dailies — I did later become a director of the somewhat junior and toothless Southam Newspaper Group in the restructuring of the company that followed Fisher's death.

Things had been pretty quiet for a while on the second newspaper front, but in June of 1977, I got a glimpse of the future. Carl O'Byrne, circulation director for the *Toronto Sun*, and Ken Wright, marketing manager for the *Financial Post* (then owned by Maclean Hunter), came to Edmonton on a scouting trip at the invitation of Edmonton city council. They talked to me about the possibility of the *Journal* printing a second newspaper, should they decide on such a launch. But given the heavy pre-runs required for the *Journal*, still operating on its two old clunkers of presses, both sides knew there was no available capacity left for a second paper. In any case, I did not want to tie the hands of the *Journal* at that time. Although the *Journal* was highly successful alone in the afternoon field, the wave of the future in newspapers was morning publication — another battle I knew I was going to have to face with the reactionary forces at head office.

The subject of printing a paper for the *Sun-Financial Post* partners came up again in August and I was quoted as saying: "Three years from now we might consider putting our new presses to work in this way, but for the time being such an operation would cause us untold grief."

Creighton then told the *Journal* that a decision about an alternative newspaper for Edmonton would be made in a few weeks, but he was upstaged by Douglas LeBel, a small-time local publisher, who announced he was planning to start the *Sunday Morning Sun* in October, with a proposed press run of 60,000. The guessing game over a *Toronto Sun* branch plant ended on Nov. 2 with an announcement by Creighton that the *Toronto Sun* group would start with a Sunday newspaper in Edmonton in April and would "expand immediately into a daily operation." Creighton promised a "cheerful, informative, entertaining, maybe even irreverent" newspaper. He went on: "We think the dear old *Edmonton Journal* has become a bit too establishment and could do with some competition."

In a tongue-in-cheek reply, I wrote to Creighton to "extend to you western hospitality and a welcome to our club.... I admire your nerve but doubt your perspicacity in the Edmonton context, so keep your eastern carpet bag packed and ready at all times."

In response, Creighton pointed out that "Southam (head office in Toronto) is the *crème de la crème* of the Western Canadian Carpet-Bag Establishment." Referring to the fact that an announcement concerning the appointment of Bill Bagshaw as publisher of the new paper did not appear on the front page of the *Journal*, Creighton said: "Those who are used to reading *War and Peace* daily I'm sure would have found the story, even on Page 121 of the *Journal*. Anyway, a newspaper that can carry enough advertising in the middle of the week to justify all those pages would welcome competition. With that size paper, you could give your carrier boys a hernia."

There was still some uncertainty over the name of the paper, as LeBel was disputing the Toronto group's claim to the *Sun* title, so that was in the hands of the lawyers.

North Hill News had agreed to print the newspaper and was planning a $100,000 press expansion to cope with it. Maclean Hunter — which, at that time, had no financial involvement in the *Toronto Sun* company — had dropped out of the Edmonton project, not satisfied with the market research done by its erstwhile partner.

That was something that puzzled me, too, and I once asked Creighton: "Did you do any research at all on this market?"

With a straight face, he replied: "Oh, yes, Don Hunt and I walked down Jasper Avenue and we could smell the money."

That may or may not have been the extent of the research done, but even if the story were apocryphal, it served the self-image that Creighton loved to cultivate.

# CHAPTER 8

Armed with a $600,000 loan from the Canadian Imperial Bank of Commerce, Doug Creighton got down to work in the fall of 1977 on the *Toronto Sun*'s first colonial adventure.

Finding an editor for the *Edmonton Sun* was the first obstacle to overcome. The man the *Sun* wanted most was Eddie Keen, a popular muckraking broadcaster whom Ross Munro had "persuaded" to resign from his position as city editor of the *Journal* some years earlier. Keen, a promoter and bandleader on the side, had grown a little too aggressively self-serving in his zeal for free publicity for himself in the columns of his own paper. Keen turned down the offer from the *Sun*, but said he'd be willing to write a column instead.

Ted Byfield also rejected the *Sun*'s approach. He was having too much fun sniping from the sidelines with *Edmonton Report*.

Others rumoured to have been considered as editor included: *Journal* columnist Barry Westgate, a brash New Zealander who had a long roller-coaster ride at the *Journal*; Eric Denhoff, the talented but totally unmanageable public relations officer for native activist Harold Cardinal; and Peter Reynolds, the creator and producer of CBC's *Hourglass* TV program. The bearded Denhoff eventually became one of the wild stable of columnists the *Sun* used to attract chest-beating attention to itself. Most of Denhoff's columns were written from a bar stool, and read that way.

The man who should have been editor, according to *Edmonton Report*, was me! My inclinations, said the magazine, in its issue of Nov. 14, 1977, "seemed to fit the role perfectly, a man of Irish name and instinct, who obviously delighted to write sledgehammer articles about politicians, brawl with the city council, make inflammatory speeches and stand ready to confront chin to chin anybody looking for a fight.... He was, in fact, the very kind of man the *Sun* needed for an editor. Unhappily, he was already working for the other side."

In the end, it was Ron Collister, the Liverpool-born former *Telegram* columnist and CBC political commentator, who was rescued from a minor *Sun* role in Ottawa and whisked out to Edmonton as editor. Collister had lost favour with the CBC after running as a federal Tory candidate in a Toronto riding — on the urging of Robert Stanfield. Collister failed to win the riding, but ended up with the largest vote count of any losing candidate. But coming out of the political closet had sidetracked his career with the CBC. It felt that Collister had sacrificed his credibility as an Ottawa commentator by identifying himself so clearly as a partisan Tory. The CBC had sent him to Washington to avoid his "contamination" in Canadian politics. In Washington, he was out of the TV limelight at a time when Ottawa was the focal point of the Trudeau-generated energy wars and the unilateral drive for a Constitution. When the CBC would not recall him from exile to Washington, he left and became a newspaper writer again, working for the *Sun*.

The kindest thing that could be said about Collister was that, as an editor, he was a great talk-show host on radio station CJCA. Administration and leadership were not high on Collister's range of talents. He was basically a solo performer.

Without an editor to pick on in the first days following the confirmation of the *Sun*'s Edmonton venture, *Edmonton Report* had to settle for Bill Bagshaw as its target. The newly appointed 45-year-old publisher, whose only newspaper experience was as a high school columnist for the *Medicine Hat News*, had helped to found CHQT. As its assistant general manager, this account executive created a large listening audience for the slightly highbrow music station and made it second in the city to rock 'n' roll CHED. The *Sun* hired him more for his community connections than for his journalistic skills. To quote *Edmonton Report*: "He is the Chamber of Commerce-Commonwealth Games-Kinsmen Club type, the kind upon whose availability all success in civic endeavour depends."

While all the speculation and hype about the newspaper was giving Creighton all the free publicity his heart desired, the *Journal* was announcing that a Martin Goldfarb survey of more than 200 of our readers, carried out in November 1977, showed that readership had increased in the past year, and this despite a 15-cent price increase.

However, many readers felt there was too much advertising in relation to the amount of news in the *Journal*. This was more of an image problem than anything else, because throughout 1977 the *Journal* had averaged 253 columns of news per day, compared to 217 the previous year. And, for the month of December alone, the average number of news columns per day was 294, compared with 214 in December, 1976. Creighton knew what he was talking about with his War and Peace wisecrack!

Apart from the *Edmonton Sun*, there were other battles being fought. On March 15, I had gone to court with an application for a writ of *certiorari* (a court order to quash a prior action) to overthrow a 60 per cent pay raise city council had awarded itself. The pay raise was voted on in a secret session of council, only a few weeks after the municipal elections. The decision was then announced in open session, as required by municipal law, on Dec. 13. The application for *certiorari* followed public uproar that led to a 24,000-name petition for a plebiscite. The petition was organized by CJCA broadcaster Fil Fraser[19]. The petition had asked for the decision raising aldermanic salaries from $12,000 to $19,000 to be put to a public referendum, as required under the Alberta Municipal Government Act. At its Feb. 14 meeting, council then agreed to accept the petition "for information only" and on March 14 it voted not to review the increase.

Also filed in district court was an application for a writ of *mandamus* (a judicial writ issued as a command to an inferior court, or ordering a person to perform a public or statutory duty), requesting the city to hold a public plebiscite on the pay raise. Both applications were in my name, as a taxpayer of the City of Edmonton, because they could not be filed by a corporation.

Explaining the actions to *Journal* readers, I wrote: "It is basically a matter of ethics, rather than legality."

Council was not subject to the regulations of the Anti-Inflation Board[20], in force since October 1975, but many of those whose taxes would go to pay the increases most certainly were, and there was natural resentment of the privileged few who could skirt around that detested board that was trying to put a lid on earnings and profits of other Canadians.

In the midst of all the thunder of public anger over the city's secret pay raise, it was disclosed that Ald. Leger, who had the ability to walk on both sides of the fence at the same time without emasculating himself, had written to the CRTC in an obvious attempt to bring pressure to bear on Fil Fraser's employer, CJCA. In his letter, Leger claimed that one alderman had said that Fraser "called us a bunch of robbers one morning." Leger asked the CRTC to obtain tapes of various Fraser shows because "remarks have been made which may be defamatory and actionable."

A day later, when *Journal* reporters interviewed a number of aldermen for a response to the legal actions, Leger said: "O'Callaghan will have his fingers and his ass burned severely."

Ald. Olivia Butti compared my action to the 1970 kidnapping and subsequent murder of Quebec cabinet minister Pierre Laporte by FLQ terrorists.

On March 21, 1978, Judge John Bracco reserved decision on the *Journal*'s bid for a public plebiscite. The city's lawyer, Bill Wilson, said the city objected to my status in launching the actions and said so far as the application for a writ of *mandamus* was concerned, "he (O'Callaghan) hasn't got direct enough interest." Nor was there any proof I had signed the Fraser petition, he said. (Nobody ever asked me that question — in fact, I never did sign the petition.)

On June 20, Judge Bracco granted my application for a writ of *mandamus* directing the city to submit its salary increase to a vote of the public. He also approved the application for a writ of *certiorari*, quashing council's decision to receive the 24,000-name petition as information only. However, he agreed that the writ of *mandamus* made it necessary to proceed with the writ of *certiorari*.

Leger was back behind his howitzer at the June 26 council meeting. He had been defamed by me in a published statement after the Bracco judgment, he said. He gave notice that he would move at the next meeting of council that all city advertising should be pulled from the *Journal* and placed in the *Sun*. He claimed that the same advertising that cost $348,127 in the *Journal* could have been placed in the *Sun* for $128,829. The difference in cost, of course, was based on the circulation spread between the two papers. The *Sun*, which did not then belong to the industry's Audit Bureau of Circulation (ABC) was claiming an average of 35,131 copies a day while the *Journal*'s daily circulation, as audited by the Audit Bureau of Circulations (ABC), was 178,693. Next day, I was quoted in the *Journal* as saying, "Surely by now he should have grasped the point that the *Journal*'s integrity can't be bought at any price."

In mid-July, without holding the court-ordered plebiscite, which it knew it could not win, council rescinded its wage-increase package and referred the issue to an independent committee headed by Justice Arnold Moir.

The case made legal history — it was the first time a newspaper, through its publisher, had sued a city council. The *Journal* had gone beyond the usual observer role of a newspaper, but the action had become necessary when an elected council attempted the destruction of democratic ethics through secretive meetings and decisions made behind the public's back. It was council's abdication of responsible leadership that lay at the root of the affair. In stepping down from its ivory tower to assume an obligation as the defender of the public, the *Journal* was simply following a noble press tradition of activism on behalf of the community it served.

# CHAPTER 9

On April Fool's Day 1978, the *Edmonton Journal* announced that a start would be made later that month on its $35-million production plant at Eastgate, about seven kilometres from its long-time downtown location. It was the 75th year of the *Journal*'s service to Edmonton and northern Alberta.

The plant would have 193,000 square feet of floor space and include the pressroom, mailroom (the marshalling yard of a newspaper's operation, where the papers are assembled and bundled and wrapped before distribution), dispatch area, newsprint warehouse storage and its own cafeteria. While pages would continue to be prepared camera-ready by the composing room downtown, the photo images would then be transmitted to Eastgate by a fibre optic link. The plates for the presses would be prepared at Eastgate. All other functions of the newspaper would remain downtown once the old presses were scrapped.

At Eastgate, the *Journal* would convert from letterpress to offset, with its three Goss Metros capable of producing up to 96,000 copies each hour.

The day after that announcement, the first daily to compete with the *Journal* since the *Bulletin* folded in 1951, made its debut. The *Edmonton Sun* had a press run of 75,000 for this Sunday edition of April 2, 1978. Publisher Bill Bagshaw said he expected to attain a weekday circulation of 35,000 and a Sunday circulation of 50,000.

There were lots of premature epitaphs for the *Sun*. At a champagne breakfast on the first morning, Dr. Charles Allard told his table companions, of whom I was one, that the *Sun* wouldn't last six months. I disagreed with him, saying that as a matter of pride, and because of its own relatively stable financial position, the *Toronto Sun* would prop up the Edmonton paper for at least two years. In fact, the *Toronto Sun* had to use its own profits for far more than two years to keep its branch plant afloat until it started to make money.

The *Toronto Sun* had other problems to deal with before my dire forecast could be tested. Not the least was the risk it faced of seeing its editor, Peter Worthington, and publisher, Doug Creighton, ending up in jail.

Worthington had come across what was classed by the government as a top-secret document. He printed excerpts from it in the *Toronto Sun*, allegedly to prove that Pierre Trudeau had lied to the country on security matters. Worthington named names from the document, his argument in doing so being that he was dealing with past history, that all those listed in the "secret" document were already known and that any possible RCMP interest in those who may or may not have been engaged in some sort of cloak-and-dagger work in Canada had long since waned.

In March 1978, the *Sun*, Creighton, and Worthington were charged by the RCMP under the Official Secrets Act with receiving and communicating a top-secret RCMP report on Soviet espionage in Canada. They were due to appear in court on April 28.

A week before that, at the annual meeting of the Canadian Daily Newspaper Publishers Association in Toronto, I moved the following resolution: "It is proposed that, while we do not necessarily support the action of the *Toronto Sun*, we do condemn the discriminatory action of the government in charging the *Sun* under the Official Secrets Act, and we ask Mr. Robinette (CDNPA's legal advisor John

J. Robinette) to examine the act as it relates to newspapers, and to advise us of representations we might make to government to make the act more in tune with the times in a democratic country where freedom of the press is an essential requisite of a free people."

That took us only a dot or a comma or so beyond a motherhood tsk-tsk in the direction of the government, but given that the *Sun* was somewhat lacking in friends at the publisher level, that was the best I could do if I hoped to get any official backing from the CDNPA. Paddy Sherman seconded the resolution, which was passed — if memory serves me right — with only one dissenter, Jack Grainger, publisher of the *North Bay Nugget.* Grainger, a cheerful freethinker, told me he voted against it mainly because he didn't like the *Sun* and he thought any comment by the CDNPA would be in contempt of court.

My original resolution had the adjective *vindictive* rather than *discriminatory* in its text, but this was changed at the request of Margaret Hamilton, senior vice-president of Thomson Newspapers. Judging the government's action as vindictive was an editorial opinion, she said. "I prefer condemnation on the basis of discrimination, which is a fact," she explained.

In introducing my motion, I had told the publishers that while freedom of speech was not absolute and could not be contained within a shifting boundary, there would always be a dispute between government and a free press as to where the boundary line of freedom should be drawn.

I said: "One assumes that the argument that will decide that issue will be based on the assumption that the document that is the basis of the charges laid was so far from being a secret document that, in the words of former prime minister

Diefenbaker, 58 copies of it were thrown into the air and picked up by various civil servants."

Whether the *Sun*'s decision to print what it did was based on courage or foolhardiness was immaterial, I said. "Whether that decision was deliberately provocative, daring the government to prosecute the *Sun*, is not for me to guess."

When I talked to Worthington after that CDNPA meeting, he stoutly denied he was determined to be a martyr to his own cause of bringing down the government of Pierre Trudeau.

"What does a paper do if it has proof that the prime minister is not telling the truth?" Worthington asked me.

"Publish and be damned," I replied.

On June 9, Ron Basford, minister of justice and attorney general, took exception to some of my remarks to that CDNPA meeting. Speaking in Penticton to a joint meeting of the Canadian Bar Association (B.C. branch) and the Law Society of British Columbia, he hotly denied my allegation that the decision to prosecute the *Sun* was based on government vindictiveness.

Basford said, "It is inconceivable to me that a man of that stature (me) could possibly believe the law operates in that manner. It implies that I, as attorney general, had allowed a prosecution decision to be discussed in cabinet, for which I clearly would have to resign.... It implies that my senior advisors in the Department of Justice are so unprincipled as to not only allow such a decision but to actively prosecute the case on my behalf. Such is not the case."

That didn't satisfy me a bit and I fired back with a column asking why a decision was taken to prosecute the *Sun*, but not the *Toronto Star*, which had the same material. The *Toronto Star* was traditionally a Liberal supporter and with the Gallup polls showing the government in deep trouble, the government could not afford to spit in the eye of the *Star*. Why was George Bain of the *Star* not prosecuted? He had been far more critical of the government on the issue of the secret document than Worthington had been. Why had Tom Cossitt, an MP who spoke long and loud on the secret document and its contents, inside and outside of the Commons, not been prosecuted? The CBC, a Crown corporation, and the second major TV network, CTV, had also made use of the document. Why were they getting off scot-free?

The federal solicitor general, Jean-Jacques Blais, told a court that publication of Worthington's column cost Canadian intelligence officers certain advantages they had held in their struggle with their Soviet counterparts. He claimed that the revelations destroyed the cover of certain informants and made others worry that the same thing could happen to them.

The defence was somewhat hampered when the courts refused to allow the *Sun*'s lawyers to see 548 documents that presumably rested in RCMP files. Blais asked the defence to accept his word that the documents were vital to Canada's security. The defence was placed in the position of trying to defend its clients without having access to the documents that were the basis of the charges.

Under Britain's Official Secrets Act of 1911, there had been only 23 prosecutions between 1945 and 1971, a period of great espionage activity worldwide. Of that total, only two involved journalists. Nevertheless, Britain had such reservations about the application of the act that in 1971, it set up a committee under Lord Oliver Franks to find ways to water down the absolute powers granted to the government.

During its hearings, the Franks committee discovered that the mere threat of prosecution often discouraged publication of certain information. The most notorious case involved the world-renowned science journalist, Chapman Pincher, who was intimidated sufficiently by such a warning that he refused to publish information from a document that showed conclusively the potentially devastating defects in the Windscale nuclear reactor[21].

Worthington's revelations in the *Toronto Sun* were hardly of that magnitude, but the declaration of the Franks committee in its 1972 report ("It is basic to natural justice that an accused should know the evidence against him.") was certainly pertinent to the Worthington case of 1978. He was never allowed to see the documents that formed the basis of the Crown's case. The scales of justice were loaded against Worthington, despite Basford's protestations to the contrary.

Worthington did not go to jail. Judge Carl Waisberg threw out the charges against Worthington, Creighton and the *Sun*. Worthington was neither a traitor nor a spy, and it was shameful that his character would be smeared by trying to ensnare him in a net more properly intended to catch enemies of this country. If Worthington is the worst this country has to fear, then we can all sleep soundly in our beds at night.

# CHAPTER 10

Roy Farran, the Winged Dagger, was one of the more colourful characters to flit through the pages of Western Canada's history since the Second World War. He had so many sidelines and careers behind him that he was difficult to catalogue and almost impossible to define with precision. The voice spoke softly in erudite wit and there was always a twinkle in the eyes as though, underneath it all, he had never learned to take himself seriously, no matter how others considered him. He was born in a border town straddling the two Irelands, so he came honestly by his credentials as a bare-knuckle brawler and a lover of tall stories, eloquently recounted in warm tones. But, unlike most soldiers, he never talked about his past exploits as a war hero; indeed, he looked more like an Anglican minister in mufti than the professional military man he once was.

Farran had a brilliant war record and a chest full of medals, many for activities with partisans behind the lines in Europe. His later service in the Middle East, at a time when refugees from Europe were trying to beat the British blockade of Palestine[22], did not endear him to the Jewish community. His brother Rex was killed when he opened a parcel addressed to Roy and it exploded in his face[23].

Farran ran unsuccessfully for the British Parliament as a Churchill Tory, then settled down to a writing career. A facile wordsmith, he turned out a shelf of war novels, mostly based on his own exploits. Of them all, *Winged Dagger*, sold the best and provided him with the capital for a new life in Canada.

He arrived in Calgary to start the North Hill News. Its giveaway circulation and its heavy advertising linage began to give the *Calgary Herald* a few fits. He bought a ranch in the lush foothills near Priddis and spent hours each summer swimming in his outdoor pool or riding the range, an accomplished and fearless horseman. He got into Canadian politics as a Calgary alderman, then followed Peter Lougheed into the Alberta legislature.

As Alberta's solicitor general, he wanted to set up an old-fashioned Borstal[24]-type reformatory for boys aged 16 to 18. He reasoned this would teach young offenders a trade, with a maximum of character-building and an accent on sports and discipline. He developed the wilderness-challenge approach in the wilds of the ghost coal town of Nordegg, west of Rocky Mountain House. Short, sharp sentences were useless, he said. He wanted to keep offenders in his juvenile penal system for at least two years instead of the 90 days most of them were sentenced to.

But when Farran and I crossed swords, it was more over hardened criminals rather than the youngsters Farran thought were worth salvaging through tough love.

In October 1978, half an hour after a hostage-taking incident had ended without serious injury at Fort Saskatchewan Correctional Institute, north of Edmonton, a photographer from the *Journal* and another from the *Sun* were ordered to give up film they had shot of riot-equipped guards who had apparently taken part in the incident. When the photographers protested, they were marched back into a building by several guards armed with billy clubs. When the *Journal* photographer, Colin Shaw, tried to phone his city editor for instructions, he was ordered to hang up the phone by Terry Downie, the prison director. Then the photographers were told to expose their film.

When a *Journal* reporter phoned Farran, who, as solicitor general, was responsible for Alberta's prisons (other than those under federal jurisdiction), Farran said: "We are playing it cool.... I don't think there's any need to be alarmed."

I thought otherwise and, the next day, the *Journal* published an editorial headed Jackboot Mentality.

"These (photographers) were not two ruffians behind bars for crimes against society," I wrote, "but two legitimate professionals going about their legal business. They did not break into jail. They were permitted to enter. They did not take part in the hostage-taking incident.... Mr. Farran claimed the *Journal* photographer 'pushed his way into jail.' Can you imagine that? Hundreds of people behind bars at the Fort want to get out and our man 'pushes his way in.' What utter nonsense!"

I followed this up with a letter to Jack Saucier, the Calgary Queen's counsel (QC) who was then chair of the Alberta Press Council. Saucier agreed to call a special meeting of the council to consider a complaint about the treatment of the photographers. (The *Sun* was not a member of the press council, but I acted on behalf of their photographer, Tom Walker, as well. The lanky Walker later worked for me at the *Calgary Herald*.)

Colin Shaw had spent 15 years in the armed forces, four of them in the Airborne Regiment. He had been a member of the Skyhawks parachute team and he had seen his share of danger and violence. But he confessed to me that despite all that military experience he felt "like a hostage in there. I felt if things hadn't gone exactly their way they would have become physical. I haven't felt that threatened in a long while."

Normally, the press council deals with complaints against its member newspapers, not complaints from the newspapers. The procedure was therefore designed to avoid a complainant having to endure the possibility of withering examination from the newspaper's representative. Once a complaint was made in writing, it was referred to the newspaper for possible remedial action, or, failing that, for a written response from the newspaper. Neither the complainant nor the newspaper being complained about was supposed to appear in person, so that the press council could deliberate strictly on the evidence before it.

But this was a special circumstance, and Farran cheerfully asked for permission to appear in person. I agreed to this proposal and was also granted the right to attend and debate the issues involved.

Farran, up to then the only cabinet minister ever to appear before the Alberta Press Council, brought with him his assistant deputy minister in charge of corrections, Bob King, and jail director Terry Downie.

Farran defended the actions of the guards and officers of the institution and stated he imposed a news blackout on events at Fort Saskatchewan to "cool the intense feelings generated." In hindsight, he said, "I admit there could have been better briefing." Photographs should not be taken of members of the tactical squad because "they perform a dangerous job for the public" and if they were publicly identified through newspaper photographs, there was a danger that prisoners or their friends outside could endanger the lives of the squad members or the lives of their families. Guards had not used excessive force in fulfilling their lawful duties, he added. The squad was not armed with billy clubs or truncheons, as claimed in *Journal* reports, "but just straight Japanese riot sticks."

Downie said he was courteous to the photographers and only wanted to confiscate their film. However, he added,

*Sun* photographer Walker insisted he wanted to expose his film. When told that the film Walker had exposed was not the roll of photos taken of the guards, Downie got annoyed and sternly told the press council: "Mr. Walker deliberately misled me and should be subject to discipline from his employers." I doubted if the *Sun* would oblige him. Personally, I hoped I never fell into the official clutches of the stiff-necked Downie.

Some press council members were disturbed at the use of words such as *jackboot* and *Nazis* in *Journal* and *Calgary Herald* editorials.

The Red Deer member of the press council, Dennis Scott, a Penhold farmer who had spent three years in a German prisoner-of-war camp — including 13 months in handcuffs — said: "Newspapers do not know what the jackboot mentality is. The press used harsh language and, in general, the correctional people and RCMP are having a difficult time, and from a citizen's point of view, I don't think they are getting a fair shake." He advocated bringing in a Japanese or German prison camp director to build a prison that would cut staff in half and reduce meals by 90 per cent. Then, he said, there would be no repeat offenders in jail.

Jail officials were rapped firmly across the knuckles by the press council for their treatment of the photographers. The manner in which they were forced to expose their film was entirely unwarranted, the press council said.

In all fairness to Farran — whom I later hired, after he left politics, to write what proved to be an elegant but ultra-right-wing column for both the *Journal* and the *Herald* — he never did take up Scott's suggestion to bring in a Japanese or German prison camp commandant to keep the hardliners at Fort Saskatchewan neat, clean and civilized.

# CHAPTER 11

On March 13, 1979, Peter Lougheed and his Tories won 74 seats in the Alberta legislature. Social Credit hung on to four. Grant Notley[25], later to die in an air crash in northern Alberta, was the only NDP member. As usual, there was not a Liberal in sight, although the closets of Alberta might have been full of them.

The size of that Tory majority gave many true democrats heartburn, no matter how proud the premier himself might have felt at the sight of all those blue-bottomed Tories arrayed in their legislative splendour and conveying the image of unparalleled voter approval.

Two days after the election, in what was intended as a letter of congratulation, I wrote to Lougheed: "The glory is yours and you are entitled to bask in its sunshine today. However, as a publisher, I face the dilemma of running a newspaper that is philosophically in support of the style of government you have given this province but that still has the obligation to give voice to all those who, in effect, lack representation and are swamped by the overwhelming mass of Tories.

"Once again, the *Journal* will walk that delicate and often unmapped borderline between approval and opposition, representing the only effective voice of caution to a juggernaut, the only possible opposition standing in the way of autocracy and paternalistic dictatorship by default of the voters.

"Unlike you, we were not elected to our position: we have to assume it, in the absence of any other effective voice to ensure that democracy remains alive. I find staggering legislature majorities depressing to a certain extent, no matter how effective the government and the leader being given such a mandate, for without a questioning army — let alone a corporal's guard of inept and dispirited losers — lined up on the other side of the floor, all those cherished ideals forged through debate and intelligent dissent fade into paternalism by neglect."

Thus, I declared the *Journal* to be the "unofficial opposition" and we took that role seriously. There were those — mostly Tories — who regarded this as an arrogant assumption on my part. They may well have been right. But my fear was that the newspaper, supposedly the surrogate for the public, had no other choice without running the risk of letting Alberta drift through that period of government with no more than yawning tokenism where democracy was supposed to be.

Some Tory supporters — then and now — look upon all journalists as mavericks who refuse to be corralled. But Tories, by nature, tend to be humourless, glaring apoplectically at the world out of countenances permanently afire because of collars that fit too snugly around their bull necks.

As we hoisted our pirate flag up the mast immediately after the provincial election, we added five extra staff to cover the affairs of the legislature. We appointed a full-time columnist, the admirable Don Braid, who — in time — kept Preston Manning and the Reform Party firmly in his sights.

(This was a watching brief he maintained from the legislature in Edmonton when he transferred his loyalties to the *Calgary Herald*. Finally, deciding he needed a change from provincial politics, he moved his family to Calgary and became the *Herald*'s city hall columnist; somehow, he never achieved in that role the same stinging pinpoint accuracy that had marked his stint as a provincial correspondent.)

During this spell of beefed-up coverage of the legislature by the *Journal*, our reporters, led by the unflappable Wendy Koenig, uncovered so many scandals involving social services that Alberta ombudsman Randall Ivany was kept busy with public inquiries that invariably confirmed the arrogance, insensitivity and incompetence of the department. Indeed, its deputy minister, the elegantly groomed Stanley Mansbridge, father of television's Peter, deemed it time to get out of his overheated kitchen and take early retirement. Certain elements of the department were out of control and, in such circumstances, it is always the head bureaucrat who must absorb the public's anger when the minister himself ducks for cover, as Blundering Bob Bogle[26] always did.

Alberta Tories railed against the *Journal*'s impudence in establishing itself as the "official opposition," although I kept on reminding them that the phrase I always used so carefully was "unofficial opposition." Being a fiercely partisan political scrapper, Lougheed himself never took kindly to the *Journal*'s self-appointed role.

The weakness of the system in Alberta in the Lougheed days was quite simply that the popularity of the man tended to bring about lopsided legislatures. The voters put their faith in Lougheed, but the same blind trust was not always accorded those who made up his cabinets.

Lougheed and Sen. Ernest Manning, another former premier, were dissimilar in so many ways, but in their leadership and sure touch both were just right for their times. Social Credit did not survive Manning for long, and the Progressive Conservatives lived on borrowed time under Lougheed's successor, Don Getty. It took Ralph Klein, another populist of a less disciplined nature than Lougheed, to bring the party back from the edge of the grave.

From an Alberta newspaper's point of view, two elections — one provincial and one federal — in only two months in 1979 should have been enough juicy fodder for any publisher to feed on, but the *Edmonton Sun* had to do it without Bill Bagshaw, its first employee. Only nine months after the first issue of the carpet-bagging *Sun* had rolled off the presses, Bagshaw was gone.

In an announcement made with Don Hunt's characteristic bluntness, the *Edmonton Sun* said its relationship with its publisher had been "severed ... effective immediately." Hunt, the *Toronto Sun*'s vice-president and general manager, appointed himself chief executive officer in Edmonton. "You can only go so long before you make changes," he said. "We're not getting our fair share of the ads.... I think we have some problems that are surmountable.... We intend to be here for a long time."

As he breezed into Edmonton, Hunt admitted that losses for the first year of the *Sun* would exceed original projections of $250,000 to $300,000. He had no idea how long he would have to stay until a new publisher was found. If he was unhappy with the *Sun*'s advertising, it also became obvious he was having even more trouble believing the circulation figures the *Sun* had been posting on its front page every day. They disappeared with Hunt's arrival and it was months before they were restored — and then considerably lower than earlier claims.

Hunt gave the *Edmonton Sun* a certain stability — using the word relatively speaking, given the turmoil it was enduring at the time — but it took him several months. He was a massive man of genial aspect. He and I were never on the same side in the newspaper wars, but the personal relationship between us was always friendly.

# CHAPTER 12

For all his naive earnestness, Opposition leader Joe Clark, who set out on a helter-skelter foray through 24 different time zones in January 1979, was a tragicomic sad sack, a Chevy Chase[27] in search of a pratfall.

The trip, to the Middle East and Japan, was supposed to be a photo opportunity to demonstrate to the voters back home that Clark could hobnob comfortably with the elite of world politics. By then, the image-makers had had their way with Clark. They dressed him nattily to a point where he looked stylish, if awkward, in a whole range of double-breasted outfits. His advisors changed his hairstyle. They helped him deepen his voice to make him appear more manly and impressive in delivery. But they couldn't do much with his tortured vocabulary that made him sound stuffy and lugubrious.

With a jeering chorus from the National Press Gallery along for the ride, Clark's organization team seemed more suited for planning a leisurely tour through the Okanagan than for the rigours of world travel. Clark never did catch up with his luggage and at one point, in Israel, he almost circumcised himself on the bayonet of an honour guard. In the middle of that miserable jaunt, Clark was quoted as saying in Tokyo: "I'm not going to win an election abroad." True, but he came perilously close to losing one there.

When he returned to Canada, he found the country in a sullen mood, but his own stock had taken a tumble as he became the object of belly laughs because of his misadventures. When Pierre Trudeau called the federal election for May 22, 1979, all the indications pointed to an anti-Alberta campaign by the Liberals, but Clark, the Alberta Tory, was in no position to benefit from a backlash in his own province. And a fellow Tory, Premier Bill Davis of Ontario, ever the opportunist, was already casting covetous eyes on Alberta's resource riches. However, Trudeau's own standing was so low that some Liberal insiders had discreetly suggested to him that he should step aside and let John Turner lead the party.

For Clark, then, May 22 was a date with destiny or oblivion, as the *Edmonton Journal* pointed out. The *Journal* didn't doubt that Clark would win, but warned: "A minority win for Joe Clark may be as depressing as a total defeat. It is now or never for him." And against a jaded and dispirited Trudeau, a minority win was all that Clark could manage.

If wishes were horses and beggars could ride, Clark would have been the consummate politician's politician. Instead, it was his fate to suffer the frustration of being a prime minister without respect, the parliamentarian who could not count when it mattered. There were nothing but alligators and swamps ahead of him for the rest of 1979. And it was evident that his own province of Alberta was not going to rush to his aid.

In a tough speech in Vancouver at the beginning of November, Premier Lougheed threatened to withhold approval of $12-billion worth of non-conventional oil recovery projects unless Ottawa came up with the domestic oil pricing deal Alberta wanted. Without something closer to the world price, as set on the Chicago market, said Lougheed, Alberta could not afford the non-conventional oil projects.

Meanwhile, Davis — looking for an issue to help him survive in a looming Ontario election — was representing himself as the "defender" of Canada against "greedy" Alberta's demands.

Lougheed was determined to stick by the rule of Canadian tradition that allowed only the producing provinces and the federal government to set oil prices. However, Davis had already forced his way to the table for a showdown poker game with Clark and Lougheed on energy. Alberta controlled 85 per cent of all Canada's energy at that time, so it should have held all the aces. However, Davis knew that with 58 Ontario Tories sitting in the Commons, Clark's position as the leader of a minority government not catering to Ontario was already shaky.

Lougheed had never had a high regard for Clark and this was evident to all the card sharps at the energy showdown. Lougheed's rage over the dilatory approach to a deal by Clark and his amiable babe-in-the-woods energy minister, Ramon (Ray) Hnatyshyn — later governor general — led to one of the rare occasions when Lougheed lost his cool. He hurled his briefing book against the wall as Clark and Hnatyshyn blathered on while Davis donned his inscrutable look, hiding behind the cloud of smoke from his pipe.

In the end, the half-hearted energy agreement with Alberta that was hammered out there but never implemented — or even welcomed by Lougheed — was not the issue that brought down the Clark government just before Christmas, 1979. It was the 18-cent excise tax that Finance Minister John Crosbie had proposed, basically to pay the cost of Clark's election promise of a mortgage tax-deductibility program. On the last day of his insecure hold on power, Clark refused to accept the advice of his aide, Nancy Jamieson, that there would not be enough Tories in the Commons to help his government survive a vote of non-confidence on Crosbie's soak-the-motorist "boodget." The downfall was engineered by Allan MacEachen[28], but the decisive vote of 139-133 against the government came when the Liberals backed an NDP sub-amendment to their own motion of non-confidence.

As Casey Stengel[29] might have said of Clark and his Tories: "Does nobody here know how to play this game?"

With Clark contemptuously tossed aside in the federal election of Feb. 18, 1980, Trudeau finally had the majority he needed to launch the major offensive of his political career — the pursuit of a made-in-Canada Constitution and Charter of Rights. But the West wanted no part of the Trudeau rule: from the Lakehead to the Pacific, only two Liberals were elected. However, all but one of Quebec's 75 seats went Liberal.

During the election campaign, Trudeau and his finance minister of a year earlier, Jean Chrétien, had avoided any specifics of the alternative to the Clark agreement on energy that they had in mind for Alberta. However, Marc Lalonde, the designated hitter on energy, and Windsor's Herb Gray, the one-track member for the auto industry, were somewhat more vocal. The uneasiness in Alberta became unbearable.

Lalonde declared that Alberta's oil belonged to all of Canada, while Davis talked smugly about "Canada's interest," when all he had in mind on energy policy was cheap oil and gas from Alberta to bolster the manufacturing dominance of Ontario. Not to be outdone, New Democrat leader Ed Broadbent accused Alberta of holding the rest of the country to ransom with its demand for a more rational oil price.

Alberta had never asked for the world price for oil. Lougheed had always maintained he would be satisfied with 85 per cent of the Chicago price. Under the Clark proposal, it would have taken five years to reach the 85 per cent level.

Just 10 days before the February polling deadline, Trudeau went to Edmonton where he spoke in reasonable terms of the "made-in-Canada" deal he would negotiate with Alberta. But he gave no details.

Herb Gray had his own view of how the Liberals would handle Alberta. If the province wasn't as "reasonable" as Ottawa wanted it to be, he said, then a "fair deal" would be arrived at by using constitutional powers to bring Alberta to heel.

At that time, Alberta was receiving only 45 per cent of the Organization of Petroleum Exporting Countries (OPEC) price for oil. However, according to Stuart Smith, a one-time Ontario Liberal leader, Albertans were already "filthy rich."

Surprisingly, Trudeau was always grudgingly admired in Edmonton. However, in his frustration with Lougheed — basically on two issues, energy and the Constitution — Trudeau made it clear he could never fathom Alberta's relationship to Central Canada and Ottawa. During one of their Harrington Lake[30] energy summits, Trudeau told Lougheed: "You'll have to stop calling me Mr. Prime Minister if we are going to be enemies."

Having demolished the tepid sovereignty association referendum that Parti Québécois Premier René Lévesque took to the Quebec voters, Trudeau had another crisis on his hands as the June 30 deadline approached on which the existing energy agreement with Alberta was to expire. Without an agreement, Alberta was planning to set its own price for oil and gas. Lalonde countered with a proposal for an increase of $2 a barrel, to last until October. That, clearly, was a stop-gap measure to keep the energy issue out of the way of the constitutional conference with the premiers that Trudeau had set for September.

The Constitution was Trudeau's beloved infant. The National Energy Program (NEP) was Lalonde's unnatural child, and Trudeau was no more than its godfather.

Lalonde made two brief visits to Edmonton after the general election. During one of them, he took breakfast at the Chateau Lacombe with the *Edmonton Journal* editorial board. After telling Lalonde that Alberta's position on energy was simply a matter of principle, the guaranteed right of a province to control its own natural resources, particularly a rapidly depleting resource it was being forced to sell at only a fraction of its true market value, I accused Lalonde: "It seems to me your position boils down solely to a matter of money."

Without so much as a blush, Lalonde replied: "That's' right. We have this horrible deficit and we have to start bringing it down. The oil business is the last cash cow left to be milked by the government." (The "horrible" deficit at that time was about $14 billion. The deficit, despite all the billions skimmed off Alberta's oil income, topped $40 billion by 1995.)

Lalonde returned to this theme of deficit financing in June in an exclusive interview with the *Journal*'s Don Braid. Brushing aside Braid's reference to principles, Lalonde said: "We're not debating a theological argument or the salvation of our souls. We're talking about a lot of money.... It is dangerous to stumble on principles."

To that end, Lalonde became convinced Alberta owned the golden goose. Commenting on a price structure he was proposing, he said in a public statement: "The Alberta government will become wealthier than anyone in his wildest dreams could have dreamed even four years ago."

Mark Rose, an NDP MP from British Columbia picked up on the theme in a letter to the *Edmonton Journal* in June. He talked of the "cool" $33 billion being handed in five years to the "profit-fat foreign oil industry in Alberta."

In person, I rather liked Lalonde. When he smiled, with his lips drawn back from those graveyard teeth, he was far removed from the bully image he always projected in Alberta. He did have a sense of humour, but his toughness, tenacity and overbearing earnestness more than camouflaged any personality endearment.

Civil disobedience in Alberta was always terribly remote, almost everyone agreed, but that did not stop public musing on Alberta's options should Lalonde impose his own unconditional surrender terms in the energy war. With Quebec having pioneered using a referendum to negotiate sovereignty association, I suggested in an *Edmonton Journal* article that Alberta might ask a similar question of its own citizens: "Do Albertans agree to let their provincial government attempt to negotiate a form of sovereignty association with the rest of Canada?" There was the enticing prospect of calling a snap provincial election just before the upcoming September constitutional conference. Imagine how Lougheed might feel, I wrote, if he went to such a conference with a referendum in his pocket giving him the right to negotiate sovereignty association with Ottawa.

This tongue-in-cheek stuff drew an outraged cry from Nick Taylor, the leader of the provincial Liberals — a party then without a seat in the Alberta legislature. The article, he said, was the result of "mixing a leprechaun with crude oil." He speculated that the "publisher of the *Edmonton Journal* hopes to be the first admiral of the Alberta Navy."

Charlie Lynch entered into the spirit of the Alberta mood with a column from Edmonton in the form of a letter to the Southam papers "from the not-so-quiet western front."

"It is hell here in the trenches, waiting for the worst," Lynch wrote. "The publisher of the *Edmonton Journal*, J. Patrick O'Callaghan, has urged the population to forswear the use of force as long as there is a chance for a peaceful settlement, but knowing O'Callaghan he really means to get the jelly ready — Irish fashion. It's reported he's already got his commission in Peter Lougheed's ARA — the Alberta Republican Army."

# CHAPTER 13

"In many instances, those who write to newspapers are nuts. If newspapers are responsible for publishing nutsy comments, they should take responsibility for the consequences."

The speaker was a Quebec lawyer, Emile Colas, and the occasion was a meeting of the Uniform Law Conference of Canada in Saskatoon on Aug. 21, 1979. What sparked the statement was a debate on a joint submission by Ontario and Alberta lawyers for a change in the libel law as it concerned letters to the editor.

The 110 delegates of the meeting included deputy attorneys general from several provinces, provincial legal staff and law reform groups.

The focal point of the meeting was the Cherneskey case. A Supreme Court of Canada majority ruling in 1978 had put the whole issue of letters to the editor in jeopardy. While most members of the public were indifferent to the entire affair, seeing it as no more than the haughty press getting its knuckles deservedly rapped, it was really the public that stood to be victimized. The ruling could have eliminated newspapers as the medium of expression for public opinion.

To those who cherish free speech, a newspaper's letters page is a public debating arena. Every journalist understands the page is used to air a wide range of opinions, most of which are not held in high regard by those who publish or edit newspapers. Nevertheless, the letters page is the most authentic megaphone for the grassroots available in a democratic society.

That voice was in peril of being muted when Morris Cherneskey, a Saskatoon lawyer who was also an alderman, successfully sued the *Saskatoon Star-Phoenix* for libel over a letter it had published in 1975. He was awarded $25,000, plus costs, against Armadale Publishers Ltd., owners of the *Star-Phoenix*. The Saskatchewan Appeal Court reversed that decision, but the Supreme Court of Canada restored the original verdict in a 6-3 decision in 1978.

Cherneskey had helped to draft a petition on behalf of 54 persons. It was directed against the establishment of an alcoholic rehabilitation centre in a residential section of Saskatoon. In presenting the petition to Saskatoon city council, the petitioners made much of the fact that it was the use to which the centre would be put by natives and Métis that they alleged would be detrimental to the area. One man told council that the establishment of the centre would turn the area into an "Indian and Métis ghetto."

In the Saskatoon newspaper's report of council proceedings, there was only a brief reference to Cherneskey contributing anything to the debate on the petition he had helped to draft. He was quoted as saying he did not think the zoning bylaws envisioned 15 people living in one place and until the bylaws were clarified, the centre should not operate.

After reading that straightforward report of the council meeting, two young law students wrote to the *Star-Phoenix* to say they were appalled by the stance adopted by the alderman. They said it was unbecoming a member of the legal profession to adopt such an approach and they hoped the "racist resistance" exhibited would be replaced by the support and encouragement they felt the project deserved.

The newspaper put the heading Racist Attitude on the letter. Cherneskey promptly sued the *Star-Phoenix* for the libel.

In response to the suit, the *Star-Phoenix* pleaded fair comment and qualified privilege. However, the defence of qualified privilege was thrown out by Justice Brownridge, and this decision was subsequently upheld by the Supreme Court of Canada. The six judges who signed the majority report declared that the burden of proving fair comment rested upon the party asserting it. The judgment said that the person writing the material complained of must be shown to have had an honest belief in the opinions expressed and "the same consideration apply to each publisher of the material."

The two students who wrote the letter had left the province by the time the case had come before the courts and, because they were outside the jurisdiction of the Saskatchewan legal system, they were never sued and never called to give evidence, so nobody could ever ascertain to the satisfaction of the courts if they honestly held the opinion they had expressed in their letter.

The courts then followed a dubious line of logic brought out in the questioning of executives of the *Star-Phoenix* that showed the newspaper people did not hold the opinions expressed in the letter from the students.

Therefore, said the Supreme Court judgment, "it appears ... to follow ... that where ... there is no evidence as to honest belief of the writers of the letter, and the newspaper and its publisher have disavowed any such belief on their part, the defence of fair comment cannot be sustained."

The majority of the Supreme Court denied that this should be construed as meaning that a newspaper was in any way restricted in publishing two diametrically opposite views of the opinion and conduct of a public figure.

What it did mean, said the judgment, "is that a newspaper cannot publish a libellous letter and then disclaim any responsibility by saying that it was published as fair comment on a matter of public interest, but (that) it does not represent the honest opinion of the newspaper."

The six members of the Supreme Court who signed that opinion included Chief Justice Bora Laskin.

However, a dissenting opinion written by Justices Brian Dickson and Willard Z. Estey had this to say: "As the columns devoted to letters to the editor are intended to stimulate uninhibited debate on every public issue, the editor's task would be an unenviable one if he were limited to publishing only those letters with which he agrees. He would be engaged in a sort of censorship, antithetical to a free press. No one believes that a newspaper shares the view of every hostile reader who takes it to task in a letter to the editor for errors of omission or commission, or that it yields assent to the view of every person who feels impelled to make his feelings known in a letter to the editor."

The Dickson-Estey opinion went on: "A free and general discussion of public matters is fundamental to a democratic society. The right of persons to make public their thoughts on the conduct of public officials, in terms usually critical and often caustic, goes back to earlier times in Greece and Rome."

Dickson, who later succeeded Laskin as chief justice, also had this to say: "It is not only the right but the duty of the press, in pursuit of its legitimate objectives, to act as a sounding board for the free flow of new and different ideas.... Many of the unorthodox points of view get newspaper space through letters to the editor. It is one of the few ways in which the public gains access to the press."

And then he got to the heart of the matter as far as any Canadian journalist is concerned: "Newspapers will not be able to provide a forum for dissemination of ideas if they are limited to publishing opinions with which they agree."

It was further pointed out that the tendency in a public controversy would be to suppress those letters with which the editor was not in agreement. The integrity of a newspaper, as Dickson noted, rests not on the publication of letters with which it is in agreement, but rather on the publication of letters expressing ideas to which it is opposed.

It is doubtful if there is an editor or publisher in Canada who would disagree with that. Nor would any of them seek special immunity from the application of general law: in the matter of comment, an editor or publisher should be in no better position than any other citizen. However, the Supreme Court's majority ruling was the exact opposite of that position: it put the publisher in a worse position than any other citizen.

According to a British court ruling, the right of fair comment is one of the fundamental cornerstones of free speech and the written word, and the courts should preserve the right of fair comment undiminished and unimpaired.

Because of the breadth of the scope of fairness when considered objectively, the issue in most cases, according to Dickson, concerns whether the defendant published the comment maliciously.

It is obvious there is a world of difference between fair comment and comment made with malice. In the Cherneskey case, the lower court's ruling that "malice is out" was not challenged either by Cherneskey's lawyer or by the Supreme Court. Dickson said that the statement made in the letter to the *Star-Phoenix* might well be defamatory, but even if it was, it was not actionable if the person publishing the statement had a good defence such as fair comment.

Unfortunately, Dickson's view did not prevail upon his colleagues at the Supreme Court. So the majority ruling swept aside the traditional idea of the newspaper as a forum for comment and discussion.

What is worse, it seemed to push the newspaper back to the dark ages of partisanship, when the only views that might be published would be those of the publisher and editor. Lord Beaverbrook, the Canadian who, in Fleet Street's *Daily Express*, practised freewheeling partisan journalism in a manner nobody had since matched, would no doubt stand up in his grave and cheer lustily at the prospect. The ruling of the Supreme Court meant that the pamphleteer would take precedence over the journalist who generally attempts a balanced presentation in news columns.

The Supreme Court ruling seemed to be out of step with the British case of Silkin vs. Beaverbrook Newspapers. In that instance, Justice Kenneth Diplock told the jury: "Those are the facts on which the defendants say they were commenting in the article, and those are the facts which you will bear in mind when you are asking yourself the question in the terms in which I put it to you: not whether you agree with the comment made on these facts, but whether you think it is a comment which any man, be he prejudiced or obstinate, could honestly hold."

Diplock pushed his point home: "So, in considering this case, members of the jury, do not apply the test of whether you agree with it. If juries did that, freedom of speech, the right of the crank to say what he likes, would go. Would a fair-minded man holding strong views, obstinate views, prejudiced views, have been capable of making this comment? If the answer to that is yes, then your verdict in this case should be a verdict for the defendants. Such a verdict does not mean that you agree with the comment. All it means is that you think that a man might honestly hold those views on those facts."

It might be stretching a point, but what if the Canadian Supreme Court judgment had been taken out of its original context to include not only letters to the editor but signed columns or even news stories? As a publisher, I doubt if I ever agreed with more than 25 per cent of the personal views of outrageously opinionated columnists writing in the newspapers I ran. Most columns of that nature are deliberately provocative, often a tongue-in-cheek stimulus to debate. But they help to form public opinion.

To accept the Supreme Court's verdict unchallenged would have meant it would have been unsafe for newspapers to publish letters to the editor unless they were either on very innocuous topics like the mating habits of racing pigeons, or contained opinions which the publisher or editor could personally endorse. And if the publisher allowed a letter to run because he agreed with its stated premise, then, – according to judicial reasoning, he could not accept for publication a letter in response that took an opposing stance.

While it was hard to understand the assertion of the majority who signed the Supreme Court's ruling that freedom of the press was not affected by it, the Supreme Court majority found a supporter in *Toronto Star* columnist Borden Spears. He felt that Justice Dickson and apprehensive publishers like me were missing that mark. Spears, who later served on the Kent Royal Commission on Newspapers, thought it was extravagant to suggest that letters would have to be purged of their traditionally vigorous, disputatious and even bigoted contributions. The issue, he said, was not the free expression of opinion, but the publication of a libel.

And a distinguished Alberta QC, while agreeing that the law of defamation was an area badly in need of reform, told me that the Supreme Court ruling merely meant that in the future editors would avoid publishing letters that might be held to be defamatory.

Another publisher felt that the judgment left open some possibility that establishment of the writer's honest belief by the editors might be a viable defence. In turn, this raised the possibility that newspapers could ensure additional protection by obtaining from the writer of a letter an affidavit attesting to his honest belief. A clumsy device, to be sure, given that most metropolitan dailies receive thousands of letters each year intended for publication. And not all of those discarded would even come under the "nutsy" category determined by Emile Colas.

An affidavit system might have helped the *Star-Phoenix* in the Cherneskey case, in view of the fact that the actual letter writers had slipped outside the jurisdiction of the Saskatchewan courts. But what an impediment it would have been to quick publication of an exasperated reader's comments on important current events!

If one accepted the view that the Supreme Court ruling had no bearing on the public and was distressing only to the newspapers themselves, then it is on a par with a statement once attributed to a Scotland Yard commander. He said: "There are only about 20 murders a year in London and not all are serious — some are just husbands killing their wives."

In the category of those who don't regard wife-killing as any more serious than littering the sidewalk, I would put the man who commented in this fashion on the Cherneskey ruling in a letter to the *Edmonton Journal*: "Albertans and Canadians should encourage their governments to reinforce the libel law so that the people, through their elected representatives, may have more clout when dealing with attempts by established, entrenched, or powerful, or monopolistic groups to discredit those in public life who do not perform in the manner, or for the purpose, that those groups desire. The same should be true for individuals. There is much recourse in a democracy to express dissent in a civil and decent manner."

He didn't explain how this "civil and decent dissent" could be expressed. The average citizen, for instance, is not in the habit of hiring a hall or putting on a $500-a-plate dinner to give his thoughts to a captive audience. When he is outraged by some aspect of public life, or the vagaries of those who choose to govern him, the average citizen only has one avenue within his reach, and that is his local newspaper's letters column.

If the ruling of the Supreme Court had been accepted as the last word on the subject, then where else could the average citizen, whose opinions do not coincide with those of his local editor and publisher, turn to express his exasperation with life in general?

Did it mean that a newspaper might be forced to throw away a letter from someone claiming to have spotted the first wild geese of spring flying north unless the publisher himself could personally verify the sighting with his rheumy old eyes?

The Cherneskey case was a sad day for free speech and the democratic expression of bold dissent, but it coincided with still another negative court thrust against a long-cherished democratic platform of free speech and expression — the right of a cartoonist to puncture the balloons of political pomposity through the art of satire.

The Supreme Court of British Columbia ruled that Bob Bierman[31], the Victoria cartoonist of biting wit, had libelled a B.C. minister in a cartoon that showed the minister gleefully pulling the wings from flies, with a tag reading Human Resources upon his chest. There was no cutline or caption to the cartoon, the basis for which was a statement by the minister that government could cut its welfare costs by giving every able-bodied man on welfare a shovel and putting him to work building roads. The lawsuit was clearly the case of a pompous minister without the slightest vestige of a sense of humour, a man who had obviously never heard of the Harry Truman advice to politicians who found the kitchen too warm for their tender tastes[32].

The minister? William Vander Zalm, then in the cabinet of Bill Bennett, but later premier of British Columbia.

We reran the cartoon in the *Edmonton Journal* and sent a cutting to Vander Zalm with the suggestion he might like to sue us too. We never heard from him. It would have been interesting to see what an Alberta court might have done with that case.

Another disturbing thing about the Bierman suit was the statement by the B.C. Supreme Court that "the cartoon depicts the plaintiff as a person with a love of cruelty who enjoys causing suffering to defenceless creatures. That was a false misrepresentation of the character of the plaintiff, as a person or in his role as minister."

Whether or not the voters of British Columbia saw that particular minister as quite the lovable or sensitive character the Supreme Court appeared to suggest is immaterial. What was upsetting was that any judge would accept that the cartoon conveyed to the ordinary, reasonable reader a statement of literal fact rather than exaggerated comment. The ordinary, reasonable readers in B.C. should be even more upset to be characterized as quite that dumb. I would doubt that there are any "ordinary, reasonable citizens" — even in B.C., a province noted for its high level of oddballs — who would be persuaded by a cartoonist that a minister of the Crown spent his spare time getting hilarious kicks from pulling wings off flies.

What the B.C. judgment meant was that the precedent created by the Supreme Court of Canada in the Saskatoon letter-writing case had been carried over into the make-believe world of cartooning. The defence of fair comment had even been denied to the artist who used satire and humour to make his point.

Surely, even judges must have occasionally glanced with amusement at the work of such as Rodewalt, Aislin, Yardley-Jones, Uluschak, Macpherson, Peterson and the like[33]. After all, the art of lampooning public figures in this way is probably older than newspapers themselves.

Cartoons are not intended as pictures of reality. They are not mirror images of anything. A cartoonist takes a facet of a public figure's appearance or character and exaggerates the devil out of it. Like Brian Mulroney's chin. How can this be a statement of fact or comment on anything but an artist's imagination running wild?

Robert Stanfield must have filled the walls of his recreation room with the originals of various banana cartoons[34], but then Stanfield was made of different character than the thin-skinned Social Credit ministers of British Columbia.

Despite Vander Zalm, hard-hitting political cartoons remain a way of life in Canada and, after a concerted effort by newspapers across the country, the sting from the Cherneskey case was also finally removed. Cartoons and letters to the editor continue to be a means by which newspapers and their readers can combine in venting their strongest feelings about those who wish to govern them. Legitimate criticism can flow on, keeping totalitarianism or benevolent paternalism — one almost as bad as the other — from the grip of those who seek power without accepting the responsibility or accountability that power in the name of the people inevitably demands.

While there was obviously no conspiracy on the part of the courts to eat into the traditional freedom of the press, it would be fair to say that the example set by the Supreme Court of Canada presided over by Bora Laskin was not sympathetic to the press. Free speech appeared to have fallen on hard times with the inhibitions of the courts, the judges going a long way toward the goal that politicians alone did not have the power to achieve — the silencing of the press. However, after Laskin's death, the Supreme Court under Brian Dickson showed far more understanding of the role of a free press.

Nevertheless, the root of the problem was not the highest court in the land, but the courts that ruled on provincial laws.

The joint Alberta-Ontario presentation to the Uniform Law Conference of Canada in Saskatoon on Aug. 21, 1979, was the first serious attempt to get agreement among the provinces for an amendment to their defamation legislation that would unplug the blockage on letters to the editor. Each province would have to make its own changes to its own laws, if political will so desired. Roy McMurtry, the Ontario attorney general, took his draft proposal to Saskatoon and when it did not get complete approval, he redrafted it for first reading in his home province.

However, John Robinette, then legal advisor to the Canadian Daily Newspaper Publishers Association, said that he and the solicitors in the Ontario Ministry of the Attorney General were of the view that the original version was preferable. McMurtry came around to their way of thinking and the wording eventually put before the legislature was the original draft.

Meanwhile in Alberta, I met with Premier Lougheed on behalf of Alberta's dailies. Lougheed was sympathetic to our point of view and arranged a meeting for me with Attorney General Neil Crawford early in December 1979. Jean Côté, then the *Edmonton Journal*'s senior lawyer and later a judge of the Alberta Court of Appeal, went with me. Crawford, an affable and efficient politician, had with him Deputy Attorney General Ross Paisley and Emil Gamache, a senior lawyer on the attorney general's staff. Crawford undertook to take a proposal to the cabinet and caucus policy committees to amend the wording of the Alberta Defamation Act as follows:

"Where the defendant published alleged defamatory matter that is an opinion expressed by another person, a defence of fair comment shall not fail for the reason only that the defendant did not hold the opinion."

This was a shortened and simplified form of the original proposal put to the Uniform Law Conference by the Ontario-Alberta delegation. Crawford led us to believe that the amendment would go before the legislature in the spring, assuming it did not get shot down in caucus. My concern was not so much the possibility of flak from the caucus, but anticipated sniping from Gamache, who was somewhat sour on the idea of any change, based on his own personal feelings about the Edmonton press.

Two months after that meeting, I was lunching with Lougheed and raised with him my continuing concern after hearing the day before that the subject of the proposed amendment had been struck from the caucus agenda list. He was surprised to hear that, because it had been agreed that the government would proceed with the amendment.

About an hour after that luncheon, I was phoned by John Scrimshaw, Crawford's aide, who told me the amendment would, in fact, come before the spring session of the legislature. Everything was in order, he said. A few minutes later, Paisley phoned to tell me the same thing.

Obviously, Lougheed hadn't wasted any time in making his wishes clear on the subject.

However, when nothing surfaced in the legislature by May 1, I wrote to Crawford, enclosing a clipping of a Canadian Press story about the introduction of legislation in Manitoba to amend that province's Defamation Act. I pointed out to him that the Alberta legislature had been in session for several weeks and reminded him of his deadline of spring for change in the Alberta act.

The reminder was unnecessary. Eight days later, on May 9, Crawford expertly steered his amendment through without any of the attendant gusts of rhetorical bombast that had dogged McMurtry's efforts in Ontario. The Alberta changes received royal assent on May 22, 1980.

In short order, amendments in roughly similar terms were approved in Manitoba, New Brunswick, Saskatchewan and Ontario. In effect, there can never again be a Cherneskey case, although the changes came too late to spare the wallets of Armadale and the *Star-Phoenix*.

The protection given under the changes does not give any newspaper any special privilege. It is just a case of restoring a principle that was always assumed to be in the act until the Cherneskey ruling. A newspaper is still bound by the provisions of the Defamation Act and no publisher has ever sought, or expected, any freedom of expression other than that traditionally accorded to all citizens. Libel is still libel, and no newspaper can escape its responsibility for publishing defamatory material, no matter whose signature appears on the offending letter or article. The amendments, however, make it clear that an ordinary citizen has the right to say his or her piece in public print, whether or not that same view is shared by the editor or publisher. They allow the columns of a newspaper to become a true debating arena once again for all shades of opinions, and that is the basis of a populist democracy.

Sir Robert Peel, a long-time British prime minister and the founder of the first British police force, once said: "Public opinion is a compound of folly, weakness, prejudice, feeling, right feeling, obstinacy and newspaper paragraphs."

Whether letters to the editor shape public opinion, or simply regurgitate opinions formed, reformed and deformed by columnists and editorial writers, is open to debate. However extreme the opinion, however violent the language in which it is couched, it can be perfectly legal. But the violence of the language may itself destroy the immunity if the courts consider it goes beyond the limits of comment.

However, in one form or another, the voice of the people must be heard. Even if those who write to newspapers are often characterized — sometimes with good reason — as "nuts."

# CHAPTER 14

Gordon Fisher climbed on a desk in the newsroom of the *Winnipeg Tribune* on Aug. 27, 1980, and announced that that day's edition would be the last. On the same day, Thomson Newspapers closed the *Ottawa Journal*. Four days later, the federal government set up the Royal Commission on Newspapers, specifically to inquire into the concentration of ownership and control of the newspaper industry.

The *Tribune*, in its closing battle with the *Winnipeg Free Press*, had made money in only one of the last 10 years of its 90-year history of valiantly striving to serve Winnipeg. The *Ottawa Journal*, a dinosaur left over from the palmier days of FP Publications, fell just short of its 95th birthday.

Fisher's great-grandfather, William Southam, founded the Southam company in 1877 for an outlay on his part of only $4,000. When the *Tribune* folded, the market value of Southam Inc., which by then had the largest total daily circulation of any newspaper group in Canada, was estimated at $500 million. Until 1945, Southam had been totally a private family company. In 1980, the hundreds of descendants of William Southam still owned about 40 per cent of the company. Indirectly, every citizen of the province of Quebec had an interest in Southam, through the Quebec Pension Plan. Canadian National's pension fund had a large financial stake in Southam. Royal Trust was another big shareholder on behalf of untold numbers of pensioners, family trusts, estates and others for whom Royal managed money.

Commenting on the past and future of Southam in 1980, Gordon Fisher said: "If I have any concern for this ship which my forebears built for me to steer, that concern is that as the number of shareholders broadens and the position of the founding family is eroded with the passing of generations, those whose wealth has been accumulated from other business interests might find us an attractive takeover prospect. That would be a catastrophe. I believe most profoundly that the size of newspaper companies is very much less important than the motives of their owners. Certainly, I don't believe the press of Canada should be owned by bankers, distillers, oil speculators and others of that breed. Nor do I believe that the newspapers of Canada should ever be subsidized by the taxpayers or be directed by their political leaders."

The closing of both the *Tribune* and the *Ottawa Journal* did not sit easily with the government or the public, and one stream of criticism came from an unexpected source — I. Norman Smith, who had retired in 1972 as editor and president of the *Ottawa Journal*.

Smith, who had joined the *Ottawa Journal* as an office boy in 1928, had said in an article in the *Ottawa Citizen* (owned by Southam) that while the closing might have been inevitable, "this surely borders on collusion." He said that nobody lost except the readers of the "great communities" of Ottawa and Winnipeg. "They will be bereft of the benefit of the editorial combat between two newspapers."

Fisher denied any collusion between Southam and Thomson in the two closings on the same day, but admitted to Smith "there was, of course, a deal."

The deal, as he explained it to Smith, followed a series of complicated manoeuvres that predated Thomson ownership of FP and the *Ottawa Journal*. Through the mismanagement of the *Montreal Star* by FP, Fisher said, the Southam-owned *Montreal Gazette* had "leaped ahead" in the market and this was devastating to the interests of FP, whose owners included two well-known Montreal families, the McConnells and the Websters. When the *Montreal Star* died in 1979, said Fisher, "we offered to the owners of FP the choice of selling their assets to the *Gazette* for cash or a piece of the *Gazette*, if they preferred to stay in Montreal."

After Thomson bought out the FP company on Jan. 11, 1980, it exercised the option FP had held to buy a one-third interest in the *Gazette*. Southam bought back that one-third interest for $15 million, a gain of $2 million for Thomson, in the arrangement that coincided with the deaths of the *Tribune* and the *Ottawa Journal*, and the purchase by Southam of Thomson's share in Pacific Press. (Until then, Southam had owned the *Vancouver Province*, and FP had owned the *Vancouver Sun*.)

"For all the obvious reasons," Fisher wrote to Smith, "such a partnership in the *Gazette* would never have been offered to Thomson if the Montreal deal had been negotiated with them. Both I and my board of directors feel fully justified in getting rid of them as a partner in a newspaper that we well understood was originally sold to us partly in trust."

Thomson, who had taken over the *Ottawa Journal* only on Jan. 11, had tried to sell it to a number of others, "but there were no takers. I believe they would have sold it to us, but that, too, would have led us right into existing competition legislation. In any case, just as we are now damned for killing two newspapers, so would we have been equally damned for merging them."

Commenting on a suggestion by Smith that Southam might have considered publishing two newspapers in Ottawa with Thomson publishing two in Winnipeg, Fisher said that was not practical.

"The truth of the matter is that in both markets the losses of the loser have been greater than the profits of the winner."

In the space of about two months in the fall of 1975, said Fisher, "we loaded all the barrels of the Southam dreadnought, aimed them right at the *Winnipeg Free Press* and pulled all the triggers at the same time. The ammunition cost us over $1 million."

In the following five years, Southam committed an additional $15 million and pushed the circulation of the *Tribune* up to between 100,000 and 110,000. But the *Free Press* maintained its own circulation at its previous level and the fate of the *Tribune* was sealed after a long summer of analysis by Southam. "Had we won, the *Free Press* would be dead instead of the *Tribune*."

Taking full responsibility upon himself for the closing, Fisher said: "I can't say I enjoyed the decision. I could not recommend that another $35 million or $40 million be thrown at the Winnipeg newspaper market." Fisher said the only way Southam could meet the commitment to the 375 employees at the *Tribune* was to close the paper and to offer the most generous separation package that had ever been offered by any Canadian company to a group of employees whose job security it could no longer protect.

Explaining the Vancouver situation, Fisher said the original Pacific Press arrangement — by which production facilities were shared between two newspapers under separate ownership — had been made between Southam and the Cromie family more than 25 years earlier. When FP bought the *Vancouver Sun* from the Cromies, it inherited the sharing arrangement.

"With the Thomson purchase of FP, we found ourselves in bed with the one newspaper company in Canada with which I found it most difficult to contemplate being a partner," Fisher wrote. "In fairness to Thomson, they recognized that we were not natural bedmates and they accepted that, with their other interests in British Columbia, they would be the ones to leave Pacific Press. They named the price ($42,250,000) and we were willing to pay it."

# CHAPTER 15

The editorial autonomy granted to Southam publishers in those days was surely stretched to its limits during the Trudeau years when Alberta was treated like the outcast of Confederation. The *Edmonton Journal*, once the defiant defender of freedom of speech in the Aberhart press-gag feud, found itself the staunch ally of Premier Lougheed as he battled against the federal Liberals who saw oil-rich Alberta as the deep pocket a free-spending Ottawa sorely needed. The battle raged fiercely and there were hints from time to time from Toronto head office that the language of dissent might be moderated a little, in view of the fact that the Liberal policies on energy had the backing of most Canadians and the bulk of Southam's newspaper empire had an Ontario base. I doubt if the Southam board, insulated from western outrage, ever understood the reasons for that outrage. However, other than mild suggestions of toning down the *Journal*'s decibel levels, Southam stuck to its traditional policy of allowing editorial decisions to be made locally. There was no interference with local management.

As part of the strategy to exploit Alberta as a subservient western colony, the federal government pushed Alberta to the brink of separation without fully appreciating the danger or the risk. The government tried to foster the idea that greedy Alberta was being piggishly ungrateful for all the help and financial assistance it had received in the past from Ottawa.

In Central Canada, the myth persisted that Ontario was really the paymaster of Confederation. The truth was somewhat different. Only three provinces traditionally paid more into supporting federalism than they took from the national cash register. According to a study done by Robert Mansell, a University of Alberta economist, over a 25-year period from 1960 on, Ontario contributed $14.7 billion to help the have-not provinces. British Columbia coughed up $3.78 billion in the same period. Alberta, a province with a population that ranks it only fourth in size in Canada, paid out more than $100 billion. The biggest recipient of federal largesse in that same quarter of a century was Quebec. It took in a net total of $91.4 billion.

Another myth that seemed to be bred in the bone in Central Canada related to some early support Ontario had given to Alberta's energy development.

The late Bill Heine, then editor of the *London Free Press*, with his blinkers firmly in place, put it this way: "Alberta is only one of 10 provinces with only two million of the 23.7 million Canadians. While it is currently floating in oil, not many years ago, it was begging for, and getting, financial support from the rest of Canada to keep its floundering oil and gas industry functioning."

I appeared on a panel in New York before an audience of U.S. energy and investment experts and bankers. Fellow panelists were: Ron Ghitter[35], who later ran unsuccessfully against Don Getty for the Tory leadership in Alberta and was later a senator; Roy Romanow, who went on to become NDP premier of Saskatchewan; and Roy McMurtry, now a retired chief justice of Ontario and former Ontario cabinet minister[36].

All went well until the sleepy-eyed McMurtry, in countering remarks of mine on Alberta's energy status, started to draw for this influential American audience a totally distorted picture of Ontario "subsidies" for the Alberta oil industry.

Lougheed was in the audience, and his face betrayed his feelings. But it was left to a tall, quiet-spoken man in the audience to set the record straight. "It is true that Ontario paid about 10 to 12 cents more per barrel than world price for Alberta oil for a short period of time," he said, "but in turn it has been subsidized by Alberta through the energy war years to the tune of at least $12 a barrel." The net benefit to Ontario, after due allowance for the extra cents it paid for Alberta oil in the early days, came to more than $50 billion, said the man who shot down Roy McMurtry.

The speaker? Geoffrey Edge, former chairman of Canada's National Energy Board.

By the summer of 1980, Trudeau was exasperated by the fact that the biggest issue facing him before his September meeting with the premiers was not patriation of the Constitution, but that of ownership, control and sale of Alberta's natural resources. He let his frustration get the better of him when he met with a group of editors in July.

"Canadians can't agree on basic values unless first they have decided on who is going to rule over the fishes," he snapped.

July was a testy month for him. He approached a meeting with Lougheed on the 24th with the anger of a man who has history in his grasp but sees it all slipping away because of lesser concerns. He wasn't the least bit interested in Lougheed's view that the Alberta Natural Resources Act gave Alberta the right to ownership of its own oil and gas, among other natural resources. To Trudeau, Lougheed appeared to be acting as if he were sealed off behind the walls of an armed fortress, expecting the angry feds, Lalonde at their head, to storm the battlements and plunder the treasure chest represented by oil, gas and the Heritage Trust Fund[37].

In an interview with the *Edmonton Journal*'s Don Braid, Trudeau said: "As I challenged Edmontonians last year ... you can run Canada just as easily as five pipsqueak guys from Quebec can run Canada."

In advance of the July 24, 1980, energy summit with Trudeau, Lougheed had outlined what Alberta was prepared to do to meet Canada's energy needs. It was willing to accelerate oil sands development, assuming the cost of social and infrastructure changes for the new towns in northern Alberta. It would take a major equity in the developments while still maintaining exploration and development incentives for conventional resources. It would provide incentive royalties for tertiary recovery and an incentive price for incremental sales of natural gas throughout Canada, with the objective of "backing out" imported crude oil. It was willing to take major debt/equity positions in energy projects outside Alberta to further the federal objective of energy self-sufficiency, and it would support additional exports of natural gas to the United States to provide the necessary cash flow to promote exploration and development.

The cost of the Alsands and Cold Lake plants would have been about $7 billion each. Even one of those projects would have generated: $800 million in business for Ontario's iron and steel industry; $370 million for Ontario metal-working firms; $325 million for the Ontario transportation industry; $740 million for other manufacturers and processors in Ontario; $370 million for Ontario's financial enterprises; and $750 million for the Ontario trade and services sector. And yet, despite this generous offer, Lalonde had the gall to remind Alberta that "sharing is what this country is all about."

Only two days before the Harrington Lake meeting, Lalonde continued setting the stage, telling a B.C. cabinet minister that "the biggest threat to Confederation is Alberta, having $40 billion in the bank." It was clear a major confrontation was in the works, with Ottawa announcing it was preparing to invoke the Petroleum Administration Act, giving it extraordinary powers over oil and gas.

Two days before the energy showdown, the *Edmonton Journal* warned: "If the prime minister insists on carrying the Lalonde strategy to its ultimate conclusion, he may yet find that the scrap of paper he is prepared to bring home from Westminster without the consent of all the provinces will be as useless as the scrap of paper poor Neville Chamberlain brought back from Munich in 1938.[38]"

Lougheed came out of the Harrington Lake meeting fully convinced he had just heard a declaration of war against Alberta. In addition, Trudeau was ready to mouth his way through a deceitful litany of public statements designed to leave the impression that he was standing alone against the obstructionist provinces blocking the path to a made-in-Canada Constitution. He was prepared to go ahead with a Canada of two levels, the upper level consisting of Ontario and Quebec, the provinces with the voting clout backed by veto rights. The lower level, one genuflection short of equality, would consist of the rest of the country.

Western fury was fanned to greater heights in November, when the National Energy Program (NEP) was introduced as part of Allen MacEachen's budget. Those who designed the policy, including "Red Ed" Clark[39], Ian Stewart[40] and Mickey Cohen[41] — who went on to become a champion of private enterprise as the head of Molson Brewery — were fully convinced that Canada would not only become self-sufficient in energy by 1990, but that it would become a net exporter of conventional oil, if it chose to do so. A totally laughable concept, dreamed up by naively idealistic Ottawa mandarins who couldn't tell an oil rig from a two-hole outdoor biffy.

Part of the reasoning behind the Liberal budget strategy was that a comprehensive energy policy, while pilloried for its blatant revenue grab, was based on the assumption that huge revenues were needed for three specific purposes: to provide security of supply; to provide opportunities through the so-called Canadianization program for Canadian companies to share in the vast energy riches; and to provide fairness to all Canadian taxpayers through a new revenue-sharing program, the money coming out of Alberta's pockets.

Under the NEP, Alberta oil was supposed to increase by $14.30 a barrel by the end of 1983. That increase was made up of $6 at the wellhead, plus $8.30 in federal taxes. In other words, of the full $14.30 increase, Ottawa would take about $9.50, Alberta only $2.50 and the industry $2.30.

Lougheed's signature never appeared on any of the NEP documents in 1980.

A few days after the NEP was unveiled, I saw Trudeau at his chilling worst. I was one of 10 senior media people invited to Ottawa for private briefings on MacEachen's budget, the NEP and the Constitution. The prime minister had never looked more tired. He came to meet the media people after a grilling in the Commons on his plans to patriate the Constitution unilaterally. He never raised his voice above a flat monotone, but anger underscored many of his answers. He rarely lifted his head to look at his questioners, but when he did those cold eyes shrivelled the hearts of the bravest.

Some of my questions he rated as too contentious and argumentative, and at one point, staring at my quivering soul through my eyeballs, he said: "Well, if you don't want to listen…!"

When he claimed to the media people — most of whom were from Central Canada and abysmally ignorant of the energy matters, which upset the two Albertans in the group — that there was no export tax on natural gas, I was infuriated enough to suggest he was dealing in distorted semantics. He retorted: "Is it just semantics if the people of Canada have to pay $3 billion?"

He didn't spell it out to those who loved to see a pushy Albertan put in his place that while Canadians were indeed to be required to underwrite this $3 billion under MacEachen's budget, the money from this domestic tax on natural gas would not be going to Alberta as part of the energy package, but to the federal treasury to help hold the $14.2-billion national deficit in check. He said the federal government had offered a better deal to Alberta than the Clark government had proposed in the summer of 1979, a statement Lougheed grudgingly confirmed to me later. "The package I offered to Mr. Lougheed was worth $30 billion over three years and this was improved by $2 billion to $3 billion last week," Trudeau told the media.

Trudeau claimed there was enough oil in Alberta's tarsands to last many generations. "It may not last until kingdom come, but it will last beyond our lifetimes." If Ottawa could get agreement with Alberta, said Trudeau, it would be of benefit to the consumer, the Canadian economy, the federal government and "certainly to Alberta." The proposal to reduce the provincial take from 45 per cent to 43 per cent was not a "drastic injustice to Alberta."

When I asked him if he saw any way out of the impasse with Alberta on energy, he said acidly: "You don't expect me to negotiate with you, do you?"

He bridled at my questions on western alienation. He denied that his unilateral move to amend the Constitution was in any way changing the face of federalism.

The prime minister was asked: "If you were an Albertan, rather than a Quebecer, would you not feel just a little bit hysterical over constitutional change that drastically alters your concept of federalism? Would you not feel emotional over your political impotence on the federal scene, and would you not be gravitating slightly toward a form of western statehood?"

To that, Trudeau replied emphatically: "The answer to all those questions is no!"

He demanded proof to support my comment that permanent veto rights for two provinces (Ontario and Quebec) as planned in his constitutional proposal would turn the other eight provinces into second-class members of Confederation.

On the Constitution, he repeated a phrase he had used answering questions in the Commons — that it was unthinkable that the British would meddle in internal Canadian affairs. When I pressed for his authority on this opinion, he fell back on assurances he said had been given to him in a letter from British Prime Minister Margaret Thatcher in June of the previous year. He deliberately excluded me from his range of hearing when I wanted to pursue the validity of that letter from Mrs. Thatcher. He spent a lot of time talking about it, but he was careful not to distribute any copies of it.

If the letter he had in mind was that of early December 1979, all it said was: "There has been no change in our policy since I saw you in June." If that was all he had to go on, then he was overlooking a visit by a British envoy to Ottawa only a few days after the June meeting referred to by Mrs. Thatcher.

The envoy was sent to tell the Canadian government that, unless the Charter of Rights and Freedoms was dropped from Trudeau's constitutional proposal, it would never pass through the British Parliament.

What exactly had Mrs. Thatcher agreed to? According to the official transcript of the media meeting in Ottawa — a transcript sent to me by Patrick Gossage, then the prime minister's chief press officer — Trudeau's response to my attempted questioning of him on the Thatcher letter went like this:

"Mrs. Thatcher gave me her word that any request we put to her would become a government bill and that she'd put a three-line whip on it to get it passed. She gave me her word to this effect when I saw her at the end of June. And, indeed, how could it be different? How could the British Parliament meddle in Canadian affairs without being accused of colonialism? Maybe that the Canadian government and Parliament are misadvised and misdirected. But who is the British Parliament to say: 'Canadians, they really don't elect the right government?'"

We now know there was no three-line whip promised by Mrs. Thatcher. (A three-line whip is a directive that binds the government party to vote on an issue only as advised by its leader.)

Whatever Mrs. Thatcher had said to Trudeau, it should be remembered that it was at a time when he had not revealed the extent of his constitutional package. Later information suggested that it was not until October that the horrified Mrs. Thatcher discovered exactly what it was that Trudeau was suggesting she had committed herself to ramming through Westminster.

When asked if he had given any thought to unilateral action on patriating the Constitution without the benefit of

Westminster, Trudeau responded as follows, according to my copy of the official transcript and tape:

"A unilateral declaration of independence? I really haven't. You know, it seems to me such an incredible misreading of the British Parliament to think that they're going to meddle — because that's what it would be — meddle in Canadian internal affairs. I just can't examine that hypothesis with any degree of seriousness."

Perhaps he couldn't examine it seriously at that November meeting with the media executives, but he obviously considered it as a serious option in the following year after the Kershaw Committee recommended to the British government that it should not proceed with automatic patriation of an amended Constitution simply because Trudeau had crooked his index finger in their direction.[42]

Trudeau told the media people that even if he patriated the Constitution without the agreement of the provinces, there would still be Aboriginal Peoples and a number of premiers going to London to seek changes of their own.

He pointed out there was a precedent for going to London to get the Constitution amended before patriation, citing the federal trip to Westminster without provincial approval to get Newfoundland accepted into Confederation.

While in Ottawa for that Trudeau encounter, I spent some time with Joe Clark, and I was struck by the contrast of attitudes between Clark and Trudeau. While Trudeau was tired and testy and showing the strain of his 61 years, Clark had never exuded more self-confidence and that at a time when everybody seemed to want his job. It was hard to know if he was totally aware of the ominous shadow of Brian Mulroney, who had sought the party leadership without ever before running for public office and who was then showing stirring interest in a parliamentary career. Relaxed and at ease with himself despite his crushing defeat by Trudeau earlier in the year, Clark told me: "I'm not ignoring Mr. Mulroney, nor am I preoccupied with his intentions." Having survived a leadership review since the February election loss, Clark did not see any real challengers on his horizon.

Referring to Trudeau's attempt to patriate the Constitution unilaterally, Clark commented: "There are uncontrollable and deep forces loose in this country."

Despite surface serenity and confidence, there must have been the realization that for all his eloquence in defying Trudeau's constitutional juggernaut, he was not really a major player in the events that were shaking Confederation to its roots.

When a disillusioned Alberta flirted with separatism that fall and winter, whatever views Clark might have had on the subject were lost in the thunder. It was Lougheed's clear statement in the legislature that the future of Alberta still rested within Confederation that offset the impact of a massive Free the West rally held in Edmonton in November 1980.

The leader of that rally, who caught the mood of more than 3,000 bellicose and rebellious Albertans at the Jubilee Auditorium, was Douglas (Doug) Christie, the Victoria lawyer, who went on to make a reputation for himself of a different kind by becoming a sort of house lawyer for anti-Jewish hatemongers like Jim Keegstra[43], Ernst Zündel[44] and Malcolm Ross[45], and for an alleged Nazi war criminal like Imre Finta[46].

It was Lougheed, not Clark, not Christie, that kept the separatists at bay. More often than not, he was depicted as a prickly Albertan, a stereotype in itself. But he was first and foremost a Canadian who believed that his own province's place in Confederation needed redefining in the best interest of the nation. During that period when Alberta was up in arms, at times defenceless politically against Trudeau's Central Canadian storm troopers, Lougheed remained a moderate even when talk of separatism moved out of the beer parlours and into the boardrooms of the major oil companies.

# CHAPTER 16

Taking the pulse of Alberta seemed to be a national pastime in 1981.

After one swing through the West, Peter Newman examined the spirit and mind of Alberta in the second volume of *The Canadian Establishment.* Newman said most observers agreed with Premier Lougheed's analysis of federal tactics on energy as an attempt to take over the resource ownership of Alberta. In doing so, Lougheed maintained, the federal government was trying to change the rules of Confederation, and Ottawa was prepared to go as far as it could push. Ottawa had counted on Albertans capitulating, but that had not happened.

Newman wrote about a number of Albertans who had made an impression of one sort or another on him, including one eccentric multimillionaire who, on rising from a night's slumber, would swing on a rope, Tarzan-style, from his bedroom into his pool down below.

Of me, he wrote: "J. Patrick O'Callaghan, the irrepressible publisher of the *Edmonton Journal*, feels the premier isn't being really tough enough. 'We've had a prime minister of Canada for more than a decade who hates the West,' he tells the stream of eastern journalists who come calling to plumb the depths of western alienation. 'Trudeau goes to western Canada with the same sort of ill humour that once upon a time emperors used to project when visiting India — as if he couldn't believe there are people out there worth considering. The Liberals offer a $4-billion Western Development Fund. We know where it's being raised. We know it's not going to be spent here. It's as if you were a highwayman, held me up at midnight, took my purse, took my rings and then said, 'Well, I'm really a kind fellow at heart — so here's 75 cents; get a bus home.'

"An Irishman who hails from County Cork and brought the silky-tongued blarney that is his birthright across the Atlantic with him, O'Callaghan (known as the Green Hornet to his staff, because he tends to wear green suits with matching shirts and parkas) has become a significant figure in Edmonton. Even though the *Journal* is owned out of Toronto just as much as its rival *Edmonton Sun*, he has managed to make the tabloid appear to be an interloper."

The natives were certainly restless in Alberta, but it was Trudeau's champagne that almost produced a call of the wild by Lougheed. The premier had insisted, ever since Sept. 3, 1981, that he was set up for the famous cork-popping champagne celebration designed strictly for the nation's television cameras. The ceremony took place after another Harrington Lake meeting with Trudeau that was as close as the Liberals and the Alberta Tories ever came to reaching a truce on energy. Lougheed had not been told in advance of the so-called "civilized toast" and photo opportunity that was supposed to end the bitterness between Ottawa and Western Canada. Many Albertans back home never forgave Lougheed for the picture. It was too much like the early Indians being bought off with beads.

There were no losers in the energy war, according to Trudeau, but that was far from an accurate assessment. Only a day before Ottawa had abandoned its march into provincial jurisdiction on energy, a parliamentary committee chaired by Liberal MP Herb Breau, with four Liberals dominating the all-party group of seven, had refused to recommend a new course of revenue-sharing between Ottawa and the provinces that would have allowed the federal government to bolster its future earnings through forced levies from the Alberta Heritage Trust Fund and Alberta resource revenues.

In addition to the Breau committee, all the provinces — except Ontario — were united in their opposition to the new "equalization" proposals.

In the wake of all that, Lougheed had good reason to tell me in a phone call from Ottawa on Sept. 3 that he was now "ecstatic" over the agreement reached at Harrington Lake. The premier accepted a proposal from Trudeau that would give Alberta a two-tier pricing structure on oil — 75 per cent of world price, to be reached gradually, for old oil, and world price for new oil.

It was further agreed to provide full world price for all oilsands and Cold Lake development.

The NEP itself was to be kept sacred from infraction. The 25-per-cent back-in clause on frontier lands stayed intact. As did the Petroleum Gas Revenue Tax. While the Federal Investment Review Agency was not technically part of the NEP, it had been used as a braking mechanism to slow down investment in the Alberta oilfields. It, too, remained inviolate.

This was the best Trudeau had to offer, and it was the best Lougheed could hope to get. Turning off the taps to Central Canada and keeping the intruder off the front porch had never been more than negotiating ploys, the two-by-four between the eyes to get the donkey's attention. It worked and, in a way, both sides were able to save face. Lougheed said he and Trudeau had agreed at their private meeting that there would be no public gloating, no recriminations.

Lougheed told me the impression he got throughout that last meeting was that Trudeau really regarded the negotiation of an energy agreement as one of those distasteful things he did not want to soil his hands on. The prime minister regarded the whole thing as "a damn nuisance," Lougheed said.

"The Constitution is Pierre Elliott Trudeau's obsession," Lougheed went on. "An energy agreement is one of those realities of governing the country, and it holds no interest for him."

It was not so much the agreement itself that made Lougheed feel ecstatic. What was of far more importance, he said, was the signal it sent to the country that never again would the federal government deal with a province in the way it had attempted to deal with Alberta. Canada could not operate as "a unitary, authoritarian state run from Ottawa."

Lougheed continued: "When I look back over a year ago, I can't help thinking that the federal government thought that pressure would build on Alberta to a point where public reaction throughout the country would have encouraged Ottawa to walk right in and take over our resources."

The tactic to paint Alberta as the "bad guys" failed in the long run. The backlash against Alberta never materialized to the extent calculated by Ottawa.

Finally, Lougheed said: "Now perhaps we can get back to managing a boom economy for Albertans. The future is very exciting."

But, for once, Lougheed was woefully wrong. The energy agreement came too late to save the proposed megaprojects of Fort McMurray. It came too late for Alsands, which was to die on the drawing board the following spring. The dream (or nightmare) of \$40-, \$50-, even \$100-a-barrel oil did not come to pass[47], not even during the Gulf War of 1991 when Kuwait's oil fields were put to the torch in Iraqi dictator Saddam Hussein's scorched earth retreat.

The prices even slithered below $10 a barrel following the energy agreement, and Calgary mothballed the drilling rigs.

Once, over lunch with *Edmonton Journal* editor Andy Snaddon and me, Lougheed analyzed the Trudeau years this way:

- 1968 to 1972: Trudeau was tied to issues of new-age government.
- 1972 to 1974: He headed a minority government and had to behave circumspectly.
- 1974 to 1978: He was trying to be "prime minister of all regions" and wanted to win the West.
- 1979 to 1980: The West rejected him twice, once when he was shoehorned out of office by Clark and then when he regained power, but without western support.

Since then, according to Lougheed, Trudeau had said: "To hell with the West."

This fits the recollection of Joe Clark, to whom Trudeau once remarked: "I came to Ottawa to save Quebec. Somebody else will have to save the West."

Was Lougheed that designated saviour? Perhaps. If nothing else, he established the case for provincial rights on the federal scene, making it clear that an Ottawa government could no longer expect to get away with its imitation of Sherman burning his way through Georgia.[48]

Lougheed's influence on Confederation was much more than a regional affair based on energy prices. If the Harrington Lake agreement was reached by a return to the co-operative federalism that Trudeau had shunned since regaining office in February of 1980, it was ironic that on the patriation of the Constitution, Trudeau seemed determined to get his way by strong-arm methods. The schoolyard bully was back. In that regard, Lougheed was something of a champion of the regions, but always with the overriding interest of the nation taken into full consideration.

He was one of the cool-headed premiers who eventually derailed Trudeau's bid to bring the Constitution home without the consent of the provinces. It was Lougheed's insistence on an amending formula that helped to make a home-grown Constitution possible. Whether we like it or not, bearing in mind the way Lougheed's "notwithstanding" clause was later used by Quebec Premier Robert Bourassa — the only premier not to sign the Constitution agreement — to save his province's unilingual sign laws from being shot down by the Charter of Rights and Freedoms, that clause had been inserted into the Constitution primarily to ensure that no single province could be forced into federal policies that impinged on provincial jurisdiction. Lougheed was determined there should be no more federal intruders on anyone's provincial porch. After the energy wars, Lougheed was gun-shy.

Only three weeks after the champagne toasts, Trudeau was handed a narrow tightrope of legality to cross the Atlantic Ocean in unilateral pursuit of his Constitution. In effect, the Supreme Court of Canada told the prime minister he could proceed with his plan to have Westminster amend the Canadian Constitution and send it home. But morally and ethically, the Supreme Court emphasized, by doing so the government would be trampling on provincial rights, and violating the tradition and convention that had motivated Canada for more than a century.

Canada had always operated under the tradition that a federal government needed provincial consent before changes could be made to the Constitution. The Supreme Court strongly hinted that for the prime minister to proceed on unilateral patriation only on legal grounds would be unconstitutional as defined by that tradition.

Trudeau was still wrestling with his Holy Grail in November 1981, when he went to Vancouver to speak to more than 1,000 of the Liberal party faithful who had paid $150 a head for the privilege of being spiritually renewed by their leader. Instead, growing bored with the proceedings and a restless audience, Trudeau tossed away his speech and chided them for having doubts about their own future.

"Worse than that," he scolded, "you're terribly unaware of what is happening in the country."

Trudeau went on: "It is often those who live at the foot of great mountains who are the last to climb those mountains.... I think you would be the last to know about your own country."

When the audience began to heckle him and one member of the crowd cried out, "Pierre, you're insulting us," the prime minister replied: "I'm sorry if I'm insulting you. I was really giving you more credit for intelligence than you deserve."

At another point, Trudeau said: "I told you, I'm just spilling, not my guts, but my heart out."

In lecturing British Columbians for not raising their sights above the timberline of their own province, Trudeau wanted all Canadians to clasp his vision of Canada to their bosoms. But all that flowed back to him in his obvious misery at their rejection of his vision was that Canadians were too diverse in their interests, too scattered in settlements across the face of the second-largest country in the world, too regional, too perverse, too different from one another, too ideologically separate, too intensely loyal to their own unshaped dreams, to accept that there was only one vision of Canada that matched all their hopes and aspirations.

He was trying to converse with ghosts.

# CHAPTER 17

The Kent Commission[49] was established 11 years after the Special Senate Committee on the Mass Media headed by Keith Davey. In its presentation to the Davey committee in 1970, Southam had stated: "In our opinion, it (press freedom) is not now threatened in Canada by government action or legislation." But in 1981, Gordon Fisher was so dismayed by the direction being taken by the three commissioners — Tom Kent, Borden Spears and Laurent Picard — that he felt compelled to declare: "We do not feel that this statement can be repeated in 1981 with the same assurance."

The newspaper industry was already under attack by a range of government advisors, sympathizers, earnest autocrats, media-meddling bureaucrats, off-the-wall idealists and good old-fashioned busybodies.

Jim Coutts, principal secretary to the prime minister, said in an Edmonton speech that Alberta "has the worst media of any province in Canada." Coutts said of the major newspaper groups active in Alberta: "They love to stir up Alberta feelings to sell papers, that make profits, most of which go back to shareholders in Ontario. That combination of a grossly biased press on the ownership side and one-party politics tends to make people feel there is something disloyal about an argument, disloyal about two points of view."

Two faceless Liberal backbenchers from Ontario backed him up by trying to move in the Commons, as a matter of "urgent and pressing necessity," that the House "condemn the three Alberta dailies which are stirring up regional dissension in order to sell more copies, the profits of which are flowing back to the monolithic press chains now in Canada." Presumably, the papers they were referring to were the *Edmonton Journal*, the *Calgary Herald* and then you would have to take your pick of the Edmonton and Calgary *Suns*.

This blatant attempt at carrying the spear for Coutts fell on stony ground, even in a Commons dominated by Liberals. And Coutts fell on his own spear a few months later when his political career came to a screeching halt in the "safe" Liberal Toronto riding of Spadina. He was defeated in a byelection by the NDP's Dan Heap, a left-tilted clergyman. So died Coutts' ambition to succeed Trudeau.

Coutts was one of the prime movers, along with Michael Pitfield[50], in the attempt to hobble the press through the Kent Commission.

The final report of the Kent Commission became a textbook for theoretical journalism student idealists, divorced from reality and willing to accept, through their own ignorance, the report as the gospel for fundamental change, without questioning the commission's reasoning, its conclusions of the political ill will that gave it momentum. As well, the report became a combined bible and lexicon for bureaucrats and politicians fretting over a free press that hounded them for the extravagance, arrogance and incompetence of government.

None of the starry-eyed naifs soaking up the Kent philosophy in journalism classes ever gave even a passing glance to the other eight volumes of the commission, containing the research data compiled for Kent. In their innocence and immaturity, perhaps this was just as well, because the research material is often at odds with the conclusions reached by the commissioners in the final report. One suspects the commissioners never wanted to be confused by the facts, having their own preset agenda of discontent.

Of all the distorted and pejorative statistics loaded into the report in order to support the biases and prejudices of the pack of disgruntled journalistic hacks and mavericks who wrote the final version, nothing was more illustrative of the sham practised by the commission than the so-called ranking of newspapers by editorial expense as a percentage of revenue.

This table was supposed to show which papers were the biggest and most commendable spenders on the editorial product, on a pound-for-pound basis, so to speak. The absurdity of this table should be evident when the small Thomson newspaper in Kamloops — long since pushed out of the daily field by a Southam upstart that began as a throwaway sheet — was listed as number two while its illustrious stablemate, the *Globe and Mail*, checked in only at the 32nd spot.

Fourth on the list in the rankings, which were calculated for the financial years of 1978, 1979 and 1980 was the *Winnipeg Tribune*. And yet it was the death throes of the *Tribune* that led to the setting up of the commission to try and determine why newspapers fail.

The *Edmonton Journal*, of which I was publisher in the years chosen for the study, came 66th in the table and the *Calgary Herald*, which I later published, was 52nd.

If a dollar calculation of the money spent on the editorial product, instead of a percentage of revenue, had been used as the yardstick, it would have shown the *Journal* and the *Herald* in the top four or five of all papers in Canada for editorial spending. Between them, the two Southam papers spent well in excess of $13 million on editorial content in 1981. The *Journal*'s total for the three years under review was $17 million. No newspaper spent more than the *Journal* on its editorial content in those years.

At the time, the *Journal* was averaging more than 300 columns a day of news and editorial content. Of course, those were the glory days for news space — within a decade, under harsh economic restraints imposed on Southam dailies by the deep thinkers at head office, the news hole in the *Journal* had shrunk below an average of 200 columns a day on average. Thank Heavens, I wasn't there to see it!

However, during the years before and during the Kent Commission's probe of the industry, the *Journal* had an enterprising newsroom. Some of the budget went to expanded coverage of the legislature in the *Journal*'s self-appointed role as "unofficial opposition." This included the sort of investigative journalism that won Wendy Koenig national recognition for her stories on children under government care being fed dog food.

In another response to hard-hitting investigative work by the *Journal*, the Alberta government had to set up a commission to look into land-buying deals that accompanied the City of Edmonton's massive annexation of procedures. Nu-West, then a major developer in Edmonton and Calgary, was incensed over some of the stories, especially those related to Don Getty — then out of politics — receiving a consultant's fee of more than six figures a year. Getty knew how to tiptoe through the corridors of power at the legislature at a time when his old cabinet colleagues were preparing to make a decision on annexation. Once, I was visited by RCMP from Sherwood Park asking me to turn over the good old plain brown envelope then sitting on my desk; Nu-West alleged it contained secret documents taken from its files. The RCMP came without a search warrant, went away empty-handed and never returned. I don't think their heart was in it. In any case, after their visit the envelope mysteriously "disappeared" from my office. Getty escaped notice in a report on the annexation activities that were being fully documented in the *Journal* at the time the Kent Commission was beavering away.

In other *Journal* activities at that time, one reporter spent two months examining the energy crisis in long-range terms, as well as searching for alternate energy possibilities. His research took him to Denver, Houston, Dallas, Baltimore, Washington, New York, Toronto, Ottawa and Montreal. Another reporter went to the Middle East at *Journal* expense — we never accepted freebies — to see how Canadian soldiers from Edmonton were faring in the UN peacekeeping operation there. Still another went to see how Canadian troops stationed at Alert, the world's most northerly military base, spent Christmas.

Five different reporters had been to Alaska at different times to study the stages of development on the Trans-Alaska pipeline project, its effects on the economy, the native land claims, the tanker route from Alaska to Washington ports and the dangers of pollution to B.C.'s coastline.

When editor Steve Hume — a poet from Saturna Island who became a columnist with the *Vancouver Sun* — had been the *Journal*'s man in Yellowknife, he logged 185,200 kilometres a year in the air covering the North.

The *Journal* sent reporters to London to Moscow and the Middle East with Premier Lougheed. Over the previous 10 years, the *Journal* had dispatched reporters to China, Japan, South America, Europe, Saudi Arabia and Egypt.

None of this came cheap, so the *Journal* was somewhat put out when, after drawing the attention of Kent staffers to its true editorial spending, the only response was a nonchalant lack of interest. "You're so rich, you can afford it," Tim Creery of Southam News told me.

In my days as publisher, the *Journal* newsroom staff had increased from 108 in 1975 — the last full year before my arrival — to 186 at the time of the Kent Commission. Of course we could afford it, as Creery said, because the *Journal* was then the jewel in the Southam crown and we intended it to stay that way.

One man who was clearly out of sorts with newspapers was Michael Pitfield, the tall, dark, ascetic secretary to the federal cabinet. Pitfield, fired eventually by the Joe Clark government, moved to the safety of the Senate.

On Dec. 18, 1981, I was spokesman for a delegation from the Canadian Daily Newspaper Publishers Association that was granted the Pitfield equivalent of a papal audience.

Preston Balmer of Armadale (Michael Sifton's publishing group) was then CDNPA's elected president and headed the group. Our delegation went to Ottawa firmly believing that concentration of ownership was the concern uppermost in the minds of those who had supported setting up the commission. But after making our presentation, we had to sit through a bleak sermon from Pitfield in which it became obvious the government was contemplating the Orwellian concept of direct intervention into the editorial side of newspapers.

In a subsequent letter to Pitfield, I pointed out that research released by the commission disagreed with the elitist view he had put forward that the public wanted more foreign news and less local coverage. It showed that Canadians were either "satisfied" or "very satisfied" with their daily newspapers and 71 percent of Canadians considered newspapers to be a regular part of their lives. Some 72 per cent commented positively on the newspapers' contribution to the communities they served. Some 69 per cent of those surveyed by the commission said newspapers were more careful to get their facts right than they had been five years earlier. Sixty-three per cent said their newspaper had either improved "a lot" or "a little" over the previous three years and only 11 per cent said they had become worse.

As I recalled Pitfield's sombre and pompous comments to our delegation, he was voicing the dissatisfaction with newspapers of three special-interest groups of readers: the elite, the academics and government.

He seemed to suggest that these dissatisfactions would coalesce to a point where some form of rules to control the press might become necessary. In particular, he complained about journalistic intrusion into the private lives of politicians and other public figures.

Pitfield voiced his unhappiness with newspapers for not giving government, as a public service, the forum he felt it must have for keeping the country fully informed on its programs and policies. He wanted such a forum without granting the newspaper the right to comment, criticize, or analyze such programs and policies. Goebbels[51] would have loved the access to such unchallenged propaganda space!

The whole tenor of his remarks seemed to be moving in the direction of government intervention designed to make newspapers more responsive to what he considered to be their obligations to both government and the public. However, when I challenged him on this, he denied he was a protagonist of any particular tack the Kent Commission should take: he was simply passing along the concerns of other people.

The hidden prospect, that some of those he served in his bureaucratic kingpin position did have intentions of taking action to remake the press of Canada into a sanitized propaganda arm of government, was frightening. Freedom of the press and freedom of speech are indivisible and paramount to all other rights in a democratic system.

In my letter to Pitfield, I said: "If the government indeed plans to move openly into our newsrooms with the Kent Commission as the vehicle for storming the ramparts, then what faith can Canadians be expected to retain in a Constitution that cannot preserve such fundamental and basic rights as freedom of speech and the freedom of the press?

"With all respect, the advice that you, as the country's pre-eminent civil servant, should be giving to your political masters, should be clear and succinct: preserve our free press, stay out of the newsroom. There can be no independence of thought, opinion, and action when government comes marching in."

I never got a reply from that haughty, but cold, fish.

By then, the commission had become a travelling circus, bolstered by shoddy statistics. Sometimes it was hard to tell the political clowns from the rogue elephants when the radical ideologues and dreaming innocents kept getting in the way of the ringmaster.

My only appearance before the commission generated so much heat and passion that I ended up in a lawsuit against a 300-pound professional wrestler who later "found religion." This formidable character, Kaye Corbett, was the heavyweight columnist for the *Edmonton Sun*. He accompanied his publisher, Elio Agostini, when we lined up before the commission on opposite sides in Edmonton on Feb. 23, 1981.

Agostini had come from a Thomson daily in the Okanagan to succeed Don Hunt. Agostini later went down to Houston in the *Sun*'s Texas adventure and stayed on as marketing director of the *Houston Post* when the *Sun* sold out to Dale Singleton, a local media millionaire.

Agostini was pretty free with the facts, telling the commission that the *Journal* "has decreased in linage in the last year by three million lines, which represents about $3 million. Their circulation for the last two years has declined, by the Audit Bureau of Circulation figures, so we (the *Sun*) are making gains."

The real truth was that the official linage figures for the industry, as compiled by CDNPA, showed that for the full year ending Dec. 31, 1980, the *Journal*'s total advertising linage was 634,308,000 — a gain of 312,000 lines. The *Journal*'s advertising revenues for that year were the highest in its history and the highest, up to that point, for any Southam newspaper.

As for circulation, the *Journal* had suffered some self-inflicted wounds in 1980, because of the start-up woes following the opening of its new production plant in May of that year. Because of continuing problems of late delivery, the *Journal* lost about 10,000 in circulation throughout the summer. However, not only did it pick up all that lost circulation, but the January 1981 circulation — the last complete and relevant figure before the Kent hearing in Edmonton — was 12,316 over the previous January and, at 187,093, represented the highest monthly average in the 77-year history of the *Journal*. (As it turned out, the February figures proved to be even higher, at 189,205, and March was in excess of 190,000.)

Agostini also claimed that, as chairman of the committee of publishers responsible for Southam News, I had "stolen" columnist Allan Fotheringham and that "one of the ways he (O'Callaghan) got him over was to ply him with more money."

(Actually, it was strong drink, not money, that did the trick! Fotheringham and I disagreed for years over the number of glasses of port we consumed at an expensive Toronto restaurant, Winston's[52] — now alas no more — during our sales pitch to each other. At the time, Fotheringham was working for FP and his column was syndicated to a number of non-Southam papers, including the *Edmonton Sun.* I persuaded Fotheringham to join Southam News because he would have a wider audience and, in any case, it was obvious to both of us that FP was about to fold. Fotheringham always claimed that if I had waited only a couple of weeks longer for the collapse of FP, I could have got him for a lot less money. Not to mention the wear and tear on my liver. Fotheringham created quite a few waves as a Southam columnist — a number of stiff-backed Southam directors thought him too irreverent and anti-establishment — but he was always good value for the money, and I still have no regrets. I wonder how many ports Doug Creighton plied him with when, years later, he enticed him back to the *Sun* organization?)

Whatever I felt about Agostini's submission to the Kent Commission, it was clear the *Sun* thought even less of my own. The day after my appearance, Corbett could not contain his venom. His column contained these acid drops:

"Kent brought his travelling newspaper inquiry show here and it died a slow death before a self-proclaimed god — J. Patrick O'Callaghan — and his stoolie, Andrew Snaddon. (Andy, later publisher of the *Medicine Hat News*, was then editor of the *Journal.*) A pack of Sunshine Girls, with their tops down, couldn't have revived this corpse. Kent and his sleepwalkers, including one-time *Toronto Star* apology writer, Borden Spears, and a couple of pasty-faced lawyers and accountants, spent more than four hours listening to

O'Callaghan and his stoolie explain how wonderful the Giant Green Bore (Corbett's standard description of the *Journal*) was and just how little they respected the *Sun*, never once admitting the Little Paper was making large dents into both its circulation and advertising area.

"One would have to stuff his head in the sand not to realize this group of failed ex-journalists on the take was merely a rubber stamp for Trudeau to exercise more control over the press in Canada. This commission isn't even entertaining. It's downright boring.

"The Irishman showed his true colour yesterday. Yellow. There he was, pontificating and belittling the *Sun* as a paper of 'kiddie porn' with its Page 3 girls and that this newspaper had no effect on both the *Journal*'s advertising and circulation figures. They both slumped dramatically in the last year.

"His arrogance became nauseating. His lies became more pronounced.... Of course, Kent and his cronies were impressed. They treat old-timers with kid gloves. They allowed O'Callaghan and his stoolie, Snaddon, to ramble on while cutting short the *Sun*'s Dynamic Duo of managing editor David Bailey and publisher Agostini. Monopolies such as Thomson, and O'Callaghan's bosses, Southam, were given short shrift by the Irishman. He couldn't see anything wrong in cutting a few people's throats such as what happened in Ottawa and Winnipeg.

"As we said before, the Irishman showed his true colour. Yellow — not green. As for Tom Kent and the rest of the sleepwalkers, they're still wandering around the Chateau Lacombe lobby, muttering, 'Wot happened?'"

That was vintage Corbett, typical of what passed for journalism in the brawling early days of the branch-plant *Suns* in both Edmonton and Calgary. There were crudely disparaging references to me in just about every issue of the *Edmonton Sun*, which I generally ignored, but Corbett, I thought, had gone too far this time. At 300 pounds, he was too big to invite him to step out into the alley, so I did the next best thing — I sued him.

But Corbett, who had been fighting a losing battle with the bottle, sank even too low for the *Sun* with a column on Oct. 31, 1981, that made all sorts of allegations about him being physically threatened by a group of Edmonton Eskimos. One of the players, whom he named, had "threatened me with a metal object and said he would stuff it where the sun doesn't shine."

Corbett lost his job and the *Sun* ran an apologetic editorial, saying its credibility had been damaged by the Eskimo column. The editorial said that over the previous few weeks it had made several severe errors concerning members of the Eskimos. "We have told you facts that we now feel are fiction. When we are wrong, dammit, we think it's only fair to admit it." It went on to "sincerely apologize" to players Hugh Campbell (who went on to become general manager of the Eskimos), Neil Lumsden, and Larry Highbaugh, and also to local broadcaster Al McCann.

The *Sun* never apologized to me. However, on Jan. 28, 1982, almost a year after his vicious column on the Kent Commission, Corbett wrote to me to apologize for "my slanderous and uncalled-for column concerning you, Andrew Snaddon and the Kent Commission.... There was certainly no need for such a column, particularly when it slandered such an outstanding newspaperman as yourself, and you have every right to pursue the matter through the courts. There can be no excuses for such a column, and obviously I was enthralled with my own rhetoric.

"My column degrading you certainly was a fireable offence, for my words were untrue. However, the column for which I was dismissed from the *Sun* was true in every aspect. There is a taste of ashes, particularly since the *Sun*'s publisher submitted to advertisers' demands, had me fired and no one within the entire *Sun* organization bothered to question it. Their silence was, indeed, deafening."

My heart was no longer in the lawsuit. Corbett had made reparations. So a few months after moving to Calgary I dropped the whole thing. Explaining my reasoning to *Journal* lawyer Allan Lefever, I wrote: "The man who wrote the column has long since disappeared into obscurity. He has already apologized to me in writing ... and has been fired by his employer. To pursue it further, when he has lost even the blanket of legal protection of his erstwhile employer, would make it appear to be no more than a vengeful act on my part against a man who is no longer of any consequence and a somewhat sad figure.... I think we should quietly let it fade away."

Corbett later made his peace with the *Sun* organization as well. The last I heard of him, he was back with the old *Telegram* survivors on King Street. Presumably he still weighed 300 pounds.

His column on the Kent Commission's "sleepwalkers ... and failed ex-journalists on the take" left no lasting impression. Indeed, saddled with the cabinet responsibility for the commission, Minister of State for Multiculturalism Jim Fleming, a lower-order minister, took his proposed recommendations to the fall meetings of CDNPA in Vancouver in 1982 and brought the house down about his ears!

To quote Patrick Nagle in the *Vancouver Sun* of Sept. 23: "Responding to Fleming, *Calgary Herald* publisher Patrick

O'Callaghan — incoming CDNPA president — said: 'We will never surrender.... If I understand this message correctly this morning, it seemed to me you said we should offer a positive response to a clumsy attempt at seduction as being preferable to being truly ravaged by a rapist.... We don't belong between the same silken sheets. We are not compatible. There is no love between us.'

"The publisher said he had no desire to co-operate with a government-authorized press council and that a voluntary press council meant newspapers had to be free to choose whether to join.

"'You are offering us voluntary compulsion,' O'Callaghan said. 'You may have to start jailing a few of us to make that point.'

"Following that exchange, Fleming ... told reporters that legislation concerning newspaper policy would be complete within the next month for presentation to the next Parliament following a November throne speech.

"'The important thing is to get the legislation out in the open,' Fleming told reporters. 'I am anxious for the debate.'"

On Feb. 9, 1983, Fleming announced that the Liberals would establish a national press council, and that. legislation establishing it would be tabled in the next session of the Commons. It would have no power beyond public criticism, the same as the three existing voluntary provincial bodies in Alberta, Ontario and Quebec. The national press council would be made up of 10 part-time members from each of five regions of the country. Three publishers, three journalists and four private citizens would serve on it. Financial support for the council would come from interest earned on a proposed $20-million endowment fund to be set up by Parliament.

Fleming's legislation would also provide matching grants of $50,000 a year for three years to help newspapers set up new out-of-province or foreign bureaus. This handout enticement had already been rejected by every newspaper group and publisher in Canada when the first trial balloon went up. It was well understood that integrity is at stake when a free press allows government to pay any of its bills.

The legislation would limit companies or individuals to owning 20 per cent of national daily newspaper circulation. The good old grandfather clause would come to the rescue of Southam and Thomson, both of whom already owned newspapers with more than that 20 per cent ceiling. About all that the proposed legislation could do was to prevent Southam taking over Thomson or Thomson taking over Southam. No one then dreamed of the possibility of Southam taking over Torstar or Torstar buying out Southam. Or Conrad Black nipping at the heels of them both.

As for Fleming's proposal to limit cross-media ownership — that is, ownership of broadcast interests and a daily newspaper in the same city — the CRTC had already received a directive from the cabinet on the same issue and blithely ignored it in the case of the Irving family in New Brunswick. K.C. Irving and his three sons — flippantly dubbed Gassy, Greasy and Oily — owned all five English-language dailies in New Brunswick, along with radio and television stations in the same publishing cities. Indeed, in four other cases that came before it in that period, the CRTC did not deny broadcast licences or renewals to those who already owned newspapers in the same communities. Another example of this cross-ownership later occurred in Calgary, when Maclean Hunter, owner of CFCN-TV, acquired a controlling interest in the *Toronto Sun*, publisher of the *Calgary Sun*. And Ted Rogers ended up owning just about everything else through print, radio, cable television spiced with conventional television, and a major telephone system. The barn door was already open.

The Canada Newspaper Act was introduced through the back door in July 1983, while the Commons was frolicking on vacation. The Liberal government had by then retreated a long way from the original Kent proposals, and what was left was more of a token gesture to the hardliners in Fleming's own party than a massive press gag.

Poor Fleming, a decent if ineffectual minister trying to do Pitfield's dirty work for him, had complained publicly he was in a "tough spot" because certain publishers were not willing to "co-operate," as he put it, with the government. Asking publishers to accept government curbs on free speech, he discovered, was a little like asking the condemned man to smile cheerfully as he walks up the steps of the gallows. He admitted that his proposals were fraught with peril constitutionally. He said he had taken great care that no group should be allowed to own newspapers whose share of circulation was more than 20 per cent of the national total. The entrenchment of freedom of the press in the Charter of Rights and Freedoms had made it much more difficult for Ottawa to act, because most legal opinion accepted that such freedom included the right to publish and to own newspapers, as well as having the freedom to write without interference for such newspapers.

Fleming was a broadcaster by background and in all the conversations I had with him, I could never get him to understand the difference between broadcasting — the flaky puff pastry of journalism — and the meat-and-potatoes newspapers. Newspapers have traditionally been unfettered by government regulation. Unlike broadcasting outlets, they do not need licences to operate. The power to grant, or to refuse, a licence inevitably leads to government control, or the risk of government control, in some form or other. The press could not survive on such sufferance.

We debated the subject of press regulation at many places across Canada and even, cheek by jowl, in my own newspaper, the *Calgary Herald*. In a letter to me dated April 19, 1983, Fleming summed it up this way: "Given that we both accept the adversarial stance in which history and tradition cast us, it is clear that we are still to some extent talking at cross purposes ... from our different perspectives we will probably have to agree to disagree."

At least, we agreed on that conclusion. We were adversaries, but never enemies.

By August 1983, Fleming was gone from the cabinet and David Collenette, the man who replaced him as multiculturalism minister, said he wasn't sure if he would have responsibility for the proposed Newspaper Act. A spokesman in Trudeau's office said no decision had been reached on the proposals. An aide to Fleming said the former minister was not told of his project's fate when Trudeau handed him his cabinet pink slip. However, if all of that suggested that the Newspaper Act was about to die on the vine, Tom Kent was having none of it when he came to the University of Calgary to debate the issue with me.

"It is vital to the public interest to prohibit, by law, the control of a newspaper by persons or corporations that have other business interests larger than the newspaper," Kent said. "Their motive, quite naturally, is to milk the paper before new media replace it; the public interest is to spend the money on providing the news."

Kent said that when newspapers are engaged in competitive fights they are risky businesses. "But now a newspaper property is about as safe as any business can be;

and it's worth more to a company the less it cares about the newspaper's role in society."

His main target was obvious. "That is why so many newspapers have been sold. It is why a conglomerate, Thomson, purchased FP (the former newspaper chain that once owned the *Globe and Mail*, the *Vancouver Sun*, the *Montreal Star*, the *Winnipeg Free Press* and the *Ottawa Journal*). FP ... was a chain simply of newspapers.... Southam is still largely a newspaper company, and it spends, on Southam News and the like, millions of dollars a year that makes for better quality papers but which it could not spend if it were a Thomson-type conglomerate, more interested in generating cash for further acquisitions to the corporate empire."

The audience of about 100 directed most of their questions to me, after Kent, in his rebuttal, rejected my conclusion that the government's assertion of a somewhat narrow and harmless regulation of newspapers was only the beginning, not the end, of government intervention.

One man asked me if I was saying that the federal government had no rights in the newspaper business while I, as a publisher, "had the only right." According to the *Calgary Herald*, which gave a full page to the debate, I replied: "If you've got to choose between wicked press barons and government, I'll take wicked press barons any time."

But that choice never became necessary — what was left of Fleming's Newspaper Act died with the John Turner government on Sept. 4, 1984. It had been introduced in the dying days of the Trudeau regime, before he took his famous walk in the snow on Leap Day in 1984, and never even made it to the debating stage in the Commons. When Brian Mulroney's Conservatives took power they followed through on a promise made in Opposition by Perrin Beatty[53] — they scrapped it.

However, the echo lingered on, even after the fall of the Liberals. Peter Desbarats, dean of the University of Western Ontario's School of Journalism and one of the most influential of the backroom boys who had worked for the Kent commission, conned the expiring Liberal government into putting up $500,000 to fund a centre for mass media studies. Such a centre had been one of the key recommendations of the commission.

The grant, made one week before the federal election of 1984, was supposed to be matched by funds from the newspaper industry. But having been bitten by Kent, the proprietors, the newspapers, the publishers and editors, knew better than to pay for a government-backed centre that was intended to provide life after death for the fugitives from the commission, who were still grimly determined to find some way to control a free press. In its pitch to the Liberal Secretary of State on behalf of Desbarats, the university had said that one of the centre's purposes would be to monitor and report on the "social responsibility function of Canada's mass media."

Eventually, the university itself somewhat reluctantly threw in the funds needed to match the government grant, but the centre never found another sugar daddy. It never had anything to show for the million dollars it scrounged for its self-serving role as the burrowing ferret digging a hole under a free press.

By and large, the general public was totally apathetic to the Kent Commission, but academic journalists, most of whom had long since fled the action of the newsrooms, continued to show their faith. The pages of the commission's main volume, with its cover showing a montage of three dead papers — the *Winnipeg Tribune*, the *Ottawa Journal* and *Montréal-Matin* — is still well thumbed by those in their cradles of left-wing purity, still not understanding the sad reality that newspapers are primarily purveyors of information, not platforms for the simplistic ideology of every half-formed graduate of a school of journalism.

# CHAPTER 18

According to Samuel Butler[54], God cannot alter the past, but historians can. In the course of human affairs, the past can be a dust heap, a distillation of rumours, an accumulation of lost opportunities, a lamentation, or even an absurdity. A remembrance of things past can often lead to regret over what might have been, but it can also echo the wisdom of having done the right thing at the right time.

Where did Peter Lougheed's thoughts alight in those quiet moments when he might have wanted to weigh the past? As Pierre Trudeau's nemesis, should he have seized the moment at the height of his political acclaim to seek the leadership of the federal Tories? Did he take too gloomy a view of his unilingual status to avoid rejection by Quebec? Did his stance on Alberta's oil rights doom any hope of support from Central Canada? In reading all the signs, did he become convinced he could not win a leadership convention? Was he really just a stay-at-home politician with no wider ambition? Only Lougheed himself could answer those questions, but many Canadians were puzzled over his reluctance to move to the federal scene.

At a private luncheon at the Chateau Lacombe in Edmonton on Valentine's Day in 1982, Lougheed told Steve Hume (then *Journal* editor), William Thorsell (then *Journal* associate editor, later editor-in-chief of the *Globe and Mail*, and director and CEO of the Royal Ontario Museum) and me why he had never contemplated such a switch too seriously.

"I have been at it (politics) since 1965," he said. "I have been premier for 10 years and they have been relatively turbulent years, and I have been right in the middle of it on the Constitution, energy, etc. There is a limit to the pressure you can put on your wife and kids." In Edmonton, he said, he could live like an average citizen walking out into the supermarket when he felt like it, pushing his wife Jeanne's shopping cart without attracting too much attention, "but everything changes when you get to Sussex Drive."

This luncheon was held in the month of constitutional agreement and there was speculation on Trudeau's possible retirement from politics now that he had achieved his main political goal. Lougheed admitted that he might still be persuaded to run for the Tory leadership, "if the wrong Liberal became leader." The strongest candidate to succeed Trudeau, Lougheed said, would be John Turner. If Turner did win a leadership convention, he would be acceptable to the West and "he would clean house with the mandarins in Ottawa."

When pushed in his definition of the "wrong Liberal" Lougheed explained it would be someone "who would want to continue the Trudeau policies that have left us in this mess, and if there were no other Tory who could beat him, then I might run." He didn't see Jean Chrétien as the "wrong Liberal leader" because there were a number of Tories who could defeat Chrétien. "If it were some other Liberal and the polls indicate I was the only one to beat him…"

He felt Chrétien wanted to be leader; by contrast, Allan MacEachen had destroyed his own chances and was no longer a significant player in the game.

When it was pointed out to Lougheed that the latest Gallup Poll had the Liberals gaining ground on the Tories despite a terrible performance by the government at a recent economic summit, Lougheed admitted candidly that the polls would eventually kill Clark as leader.

Despite that, he said, Clark would run in still another leadership contest "because of Maureen's state of mind. She (Clark's wife, Maureen McTeer) is a very strong-willed lady and Joe pays attention to her." McTeer still believed that Clark would prove himself worthy of the highest office — if only the electors would give him another chance. If the party forced a leadership convention on Clark, Lougheed said, there would be four determined candidates — John Crosbie, David Crombie, Brian Mulroney and Clark himself.

If the Tory convention preceded the Liberal one, Crombie — once and always the "tiny, perfect mayor of Toronto" — would win, Lougheed said. If the Tory convention followed that of the Liberals, it would depend on whom the Liberals would elect. If the Liberals called in Turner, Lougheed thought the Tories would choose Mulroney. If the Liberals picked Donald Macdonald,Lougheed thought Crosbie would win. And if it were Chrétien, he saw Clark as the Tory winner.

Lougheed made it obvious he would be happy to see Turner not only as Liberal leader, but as prime minister as well. His second choice would be Macdonald — whose royal commission, appointed by Trudeau, later supported Lougheed's last hurrah, free trade. Lougheed did not think anyone on the Tory side could beat Turner. Of Turner, Lougheed said: "He is not as personally ambitious as he used to be and is much more concerned about the country."

Another surprise, in retrospect, was Lougheed's personal choice of a Tory to replace Clark. "You haven't asked me about 'my' candidate — Darcy McKeough," he volunteered. (McKeough, the Chatham strongman of a Bill Davis government, eventually left politics to head Union Gas, but was forced out of that position when Unicorp absorbed Union Gas.)

Conceding that McKeough could not defeat Turner, Lougheed would not elaborate on a comment he made about Davis — "There is so much jealousy there." Saying only that "Davis didn't project," Lougheed clearly put the Ontario premier at the bottom of his list of possible federal Tory leaders. The public's perception of Davis, said Lougheed, was "of a cat that swallowed the canary."

Clearly in Lougheed's mind, Clark had played a relatively insignificant role in the battle against Trudeau's hell-bent dash toward a new Constitution. In a way, despite his strafing of Trudeau's autocratic meddling with legality and tradition, Clark deserved better than that, but being a short-term prime minister who came and went so quickly as never to leave a footprint on history, he was overlooked and ignored by those who carried guns with heavier power.

Trudeau got his Constitution, but in the end he had to do it the Canadian way, getting the consent of nine provinces, bitterly and grudgingly given, after a series of high-pitched meetings in Ottawa. He got his Constitution without Quebec, thus sowing the seeds for the tragedies of Meech Lake and Charlottetown.[55]

When Quebec Premier René Lévesque stalked out of the February meetings without putting his signature to the final agreement, he dismissed the new Constitution in scathingly contemptuous terms as a "lawyers' package." His anger stemmed partly from a perception that he had been betrayed by the other provinces. Only Ontario and New Brunswick had supported Trudeau's plan for patriation of the Constitution, and the eight dissenting provinces had an agreement that none would move from their common front position without first informing the other seven. However, after a compromise cooked up by the kitchen cabinet of Chrétien, Roy Romanow of Saskatchewan and Roy McMurtry of Ontario, Lévesque missed the 8 a.m. breakfast meeting of the group of eight on the final day, when it was agreed to put the alternative proposal to Trudeau. It was assumed that Lévesque, a notorious laggard in the mornings, had already been informed of the switch in strategy and tacitly agreed to it without the tiresome necessity of having to attend breakfast. By the time he did show up, half an hour later, the die had already been cast; to his dying day Lévesque believed he had been sold out.

The bitterness at the finish was no more than a carryover of the tone set by Trudeau at the opening dinner he gave for the premiers. Before they had even started to eat, Trudeau told them they might as well accept that they were all "political enemies." The nastiness of that comment permeated every meeting that followed. Lougheed, who had been known to refer to Trudeau in private as a "bastard" while still retaining a grudging respect for him, felt the meetings never recovered from that far-from-rousing start.

Trudeau, the arsonist of Confederation, scattered the ashes to the winds of history. His initial unilateral approach to patriation produced outrage from coast to coast.

In the Commons, at one stage of the rocky road to Westminster, he called the Opposition "fascist." He embarrassed the British Parliament by treating it as an unwilling agent of change for the Canadian federal government. But he got his Constitution, tattered and flawed, by forcing Quebec into the exile of the spurned prodigal.

# CHAPTER 19

The story of the Weasel and the Worms began on April 19, 1982, only two days after the Charter of Rights and Freedoms entered our lives at the royal assent stage of the Constitution Act. I was in Toronto attending the annual meetings of The Canadian Press and the Canadian Daily Newspaper Publishers Association. I was told in a phone call from Edmonton that four officers of the Combines Investigation Branch had swept into my office. They were armed with a certificate of authorization signed by Dr. Frank Roseman, a member of the Restrictive Trade Practices Commission. Not only were they empowered to examine anything they might find on *Journal* premises, but they also had the right to search any premises occupied by Southam Inc., parent company of the *Journal*, anywhere in Canada.

Two years later, writing the judgment of the Supreme Court of Canada on the nation's first test of Section 8 of the Charter ("Everyone has the right to be secure against unreasonable search and seizure.") Justice Brian Dickson said of that order: "The authorization has a breathtaking sweep; it is tantamount to a licence to roam at large on the premises of Southam Inc., at the stated address and elsewhere in Canada."

The leader of Roseman's Raiders was Michael J. Milton. With him were Michael L. Murphy, J. Andrew McAlpine and Antonio P. Marrocco. I am sure they were all fine upstanding citizens, a credit to Lawson A.W. Hunter, then director of investigations research of the Combines Investigation Branch. Forever around the *Journal*, they were known as the Weasel and the Worms. The group sobriquet appealed to my worst instincts, but I can't take credit for the dubbing. It was done by the *Journal*'s brilliant young lawyer, Allen Lefever.

This tall, pencil-slim, black-moustached and soft-spoken man could be a smouldering volcano on matters of government encroachment on the precious freedoms that Chrétien had touted to me as the major ingredients of the charter, but Lefever and I agreed there was a wide gulf between Liberal theory on a brave new world of freedom, and government application of that theory.

So battle was joined, with Section 8 as the flag we rallied around. However, there were other precedents for our refusal to submit meekly to the government raid on my office.

In 1765, in a British case (Entick vs. Carrington), the secretary of state issued a warrant authorizing a search and seizure of papers in the plaintiff's home in the expectation that such documents would be found to link the plaintiff with seditious papers then being circulated. The judgment of the court in that case read in part: "We can safely say there is no law in this country to justify the defendants in what they have done: if there was, it would destroy all the comforts of society, for papers are often the dearest property a man can have."

I doubt if anything the Weasel and the Worms might have found in my files could ever be classified as "seditious." However, just in case I was wrong, Lefever went off to get an injunction holding up the search, while *Journal* business manager Brian Storey kept the raiders at bay. Lefever got his "stop-work" order on April 20 from Justice B. Feehan.

Lefever next trotted off to the Court of Queen's Bench for an injunction to have the search terminated, but Justice Department lawyer T.C. Joyce argued that Justice R.C. Cavanaugh did not have the authority to grant such an application. However, Cavanaugh disagreed with that assertion and gave Lefever two weeks to prepare arguments because "this is the first application along these lines. It is unique; it is brand new." In the meantime, the search could proceed, but all documents would have to be sealed.

On May 20, ruling on the *Journal*'s application under Section 24 of the Constitution ("Anyone whose rights or freedoms, as guaranteed by this charter, have been infringed or denied may apply to a court of competent jurisdiction to obtain such remedy as the court considers appropriate and just in the circumstance."), Justice Cavanaugh again said the search could continue, but he added the rider that the *Journal* could take civil action to claim damages if the search revealed nothing incriminating.

The next day, the *Journal* applied to the Alberta Appeal Court for a temporary injunction to halt the search. The court — consisting of Justices S.S. Lieberman, W.J. Haddad and R.H. Belzil — ruled it would not prevent the search, but it set certain limitations. The judges ordered that copies of any seized documents be deposited with the clerk of the court.

All of this was taking place at a time when Tom Kent's Royal Commission on Newspapers was burrowing into the entrails of the newspaper industry. Earlier that month, the Southam and Thomson companies had been charged with collusion in the closing of the *Winnipeg Tribune* and the *Ottawa Journal* on the same day.

Before those charges were subsequently thrown out of court, more of Hunter's henchmen descended on Southam's Toronto head office. They came upon Southam vice-president Bill Carradine — the man who had inherited my green furniture when I moved to Windsor — tearing up some notes. Just for the hell of it, presumably, they charged him with destroying possible evidence. For all I knew, Bill being a diligent husband and a very meticulous note-taker, it might well have been that he was tearing up that day's discarded grocery list.

Carradine and I were not close friends, but he was a decent and honourable man, and I thought he got a raw deal from the Combines people, so I phoned and told him so. After the ridiculous charges against him were dropped, I wrote to him on Jan. 4, 1984, as follows: "Thank God sanity has finally prevailed. Had the Crown not stayed the proceedings against you today, it would have been more of a measure of its vindictiveness than the course of true justice. Perhaps you can now sleep with a clear conscience at night knowing that you have been given a clear bill of health morally, ethically and in every other sense. It has been a difficult period for you and one has to wonder about a system of justice that can keep charges dangling like the sword of Damocles[56] over the head of an innocent person for years. To say the least, justice has a cold heart."

Carradine's reply surprised me. "I remember very clearly when the original charge was laid and the accusations splashed all over the newspapers that you were the only one of our publishers who phoned me to express support and to say that the charges were obviously trumped-up harassment on the part of government and that right would eventually prevail. The fact that not a single other publisher phoned me at that time still sticks in my memory and it is therefore particularly heartwarming to have your letter and to recall that support I had from you at a time when my spirits hit a pretty low level."

Obviously, the publishers were not exactly rushing to the barricades to support the senior vice-president of Southam. It's a cruel world out there, Bill.

Armed with the blessing of the Court of Queen's Bench to proceed with a limited search, the boys from

Ottawa were back in my office on May 21. Four days later, in Alberta's Court of Appeal, roly-poly Chief Justice Bill McGillivray, speaking for himself and for Justices D.C. Prowse and J.H. Laycraft — another Alberta chief justice in the making — extended the court order to continue the search. But they also directed that all documents be placed in custody of the clerk of the court and with no permission to make any notes. This order was to stay in effect until September, when the Appeal Court was due to rule on whether a Queen's Bench justice had jurisdiction to hear the matter or whether it should be dealt with in federal court.

On Aug. 13, the federal department of justice abandoned its appeal that would have argued an Alberta court had no jurisdiction over the federal Combines Investigation Act. However, the department said it would continue its appeal in other elements, arguing Justice Cavanaugh erred in stopping the original search and in placing all seized documents in the custody of the courts until the disposition of the whole affair by a higher court.

In his factum for the Appeal Court hearing, Lefever wrote on Oct. 29, 1982: "The search or seizure power entails an inquisitorial fishing trip where no specific allegation exists that a criminal activity is about to be committed."

By then, however, the sands of the hourglass of my tenure at the *Journal* had run out. I was off to Calgary as publisher of the *Herald*, the second of Southam's Alberta gold-dust twins. However, William Newbigging, my successor as publisher of the *Journal*, did not skip a beat, instructing Lefever to carry on the battle against the Weasel and the Worms.

On Jan. 31, 1983, Alberta's highest court declared that the raid on my files was unconstitutional.

In the judgment written by Justice D.C. Prowse, allowing the *Journal*'s appeal, it was stated that parts of Section 10 of the Combines Act were inconsistent with the provisions of Section 8 of the Charter of Rights and Freedoms and were therefore of no force or effect. The clerk of the court was ordered to return the documents in his possession to the *Journal* in 10 days in the event a stay was not sought and granted.

The ruling of the court was unanimous, with Chief Justice McGillivray, Herb Laycraft, J.A. McClung and J.A. Kearns agreeing. Prowse's eloquent written judgment said that Section 8 did not confer powers of search and seizure on the government of Canada or the provinces, "but rather it is a limitation upon powers they derive from other sources."

The roots of the right to be secure against unreasonable search and seizure, said Prowse, "are embedded in the common law, in statutes subsequently enacted, and in decisions of the courts made as the society in which we live has evolved."

The issue on the appeal was confined to the application of Section 10 of the Combines Act to an inquiry "relating to the production, distribution and supply of newspapers and related products in Edmonton" for the purpose of determining whether an offence has been, or is about to be, committed under Sections 33 or 34 of the Combines Act.

Condensing some of the legalese, these sections say that "every person who is a party, or privy to, or knowingly assists in, or in the formation of, a merger or monopoly, is guilty of an indictable offence and is liable to imprisonment for two years.

"Everyone engaged in a business who ... engages in a policy of selling products at prices unreasonably low, having the effect or tendency of substantially lessening competition or eliminating a competitor, or designed to have such an effect, is guilty of an indictable offence and is liable to imprisonment for two years."

So there you have it: the poor old publisher had finally found out that he had been faced with the prospect of two years in jail, and no one to that point had told him what he was supposed to have done!

Prowse went on: "I have not attempted to set out an inclusive list of safeguards which, if applied, will result in a search and seizure that satisfies Section 8 of the charter. I have merely dealt with some obvious omissions in the present case."

Alberta Chief Justice McGillivray made it plain during the hearings that the sweeping powers of the Combines people to go on a fishing expedition in uncharted waters concerned him immensely. Nevertheless, the 5-0 decision by the Appeal Court of Alberta was still not good enough for the federal government. It took the matter to the Supreme Court of Canada.

So off we went to Ottawa, Allan Lefever's moustache bristling in anticipation of delivering the final comeuppance to Lawson Hunter's harried raiders.

Just two weeks after Brian Mulroney's general election victory in September 1984, the Supreme Court wrote the last chapter of the Weasel and the Worms saga. In another unanimous ruling, it declared that the raid on my offices at the *Journal* was unconstitutional. Not only did the Supreme Court support the Alberta top court's judgment, but it also granted the *Journal* costs against the government.

Bora Laskin was chairman, but he took no part in the judgment written by Justice Dickson, the ailing Laskin's eventual successor. Dickson said that the government had made no submissions capable of supporting a claim that even if searches were "unreasonable" within the meaning of Section 8 of the charter, they were nevertheless a reasonable limit as "demonstrably justified in a free and democratic society."

The purpose of the charter, said Dickson, was to guarantee and to protect, within the limits of reason, the enjoyment of the rights and freedoms it enshrines. "It is intended to constrain governmental action inconsistent with those rights and freedoms; it is not in itself an authorization for governmental action."

Nothing had been established to identify the point at which the interests of the state come to prevail over the interests of the individual in resisting such searches, said Dickson. To define the proper standard as the possibility of finding evidence was a very low standard that would validate intrusion on the basis of suspicion, and authorize fishing expeditions of considerable latitude.

It had taken more than two years, but the *Journal*'s determination ensured for all time that never again could such "breathtaking" raids be made on newspaper offices. Big Brother has no authority to poke his long nose into the environs of a free press. The "comforts of society" are preserved under democracy.

I never found out details of any alleged wrongdoing on the part of the *Journal* or myself, and under the Combines legislation in question the name of the informant or accuser is never revealed. Suspicion, naturally, falls heavily on the *Toronto Sun* organization because the offspring tabloid in Edmonton was hurting in its circulation and advertising war with the *Journal*.

As a postscript to the Weasel and the Worms, a few months after the *Journal*'s Supreme Court victory, I finally met Lawson Hunter at an Osgoode Hall Law School lecture series at York University in Toronto. By then, he had left the Combines branch and was about to join the Ottawa law firm of Fraser & Beatty. He proved to be personable, witty and engaging.

He told the lecture audience that "for all the grandiose philosophy evoked by our concept of a free press, the newspaper industry is also a business."

He went on: "We must be very clear about the distinction between government intervention to control ideas and news, and government intervention because an industry is operating in a way that denies freedom of choice in the market place or restrains competition among competitors."

He cited the quashing of search warrants in two instances during search-and-seizure visits to Pacific Press, publishers of the *Vancouver Sun* and the *Province.*

He then referred to the cases of Hunter vs. Southam and Hunter vs. Thomson Newspapers Ltd arising from the Kent Commission. The central issue in all these cases, he said, was the constitutionality of the act's search-and-seizure provision, but constitutionality was decided under Section 8 of the charter. That is, the cases were decided under the search-and-seizure provisions of the charter and not under its freedom-of-the-press provision. And, in each case, he said, the Combines people were carrying out business investigations of those companies. There was no evidence of the government investigating any of the newspapers for their editorial policy, and there was no attempt to confiscate reporters' notes.

(Charges of collusion against Southam and Thomson, arising from the closing on the same day of the *Winnipeg Tribune* by Southam and the *Ottawa Journal* by Thomson, were dismissed on Dec. 11, 1983.)

Pat O'Callaghan as a young boy

Pat O'Callaghan – RAF

Pat O'Callaghan with Prime Minister Brian Mulroney
at the *Calgary Herald*

Joan and Pat O'Callaghan – France

# CHAPTER 20

When Gordon Fisher asked me to go to Calgary in 1982 to take over the *Herald*, with its brand-new, state-of-the-art plant, on the retirement of Frank Swanson, I told him I wasn't interested. I was having too much fun in Edmonton.

He kept up the pressure, his main selling point being that Calgary was an exciting city and it needed an exciting paper. I brooded over it for weeks, trying to tell myself I was only a few months short of the seven-year itch so far as my stay in Edmonton was concerned. In that period of time, I had presided over the building of a production plant that was far ahead of its time. I had battled with the City of Edmonton in and out of the courts, and I was embroiled in another precedent-setting legal encounter with the government of Canada. Then there was the no-holds-barred rivalry with the upstart *Edmonton Sun.* On top of that, there was the continuing editorial war with the Trudeau government in its assault on Alberta's oil riches and its rush toward a new Constitution. And there was the fight for press freedom in face of the Kent Commission. All in all, it had not been uneventful, but maybe it was time to fire up the engines for still another move and a new perspective. I told Fisher I would go to Calgary later in the summer.

One of my last speeches in Edmonton was on March 17, a day when Irishmen don't normally need to deliver dry political sermons to develop a thirst! Wanting to go out on a high note in a year when Alberta was on a downer because of the energy and constitutional woes, I told the Chamber of Commerce that the future for Alberta was unparalleled in its magnificence if we could only cope with the prospect instead of being frightened by the weight of the immediate problems.

The speech came 13 days after Didsbury voters, spooked by the intransigence of Trudeau, Lalonde and MacEachen on Alberta's energy plight, had voted Gordon Kesler into the legislature in a byelection. Kesler, an oil spy, a rodeo rider and chuckwagon driver, was a separatist, the first ever elected in Alberta. He represented the Western Canada Concept, and I told my Edmonton audience not to be panicked by this manifestation of protest, of grassroots resentment, of "contempt for a central government that has debased a nation of ungovernable regions into believing that it should be compressed into the narrow funnel of an identity that does not exist outside of Ottawa, Montreal and Toronto."

My boosterism on Alberta's radiant future fell a little flat because by May, Alsands — the last of the great megaprojects planned for Fort McMurray — was dead. One by one, as Ottawa offered no encouragement of price that would stabilize the uncertainty inherent in any of the projects that were so desperately needed to tap the oilsands promise, the partners in the $10-billion consortium got cold feet and empty wallets.

When I arrived in Calgary, instead of the exciting city promised to me by Gordon Fisher, it was quiet as the grave, not even mourners left to walk the streets. Even Mayor Ralph Klein's "creeps and bums"[57] had deserted the oil capital of Canada.

Alsands was not the end of Calgary's bleak downturn. Already hovering on the brink of total collapse was Dome Petroleum, once the biggest success story in the oil patch. Four years earlier, I had sat through a long dinner at the Edmonton Plaza Hotel, along with Donald Macdonald, a former Liberal energy minister. We had listened to one of Jack Gallagher's relentlessly upbeat dissertations on the wealth that lay beneath the ice of the Beaufort Sea waiting to be harvested by Dome. At the end of it, as we were walking out of the hotel, Macdonald said: "Patrick, you have just seen Canada's greatest snake oil salesman at work."

Gallagher, a handsome, trim, white-moustached man, ebullient, fulsome, energetic and bursting with life, loved being the centre of attention. It is easy now to write him off with Napoleon's cruel *bon mot*: "Glory is fleeting, but obscurity is forever." Nothing could be more inaccurate.

In his heyday, Gallagher was a symbol of the times, a happy geologist who believed that the vast pools of oil and gas trapped beneath Arctic ice would eventually produce more exciting finds than Leduc, Redwater, Black Diamond, Lloydminster, Cold Lake or even the tarsands of Primrose Lake and Fort McMurray. Gallagher was a dreamer who believed in his own vision.

In pursuit of that northern dream, by 1978 he had three deep-sea rig ships, Explorers I, II and III, operating out of Tuktoyaktuk with seven supply ships to back them up. The tonnage of Gallagher's private fleet — through Dome's subsidiary, Canadian Marine Drilling Limited — exceeded that of Canada's entire navy.

But the dream died when the Berger Commission[58] placed a 10-year moratorium on development of the Mackenzie Valley, thus cutting off a possible pipeline to carry Arctic oil south. It was ironic, in a way, that the commission, set up by Jean Chrétien, the Liberal minister of Indian Affairs and Northern Development at that time, should set Dome on the path to ruin, because its earlier success had been built on shrewd exploitation of the "Canada-first" provisions of the Liberals' National Energy Program (NEP).

In responding to Lalonde's siren song, Dome had vastly overextended its investment resources and by mid-1982 it was strangling on its own debt load. The rush to cash in on acquisition of foreign-owned oil companies being squeezed out by the NEP was masterminded by Bill Richards, Gallagher's second-in-command at Dome, while Gallagher spent his time wowing the money men with his "snake oil" slide shows.

By 1982, Dome was land rich and cash poor. In addition to its Arctic interest, its holdings in the western sedimentary basin exceeded those of all other oil companies combined. As the NEP started to choke the oil business and OPEC smothered Alberta's exploration initiatives, things got so bad for Dome that it couldn't afford to rent a rig for all its promising oil territory, and no other company wanted to enter a joint venture for fear Dome would go belly up without paying its share.

In the end, the banks stepped in. Bill Mulholland, the pint-sized Napoleon of the gold and glass towers of Bay Street, used the Bank of Montreal's muscle to extract a price for keeping Dome going as long as it could. His price: the heads of Gallagher and Richards.

Mulholland got the heads dripping on a platter, but Dome was doomed in any case.

Bob Blair had also followed the early Dome strategy of trying to benefit from Lalonde's Canadianization incentives, but Blair avoided the excessive recklessness of the high-flying Richards. Blair, who once donned a trapper's jacket fringed with beads to impress a National Energy Board hearing into applications for a northern pipeline — the Bay Street boys showed up at the same hearing in Yellowknife in their dark banker suits — built up his stake in the oil and gas business, including major developments in petrochemicals, through a series of shrewd moves while wearing his Canadian heart on his sleeve to become the darling of Ottawa's Liberals. (It is ironic how quickly that patriotism faded when Li Ka-shing[59] came calling with his Hong Kong dollars to buy a controlling interest in Husky from Blair's Nova.)

While the federal government was behaving like a banana republic in trying to force foreign investment out of the oilfields, Alberta could only fume at this assault on the assets of friendly neighbours who had chosen to take risks in the western wilds in the early development days, risks that Central Canadian financiers had coldly shunned.

So when I went to down-in-the-dumps Calgary in August 1982, the city wasn't wearing its happiest face. When it had been announced that I was leaving Edmonton, an unknown "admirer" had written to me as follows: "How can you face the Almighty God when you have destroyed Mr. P. Trudeau's reputation? ... You had better make restitution, or you will never save your soul." All the signs of economic gloom to the contrary, my coming to Calgary was hardly part of that process of restitution, unless Gordon Fisher knew something I didn't.

Nick Taylor, the quipster who ran the provincial Liberals out of his back pocket, had welcomed me to Calgary with a sly dig at Joe Clark's Israel policy. Of my change of cities, he wrote: "It's like moving from Tel Aviv to Jerusalem because most people in Calgary believe that our premier was born in a manger somewhere out there on the west side of town."

If Lougheed still had enough straw left in his mouth from that stable on the west side of town, he had no desire to spit any of it out to play the role of saviour of the federal Tories the next time I made the proposal in the *Herald* — on Oct. 6, 1982. In suggesting that a fall vote in Alberta might free Lougheed for a run at the federal leadership in 1983, I said that what some Tories envisaged was a "party led by a man who would surely be a messiah rather than his tentative gospel preacher."

But Clark, the tentative gospel preacher, had no intention of giving up his pulpit to Lougheed; and Lougheed, after 17 years of politics, was sticking to his earlier statement that he was simply tired of it all. Obviously, Jeanne Lougheed wasn't bothering to check the wallpaper samples for that house on Sussex Drive.

With a Tory leadership review already planned for Winnipeg early in 1983, Clark had no intention of making the sacrifice Capt. Lawrence Oates made when he realized that the Scott expedition to the South Pole was hampered by his own frost-bitten feet. Oates tried to resolve that problem by disappearing into the blizzard night to give his friends a chance to survive. Given the fierce desire of Clark to become prime minister again, there was little likelihood of him following the noble instincts of Oates and disappearing in the direction of Portage and Main, decked out in his fur-lined boots and parka.

When Peter Pocklington, the somewhat erratic owner of the Edmonton Oilers, offered his own services as prime minister for a dollar a year (about what he would have been worth), Clark responded that he had no intention of using the Winnipeg review convention to call a full-fledged leadership conference.

John Crosbie earned the ire of Tory house leader Erik Nielsen at a caucus meeting for expressing doubts in public about the capability of Clark leading the Tories back to power. Calgary South MP John Thomson came out of the Tory closet with a direct appeal for a leadership convention.

While the followers were already sharpening their knives, Clark refused to accept he was the millstone around the neck of the party.

Obviously, 1982 was not a good year to be an Albertan, a political leader or an oilman, but even in the seemingly moribund city of Calgary, life was never dull for a publisher trying to cope with a new command.

# CHAPTER 21

Junius[60], who for years has been admonishing loyal readers of the editorial page of the *Globe and Mail* to "neither advise nor submit to arbitrary measures," also believed — although the *Globe* never tells us — that "there is holy mistaken zeal in politics as well as in religion. By persuading others, we convince ourselves."

There was never any mistaking the fervour that Joe Clark brought to his politics, but he revered the Junius dictum — he was always trying to persuade others to accept what he had already convinced himself was a self-evident truth. It was his flawed political wisdom, forged in mistaken zeal, that brought him to the Winnipeg convention in January 1983, demanding from the Tories better than 66 per cent support for his leadership. If he didn't get it, he said, he would call a full-scale leadership convention. In fact, he got 1,607 delegates voting to leave things the way they were — a 66.9 per cent vote in his favour. But after his bold and reckless challenge, it was too wafer-thin a margin of victory for him to ignore. In a sense, he had cornered himself into calling a leadership race that he couldn't win, thus opening the door to the Brian Mulroney era.

Mulroney had spent the summer of 1982 speaking to enthusiastic audiences all across the country. Everywhere he went, Mulroney declared himself a Clark supporter. He never missed an opportunity to say that the party, in picking Clark in 1976, chose "wisely and well." Mulroney said he would do everything he could to bring about a change of government, but then he always added the rider: "Mr. Clark's reconfirmation as leader is an important part of this process.

His subsequent re-election as prime minister will be good for Canada." Isn't that what a good party man is supposed to say about his leader? But Clark was set to take the bait, not seeing the hook being floated under his nose.

Historians will have to wrestle with what might have been if Clark had stuck to the letter of his own 66 per cent guideline and, by doing so, denied Mulroney the chance for a leadership rematch in Ottawa. The shootout planned for June 10-12 should have given the party the opportunity to expand from warring cliques into a united army dedicated to mopping up the beaten remnants of Liberalism, but as usual it was ready to fumble the chance.

When Premier Lougheed came to see the *Calgary Herald* editorial board in May, a month before the leadership convention, he was emphatic in his refusal to become a candidate. After the board had gone, and he was relaxing alone with me in my office, he told me there was no substance to the story that had surfaced in 1976 that it was his wife, Jeanne, who had convinced him for personal and family reasons not to run for the Tory leadership when Robert Stanfield had bowed out. He said he could not have left Alberta at a time when there were serious problems arising at the federal level on energy.

An article I had written in February had prompted Jeanne Lougheed to ask the premier: "What would you do if Joe Clark came to you and asked you to run if he stepped down?" His response to her was that she didn't have to worry about getting an answer to such a hypothetical question because Clark had no intention of stepping down — "Maureen wouldn't let him!" However, either deliberately or by oversight, Lougheed left unanswered what his response might have been if Clark made that approach to him.

When he was pushed earlier by the editorial board to state whom he might support at the June convention, he demonstrated his own brand of circumlocution, but the inference to be taken was that Clark would not be his choice. Later, alone, he told me he thought Clark would win, "but what good will that do?"

He had made it clear to the board who would not get his approval: Bill Davis. "I don't know how I can support him, given his attitude on the energy question. I was very disturbed by that." He said Davis had never grasped that a healthy Alberta meant a healthy Ontario.

Davis certainly had designs on the leadership, but when he put out feelers it became evident Alberta Tories would have none of it. An article I wrote for the *Herald* a few days after the Lougheed visit to the editorial board was blamed by some Davis backers for his decision not to stand. The article was headed: Don't Call Us, Bill Davis — We'll Call You! The Lougheed people, it is said, hooted with glee when they saw it and rushed copies of the article to Davis in his Queen's Park office while he was still pondering his decision.

Davis didn't just bring down the Clark government in 1980 — he more or less wrote the book on denying to the oil-producing provinces the legitimate market price that Davis had always demanded for his own province's resources and manufactured goods.

The article said: "His vision of Canada is no broader than that of his own background — a parish-pump, small-town lawyer-politician, comfortable in an assumed folksiness, with an obsession for moulding policies to fit the prevailing polls.

"It was the support of Davis, along with that of New Brunswick Premier Richard Hatfield that sustained Trudeau in his last-hurrah gallop toward a Constitution that nobody wanted. In return, Davis got his cheaper oil.

"For the sake of the Tories, who have federal power almost within their grasp, the dual tragedy is that Clark still sees himself as a man of destiny and is destroying the party, and Davis sees himself as the champion of Confederation from a base that is more rigidly parochial and blurred of vision than anything seen in Mackenzie King's clouded crystal ball. Doesn't Canada deserve better? It should be spared the regional divisiveness of a bid for federal power by Bill Davis."

That's hardly the stuff you want to see in a letter of recommendation when you go looking for a new job. Davis used the occasion on an off-the-record black-tie dinner at the Ranchmen's Club in Calgary on Sept. 6, three months after the Tory convention to seek a measure of revenge.

He started out trying to woo an audience he knew was hostile. The theme of his speech was that a Canadian economic recovery was at hand and all would benefit from it. However, he wandered off the topic to suggest he had had an unfair press in Alberta, and more particularly from the *Herald*. Somebody must have told him I was present, because he mentioned my name several times. He said that I had completely misunderstood and misrepresented his position on energy. Each time he fired off one of his zingers intended for me, he turned for emphasis to the table where he thought I was sitting. I don't know who the poor individual was that he transfixed with his outrage in this way, but when Davis kept hitting the wrong target, like a demented Scud missile gunner, there were some embarrassed titters around the room.

Davis denied that Ontario had opposed world price for Alberta oil, but then he began to waffle, realizing the audience at the Ranchmen's Club was somewhat more knowledgeable on the subject of oil than the average group of Ontario voters he was used to hoodwinking. He said he had done everything in his power to support the party leader (Clark) during the 1980 election that followed the end of the nine-month Tory government. He said he had been unfairly ridiculed for disappearing from the country (on a Florida vacation) when it was suggested that he should have been on the stump for Clark during the winter election. He said he would have given Clark any help he wanted, but Clark never asked for it.

The impression he gave to that audience largely composed of Alberta oilmen was that he was not happy to be seen as the accomplice (unwitting or otherwise) of Trudeau and Lalonde. Some sensed that he actually regretted what he had helped to set in train with his connivance on the energy war.

In this regard, it is interesting now to recall the words of David Peterson, then the Ontario Liberal finance critic, when the Davis government slapped an *ad valorem* tax on gasoline and diesel fuel in 1981. Pointing out that the tax would put more money into Ontario's coffers than the producing provinces ever got, Peterson said: "Ontario will get massive windfall profits while Davis sits on the sidelines, laughing, parading as the champion of cheap energy."

But Davis was not laughing that night at the Ranchmen's Club. After declaring his great friendship for Lougheed, he said he would have backed the Alberta premier in 1976 if Lougheed had chosen to run for the leadership. He didn't put the same pledge in the context of the 1983 contest, but he admitted he had considered running himself. He said he had taken extensive soundings. What finally persuaded him not to run, and what "made me very sad was the sort of editorial writing by Mr. O'Callaghan" that made it obvious he would not enjoy Alberta backing. He did not say if he had ever approached Lougheed for his support for such a bid.

The political lives of Davis and Lougheed sometimes ran along parallel lines, but more often there was discord between these two Tories whose regional demarcation lines so often excluded each other's interests.

It would have to be said that in their time, Lougheed, Davis and René Lévesque formed a powerful trio of provincial leaders who put an indelible mark on the history of Canada. Each was a man of determination, Davis less obtrusively so than the others. While Davis was the epitome of bland Canadianism, the style befitting the man who influenced national events simply by drawing attention to the political thump of the province he led, Lougheed bore the scars of many wounds earned honourably in too many wars with Ottawa. But Davis and Lougheed and Lévesque had influenced governing patterns by the manner in which an ungovernable country deals with the sum of all its wayward parts.

All three operated on the national scene at a time when Canada was confused and groping for its own identity. All three, in different ways, helped to write a scenario for what was supposed to be the progressive Canada of the future. Unfortunately, the missing link between regional and national interests made it impossible to achieve an enduring balance. It is a link that may never be found.

The Tories were clearly at the crossroads in 1983, and the path to the federal leadership was littered with candidates determined to self-destruct along the way. Nobody's hands were quite clean, with Clark and Mulroney matching winos against nine-year-olds in an excessively bad-taste search for Quebec delegates' votes[61].

Clark, despite having the prestige of being the current leader and being a former prime minister who had once defeated Trudeau and the Liberals, was the most vulnerable of the serious candidates at the Ottawa convention. If, indeed, he had topped the final ballot, the biggest winner would have been the sagging Liberals, not the Tory party. In the end, the Tories gambled on Brian Mulroney, a man who had yet to prove he had more substance than shadow, more character than charisma and more staying power than sheer hunger for political power.

# CHAPTER 22

Brian Mulroney once celebrated his birthday at the White House. When asked by President Ronald Reagan what birthday he was observing, Mulroney told the president he was 49. Reagan paused for a moment and then chuckled: "What can I say, other than, 'Good luck, kid.'"

Mulroney told me: "I now have that Good Luck, Kid embroidered on my pillow and I sleep on it every night."

But did he have that Good Luck, Kid stitched to his heart?

If he had the luck of the Irish, then in his case it was all bad. To his Irish genes he also owed his pugnacity. His ability to hate and get even was something he borrowed from either Trudeau or the Kennedys. Or, more likely, from a long-dead black Irish predecessor. Above all, he hated the national press with a ferocity that was searing. This was puzzling for a man who started out as a media junkie.

The media were clearly on his mind when he phoned me on Jan. 25, 1986. An Angus Reid poll had his government in deep trouble after less than two years in office. For this, he blamed a rash of minor scandals, which he said the CBC delighted in airing day after day. He felt the swift resignation of John Fraser should have disposed of the minister's error of judgment in the StarKist tuna fish affair[62]. When I said Fraser had shown class by stepping down so swiftly, whereas Suzanne Blais-Grenier[63], the indiscreet traveller, had not, he snapped: "Don't mention that woman to me."

His troubles with the polls stemmed from distorted perceptions force-fed to Canadians by the National Press Gallery, he said.

"When I came here (to Ottawa) three years ago to announce my candidacy (for the Tory leadership), 298 out of the 300 people in the press gallery laughed at me, said I hadn't got a chance. When I came here as leader of the Opposition, they said Trudeau would chew me up and spit me out. When Prime Minister Turner called an election, his party was 14 points ahead in the polls, and I got the biggest majority in the history of Canada."

He said the press gallery continually ignored the "big-ticket items of this government." He listed these as "national reconciliation, the energy deals with the West, and on the East Coast, the 450,000 new jobs we have created."

On the subject of free trade, he declared: "We are not only going to push for free trade, we are going to goddamn well do it!"

He went on: "Look it! Ontario has the auto business. It has all of the auto parts business. It has the auto pact to protect it. Everything is tremendous for Ontario, which wants to keep everything to itself as it always does. But I have to go ahead and do these goddamn things for the rest of the country. We can't allow one province to block it."

Finally, he said: "You know me, Patrick. I'm an Irishman from the wrong side of the tracks. We're pretty tough. We never give up. We never stop fighting." But while flexing his muscles, he also pondered ruefully and with genuine sadness the manner in which the free trade debate was shaping up. "This country has lost the art of being civil in politics," he said.

A cabinet shuffle at the end of June cost Alberta an ally in Pat Carney, a popular cabinet minister who had been well received in energy circles. She lost the fight in cabinet to drop immediately the Petroleum and Gas Revenue Tax, as promised in the 1984 election, and Mulroney decided to throw her into the free trade fight instead. The impression left with Alberta was that energy was now a low priority. Not only that, but Carney's replacement as energy minister was Marcel Masse, a closet separatist and still another francophone from a consuming province stepping into the shoes of Lalonde and Chrétien. It was not a happy prospect for an industry in need of help.

Apart from quoting Greek philosophers to bewildered Alberta oilmen, Masse's only initiative was to demand more jobs for francophones in the top management positions of Petro Canada.

Alberta's mood was soured even more by Mulroney, who paused, while signing a $225-million aid package for Nova Scotia's Venture gas field, to say: "No province has benefited more from our energy policies than the province of Alberta." This was news to Albertans, and they gave Mulroney their response in a fall byelection in the Pembina riding. Surely it rated a line in the *Guinness Book of Records* that the Tories had lost 34,000 voters there in the two years since the general election.

The Tories did hold the seat by the skin of their teeth, but Mulroney was forced to hit the campaign trail in the dying stages of the byelection to ensure they did so. For his trouble, he had to endure obscene heckling from strikers from Gainers, Peter Pocklington's meat-packing plant in nearby Edmonton.

Walter Van Der Walle just edged out Ivor Dent, the former NDP mayor of Edmonton. Doug Christie was a distant fourth, running on a western separatist ticket.

But it wasn't only Alberta that was feeling a sense of alienation from the federal Tories.

A committee of 75 civil servants from three different departments had recommended that a tender from Bristol Aerospace of Winnipeg be accepted for a billion-dollar contract to service Canada's new fighter, the CF-18. Bristol's bid was superior technically to a bid from Canadair of Montreal, the committee agreed. And Bristol's bid was lower than Canadair's. But the Quebec caucus of the Tory party swung its considerable weight behind Canadair.

Going against the advice of its own impartial committee of civil servants, and defying all business and economic logic, the government made a highly charged political decision to give the contract to Montreal.

If Mulroney was writing off the West, it didn't stop him telling me in a phone call on Nov. 22, 1986, that he still regarded himself as the "best goddamn friend Alberta has ever had."

He called me at home, just after my daughter Fiona and I had got back from a Calgary Flames hockey game. After thrilling the 15-year-old by chatting with her about his children, the youngest of whom, Nicholas, he had brought with him to Calgary to tour some of the sites for the Winter Olympics, he moved on to the subject of Alberta, bristling a little at my comment that the province would prefer something more tangible than the rhetoric of fine words to prove his undying love.

In these phone calls to me, Mulroney's view of the people in the political spotlight was always coloured by his highly subjective perceptions, as he proved when he got on the subject of the CF-18 contract. I told him the decision to shaft Winnipeg was unforgiveable and it was all the more damaging in the light of the attention the city had always had from the Liberal government, with Lloyd Axworthy[64] acting as the godfather of the province and channelling hundreds of millions of federal dollars into the city.

He agreed with my analysis that if an election were being held then, not a single Tory would hold his seat in Manitoba. However, he told me that Howard Pawley, then NDP premier of Manitoba, had told him the same thing when Mulroney intervened in the debate over French-language rights in the province. Pawley's prediction would have been dead-on, he said, had an election come on the heels of that intervention.

"But you have to be patient," Mulroney said. "Circumstances in politics change quite rapidly."

Lloyd Axworthy was always low on his hit parade. "Axworthy is viscerally anti-American," Mulroney said. "He's basically a hater. He hates Americans, he hates Tories, he hates business, he hates the oil industry, he hates everybody, even the West, unlike his brother, Tom, who's not a bit like that." (Tom Axworthy had been on Trudeau's staff and later co-authored a book with the former prime minister.)

# CHAPTER 23

It was the battle against Central Canadian interventionism that had given Ted Byfield his audience and helped him to coin money with *Alberta Report*. But by 1986, the waning of the energy war left him adrift, unsure of the next targets for his poison-tipped essays.

With plenty of money in his pocket, he took time out from the fray to meditate, to contemplate the books he wanted to write on the history of Christianity and other religions. He chose an expensive boat as his monastic cell, but continued as an iconoclastic observer of the Alberta scene all the way from Vancouver harbour. His son Link became publisher during Byfield's brief sabbatical, and Ted was identified on the magazine's masthead as president and chairman of Interwest Publications, owners of *Alberta Report*.

However, things quickly started to go downhill in Edmonton and Ted rushed back to assume an untitled role as the puppet master for Link. The son should not be held totally accountable for the downturn because it was Ted's own grand strategy that was mostly responsible for the decline. Before he had gone off to commune with his soul in Vancouver, Ted had put on the market a magazine to serve all four western provinces. What was good for Alberta, he reasoned, was good for all of the West, with his own vitriolic column the straw to stir the drink.

What was called *Alberta Report* in one province — outside of Alberta's capital city, where it remained *Edmonton Report* — became *Western Report* in the three other provinces west of the Lakehead. All the issues carried virtually the same editorial material, with only meagre allowance for local topics in each province. The purpose of going beyond its Alberta roots was to attract national advertising — that is, advertising that needs more than a local market base. Such "national" advertising up to then had mostly gone the way of *Maclean*'s magazine in the weekly field.

However, Byfield found there was a major price to pay for this expansionist strategy: he began to lose some of the magazine's core audience, the Albertans who bought a magazine they had felt was giving them a specific perspective on their own province. The erosion of the Alberta-first attitude was evident in many editions of the new *Western Report*, even when it was wearing the disguise of an *Alberta Report* nameplate.

In one issue I checked in June 1986, there were 42 features or stories spread across 54 pages, and only 11 of them had direct interest for Alberta. The grandiose concept of *Alberta Report* as the magazine of the West, thumbing its nose at *Maclean*'s, the eastern intruder, began to founder on the rocks of Byfield's egotistical ambition.

When I mused along these lines in the *Calgary Herald*, Byfield used the columns of the Edmonton and Calgary *Sun*s to brand me as the prophet of doom. "Not for nothing do they call him Jeremiah," he wrote. (Not even my mother called me by my given first name, Jeremiah,)

My record as prophet demonstrated a curious inconsistency, Byfield wrote. "He is not wrong some of the time. He is not wrong most of the time. He has simply never been right."

Then, with a typical rhetorical leap that stood all logic on its head, he spoke of "Southam reversals" caused by my publishing days at both the *Journal* and the *Herald*. The consequences to the bottom line were so severe, he stated, that a formidable takeover move developed against Southam "predicated on that fact that its profits had become so pathetic, particularly in the newspaper division."

Despite giving it my best shot, as outlined by Byfield, I didn't bring down the company all by myself in 1986. It managed to hang in there. The annual report for that year showed that Southam's overall revenues were just under $1.3 billion — an increase of $115 million on the previous year. Net income of $67 million was 79.3 per cent over the previous year (up from $37 million). Dividends for the year were up by 24 per cent. In the newspaper division – that "pathetic" performer, according to Byfield — revenues of $648 million were $48 million better than the previous year, and the operating income of $83.5 million was $14 million above 1985. And the *Herald* and the *Journal* were still the company's top earners.

What price failure?

Chewing on the bone of his discontent with my somewhat negative analysis of his western magazine strategy, Byfield took still another swing at me in his June 16, 1986, column in *Alberta Report*. In the process, he also gave his reasons for the transformation of *Alberta Report* from a magazine almost all of whose news emanated from Alberta, to a magazine trying to cover four provinces.

He blamed three severe economic reversals: first, the National Energy Program ("one of whose purposes, it now seems indisputable, was to arrest the growing economic power of this province because it threatened the Canadian status quo"); second, the decline of the cattle and grain industry; and third, the collapse of the international oil market.

All of these things combined began "hitting us a year ago February, when national advertisers, aware that Alberta was not the boomland it had been, began diverting their dollars back to Ontario. We remained profitable, but that trend was downward, and it became evident that if we did nothing about it we would soon be defunct."

That was understandable, but then he wandered off the rails again to suggest that his search for a regional presence, rather than a single provincial base, had failed because of resentment by the eastern media. "We must always remember that the 'eastern' media include nearly the whole of the western media. All can be counted on to oppose any movement toward any unification of outlook in the West."

But the real key to Byfield's article was contained in this heading: Why Southam's Branch Office Fears A Trend To Western Unity. This was a familiar theme of Byfield's and in that particular column he developed it this way: "The *Calgary Herald*, wholly owned by Southams in Toronto, spread over half a page an attack on this magazine over the signature of its publisher, deploring and deriding our western content. Why, he asked, should Calgarians care about the affairs of Winnipeg or North Battleford or the British Columbia coast? If the man ever left his Southam ivory tower long enough to take a look at the agony of the city he's supposed to serve, he would very rapidly have his answer. But of course he will not. He looks instead to Toronto, where his own fortunes are decided, and he will vanish from the West at the snap of a Southam finger. The rest of us, meanwhile, stand or fall with Alberta. But Alberta and all the West, if they are to stand at all, must stand together. That is the change we have worked in the perspective of this magazine. That is also the change we seek to work in the perspective of Western Canada."

All very nobly virtuous, of course, and worthy of a couple of inspiring choruses of *Land of Hope and Glory*, but the idea of Southam snapping its collective fingers to draw me from the West was enough to make any sober-sided director of the company laugh hysterically. With only about 2,900 kilometres separating Calgary from the Southam head office on Bloor Street, there were some in that real ivory tower who felt I was already uncomfortably close. In all fairness, the late Gordon Fisher used to ask me plaintively: "Why do you never visit us?" But nobody else at head office was prepared to extend the same invitation.

A day after his outburst in *Alberta Report*, Byfield told reporters that *Western Report* was not in trouble, despite layoffs of clerical and sales staff. A number of editorial freelancers had been let go, but he denied the magazine was closing its Vancouver office. He said *Western Report*'s circulation was about 8,000, while *Alberta Report* had 52,000 subscribers. (This latter figure was a drop of 20 per cent from *Alberta Report*'s palmier days.) By any conservative estimate, Byfield's *Western Report* had then cost Interwest about $2 million, a large sum for a small but one-time profitable publishing enterprise.

*Alberta Report* survived that 1986 crisis because a number of Albertans felt Byfield's voice was pertinent to the times. One of those saviours was Jim Gray, the articulate Calgary oilman and booster of the Triple-E Senate proposition[65], who had made a mint of money when Canadian Hunter brought the huge Elmworth gas field on stream on the Alberta-B.C. border. A major interest in Canadian Hunter was then held by Noranda.

However, a year later, the irascible pamphleteer was having more red-ink problems. Although a frequent and abrasive critic of the Alberta government — too left-leaning for Byfield's taste — it did not stop him from taking a $250,000 loan from the Alberta Opportunity Company (AOC), a provincial government agency. When the news leaked out, it inspired the following *Herald* editorial on Nov. 28, 1987:

"Clearly, this scourge of the Alberta government (*Alberta Report*) does not share a newspaper's abhorrence of government involvement in its operation. A newspaper is not a propaganda machine; it has no political master. It has no God-given right to exist. Because democracy has enshrined freedom of speech in the Canadian Charter of Rights to bolster the traditional independence of the press, this newspaper — any newspaper — needs no government to license it to operate. The flip side of that independence is that no newspaper can take government subsidies as an insurance against failure.

"But *Alberta Report* is not a newspaper. It is a news magazine, a scavenger of newspapers, picking their brains and their finished products for story ideas to serve up as rehashed analysis. It has no such compunction when it comes to accepting money from government. Neither, apparently, does it see the dichotomy in its editor saying that the government loan will have no effect on editorial policy while the president of the AOC says that 'the taxpayers' money should not be used to do other businesses harm.'

"When the camel is in the tent, who knows where it might want to set down its big feet? What price editorial freedom and integrity? How about $250,000?"

When you stick a pin in a Byfield, the whole family bleeds and it was son Link who rushed forward with the bandages on Dec. 14. Under the heading on his Letter from the Publisher column — Why The *Herald*'s O'Callaghan Fears This Magazine — he ran the editorial from the *Herald* in full.

"Though unsigned," he wrote, the editorial "bears the trademark ferocity of that bombastic old soul, J. Patrick O'Callaghan." My anonymity thus unveiled, he went on: "No matter how pathetically absurd the pretext, an O'Callaghan condemnation is always good reading. It is a fact that

O'Callaghan diatribes against this magazine have been something of an annual event for the past 10 years."

Dealing with what he said was the *Herald*'s editorial charge — that borrowing money from an Alberta government agency made *Alberta Report* "merely a public relations firm for the Getty cabinet" — this chip off the Byfield block dismissed it as "typically cheap, charming O'Callaghan plonk."

Then he went on to reveal something his father had carefully kept quiet — that the $250,000 loan from the Alberta Opportunity Company was not by any means the first to the magazine. It was at least the third, he suggested, and excusable on the grounds that while that "velvet coffin" — the *Herald* — had a sugar daddy at Southam head office in the event of a cash shortage, *Alberta Report* had few hard assets against which to borrow from banks and to fall back on higher-risk lenders like the AOC.

He wound up a progress report that had a false ring to it underneath the bravado with this stirring paragraph: "Pat O'Callaghan, then publisher of the *Edmonton Journal*, watched us grow under his nose. We grew because his newspaper, with its pompous, lazy, left-wing, public-utility mindset, did a lousy job. Not that a pipsqueak like us will ever put Southam out of business." That last sentence was at least reassuring to both Southam and me!

My exchange with the Byfields on the AOC loan gave CBC Edmonton the idea that getting Ted Byfield and Pat O'Callaghan together on the same early-morning radio show would help its listeners to wake up in fighting mood. So on Dec. 21, 1987, together in purple prose on the air waves although 322 kilometres apart geographically, Byfield and I were asked to explain our vastly different positions on publications accepting money from government. Byfield first extracted a promise from the interviewer that "for every minute he gets, I get an equivalent minute."

Then he was off and running. The *Calgary Herald* did not exist, he said. It was just a branch plant of the Southam company. Southam had persuaded the Trudeau government to give it protection from the American takeover, he went on. It got radio licences at the drop of a hat. Southam owned Coles Book Stores and then needed bookstands at government airports and Southam pulled government strings to get them. On the subject of the rumoured takeover bid following the death of Gordon Fisher, Byfield said the company got the Ontario government to look the other way because "the whole thing stank to high heaven. What was the payoff for that? Is the *Calgary Herald* pusillanimous on free trade because Southam is beholden to the Ontario government?" (To round that misshapen logic into recognizable form, it should be pointed out that the *Herald* was the federal government's strongest editorial supporter on its free trade initiative and I wrote most of those editorials myself. So poor David Peterson must still be waiting for his payoff.)

Byfield in full flight is a sight to behold and to listen to. When I dared to point out, in response to some acid comments made in *Alberta Report* over the supposed decline of the *Edmonton Journal*, the many awards it had received over the years, including the only Pulitzer Prize ever awarded outside the United States, Byfield threw all reason to the winds of the airwaves.

The *Journal*, he said, "wins prizes from organizations Southam itself controls." (That must have given former governor general Roland Michener, himself an Albertan and founder of the public service awards given in his name, food for thought. And a whole host of the Pulitzer family surely turned over in their graves with a collective sigh.) "Southam gives them the prizes," Byfield went on, "because Southam owns half the media." Not quite, Ted, not quite.

Byfield also blurted out in that broadcast that, in addition to the various loans taken from AOC, a group of Alberta businessmen had recently invested more than $350,000 in the magazine.

It would not be too difficult to guess that some of Byfield's admiring backers went on to become members of Preston Manning's Reform Party, which Byfield helped to found. Byfield, along with Manning and the late Stanley Roberts — a political gadfly who had been a Manitoba Liberal MLA and many other things — organized the Western Assembly in Vancouver in 1987. Byfield was the keynote speaker at the assembly, which gave birth to the Reform Party. Some delegates had hoped he would run for the leadership, although I doubt he himself had any ambitions along those lines. He was too much the maverick.

Nevertheless, despite the financial efforts of his friends, and government loans, he was clearly living on borrowed time. In 1990, Interwest Publications Ltd. reported an accumulated debt of $4 million and went into voluntary receivership as a condition of sale to a group of Calgary oilmen, led by Don Graves. To compound Byfield's problems, according to his son, Link, Ted was the biggest loser in the failure of Interwest; he had an estimated $500,000 invested.

Graves became chairman of the reorganized company. Link Byfield took on the title of editor-publisher. Ted got the title of president and continued to write his back-of-the-book column, although some of the verve had gone from it.

It was really the end of an era. It just couldn't be the same anymore now that the old soft-shoe act of Byfield and

O'Callaghan had been dissolved. We really deserved each other and each, in his own way, revelled in the swordplay.

# CHAPTER 24

When Michael O'Malley has a complaint, he goes straight to the top.

Detecting an "incredible open scandal" — his words, not mine — he wrote to Pope John Paul II saying that the Catholic bishops of Canada more or less ignored Church canons 1041 and 1042. These are the canons that order them "to refrain from public heresy and schism."

Having thus branded them all, by implication, as heretics, he went on: "The Canadian Conference of Catholic Bishops have been so infiltrated by secular feminists that the magisterium of the church has been surrendered to a national opinion which promotes, with the full approval of the bishops' authority, sexual immorality and women's ordination, and attacks on the family, and spreads contempt at the universal magisterium of the Church."

Immorality is where you find it, I guess.

The linking of women's ordination and immorality in one sub-clause of his letter of Jan. 20, 1986, to the pope is not just coincidence. O'Malley told a Calgary judge in a defamation suit against me that not only was he unmarried, but he was totally celibate, a philosophy and state of grace he outlined in relished detail. While remaining aloof from all feminine wiles, he was clearly not in favour of advancing the cause of women in the Catholic Church, either. The Roman Catholic bishops and priests of Canada, with Calgary's own Bishop Paul O'Byrne — a Barry Fitzgerald[66] look-alike — in the vanguard, found their Christian charity stretched to the limits when the subject of O'Malley surfaced.

(By way of explanation: he used to be Michael Malley. He told a judge he had changed the name to O'Malley to "reclaim my Irish roots.")

"Holy Father, what is going on?" he asked plaintively in his letter to the Vatican, after outlining how he had to go to the Papal Pro-Nuncio[67], Archbishop Angelo Palmas, when he got no satisfaction from the Canadian Church over his complaint that the rule allowing women to perform certain ministries outside the sanctuary but forbidding them to serve the altar within the sanctuary was being violated. O'Malley doesn't want women that close to the eyes of God.

O'Malley described himself as an anti-abortion crusader. He quit a $25,000 a year job counselling emotionally disturbed children, he said, to work full-time for Calgary's Coalition for Life, but even that dedicated organization wearied of him after two years as its self-ordained spokesman. Its board refused to back him in his confrontational approach to the *Herald* and he was forced to resign.

So he set up a branch of the Toronto-based Campaign Life Coalition (often called simply Campaign Life) and installed himself as president, keeper of the nation's morals, guardian of the Catholic Church's rigid authoritarian principles, public scold and general nuisance.

Not being terribly sensitive or selective in his choice of targets, he made life miserable for his own clergy, for the courts, for hospitals and doctors who performed abortions, and for the television networks and those who license them. He chained himself to hospital surgeries, blocked doorways to abortion counselling offices and appeared in court on numerous occasions, craving publicity and attention. He was convicted of public mischief, but proudly told Judge Blair Mason in the defamation suit against the *Herald* that he never paid the fine. As he explained it, the Vatican had decreed that any citizen had the right to disobey unjust laws. The courts showed a reluctance to impress on this pest to society that not even the Vatican had the right to interfere with Canadian law. In one of his many clashes over the years, even with those of the same side, he was called a "lone wolf" by the vice-president of the Alberta Federation of Women United for Families. Hermina Dykxhoorn dismissed some of his criticisms as the uninformed ramblings of a renegade crusader.

O'Malley once accosted me at the church doorway as I was leaving St. Mary's Cathedral in Calgary after a Good Friday service. Presumably, he wanted to debate my stance on abortion, although I had never expressed a public opinion on that subject.

Tired of telling him that the *Herald* did not exist exclusively to service the demands of any special-interest group, and tired of the incessant browbeating by letter and phone to which he subjected *Herald* editors, reporters or columnists whose views or professional decisions did not support his extreme position on abortion, I finally wrote a memo to staff listing guidelines on how to deal with fanatics.

O'Malley always accorded himself a legitimacy claimed through association with organizations dedicated to the pro-life cause. But it is a legitimacy he and others consistently abuse, because they cannot accept any compromise that would attempt to bridge the two extremes of pro-life and pro-choice. He was totally contemptuous of the society that set laws with which he was incompatible, but used the courts to harass others. (Ald. Barbara Scott told the defamation hearing that she had received numerous writs from O'Malley. She never read them, she testified, passing them to the city solicitor to deal with. She said in evidence that his nuisance suits against herself and other elected city officials and staff had cost the city about $100,000 in legal costs. O'Malley had virtually no expenses — he acted as his own legal counsel.

It should be remembered that on Jan. 24, 1986, the date of my statement of guidelines on fanatics, Canada already had an abortion law. It had been in force for many years and the *Herald*, while offering no official editorial view for or against abortion, simply supported the law as it stood. Admittedly, that law, like most of the political compromises Canada offers on controversial issues, had elements of weakness that made it virtually inoperable. But I never considered it an offence to support an existing law.

Given O'Malley's militant Catholicism, it is important also to remember that the abortion law, such as it is, is the product of a government led by a Catholic prime minister, Pierre Trudeau, and upheld in succession by governments led by three other Catholic prime ministers — Joe Clark, John Turner and Brian Mulroney.

While respecting the right of both factions to publicize their positions on abortion, it did not necessarily follow that the *Herald* was obliged to record for posterity every word the ubiquitous O'Malley uttered. We saw no compelling reason to rush into the press room shouting "Hold the front page!" every time O'Malley so much as sneezed. In effect, my memo told *Herald* staff not to deal with O'Malley unless he was the central figure of a genuine news story. General news of the pro-life movement should be obtained from other sources. The O'Malleys of this world are driven by their obsessions, but the public needs protection from those who would use a free press as a propaganda tool for their own personal fanaticism.

Given the heave-ho from the columns of the *Calgary Herald* did not deter O'Malley and soon he caught the ear of the *Globe and Mail*. Under the heading Paper Writes Off Anti-abortionist, and an overline, Letters Got On Publisher's Nerves, the *Globe and Mail* ran a story on April 19, 1986, that owed much to O'Malley's faithful copying machine.

Said the *Globe*: "For nearly two years, he (O'Malley) has pursued reporters and editors with letters and phone calls. He has written to Mr. O'Callaghan at least six times (with copies circulated extensively) and has received in return what are probably six of the most colourful and vigorous letters written by any Canadian publisher since Bob Edwards[68] ran the *Calgary Eye Opener* in the first two decades of this century."

Maybe we should have called reporter Murray Campbell to the trial in Calgary, because at least four of the letters referred to, along with the *Globe* article and a piece from *Alberta Report*, constituted O'Malley's case that he was defamed. (Judge Blair Mason mused out loud why, if the *Globe* piece were considered defamatory by O'Malley, I was being sued and not the *Globe*. Good question, but no answer.)

O'Malley did even better in finding an ally in Ted Byfield. Of all days, Byfield chose St Patrick's Day, 1986, to run a signed column headed Now If Paddy The Publisher Himself Were To Get Pregnant....

Assuming that I was personally opposed to abortion, Byfield told his readers he was puzzled why I didn't write about it and why I had had O'Malley thrown out of the *Herald*.

His imagination in full flight, Byfield penned this wild-eyed prose: "He (O'Callaghan) is telling us that he would never have one (a baby) himself. He is declaring, with neither fear of the consequences nor favour for any, that if he finds himself pregnant, he will carry the baby to term. Having carefully examined his conscience Paddy O'Callaghan has decided he will never have an abortion."

In retrospect, I should have set Byfield's mind at ease. After all, even in 1986, I was past the age of child-bearing.

Two weeks earlier, *Alberta Report* had accused me of fence-sitting on the issue of abortion — "a restraint uncharacteristic of the only publisher in the West given to signed full-page editorials on issues such as capital punishment (he's an abolitionist.)"

O'Malley had taken his case to *Alberta Report* on that occasion after another blow-up with the *Herald.* His central target, of all things, was CBS Television. The American network had aired a much ballyhooed episode of the *Cagney and Lacey*[69] series about two policewomen. The episode allegedly took a pro-choice stance.

When O'Malley complained to the CRTC, he demanded that the *Herald* run a story about his protest. When the *Herald* refused, it was again accused of censorship.

Without skipping a beat, O'Malley next moved on to the Alberta Press Council. In a letter dated April 14, 1986, he urged the council to reprimand the *Herald* "for its complete censoring of a pro-life spokesman (himself, although now without an organization to speak for) and hope you will recommend the *Herald* give balanced coverage to the abortion issue, with fair pro-life coverage, and recommend that the *Herald* employ at least one pro-life columnist to present the other side and balance all the other columnists." No doubt, given the right coaxing, the unstoppable O'Malley would have volunteered his services as that columnist!

As was usual with all such O'Malley complaints, his letter was accompanied by a whole sheaf of documents and clippings. In fact, I actually had it weighed — so help me, in addition to his three-page single-spaced letter, his documentation weighed 800 grams (about 1.8 lbs.)!

In replying to the press council, I pointed out that the *Herald* files were bulging with clippings quoting O'Malley or reporting events in which he had been involved. Once we even ran a fairly flattering background analysis of him on one of our main editorial pages.

"One is tempted to describe Mr. O'Malley as a full-time professional, religious fanatic and polemicist," I wrote, "an extremist on the subject of abortion who carries the extra burden of believing it is his mission in life to convert the heathen at whatever cost."

As one of my supporting documents, I attached a copy of a letter Alan P. Norton, a senior member of the board of directors for Calgary Pro-Life Association, had written to Ted Byfield after the "Pregnant Paddy" column.

Norton objected to *Alberta Report* referring to O'Malley as "the chief spokesman for the pro-life movement in Calgary."

"The most vocal, irritating, outspoken and vociferous he is. The 'chief spokesman' he is not," Norton said.

Norton's letter to Byfield also said, "Some members of the pro-life movement are concerned that O'Malley's continuing tirade may begin to close doors to the media that have taken years to open. I can only thank Mr. O'Callaghan for having the fortitude to exclude O'Malley and not the entire pro-life movement from having access to the paper."

Another point that caused Norton anguish in the O'Malley affair was outlined by him in the 1991 trial. It revolved around a doctored letter O'Malley had taken to Norton, a printer, to have set as part of a newsletter he wanted to publish in his new role as president of Campaign Life.

The so-called letter from me was actually a cunning mix of five letters written to O'Malley in reply to various letters from him. These extracts had been cut and pasted together to give the impression of being a single letter, but they were actually snipped from letters dated Aug. 30, 1984; Sept. 5, 1984; Jan. 17 and 22, and Feb. 3, 1986. He put the *Herald*'s letterhead on top and the signature from one of my original letters on the bottom and photocopied the whole to give the appearance of being one single letter. Nothing was in context, nothing in sequence, and the total effort was right out of the Josef Goebbels school of faked correspondence. (In court, he said he was simply "editing" the letters, a function he felt any newspaper would understand.)

Norton refused to print the phony letter, but another printer raised no objections and the newsletter duly went out to all O'Malley's admiring fans.

O'Malley dropped off another of his "care" packages to me on March 27, his letter again tossing in his standard threat to report me to the press council. He said he was planning to extend his complaint from the "uniform" view of the *Herald* supporting abortion to "this genuine suppression of news."

His package, in addition to a brief by the Calgary Birth Control Association (CBCA), to which he naturally took exception, included seven photocopied newspaper clippings. One included a picture of himself on a story headed Pro-lifer Urges Equal Footing. This was a reference to his bid to stymie a council grant to the Birth Control Association. Another clipping from the *Herald* was headed Pro-lifers To Picket Opponents' Offices and mainly consisted of quotes from O'Malley. A third *Herald* clipping, headed Agencies' Funding Requests Put On Hold, contained the information that the city's community services committee dismissed a complaint from O'Malley that the CBCA was "using tax dollars to promote abortion and sexual promiscuity." It also contained the information that the committee — headed by

Ald. Scott — had rejected a request by O'Malley to turn down the CBCA's request for a grant of $179,463.

For a man complaining to the press council about "suppression of news" about himself, he seemed to have got his name and face into a lot of *Herald* clippings!

The press council rejected every complaint O'Malley made about me, but he had an explanation for that too. He told Judge Mason's court that not only was the press council, like the *Herald*, totally pro-abortion, but — quoting Byfield as his authority — it was fully in the pocket of Southam.

Four days before Christmas 1987, a 16-page epic from O'Malley was dropped on my desk, like flotsam from some litigious wreck. This time, I was accused of "a number of untrue, disparaging and defamatory imputations directed toward my character and competence in my calling as a pro-life activist and spokesman; imputations which amount to serious libels." Supporting all of this was a collection of paperwork, impressive in bulk, if nothing else.

His letter not only accused me of a vendetta "designed to defame and injure me in my professional reputation and career" but also linked Catherine Ford with me in this dastardly plot. Catherine, the brilliant, if sometimes capricious, columnist and associate editor of the *Herald*, was alleged to have told O'Malley he was an "irrational extremist" when she refused to publish one of his copious letters to the editor.

O'Malley gave me two weeks on which to supply him with a draft of a letter of apology and retraction. Otherwise, he would proceed with an action for libel, naming me personally, along with the *Calgary Herald* and Southam. He expanded his range to include Catherine Ford as a defendant, but she was later dropped from the suit.

When his statement of claim was eventually received by me, it ran to 16 pages, all prepared, typed and hand-delivered by O'Malley himself. There were various other attachments, adding another 20 pages. The most curious of these was a letter addressed to "Dear God O'Callaghan." It was unsigned and carried this postscript: "Michael O'Malley has no inkling I am writing this reply to your insidious letter to him. Being a true practising Catholic, I am sure he would ask me to ignore that heretic (me, I guess) and forgive his troubled mind." The sentiment might have carried a little more weight had the typing not borne such a striking resemblance to that on the letter from O'Malley to which it was attached. Some of the more flattering quotes from the letter to "God O'Callaghan" ran as follows:

"The flexibility of your mindset is impeccable, categorizing people for life according to your indisputable doctrine. After all, you are a practising Catholic, you go to Mass, receive the Eucharist, you are the poor Publican, how dare that Pharisee Malley try to tell and remind you, a holy Catholic, about the Church's teaching on respect of life, you are God, you will tell that vituperative unbalanced Pharisee about respect for life.

"So God O'Callaghan, what is this utter garbage that you spout in print? You feel confident in your malicious degradation of a person because you have the $$$s to back you up if things should come to a head. Why don't you throw away your mangled mind and try to bring some reason into your demented, so-called free press?

"We the concerned society are heartily sick of your sick mentality. Ha! Practising Catholic! So was Judas, but you know what he did, you seem to be following in his exact footsteps.

"Not every newspaper has an insulting jackass for a publisher. So I am growing hoarse trying to pound logic and common sense into the closed mind of a fanatic jackass."

And that's just the good stuff!

The trial began in Calgary on June 3, 1991, and took up 10 days of court time. O'Malley called no witnesses and had a subpoena demanding the presence of Bishop Paul O'Byrne thrown out by the judge. Acting as his own legal counsel, O'Malley hammered away on his "David vs. Goliath" theme. One of the things he had trouble explaining to the judge was the irritatingly cute dodge he pulled out of his manual of urban guerilla dirty tricks, of having several fake phone numbers listed in the Yellow Pages phone directory to confuse anyone trying to look for abortion counselling.

It was not until 1992 that the case was finally disposed of, totally in the *Herald*'s favour. The judge awarded costs in our favour.

It is always difficult for a newspaper to deal with self-righteously pigheaded troublemakers of the O'Malley kind because their own propelled omniscience gets in the way of understanding. No newspaper can allow itself to be available on demand to all who need a propaganda platform or a religious pulpit.

I had seven years of trying to deal with the scourge, but O'Malley was beyond the reach of balanced perception. I couldn't help him, but I'm not alone in that. When he appealed to higher authority, even the pope could not come to his aid. O'Malley was just one of the many oddballs, eccentric nuisances who make life miserable for those who publish or edit daily newspapers.

Over the 17 years I spent as a publisher, I was often asked what it was that a publisher did, or was supposed to do. Frankly, I never saw a job description for a publisher, and no two publishers had the same appreciation of what their job was supposed to be. Starting out as a publisher, I would never have guessed that so much of my time would be spent on the care and handling of religious fanatics, mischievous crackpots and malicious busybodies.

Perhaps, taking a leaf out of O'Malley's book, I should despatch my own letter to the Vatican. Following O'Malley's episcopal style, I might be emboldened enough to say: "I write in full confidence and hope in appeal to the paternal solicitude of your priestly heart for the welfare of all the children of the faith in the Roman Catholic Church in Canada, even those misbegotten sinners who have the misfortune to publish daily newspapers. Holy Father, please help us! And failing that, grant me full remission of my sins for having served my penance in the shadow of the indefatigable Michael O'Malley."

To be fair to O'Malley, in 1995, when the more violently unstable elements of the pro-life movement began using guns to make their point, O'Malley told the *Herald*: "I just hate what's going on."

# CHAPTER 25

The parade of villains, charlatans, oddballs, harmless kooks, wastrels, publicity-seekers and other assorted characters that passes endlessly in front of any newspaper makes for an interesting life, to say the least of it. It was never dull.

Dalton Camp[70] wrote in the *Toronto Star* in June 1983: "A man named J. Patrick O'Callaghan, no less, is the publisher of the *Calgary Herald*. Those of you who are disappointed to learn this, having thought of him as an Irish poet, will be consoled on learning the man has a way with words which transcends poetry."

Even allowing for the dripping sarcasm, not everybody in Alberta who read my signed articles and editorials during the tumultuous years of the energy and constitutional wars, thought of me in quite that way, either.

One persistent correspondent, who seemed to read everything I wrote without agreeing with a word of it, remarked: "You are ignorant, O'Callaghan, but the one constant strain running through the history of the Irish is ignorance. You are stark, raving mad — bonkers!"

Another equally colourful critic sent a scrap of brown wrapping paper on which he — or she — had scrawled: "You are the Irish con. You should be shot in the ass."

In a letter to the Alberta attorney general, a reader who disagreed with a *Herald* editorial criticizing the Alberta government for trying to curtail the use of French in the legislature, said: "I fail to see how even a non-Canadian, racist, island savage Irishman such as O'Callaghan can object to such a law. The French get everything they want and if

O'Callaghan writes an editorial abusing the legislators who enact such a law, put the son of a bitch in prison."

One man used to clip everything I wrote in the *Journal* and send it back to me with the word *bullshit* inscribed on it. Finally, he expanded his vocabulary to the editorial comment: "Pure bullshit!" Such is progress, or the belated benefits of higher education.

There was one woman I have never met, who carried on a one-sided correspondence with me for years. Although she had only seen newspaper pictures of me she wrote: "Are you to blame if you radiate such an irresistible aura?"

When I left Edmonton in 1982 to become publisher of the *Calgary Herald*, she wrote: "It is gone, that bright gleaming, that persuasive aura, a mind/voice/spirit, which once illuminated your paper. I am filled with a deep melancholy, a fragrant regret, as when my roses scatter petals on the wet lawn ... you walked out with a clatter of spurs."

Is it poetry you want, Dalton Camp? Or crushed rose petals on your New Brunswick lawn?

After seeing a 1991 episode of CTV's *The Shirley Show*[71] episode on which I was a panelist, the same woman tracked me down by letter in Toronto. "Put on more weight, lad: it becomes you," she wrote. "Wear the suit you wore in that 1985 photo in the *Herald* and tint your hair before an appearance. And make them supply you with a better chair, that you may be more comfortable.... When you smiled, ducking your head like a boy, it was amazingly lovely. Why did you hide that person all those years?"

Sheer modesty, I guess.

In the spring of 1990, I was a judge for the Western Ontario Newspaper Awards. One of the entries was from an off-the-wall columnist who submitted a piece he had written about a man who earned $10,000 in a Kitchener contest which I can only describe in the words used by the columnist in his explanatory letter to the judges: "A ludicrous subject that, for maximum effect, had to be played straight.... By taking a direct, on-the-scene approach, I tried to give a sense of what it was like to watch a fellow human being actually eat pig manure.... The challenge was to keep from being offensive; no easy task."

In his delicate outline to the judges, the columnist did not spare us the ultimate in how low some will sink for money. In this case, the man doing the sinking in something that any self-respecting pig would not mention in drawing-room company was first covered in honey and feathers and, after being thrown face down into the vat, he had to grope around for an apple, which he then ate, core and all!

Now that's class journalism of the tell-it-as-it-is school. After a while, even the crazier of the people whose doings we faithfully report to our readers take on a level of sanity that defies all belief.

I once had to change my private phone number at my Calgary office because a nutty religious fanatic, the blue lady who did a striptease at centre field in freezing temperatures when the Grey Cup game was played in Calgary many years earlier, got hold of it and phoned me repeatedly. One of her demands, all made in an escalating screech, was that the *Herald* should run a cartoon for saints only. The same woman used to have herself listed in the Calgary phone book as Saint Nadia, although in her frequent phone calls to various people at the *Herald* she invariably referred to herself as "God." In one of our conversations before Alberta Government Telephones came to my rescue by changing my private number, she asked me if the *J* in J. Patrick O'Callaghan stood for Jesus. In the hope that I might qualify for instant beatification — at least in her book — and get her off the line at the same time, I lied a little. The heavens did not fall.

Then there was somebody signing herself Granny Wall and writing from a ranch in Redmond, Ore., who wanted to dash off a weekly column for me. Describing herself as "an old curmudgeon philosopher with direct access to Supreme Intelligence," she sent me some sample columns. This was part of one:

"Last night before I went to sleep, I interviewed Jesus. Yes, I actually interviewed Jesus through spiritual contact.... Jesus informed me that his name is not Jesus Christ. He said he would go with Jesus of Nazareth but not with Jesus Christ. So I asked my first question: 'Why does everyone call you Jesus Christ if that is not your real name?' Jesus: 'If I recall correctly, one of my buddies gave me that handle. I think it was Simon, but I'm not sure. It was after I left the physical plane, so I couldn't object.'"

In another column, she promised to interview others "who have left the physical plane. There will be questions with answers from people like Moses, Confucius, Brigham Young, FDR, Jimmy Hoffa[72] and many others." I never had the heart to ask her if Jimmy Hoffa had told her where he was buried, nor how he came to be linked with the others who had lived more admirable lives, but history does have a precedent for off-kilter associations of that sort. Bad King John — the British monarch who lost the crown jewels in The Wash[73] and later was forced by his nobles to sign the Magna Carta — was eventually buried in Worcester Cathedral, his tomb placed between those of two saints so that when the Last Trumpet sounded, he would at least have a fighting chance of sneaking into Paradise between the two holy men. It would take a whole regiment of holy men to achieve the same trick for Hoffa.

Pity the poor publishers and editors, having to fend off those of somewhat warped views who truly believe there is an expectant world waiting breathlessly for the wisdom they wish to impart. The letters-to-the editor page is generally the place where those with a chip on their shoulders find an exclusive battleground. If that is so, then the press councils of Canada should not be overlooked as the landing beaches for the second front.

Ontario, prodded by Beland Honderich of the *Toronto Star*, moved first to organize a voluntary provincial press council in 1972, but the Alberta Press Council beat Ontario to the punch to be first in action. The *Edmonton Journal*, with Ross Munro the main inspiration, and the *Calgary Herald*, led by Frank Swanson, persuaded most of the province's dailies to give their support to this monitoring process.

However, even after more than two decades of acting as the guardians of the public's right to get fair treatment from Canada's daily newspapers, the function of a press council remains largely misunderstood. A press council is not a punitive body. It has no authority to impose fines or any other legislated punishment for those who fall short of the public's standards of journalism.

A press council cannot act as a tribunal dealing with matters that lie more properly within the jurisdiction of the courts. A press council deals in matter of taste and fairness, not in crime and punishment. While a press council tries to build bridges between a reader and a newspaper, that does not preclude members of the public from seeking a court-imposed resolution of complaints.

Because of the nature of their business, often exposing what lies under the stones of those who are in the public eye, journalists are always conscious of the risk or threat of a lawsuit when they pick away at the maggots their investigations often turn up. It is not that the public is naturally antagonistic toward newspapers. If anything, with some notable exceptions, it tends to regard the press in a familial sense, indulging in a stern, old-fashioned paternalistic manner when its offspring appear wayward.

Nevertheless, there are enough of the rich and powerful, defending their territory and their carefully acquired names, along with a whole host of bloody-minded troublemakers, willing to hamper the press in its self-appointed role as society's sieve through which passes even the tiniest particles of dirt.

The heavy-handed Reichmanns, before their fall from entrepreneurial grace, almost put *Toronto Life* magazine out of business with the heaviest of libel chills[74]. And they followed that up by ensuring that a magazine article tracing the family's roots could never be turned into a book without incurring the legal wrath of the Reichmanns. Also succeeding in banning a book were the Bronfman bully boys from the family's secretive holding company. One of the top brass of the Bronfmans scared off a book publisher with a letter warning in less-than-subtle terms that the author and the publisher had better beware of the legal hornets' nest the *Globe and Mail*'s Kimberley Noble might stir up if she were to get even one of her facts wrong. So one of Canada's best investigative business journalists was left with an unpublished manuscript sitting in her bottom drawer.[75]

Conrad Black is another past master at firing warning shots across the bows of any who take his name in vain.

On top of all that, there are the activists of many causes who see themselves as counterpoints to elected governments, the dozens of snivelling special-interest organizations whose exaggerated expectations have helped to make Canada one of the most overtaxed countries in the Western world. They all want a piece of the pie they never baked, and they take up the time of the courts while holding newspapers accountable as their unwilling but active propagandists.

The 1982 Charter of Rights and Freedoms would appear to have guaranteed freedom of the press, cocooned in the blanket freedom of speech granted to all Canadians, but for more than a decade journalists have been debating whether the charter opened more doors to newspapers or closed some off.

Despite all that, it is still true that most members of the public seem to have adopted the attitude of the British playwright Tom Stoppard toward the press: "I'm with you on the free press; it's the newspapers I can't stand." Nevertheless, it is not the relatively stable majority that makes life miserable for those trying to give an accurate picture of what is really bland in a nation lacking a spark of initiative. The problem is an off-the-wall minority that is split into so many different categories of self-serving Hegelian idealism that the poor journalist can never keep track of them as they vie with each other for public notice.

How did our newspapers, given their swashbuckling pioneering days, ever come to surrender their souls to those who shout the shrillest, while evolving into such dull parish-pump recorders of passing time, unwilling to tread on anybody's toes?

Unlike the American press, Canadian journalists don't have the protection of a First Amendment. Our charter guarantee of freedom of speech is to a large extent a promise without substance, more an idealistic principle than a defined right. We are hemmed in by laws and regulations that make the pursuit of truth and information something of a war game at times.

We have an access-to-information law that is a bad joke: it amounts to news management by government. Bureaucrats are skilled in the arts of obfuscation, taking months to find any document that a good librarian could locate in a matter of minutes. They find reasons to charge exorbitant sums for even the simplest document search, thus making it impossible for all but the rich news organizations to follow through with legitimate inquiries. The bureaucrats, unfortunately, systemized and unionized until all the life has gone out of them, are the offspring of a nation which insists on over-governing itself.

The courts are not as supportive of a free press as they might be. A judge in Edmonton ruled in 1986 that members of the press do not have a distinguishable identity in society. As a result, Justice Howard McCallum ordered that an *Edmonton Journal* reporter, Marilyn Moysa, would have to reveal sources to the Alberta Labour Relations Board, for a story the *Journal* published concerning a union-organizing attempt at the downtown Bay store. The union, through the Labour Relations Board, wanted to get from the reporter the names of those who clearly did not want to join the union.

The dilemma thus posed for a conscientious reporter was this: she could do as the court ordered and seriously damage those who had confided in her on the understanding their names would not be given , or she could refuse and put herself in contempt, thus facing a fine, or jail, or both.

The Labour Relations Board was one of more than 20 such quasi-judicial tribunals in Alberta at the time, many of them stacked with political appointees, natural creatures of patronage and pompous power. Most of the boards were not bound by normal rules of evidence and court procedures. Their powers needed to be curbed, not expanded, and yet here was a judge ordering a reporter to violate a cardinal rule of a free press — the protection of sources. And all to please a vindictive union trying to stamp out democratic dissent by employees opposed to being organized.

Perhaps it is unfair to castigate the judge who was only interpreting the law as he saw it. Nor should one totally blame the union for exploiting a law as it exists. It is the continuing uncertainty and confusion of the Charter of Rights and Freedoms that has forced the courts to become the arbiter of high-sounding ideas that are so unspecific as to need clarification until the cows come home.

The Moysa case came at a time when the rules of the game were always changing for the worse. It was an offence to publish the names of young offenders, even if they went on a spree of murder, mayhem, rape and robbery. Newspapers could not mention search warrants being executed unless every party to such a search gave consent, including the party under scrutiny.

Even the so-called right-to-reply legislation then in use in some other countries was being dusted off. Such compulsory right of reply violates any freedom of speech Canadian journalists might have. Journalistic ethics require that all sides of a story be reported fairly and mistakes corrected when they occur. When ethics fail, as sometimes they do, and mistakes are not corrected adequately, then there are laws of defamation, and press councils, to ensure that such imbalance, or incorrect information, be put right. But why should a newspaper be forced to acquiesce in giving away part of a precious freedom it has taken centuries to accumulate?

Forcing a newspaper to print something against its professional judgment is as bad as denying it the right to print something that officialdom does not want aired in public.

The Moysa case never went to a press council, but the way in which it was handled in the courts suffices to emphasize the necessity for the sort of declaration made by Chief Justice Brian Dickson, in another case involving the *Edmonton Journal*. Writing the judgment of the Supreme Court of Canada in the search-and-seizure case that arose from a raid on my office at the *Journal*, Dickson said: "The Canadian Charter of Rights and Freedoms guarantees the rights set out in it, subject only to such reasonable limits prescribed by law as can be demonstrably justified in a free and democratic society."

Were such "reasonable limits prescribed by law" evident in the manner in which Marilyn Moysa was treated by the courts? That's for others to judge, not me. Her case dragged on through further court proceedings, with the union pursuing her all the way. Marilyn stuck to her guns and kept her lips sealed. She was never fined and never went to jail. Perhaps, in the end, even the court was ashamed of itself, choosing not to impose a judgment of contempt upon her.

Of all the institutions in a democracy, perhaps the oddest of all is the newspaper. For some reason, in addition to those genuinely seeking to be informed and entertained, it also attracts to its fringes more than a fair share of fanatics, misfits, the unbalanced, the bigoted, the misbegotten, the wayward and the empty-headed.

And that is where the press councils come in.

The ambiguous nature of a free press was outlined in this fashion in the Ontario Press Council's annual report for 1990 by its chairman, former Supreme Court of Canada Justice Willard Z. Estey: "It is difficult to precisely describe and define the players in the game, their rights and obligations to the community and the reasonable limits which civilization has placed around the press while at the same time struggling to assure its freedom. All of this is predicated on the early recognition in the free society of the scarcity of the freedom of expression."

Estey believed "the over-exuberance of the bureaucrat, mandarin or regulator is evident everywhere in our daily life." To counter that, he said, "virtually the only pruning mechanism outside of the political process for reducing the size of the state and trimming its tentacles when they threaten to strangle us is the free and independent press."

In their turn, because they are free of government involvement, press councils have a role to play in protecting the public from the over-exuberance of the newspapers. While the newspapers exercise their own form of self-restraint, backed by the thoughtful deliberations of press councils, such lapses of self-restraint tend to be acceptably low despite the constant attempts by those in public life to diminish and belittle the performance of a free press.

In analyzing the nature of the complaints it received in 1990, the Ontario Press Council's annual report revealed that there were only six complaints concerning advertising, compared with 59 complaints about news stories. By far the biggest number of complaints — 32 — argued that stories were erroneous or misleading. There were only three allegations that stories had been distorted or falsified.

What is striking is that there were 43 complaints arising from comment, based on perceptions that comment, rather than news stories, might have been biased, derogatory, dishonest, erroneous, irresponsible, misleading, objectionable, plagiarized, pornographic, racist, reprehensible, promoting hatred, sexist, unethical, unfair or unreasonable. Only 10 of those complaints actually reached the adjudication stage in 1990.

Trying to deal with complaints of this nature can be a nightmare for an editor, because readers insist on judging hard-hitting commentary solely through the narrow funnel of their own biases and prejudices.

A few months after I became publisher of the *Calgary Herald* in 1982, I got embroiled — through the Alberta Press Council — in a standoff with an irate correspondent named Achim N. Lohse. It was all over a column written by Pat McMahon. The column was typical McMahon. He saw himself as a "smoking gun," a devotee of distinct — if sometimes irrational — opinions and he had a faithful following in those days.

On this occasion, McMahon (later killed in a car accident in Victoria) was stirred up by an apparent rise of western separatism. In commenting on various statements made by Gordon Kesler, the only declared separatist ever elected to the Alberta Legislature, McMahon began his piece this way: "Isn't it interesting how the separatists among us are so intellectually bankrupt they can't appreciate the exquisite irony of their position? They hate their country so much they want to destroy it."

Giving the *Oxford Dictionary* definition of a traitor as "one who is false to his allegiance or acts disloyally to his country," McMahon got a little carried away with his florid verbosity. Branding separatists as traitors would steal "an important part of their country — their birthright" — from other Canadians, McMahon declaimed: "I don't know why it isn't a hanging offence, but it isn't."

McMahon then went on to list quotations from Kesler's speeches to make his case that the leader of the Western Canada Concept (WCC) was not only a traitor, but as an illustration of the things "Kesler and the mental heavyweights in his merry band might do if they ever got their mitts on the

Heritage Fund." The Heritage Fund, set up by Lougheed's Tory government, was Alberta's rainy-day insurance against the eventual decline of oil revenues.

(To be fair to Kesler, he was never comfortable with the separatist plank hammered into the WCC political platform by the more loony of his followers and he later disavowed it. For his sins, they kicked him out of the party. He quit politics after defeat in a provincial general election and returned to his old ways of making a living — as an oil spy and a chuckwagon driver at the Calgary Stampede. The WCC soon plunged into oblivion.)

Lohse took McMahon's column at face value and complained to the Alberta Press Council in a lazily drafted letter of condemnation that seemed totally lacking in detail, other than to claim the column was inflammatory. He also sent a letter to the *Herald* with a dire warning in the postscript: "Either print this letter as a whole or not at all. I do not want my meaning distorted nor my prose mangled by gratuitous editing."

In responding to his complaint to the press council, I told him we would have been happy to have allowed him to write a letter for publication disagreeing with McMahon's column, but we had no intention of allowing him to call McMahon a "rabid fascist" in our own columns as he demanded. Newspapers have always given a longer leash to their critics than their critics have to newspapers, but even democratic dissent has its outer limits.

I asked Lohse what he found inflammatory about the column, quoting to him one *Oxford Dictionary* definition of the word as meaning "to tend to inflame with desire or passion." McMahon, I pointed out, was certainly passionate in the expression of his belief that those who want to destroy the country should be classified as traitors, but he did not suggest the law should be changed to dispose of them in summary fashion.

As for the quotes from Kesler, I told Lohse, at least McMahon had the good taste not to use the one Kesler was best known for: "If we're all lucky, Trudeau will have a heart attack within the next five minutes."

The correspondence deteriorated even further into a battle of quotations from the *Oxford Dictionary* on the meaning of the word *inflammatory*. Lohse insisted that the column was "an invitation to extra-legal violence and thus seditious as well as inflammatory." He found my defence of McMahon "grotesque," saying there was no journalistic "right" to incite people to murder. The column, he said, "might well push some borderline psychotic over the edge."

I doubt if Lohse got any satisfaction from the affair, but he does deserve some limited measure of sympathy. Clearly, he was one of those impassioned, if arrogantly pompous, readers who are convinced that their local newspaper is at least subversive, and that no matter how reasoned the arguments put up to counter such subversion, the newspaper always wins. That is an image a newspaper can never overcome, the idea that it is beyond all measure of control and public reason.

This shows why it is imperative to allow a reader who closes his mind to all rational explanations the right to a further and impartial safety valve. The courts can take care of the defamation suits and mete out appropriate penalties if necessary, but voluntary press councils and newspaper ombudsmen can play key roles in mediating matters of taste and accuracy.

The public needs a sympathetic shoulder to cry on occasionally, because newspapers tend to be stocked with faceless bureaucrats. Newsrooms generally hate ombudsmen, because they have a right given to them by the publisher to question reporters and editors on the way certain stories were handled and published. The ombudsmen I appointed at both the *Edmonton Journal* and the *Calgary Herald* also had the mandate to write critically in their own papers when the newspaper failed the public through sloppy reporting or editing. I never asked to see such a column in advance, and there were times when I was used for target practice by an ombudsman because of my own journalistic sins or woeful decisions. Mea culpa!

No matter how hard they try to be responsive to their public, newspapers will never totally make amends for the transgressions determined by their readers. However, it is necessary to distinguish between those who are outraged or aggrieved by something they strongly disagree with, and those who abuse the system, especially the courts, in a malicious way to tie up the newspaper in legal red tape.

Newspapers spend hundreds of thousands of dollars each year simply preparing responses to what are clearly frivolous or mischievous lawsuits, designed either to embarrass or harass a newspaper. Other media have similar problems, but to a lesser degree.

In 1986, a libel suit against CBC Radio for a documentary criticizing the investigation that led to the wrongful murder conviction of Donald Marshall a Micmac Indian, was dropped only hours before the case was to go to trial. John McIntyre, the former chief of the Sydney, N.S., police, set the suit in motion shortly after the November 1993 *Sunday Morning* documentary drew attention to the shortcomings of the 1971 investigation and trial that sent Marshall to prison for 11 years for a killing he did not commit.

Marshall was retried and acquitted in 1983, after three witnesses from the first trial changed their testimony. Marshall received $270,000 from the Nova Scotia government in compensation. After the suit by McIntyre was launched, his lawyer approached the CBC and asked that it be settled out of court. Otherwise, the lawyer warned, it would be a long and costly libel trial. The CBC refused to settle.

Three years later, when McIntyre dropped the suit, no reason was given. The CBC refused to speculate on its own account, although it was obvious the suit was intended to freeze any further comment the CBC might want to make on the police handling of the Marshall case.

However, Dan Henry, the CBC lawyer, did say the case was a "comment on the state of libel law in this country," which sees "large sums of money spent on legal actions gobbling up editorial budgets." Henry added: "Is that the price of freedom of expression?"

He is not the only representative of a news medium who has asked the same question. And the answer is always the same.

Often, such actions are intended to muzzle the press. One instance I recall, of how far some people will go to put themselves in a better light at the expense of the truth, involved not poor reporting by a newspaper, but the fact that it was too accurate in its reporting.

It began on June 6, 1984, when the *Calgary Herald* ran a story under the heading Ambulance Owner 'Doped,' Jury Told. Everything printed was said in court, was reported accurately and properly, and was therefore privileged. However, on Aug. 16, a Calgary lawyer wrote to the *Herald* on behalf of a private ambulance owner in what was an obvious attempt to rewrite the official court record.

The whole thing arose from the trial of a 20-year-old woman who had been accused of stabbing her common-law husband to death. (She was eventually acquitted.) In his closing argument, the defence lawyer said the man might have lived if it had not been for the haphazard way he was treated by ambulance attendants. In evidence, two ambulance attendants admitted they didn't know how to handle a stabbing victim. One said he was "in way over my head."

An RCMP constable told the court that, in addition to the ambulance attendants' incompetence, the ambulance proprietor was "somewhat doped up." He had trouble climbing the stairs, likely because of some medication he was on. In checking the official transcript of the trial, it transpired that the full quote of the RCMP constable was: "I don't know what injuries he (the ambulance owner) has, but at the time he was on medication and somewhat doped up." Furthermore, according to the official transcript, the constable told the court that in his opinion, the ambulance proprietor was intoxicated when he went up the stairs to see the stabbing victim. In response to a question from the judge, the constable repeated his assertion.

Another constable, while unwilling to state the proprietor was intoxicated, said: "I noted when he came up the stairs he was shaking and he was helped up the stairs and limping on one leg. He was helped by two other men that were his attendants."

One of those attendants said in evidence: "He (the ambulance owner) was impaired, but whether it was from pain killers I'm not sure." When asked to explain what he meant by "impaired," the witness said: "By impaired, I meant that his walking wasn't normal." He also indicated his employer was slurring his words. However, he could not say for sure whether the man was impaired or intoxicated, but he also could not say if he was stone sober.

After further court actions over the validity of an amended statement of claim by the ambulance owner, his lawyer said his client would settle out of court, with the *Herald* for $75,000. He got an emphatic No from the *Herald.*

The total argument, as became obvious during subsequent examinations for discoveries, was not over the accuracy of the *Herald*, but over the accuracy of the evidence actually given in court. No newspaper has control over what is said in court; it can only report what is actually said there. It is up to a judge and jury to decide who is telling the truth and who is lying under oath.

This was an argument that was never accepted by the complainant, and the matter remained unresolved to his satisfaction up to the time he died a few years later.

Under the broad heading of Pernicious Nuisance I would put the case of Alphonse A. Kennedy. The target for his arrow was a column written by Larry Wood, a *Calgary Herald* sports writer, and published in January 1984. In the first paragraph of that column, a tribute to the venerable sports writer and author Jim Coleman, Wood wrote: "There was a time a few years back when Jim Coleman, more affectionately known among his peers as Jeems, figured he'd be passing from this world while bent over a battered Underwood typewriter churning out the word on the wide world of sports."

This prompted a letter from a Calgary law firm, saying it acted on behalf of Kennedy. It seems he had written a book in 1982 entitled *Destiny Is The Power* and claimed infringement of copyright by Larry Wood in using the phrase "more affectionately known among his peers as Jeems."

The *Herald* dismissed this claim in a two-sentence letter.

By July, another letter informed the *Herald* litigation would begin immediately. The letter contained a less-than-subtle hint that we might want to attempt a settlement prior to further costs being incurred. Our lawyer then wrote to Kennedy's lawyer to say he had talked to Coleman, who told him the nickname Jeems had been bestowed on him while he was working for the *Globe and Mail* back in the 1950s, at least 30 years before Kennedy's book was published.

A few days later, Kennedy himself wrote to tell us he had severed all connections with his own lawyer. He told the *Herald* it could evade responsibility for any settlement with him by stating its profits came from advertising, not from Wood's column. I'm not sure of the point of that, but when he got no response from us, he sent another letter — responding to the letter we had sent to the lawyer he had dismissed. Now, Kennedy told us, he was no longer objecting to the use of the word Jeems as a diminutive of Coleman's first name, but to the words "affectionately known among his peers." He had researched that phrase and, according to his understanding, nobody else had ever used it. It was his copyright, he claimed. His letter concluded: "I'll see you in court."

In April 1985, we were compelled to attend an examination for discoveries. After a disagreement, when Kennedy said he was going to call Wood as his witness to testify against himself, trial was set for July 2 in the small claims division of the Calgary courthouse. This was after costs of $75 had been assessed against him, with a court order that this would have to be paid regardless of the outcome of the trial. Needless to say, the judgment of the small claims court was also in the *Herald*'s favour, with costs awarded against Kennedy.

But he was still not done with us. He then served notice of appeal against the judgment. The appeal was also dismissed, again with costs awarded to the *Herald*. But there was never any hope of a penny being recovered from him.

The irony of this whole silly episode is that we won, despite our lawyer, who put the wrong date for the appeal hearing in his engagement book and failed to show up in court.

The case was a demonstration of the underside of democracy, where the benefit of the doubt goes to the so-called underdog, even when his barks are beyond the bounds of reason. Absurdity triumphs as we tilt the playing field in a misguided attempt to provide "equality" within the law for those who shake a futile fist at the press.

Although it would be unfair to try and put James Gray in the same category as Alphonse A. Kennedy, I have never had much luck with authors during my years in Calgary. Gray has written a number of books about the pioneer days of the West, and one of his better-selling works was about the brothels of Western Canada. I have never had the nerve to ask him the nature or the substance of his research on that red-light topic.

To be honest, I never had the nerve to ask him anything because I found him irascible, and I heard from him often enough when the *Herald* irritated him. Gray is an excellent craftsman, and his books are carefully constructed, the prose emphasizing clarity. Any time he advanced an opinion about the poor quality of the *Herald*, you could be sure he would throw in references to his days as an editorial writer at the *Winnipeg Free Press*. He used our library facilities for research for many of his books and berated *Herald* staff from time to time, constantly invoking his own editorial ethics while ignoring the years he spent as a flack for an oil company.

On March 7, 1984, Gray dashed off an angry letter to St. Clair Balfour, chairman of Southam, to suggest that "the quality of the prose being inflicted on the customers (by the *Herald*) posed a threat to the company's bottom line."

He went on: "As one who has learned his trade under George Ferguson and J.W. Dafoe, I am simply appalled at what O'Callaghan has done to the *Herald* editorial page." Enclosing a copy of an editorial on which he said he "had gagged all the way on a flight to Palm Springs," he asked Balfour: "Is there a city editor anywhere in your employ who would hire the perpetrator of this kind of flatulent claptrap as a junior office boy? There are adages floating around about cobblers sticking to lasts. May I suggest anchoring Mr. O'C in the business office and restoring editorial writing to editors who can write."

Balfour sent Gray a polite reply saying he did not share Gray's concerns over the quality of editorial writing in the *Herald* and suggesting he should have taken his complaint directly to me as the publisher of the *Herald*. Then Balfour said: "He (O'Callaghan) would have replied in his eloquent Irish way that he had already commented critically on the piece to which you refer."

Balfour concluded his letter to Gray: "I am sending him (O'Callaghan) a copy of your letter and my reply. I'm sure you will hear from him directly — in impeccable English."

Gray was right about the execrable quality of that particular editorial; it should have been spiked as unworthy of publication. I was just as upset as he was — after I saw it in print.

In a reply to Gray, I wrote: "Were I not bound by the oath of editorial anonymity, I would be happy to declare there is not a single syllable in that editorial for which I can claim parentage — but having taken that vow of editorial silence, I can't even admit it is a bastard son." However, I had to accept responsibility for every opinion expressed on the editorial page "even those not couched in a manner more redolent of grace and style."

More than a year later, Gray took his umbrage a step further, this time over a columnist's review of a book documenting the history of the Calgary Stampede. What upset Gray, the author of the book, began with this particular sentence in Pat Tivy's column: "The author was hired by the Stampede board to tell their story — but indeed, he tells me the board kicked in a few extra bucks to help the publisher buy top-quality paper so photos could be reproduced through the book."

However, the columnist then went on to say that while Gray had had remarkable access to the Stampede's records, he had spent little time examining the show's shadowy side. Tivy detailed some of the shady incidents involving the Stampede, including the shoddy treatment of residents of the Victoria Park community over the location of the Saddledome.

Tivy ended the column by saying: "Despite its few faults, the book is undeniably the best book about the Stampede ever written."

Despite this flattering conclusion, Gray was beside himself with anger, claiming Tivy had cast aspersions upon his integrity and his reputation. Tivy, he said, had only talked to him for 90 seconds, and he had made it clear to Tivy he did not have much access to Stampede files, other than annual reports and minutes of board meetings. Most of his material, said Gray, had been obtained from the "public record" — obviously a euphemism for back copies of the

*Calgary Herald*! He said he had listed various scandals in his book, but Tivy must never have read it.

We published his letter and this was followed by a letter from Gray's lawyer claiming Tivy's statements were libellous. The alleged libels were contained in the letter from him that the *Herald* had published, so his complaints had already had a public airing. Even as Gray's letter was descending on our desk, he was already penning an even more indignant complaint to the Alberta Press Council along the same lines. Not done yet, he then fired off a second complaint to the press council over the way his letter had been edited for publication in the *Herald*. He did not mention in his second letter to the press council another piece of discreet editing done on his epistle to the *Herald*.

His original had begun: "Apart from demonstrating the art of picking fly shit out of pepper…" The colourful phrase did not make it into the sanctified columns of our family newspaper and I take full responsibility for use of a blue pencil on that one.

In February 1986, the press council told Gray that, in view of his lawyer's letter alleging libel, its rules prevented it from hearing any matters which are, or may be intended to be, disposed of in the courts. Before it could hear his complaint, it needed a written undertaking from him or his counsel that he had no intention then, or in the future, of taking any legal proceedings in the matter.

Nothing further was heard until April 11, 1986, when a letter sent to the press council by Gray's lawyer had this to say: "I have now spoken to my client regarding your letter of Feb. 16, 1986. We feel that the Alberta Press Council, in the opinion of Mr. Gray, is a 'toothless, bog-spavined watchdog.' It is obvious that the Alberta Press Council does not wish to become involved in any proceedings which would involve a powerful member such as the *Calgary Herald.* Needless to say, neither Mr. Gray nor myself are impressed with the courage of the Alberta Press Council. Where does this policy, as enunciated in your letter of Feb. 16, 1986, originate from? If it is written policy I would be pleased to receive from you a copy of your policy guideline. I look forward to hearing from you."

The press council did, in fact, respond, more politely than I might have been inclined to, but the exasperation of the press council began to show through in the final paragraph of its letter of reply: "Should there be any further correspondence from Mr. Gray or yourself concerning this matter, we would hope and expect that it will be couched in more temperate and rational terms than those most recently directed toward us."

I never heard from Gray after that; perhaps he went on to perfect the art of picking fly shit out of pepper. I wonder if that is something he learned at Dafoe's knee?

Perhaps one of the strangest lawsuits I was involved in came from lawyers representing Colin Thatcher, the former Saskatchewan cabinet minister convicted of murdering his former wife, JoAnn Wilson.

The suit arose from the coverage of his trial by Peter Calamai, then of Southam News and later editorial page editor of the *Ottawa Citizen.* Calamai won a National Newspaper Award for that coverage.

Thatcher claimed to have been defamed by Calamai; by Calamai's employer, Southam Inc.; by the *Calgary Herald*, of which I was then publisher; by the *Edmonton Journal*; and by the *Montreal Gazette.* He also claimed defamation by Don Sellar, a former *Herald* reporter and Southam News correspondent, later ombudsman for the *Toronto Star*, and by

Heather Bird, a Saskatchewan reporter who had also covered the trial.

Thatcher claimed to have suffered serious injury to his reputation, both inside and outside Saskatchewan, as a result of certain articles by Calamai, Sellar, and Bird. Amid the comments complained of were these:

■ "He was an anachronism, a throwback to the swaggering land barons who played to win, without bothering about rules or public images."

■ "Varooming around Regina in a canary-yellow Corvette, Thatcher wallowed in the symbols of prestige and power. For eight months, he enjoyed the high-flying life of cabinet minister until the stink of patronage and questionable expense accounts sparked his dismissal."

■ "A week later, Wilson was dead, hacked two dozen times by a sickle, and shot, execution-style, in the temple at close range."

■ "Colin Thatcher had a hatred for JoAnn Wilson that was almost breathtaking."

■ "The final chapter was murder."

■ "Known as the J.R. Ewing[76] of Saskatchewan, Thatcher is a violent, volatile man, fuelled by money and driven by power. Thatcher never forgave Wilson for the public humiliation she inflicted on him by deserting him for his best friend. That hatred grew to an obsession during their long, messy, bitter divorce."

■ "Thatcher stalked her for one week with his gun. It may never be known if he did the actual killing or paid someone to do it for him."

■ "The savagery of the beating is what makes people believe Thatcher killed JoAnn...Thatcher was the only person in the world who hated JoAnn enough to kill her that way."

And so on. All pretty hard-hitting stuff, but this was all written about a man already convicted of murdering his ex-wife. It was significant that toward the end of that lengthy affidavit by Thatcher in support of his notice of intent he had this sentence: "The plaintiff denies that he killed or inspired with others to kill JoAnn Wilson." No doubt the word *inspired* was meant to be *conspired*. Blame careless legal drafting for that error of language. The point of significance is not the misuse of the English language, but the apparently blatant attempt by a murderer whose appeal had already been dismissed, to find still other legal means of asserting his innocence publicly. Perhaps that was the real reason for the notice of intent, rather than any slim hope of collecting damages for defamation.

The affidavit claimed that many of the words objected to in the statement of claim were blasphemous and libellous. Thatcher sought damages for defamation of his personal character, defamation in his profession; plus general damages for defamation and each and every innuendo; special damages to be determined at the trial; and costs.

Perhaps I am a touch cynical, but I find it difficult to imagine how Thatcher, to quote his affidavit, could claim: "I have sustained serious injury to my reputation from inside and outside Saskatchewan."

What reputation could Thatcher possibly have in the eyes of his former cabinet colleagues in Regina? Surely he was not worried how his fellow inmates at the Fort Saskatchewan Correctional Centre, north of Edmonton, might feel about him; he had no reputation to protect, and nobody knew it better than those behind bars with him.

As for the lawsuit, it rests somewhere in no man's land.[77]

# CHAPTER 26

My relationship with Doug Creighton was a little like that of an old married couple who still have some hidden affection for each other, but who are only too conscious of each other's foibles and weaknesses of character.

Sacha Guitry[78] once said: "There are women whose infidelities are the only link they still have with their husbands." Creighton and I were faithful to each other in our own way, I suppose.

At a cocktail party, Creighton hosted at Winston's in Toronto to launch Allan Fotheringham's book *Birds of a Feather*, Creighton introduced me to a puzzled Alan Eagleson[79] in this fashion: "This is Patrick O'Callaghan, one of my best friends. But a son of a bitch!"

So it should come as no surprise that he once sued me.

It all goes back to a column I wrote for the *Calgary Herald* on Jan. 29, 1987. It was during the buildup to Canada's final debate on capital punishment. The *Calgary Sun* was almost slavering at the mouth at the prospect of the hangman being brought out of retirement. I am an abolitionist. One of the first editorial policy changes I made on taking over both the *Edmonton Journal* (in 1976) and the *Calgary Herald* (in 1982) was to switch away from support for capital punishment. Some 80 per cent of the readers of both papers in this fundamentalist eye-for-an-eye province disagreed with me. So much for eloquent advocacy!

In early 1987, in the middle of the agonizing over Mulroney's campaign pledge to hold a free vote on capital punishment, an RCMP officer, Const. Gordon Kowalczyk

— apparently trying to question the driver of a stolen truck — was shot to death near Calgary's airport. The *Sun* hit its stride immediately, "drooling wantonly with unbridled passion for bloodthirsty headlines that is its stock in trade," as I so gently put it in a column headed Sensationalism Betrays Ethics.

In addition to the RCMP murder — for which a man was later convicted and sentenced to life imprisonment — the *Sun* also had an earlier field day when a drugstore owner in Calgary shot to death a junkie attempting a holdup for drugs. The would-be robber was chased down a street in broad daylight and blasted in the back; the *Sun* approved of this frontier justice.

My signed piece accused the *Sun* of an orgy of sleazy journalism over the death of the RCMP officer and went on: "The death of any police officer in the vital task of protecting society is an act of unforgiveable savagery, the more so because Canada is not a gun-happy nation of outlaw Rambos[80]. But should a newspaper become the agent of society's revenge, playing to the baser instincts of a responsive audience that would bay at the moon if enough emotional rhetoric were forced down its gullet?"

I then went on to detail the score card for the *Sun* in bloodthirsty stories in the two days following first news of the Kowalczyk murder.

On the first day, there was a head-and-shoulders picture of the dead officer filling the front page under the one-word headline: Manhunt. Inside, as the *Sun*'s vigilantes rushed to their saddles, were these crowd-pleasers:

- Killer Hunted;
- Fears Came True;
- You Said It (street interviews with six bystanders);
- June Targeted For Death Vote;
- Vets Push For Noose;
- It Just Doesn't Make Sense (a column of pre-digested superficialities by *Sun* columnist Jack Tennant);
- Let Death Return (an editorial demanding the return of the hangman);
- And, of course, the inevitable in the *Sun*'s armoury of cheap gimmickry, a cut-out coupon for its readers to send to the prime minister to bring pressure to bear for a Commons debate on capital punishment.

On the following day, the whole of the front page of the *Sun* was taken up with a headline dripping in blood-red ink saying Help Find This Killer. Another headline proclaimed. You Demand Death Penalty. Then there was Murder Hot Line and 1,000 Set For Service — a reference to plans for the Mountie's funeral. You Said It showed up again, this time pinning down six hand-picked local MPs to support the return of the executioner. Just so there was no doubt in any *Sun* reader's mind, there was the heading "Calgary wants death penalty." And once more the Let Brian Know coupon.

If it's blood and guts you want, I told *Herald* readers, then the *Sun* is for you.

"Newspapers, for the shoddy purpose of circulation, should never pander to the mob instinct of a lynching party," I wrote.

Commenting on the fact that the Mulroney government was already committed to a debate on capital punishment, I wrote: "If Canada were a violent society, a rush backwards in time to the clanging trapdoor and the quicklime of the grave might be society's response. But Canada is one of the least violent of western nations." I then gave statistics to support this argument.

Citing capital punishment as a deterrent to murder is simply a myth, I said. "The existence of a death sentence would not have saved Const. Kowalczyk from his cruel fate. In fact the gallows cheapens life in its casual attitude to death. It does not reform, it does not bring the innocent back from the dead, it does not change or modify or dissuade from their purpose those with murder in their hearts. So all that is left is a reflection of society's most ignoble emotions, a thirsty bloodlust disguised as justice, cloaked in self-righteousness, for the purpose of revenge."

Parliament should not be stampeded into a decision of a life-or-death nature by the cheap tricks of a circulation-hungry newspaper oddity like the *Sun*, I said.

"The frenzy of a shabby newspaper catering to the cruder elements of red-necked mouth-breathers fills any self-respecting journalist with loathing and shame. Capital punishment is an issue that deserves responsible debate: gutter journalism contributes nothing of value to such discussion. Surely Canada is far too mature for this sort of besotted journalism."

Creighton did not keep me waiting long for his comments. The offending article had been faxed to him by *Calgary Sun* publisher Jim Tighe (later a *Toronto Sun* publisher) and Creighton phoned me on Feb. 2 "more in sadness than anger," as he put it.

He started by saying: "I think you really reached the lowest point in our relationship with your piece of Jan. 29. Do you really think we were 'drooling with the unbridled passion for bloodthirsty headlines'? Do you think we are 'having an orgy of sleazy journalism'? Do you really feel we want to become 'an agent of society's revenge'?"

I replied that I never wrote anything I didn't believe in. In the Steven Kesler affair — the drugstore owner who shot the junkie — the *Sun* violated every journalistic rule of fair play, elevating a gun-happy druggist to the role of an avenging angel. Much of its coverage of the Kesler incident was in contempt of court, making it impossible for the Crown to prosecute without ruffling the stirred-up public's animosity toward the dead man and sympathy for the accused. It had all the appearance of a stacked trial. But Creighton did not want to hear about that.

"I have turned your article over to our lawyers to see if we should sue," he said.

He followed up the phone call with a letter to John Fisher, president of Southam Inc. Explaining his own background as a journalist, Creighton told Fisher: "I hope you will understand I can't let remarks from an old — and now former — friend of mine, Patrick O'Callaghan, go unchallenged."

Being sued, along with the *Herald*, for damages under the Defamation Act put me in a rather exclusive club. A search for precedents under Commonwealth jurisdiction for one newspaper suing another for defamation revealed only two instances where litigation was undertaken. The first was the case of Robert Maxwell, then the owner of a tabloid, Britain's *Daily Mirror*, suing the saucy *Private Eye* magazine for alleging that Maxwell had bribed British Labour politicians by paying for their travel on various international trips. The second case involved an ethnic newspaper suing *The Economist* magazine for statements suggesting the paper was financed by, and became the voice of, the Soviet Union to the Greek community in the United Kingdom. But neither case was an exact parallel of one daily newspaper suing another.

Once, when Creighton and I discussed the case over a drink, he came up with a new wrinkle. At the time, I had just retired as publisher of the *Herald* and was Southam's visiting professor of journalism, on loan to the Ryerson School of Journalism.

"When the judge and jury rule in my favour," Creighton told me, "I'll turn the money over to Ryerson to pay for a scholarship in your name."

"I don't think you can get much of a scholarship for $10," I answered. That was about all his suit was worth. "It wouldn't even pay for two of your beloved martinis."

We went through the examination for discovery process and a trial date was set, but I never got my day in court after spending three years polishing up my ad libs. Next to me, the most bitterly disappointed man when the suit was dropped was Everett Bunnell of Parlee McLaws. As the *Herald*'s senior lawyer, he was rubbing his hands with glee over what was shaping up as a showcase trial for the newspaper industry. The *Herald* newsroom was dismayed when an out-of-court deal was cooked up by Kevin Peterson, my successor as publisher of the *Herald*, and Ken King, his counterpart at the *Calgary Sun*.

These new-breed managers thought the public brawl between Creighton and myself rather unseemly. The suit was solely Creighton's idea in the first place and the *Calgary Sun* was always rather gun-shy of it, not wanting to have its ethics and standards examined in a courtroom. So King went to work on Creighton, and it was agreed between the *Sun* and the *Herald* that the suit would be dropped and that a joint scholarship would be created at Calgary's Mount Royal College[81]. This scholarship, announced in both the *Calgary Sun* and the *Herald* in November 1990, would be named the *Calgary Sun/Calgary Herald* J.P. O'Callaghan Journalism Award of Excellence. There was no apology by me, no under-the-counter deal on costs, to the best of my knowledge. I did not withdraw a word I wrote in that column.

When I was asked if I would agree to the settlement, I held out briefly for an added incentive: two seats, three times a year, in the *Toronto Sun*'s box at the SkyDome[82] for Blue Jays games. But I gave in gracefully on this point when it became obvious Peterson and King had no desire to fuel the fighting spirits of two battle-scarred old warriors.

# CHAPTER 27

It was a raw November day in 1987, bone-chilling rain tumbling out of a grey Toronto sky, the sort of day when you walk along with your head down, anxious only to get with the minimum of discomfort and the maximum of speed to somewhere dry and warm.

Joan Abeles, then manager of promotional and educational services for the Canadian Daily Newspaper Publishers Association, was clutching my arm and I had Peter Wright's *Spycatcher*[83] tucked safely under my other arm, wondering what James Bond might have made of the dullest book ever written on his secretive profession.

As the uniformed figure in the fur hat rotated the revolving doors at the entrance to the Four Seasons Hotel to speed our entry, there appeared to be more brave souls than expected standing outside in the wintry wind. When we crossed the lobby to the elevators, it soon became obvious that the whole bank of them was immobilized. In the manner of exasperated tall tower users everywhere, I jabbed at the button to force an elevator to obey my imperious command. Nothing happened. Then a bystander volunteered the information that the elevators would not be working for a while. The man had a tiny ear piece connected to a thin black cord. There were other men and women standing around in the foyer, more conspicuous than anonymous, all with their ear pieces and the distinguishing identifying symbol in their buttonholes.

It was VIP time.

"Is somebody important coming?" Joan asked. "Who is it?"

There is only one way to find out these things — go to the well-informed. So I asked the doorman.

"The prime minister of Canada is due to arrive in a few minutes," he told me, his voice a little bubble of excitement.

"Is that all?" I responded, with an air of insouciant indifference, more for the benefit of Joan — then a Liberal, the daughter of a distinctly Liberal father and a determinedly Liberal mother — than out of any sense of disrespect for either the office or the man filling it. "It's only a Tory prime minister," I told Joan, tongue slightly in cheek. "Let's go and get a drink until they switch on the elevators again."

"Now just a minute," she said. "I've never seen a prime minister in the flesh."

So we stood in front of the silent elevators, waiting for the great man's arrival. We scanned the foyer. Apart from hotel staff — the manager was nervously rehearsing his greeting — some photographers, and the security people, who might just as well have been in uniform for all their inability to disappear into the scenery, the entire welcoming crowd consisted of Joan and I and one other couple.

As we waited, the female half of the other couple approached us. "Are you Canadians?" she asked.

We were, we admitted.

"I can't believe it," the woman said. "You mean your prime minister will just casually walk in here? We're from Cleveland, Ohio, and we once saw the president of the United States. But we couldn't get anywhere near him. And now we're going to see your prime minister up close. I am totally amazed."

"We don't believe in making too much fuss, "I said. "We're a very low-key country."

A few minutes later, there was a little murmur of excitement and the manager straightened his shoulders and cleared his throat. The knot of security people near the entrance congregated like birds about to compete for crumbs. The other guardians of prime ministerial flesh who were scattered around the foyer kept the vast welcoming throng of four people under careful scrutiny. After all, was that really a book I had under my arm? And what might Joan have concealed in that massive gathering bag that accompanied her everywhere?

The manager's welcoming words and handshake out of the way, Brian Mulroney, always the consummate politician, looked around for his public. There we stood, all four of us, shoulder to shoulder in solid array. I was the only one he had met before, so he made a beeline for me and squeezed my hand. We chatted briefly about *Spycatcher* and made small talk. I introduced Joan to him, cautioning him that she was a Liberal. He charmed the pants off her, that Irish cobbler's leprechaun grin spreading across his handsome face. I held Joan's Liberal elbow in case she swooned. Then I said to Mulroney: "I've only just met this couple so I can't introduce you." As he moved his half-acre smile in their direction, I said with a hint of sarcasm: "You don't need to waste too much time on them, sir, they're from Cleveland, Ohio, so you can't get their votes."

Mulroney chatted with the Americans just as amiably, pointing out that he had worked for the Hanna Corporation of Cleveland, when he was president of the Iron Ore Company of Canada in Schefferville, Que..

After he had gone, the Cleveland woman, just as enraptured with him as Joan, said to me: "He knew you! He called you Patrick as soon as he spotted you!"

"Canada is a small country," I replied modestly. "He knows everybody."

Later that night, Joan and I were having dinner in Truffles[84], our favourite dining room in Toronto, when she excused herself. She was gone a long time and I began to wonder if I should organize a search party before the Grand Marnier soufflé collapsed and the chef contemplated suicide.

When she finally returned, she was all aglow — a not unnatural state for her — and I said accusingly: "I know where you've been. You had to phone your mother to let her know you met the prime minister. And you a good Liberal! I hope your father hasn't disowned you."

Five months later, when I was introducing Mulroney to the head table guests before a Canadian Daily Newspaper Publishers Association luncheon in Toronto, he did not wait for me to give her name. "Hi, Joan," he said, "so nice to see you again."

That was typical Mulroney, the day he won over a Liberal voter to his Tory cause. He was the most handsome, most personable leader the federal Tories ever had. He had political charisma and the impeccable presence. He was a man of prodigious energy. He had grace and wit, a crackling electric persona that reached out to spark those around him. Canadians of that day felt they needed such a leader, someone to brush off the cobwebs of Trudeau's congealing autocracy. They wanted to respond to his call for ethical governance, and they rallied to his heartfelt promise of healing regional scars. But in the end, they turned on him, soured by his personal extravagances and the smell of corruption that surrounded him without ever quite touching him personally.

"I want to tell you, Patrick," he said firmly, "that while it is always difficult to predict what will happen when you are two years into a mandate, I will still be around two years from now and I will still be prime minister. You can be sure of that. Bet your mortgage on it."

However, he was gloomy about the scandals besetting his cabinet and the favourable press Liberal leader John Turner was getting as he hammered away at the government on its sore spot.

"I get no pleasure from it," he said, meaning the scandals. "Any more than Trudeau did. And he had far more of this sort of thing to deal with then I had. When I led the Opposition, I made no comments of such a personal nature. There was no digging of dirt, no trafficking in petty scandals. Turner has sunk to a new low."

Shifting gears, he said: "Two years from now you will see the greatest ever campaign. When I am finished they will have to hold a tag day for Turner and Broadbent. When I am down to 25 per cent (in the polls), I know why I am there. Our own polls showed us Bissonette cost us 16 per cent and Sinclair 10 per cent." (André Bissonette, secretary of state for transport, had been fired by Mulroney in January 1986 for questionable land flips involving a company called Oerlikon. He was acquitted in February 1988 of charges of fraud, conspiracy and breach of trust. Sinclair Stevens left cabinet in May 1986 after allegations of conflict of interest in the handling of his personal affairs. A commission of inquiry later concluded that Stevens violated federal conflict of interest guidelines 14 times while industry minister.)

While news of the government's achievements went unmentioned, Mulroney complained to me, "the goddammed Claire Hoy" — who had been writing a series of blistering and highly personal attacks on the prime minister for the *Toronto Sun* — "reduces the (press) gallery to his level. He has scared the bejesus out of the gallery. We have been badly hurt by the unfairness of the gallery."

(Hoy's go-for-the-jugular style of journalism was a topic to which Mulroney returned time and time again in conversations about what he perceived to be the failings of the national press. Later, when Hoy wrote a vicious book about the Mulroneys, *Friends in High Places*, it topped the lists in bookstores for months. Some of Hoy's most bilous material didn't make it into the book, vetoed by his publisher, Key Porter. Hoy lost his column in the *Sun* when he refused to move to Toronto. Paul Godfrey, his publisher and a longtime Tory activist in Toronto, wanted to stop Hoy's diatribes from an Ottawa base.)

In that 1987 phone call to me, Mulroney also had his knife out for Don McGillivray, the hayseed dean of Southam News. McGillivray had not written anything objective for months, Mulroney said. He contrasted this with the favourable coverage of his South African tour by Michael Valpy of the *Globe and Mail*.

Turning to his relations with U.S. President Ronald Reagan, Mulroney said: "By God, Patrick, I'm going to ask you to have dinner with him. You're the only guy at Southam I'm still talking to." (Mulroney kept his promise of inviting me to dinner with Reagan in Ottawa, although it turned out to be more a cast of hundreds than an intimate tête-à-tête. The most memorable part of that evening was watching Nancy Reagan giving her impression of the adoring presidential wife. While her husband was reading his inconsequential speech, she never took her eyes off him, and I swear she never blinked in all of 15 minutes. Quite a performance!)

Mulroney was back to the subject of the press again when he phoned me at home in Calgary in the middle of a baseball game I was watching on television on June 23, 1987. The Blue Jays were ahead 8-2 at the time, so I wasn't missing much. While he still had a particularly low regard for Southam News, he had now come to the conclusion that the government was in control of its own destiny.

"For the first two years," he said, "there was focus (by the press gallery) on trivia — my haircut, my shoes. There was no attempt to analyze what we were doing as a government. But now the public knows we are concentrating on the major issues, that we are a decisive government."

He went on: "The other night I switched on *The Journal* to watch a discussion on Michael Wilson's[85] white paper (on tax reform). They had William Thorsell[86] debating with John Ferguson and Dian Cohen[87] with Pamela Wallin[88]. Thorsell dealt with the substance of the white paper and, as it happens, he liked it. But that is immaterial. Remember, we are talking about tax reform, but that didn't stop Ferguson from talking about my Guccis[89]. I had to restrain Mila, who was watching with me. The Ottawa people are simply mean-spirited. The outside press is professional, prepared to examine policy and to criticize or praise it, but without any attempt at personal attacks."

If the one-dimensional journalism on the subject of Mulroney was all the rage in the press gallery, he soon gave them something more substantive than his personal quirks and shortcomings to work on — free trade.

If it was, as he said, an idea whose time had come, it was soon to become his Gabriel's trumpet call for a government needing an election issue. The future of the country was firmly set in his priorities, and the issue of free trade was a popular one in Western Canada, because Alberta, Saskatchewan and Manitoba were more natural trading partners continentally north to south rather than east to west. His initiative was also welcomed in Quebec. But it was not an issue for the faint-hearted or for entrenched unions who could not face the competitive threat from outside Canada's protective tariff walls.

Free trade was also something John Turner could sink his teeth into and, clothing himself in the righteous cloak of "nationalism," he roused himself for his last hurrah with a grandstanding show of indignation. In the process, he hijacked what should have been an NDP-trade union campaign and drove Broadbent down in the popularity polls. Furthermore, Ontario Premier David Peterson, tiresomely regional to some as he represented the province that did 50 per cent of Canada's trade with the United States under the protective umbrella of Ottawa's restrictions, had an enormous stake to defend and he never lost sight of that immense burden of provincial leadership. In doing so, he seemed determined to deny Canada the full measure of its ambition and growth potential.

On Dec. 12, reaching me at the *Herald* on a Saturday morning, Mulroney was in a jubilant mood over free trade. He hedged his bets when I asked him if, as everyone speculated, he would call an election on the issue. "The Liberals and the NDP want an election on free trade, but I've got all the mandate I need — I've got a five-year mandate. Four years will be up next Sept. 17 (1988) but I don't know any reasons I'd go before then. If I found a bonanza, then I'd go." It was obvious, although unsaid, that he already regarded free trade as that bonanza.

He had some scathing comments about Premier Peterson and the *Toronto Star*'s reporting of the free trade negotiations being handled by Simon Reisman[90]. The *Star*, Mulroney said, had excised from an Ontario government report, everything that suggested it might be a good deal for Ontario. And Reisman, according to Mulroney, had described

Peterson as "the most selfish son of a bitch I have ever met. The man is a hypocrite."

Mulroney referred to a television news clip of the previous night in which Peterson was asked to respond to the prime minister's comment that the deal was a win-win situation for both Canada and the U.S. Peterson's response was predictable: "It is win-lose situation. They (the Americans) win, we lose."

Mulroney said the next question was cut from the interview. The interviewer allegedly said to Peterson: "Have you read the (new) free trade document yet?" And Peterson replied: "No, I plan on reading it this weekend." When told it contained substantial changes from earlier documents, Peterson said: "My mind is already made up."

The prime minister said Peterson thought he had some kind of veto on free trade, but as "the talks became more complex, we pulled the rabbit out of the hat and Peterson found he was stuck with the rest of us."

At a meeting of the first ministers, Mulroney said, Peterson tried to convince Don Getty that free trade was bad for Alberta. Getty replied: "Are you out of your mind?"

At a time when Ontario was greeting with open arms a proposal by General Motors to spend $2 billion on expanding its plant in Oshawa, Peterson told the first ministers, in their closed session, of his objections to American investment in Canada.

"Goddammit, David," Getty said, "if you don't want that two billion we'll take it."

Mulroney said the people of Ontario had always had a perception of themselves as being more Canadian than anyone else — "the Robarts[91] syndrome" — and they always took the stance of the "national interest."

"Now they're discovering Peterson is turning Ontario into the dog in the manger of Confederation."

Mulroney went on: "I'm going to have to tell David Peterson that if we don't get a comprehensive agreement on trade, then the auto pact is dead. A comprehensive agreement is the only thing saving the auto pact. Reagan told me that himself. He said the governors of Michigan, Indiana, etc., felt the auto pact was unfavourable to them. I told Reagan the auto pact was untouchable. I saved Peterson's ass for him.

"Peterson's vision of Canada sees a maître d' from Quebec, a farmhand from Saskatchewan and a shoeshine boy from Newfoundland. And there is wealthy Ontario.

"Do you know, Patrick, that when we (the first ministers) met in Toronto that poor little guy from New Brunswick (Premier Frank McKenna, who had ousted Richard Hatfield's Tories and whose Liberals took every seat in the legislature in the process) was simply awestruck as he gazed up at those gold buildings in Toronto and got out of the way of all those expensive cars. Peterson said to him: 'Look, Frank, leave all this to us; it wouldn't be good for you. Go back to the woods of northern New Brunswick and starve.' Well, if I have to go on the campaign trail on free trade and take Peterson on, he's going to discover that I'm a tough, miserable, Irish politician, and it will be a long, cold winter for him."

Then the bravado went out of his voice and he said: "I don't give a goddamn what happens to me in the next election. I just want them to say: 'Jesus, this guy did his best for Canada.'"

Eighteen days after this freewheeling monologue on free trade, Mulroney phoned me at home to wish me the compliments of the season. Recent polls had shown an eight-point climb in popular standing for the Tories and he admitted: "I'm always cheerful, my friend." But it was free trade still, not the polls, that he had on his mind, although the two were inextricably bound together.

"It was clear to everyone but (David Peterson) that Ontario's interests are best served by this agreement," he said. "There is a whole region of the country — Western Canada — that knows Trudeau sold them down the river. Peter Lougheed told me on Oct. 5, after Turner's threat to tear up the free trade agreement if he is elected, that the Liberals would never again win a seat west of the Lakehead."

I questioned that analysis, pointing to Lloyd Axworthy's continued survival in Winnipeg.

"Axworthy is a mean, splenetic bastard," Mulroney replied. "Personally, I like him, but he heads the vicious left-wing element of the Liberals."

Nor was he happy with a meeting he had had with Linda Hughes, editor — later to become publisher — of the *Edmonton Journal* and her editorial board. Free trade had occupied their agenda. He said he found the editorial writers to be "cute little NDP types — not vicious, but certainly left-wing."

# CHAPTER 28

In a phone call to me on Dec. 30, 1987, Brian Mulroney said: "I'm looking forward to coming to Calgary and having lunch at the Petroleum Club."

"Don't bring Pat Carney with you," I replied.

No offence to Pat Carney, of course. After all, I had once marched into the ballroom of the Westin Hotel in Toronto, with the head-table platoon for a Canadian Press annual dinner, carrying her bulky purse. (She had fierce back problems and when she spoke to the publishers of Canada and their guests at the CP dinner she had unobtrusively kicked off her shoes to ease the strain on her aching muscles. She couldn't even carry her own bag.) Carney, as energy minister, had gone out to Calgary in 1984 to give the oil industry the good news that the National Energy Program (NEP) was being put to death. But she was not permitted to have lunch in the public areas of the exclusively male Petroleum Club and had to be booked into a private room to eat. She never forgave the Petroleum Club.

That rule — barring women from lunching there and allowing them on the premises only for evening social occasions and if escorted by males — had stood since the club opened in 1947.

The phone call from Mulroney came just over a year after I failed in my first attempt to persuade the club to admit women into membership. And a few months after the phone call, I was once again deeply involved in plotting to crack the male bastion. Carney wrote to me to ask: "Is the club ready to come into the 20th century yet?" At that time (May 1988) I hadn't got an answer for her.

Back on June 23, 1986, I had written to Don Barkwell, then the president of the club, to tell him I was transferring a membership held under a *Calgary Herald* block of shares to another employee. Normally, notices of such transfers were a formality, processed by the club manager and eventually voted upon by the membership. But, as I pointed out to Barkwell — who was executive vice-president and chief executive officer of Norcen Energy Resources — this particular share transfer might cause complications, hence the letter to him. Kevin Peterson, general manager of the *Herald*, was giving up his share in the Petroleum Club to take membership in the Ranchmen's Club. Like me, Kevin held strong feelings about the Petroleum Club's ban on women, more personally because his wife, Sheila O'Brien, then a vice-president of Petro-Canada, could not qualify for membership although her husband could.

I was attempting to change the club's rules by asking for a transfer of Peterson's share to Catherine Ford.

Ironically, Catherine was a more frequent user of the Petroleum Club than most members — but only, of course, as a guest of the man later to be her husband, Les Elhatton. (To be honest, Joan Abeles and I found the Petroleum Club pretentious and stuffy, and we much preferred the Ranchmen's toasted lobster sandwiches and the famous Palliser bread and specially-made local cheese for our lunches.)

Catherine, granddaughter of the late Clinton J. Ford, former chief justice of Alberta and the Northwest Territories, was hardly a sacrificial lamb. Never one to mince her words before serving them up piping hot, she had once written a column for the *Brampton Times* during the explosive political period of René Lévesque's groping for a sovereignty-association referendum. The column's heading — Go Suck A

Lemon — left no doubt about where she stood on the Quebec question.

She and trouble were never far apart. Blame her Irish mother for that! When Les Elhatton died in 1988, after only a few months of marriage, his obituary notice in the *Herald* asked for contributions in his name to the Calgary Birth Control Association instead of flowers. That had been his wish. The funeral service was to take place in St. Mary's Cathedral, but the parish priest told Catherine's family the day before the funeral that it would not take place there unless another obituary notice were published without reference to the birth control association. "Finally," Ford told a *Globe and Mail* interviewer, "I just agreed to change the obituary. If it came down to a choice of picking my husband's favourite charity or carrying out his wish to be buried in the Catholic Church, freedom of speech stops at the church door." I arrived in Toronto the day after the funeral from International Press Institute meetings in Istanbul and was promptly quoted in the *Globe* as saying the church's actions were insensitive and cruel. I followed this up with a stinging letter to the priest concerned, Father Bill Stephenson — my own parish priest, no less, and otherwise a very decent, down-to-earth man — and also sent a copy to Bishop O'Byrne, whom we suspected was the real instigator of the threatened ban. Furthermore, I told our advertising department to bill the bishop, not Catherine, for the cost of the second obituary. But Catherine had the last word anyway. She told the *Globe*: "Les is probably somewhere laughing about this whole thing. He's probably saying, 'I married this outspoken woman and she can't even bury me without a controversy!'"

So that was the type of woman who was more than willing to be thrown into the fray back in 1986 as we attempted to break the sex barrier at the Petroleum Club.

In my letter to the club president, I told him I appreciated that "an outdated four-letter word" contained in Section 10 of the club's rules might make the transfer of a *Herald* share difficult. Therefore I was also proposing, seconded by Les Elhatton, that the word *male* be deleted from the first line of Section 10 and that all other references in the bylaws that prevented females from becoming full members of the club should also be amended or deleted. The effect of those simple changes would have been to allow full equality, without distinction on grounds of sex, to all those otherwise considered by the club as qualified for consideration as members. In the case of Catherine Ford, it was not a case of waiting for a vacancy to occur, because the *Herald* already had a share ready for her.

My letter drew attention to the fact that while the club was founded to cater to an industry that was then considered a male preserve, at least in its upper echelons, women were now found in growing numbers in the executive suites. The Neanderthal rule of the club barred such women from membership while their male colleagues of equivalent rank were automatically welcome. The discrimination was no longer tolerable, I told Barkwell.

Ford, I said, was a reputable and respected columnist, a senior member of our editorial department and part of our management team. I noted that several of her male colleagues already held company membership in the club.

On July 3, I got formal acknowledgment of my letter, but Barkwell made no mention of what he proposed to do about my request to transfer a share to Ford. However, he did say the question of opening full membership to females was on the agenda for his year as president, and it had been discussed at the board's most recent meeting. It had been referred to both the house and membership committees.

After receiving reports from those committees, he said, the board would consider taking the issue to the full membership.

Revelling in the whole affair, Ford could not resist taking a shot or two in her column at the anachronistic attitudes of the club. That did not endear her to the more hidebound of its members, and there were many of those. They posted an eight-by-ten photo of her above the urinals in the men's room and across the photo some loutish, but anonymous, soul had written: "Would you want this woman in your club?"

On Sept. 15, 1986, I wrote to Barkwell again, telling him that I had just appointed Ford associate editor of the *Herald*, the first woman to hold that title. If a man had been appointed associate editor, I would have wanted him to have a membership in the Petroleum Club; I expected no less for Ford.

Meantime, Barkwell was doing his own lobbying with the board to find some way around the men-only bylaws. He phoned me a few days later to say that the question of admitting women as members came up every year and "it gets a little more momentum." He said it was "almost positive" that he would take the issue to the shareholders later in the fall and that he would call a special meeting for this purpose. "I think it will pass," he added.

He said a number of members liked things the way they were, although "no one is against women." As president, he said, he could not take a stand on the issue and would have to be neutral if it came to a vote. I told him I would be happy to speak to such a resolution if it would help to take the heat off him.

Some 322 kilometres farther north, the Edmonton Club — founded in 1899 — decided to amend its constitution to allow women into membership, but it was done with a certain patronizing smugness. Club president Robert Sherman explained: "Women have been coming to lunch with members over the past few years and they've been fitting in very well."

To which the *Edmonton Journal*, in a sarcastic editorial, commented: "How nice! They've passed the test. But tell us what happens if all the little gals start slurping their soup?"

An extraordinary meeting of the shareholders of the Calgary Petroleum Club was called for Nov. 17 to discuss the issue of women's membership. In a document dated Oct. 7, signed by the president and sent to all 1,700 shareholders, a whole flock of amendments were listed, but even at this late date in its flirtation with progress the board could not go all the way — it wanted to reserve the entire lower basement area (with the exception of the President's Room) for male members. This area encompassed the "quiet room," the card room and the pool room. Boys will be boys, and they didn't want the little ladies spoiling their fun!

Voting was to be by ballot, and it would take a two-thirds majority to effect any changes. Indications were that the changes would pass, because some of the American-owned oil companies were putting pressure on their local people.

But it wasn't just the Americans turning up the heat. Petro-Canada — backed by having enough memberships to start a club of its own and being pushed by all political parties — let it be known that they wanted a change and would urge those of its executives holding membership shares to turn them in if the vote failed.

Bill Hopper, the Petrocan chairman, told me he rarely lunched at the club — at noon, Calgary time, it is already 2 p.m. in Ottawa, so "I end up eating lunch at my desk most of the time." Nevertheless, luxury brown-bagging didn't stop him getting dumped on by the boys of the old brigade. There was a widely held perception that Petrocan, operating out of its own despised Red Square[92] and not exactly the most popular oil company with the "in" set in Calgary, was trying to influence the vote with the blackmail threat of getting its own multitude of members to quit.

The proposed vote was also a hot topic outside Calgary. The *Globe and Mail* ran a news story on Nov. 10, quoting Ada Rawlins, public relations director for the Independent Petroleum Association of Canada, as "still seething" over the earlier ban on Pat Carney. She claimed, however, there had been little pressure from women wanting to join the club. "To most of us, it's a joke that we can't get in. Some of the members I've talked to are a little ashamed about it."

Because it was deeply involved behind the scenes, the *Herald* itself had run only a couple of straightforward news stories on the proposed vote, and most of our columnists had restrained themselves from being overly critical, cynical or sarcastic.

There was a surprising air of tension at the club on Nov. 17. There was a rigid system of checking for voting eligibility when I got there early, accompanied by Kevin Peterson, still clinging to the share membership earmarked for Ford. Also with us were Don Babick, the *Herald's* marketing manager and later publisher of the *Edmonton Journal* and *Pacific Press*, and Ken Turner, the production manager. Turner, a big, affable, slow-talking, avuncular ex-compositor farm boy from Saskatchewan, told me he had a crisis of confidence. He knew my feelings on the issue, but did not think he could support me. "Do what you think is best," I told him. I never did ask him how he voted and he never told me, but he later gave up his own Petroleum Club membership in exchange for my company membership in Bearspaw Ridge Golf Club.

After Barkwell had outlined the rules of the meeting, he said the proposal was being brought forward by the board without any recommendation or rejection. Board member Bill Gatenby, chairman of Texaco Canada, moved the recommendation as a matter of form, and I rose to support the motion, the only person to speak in favour of it. In fact, I was the only one to speak either for or against it: everybody's mind was already made up. Saying I didn't believe in special privilege for men or women, I said women must be accorded the rights of their status as earned through their career performances or their impact on public life. Discrimination by sex must end.

I went on: "I believe in all sincerity that the Petroleum Club needs to take recognition of a self-evident truth: that you can't hang on to the hands of time forever, to stop it marking the passage of the hours. I fear no evil or intrusion by this change, nor should there be any feeling of sacrifice in what would be expected of male members under a change of rules. But I would urge you to consider how you vote, not under any sense of external pressure, but simply from the depths of your own conscience and reason." I sat down to utter silence, knowing that my words had fallen mostly on deaf ears. It was clear I was the odd man out.

They took a long time to tally the votes, and Les Elhatton and I sat glumly in the bar until the club posted a notice in the form of a press release: "On behalf of the membership of the Calgary Petroleum Club, we wish to announce that at an extraordinary general meeting held today, a resolution providing for female membership was defeated." Under the bylaws, the actual vote did not have to be announced. The figures were tallied by independent accountants and handed to the president. It was not difficult for him to estimate that the amendment had not garnered the required two-thirds out of the 700 votes cast required for it to pass.

Over the next few days, Bill Hopper announced that most of his executives would be resigning from the Petroleum Club. Most, but not all. In a telephone call, he told me: "I expected it. It's inevitable this would happen. The club is full of farts. Old farts and young farts. A lot were disturbed by your strident speech. Talking to Bill Siebens, the incoming president, is like taking to a wall. I've taken a lot of flak, but we fought the good fight with the Rideau Club (in Ottawa) before this. Bill Siebens is even on my board. He's hell on wheels when you suggest trying to alter the character of the club."

Hopper said he had had a hundred letters from all over the country supporting his stand, and some contained the cut-up cards of other oil companies as a gesture of displeasure to those who had not encouraged their members to quit the Petroleum Club.

In Calgary, however, as one oilman told me: "A lot of us still consider Petrocan a rapist federal industry, so we're certainly not going to follow their lead. They're too big to be ignored, but they don't have to be taken as an authority. And it bothers me that they're talking so strongly about this now when they knew our policies at the time they bought their memberships."

Three days after the vote, when I walked into the Petroleum Club to attend a private function, the executive vice-president of a major energy company first shook my hand and then said: "There are only two people in this club we wanted to get rid of. Bill Hopper was one and he's already gone. When are you going?"

"Not until we get the rule changed," I replied.

Were Hopper and I the villains of the piece? *Alberta Report* certainly tried to paint us that way. It wrote: "The gentlemen of the club took quite a whipping in the press and, although unrepentant, they were nonetheless embarrassed. Thus they are now trying to make themselves understood. 'None of us are proud of the Carney incident, and most of us have accepted the fact that women are playing big roles in the oilpatch now,' says one oil company executive who voted against the proposal. 'We were ready to open things, but then the *Calgary Herald* and Petro Canada started telling us what we should do. They were trying to coerce us into allowing women to join. Oilmen, being a fiercely independent bunch, resented it. So you see, it wasn't an anti-women vote. It was a vote against the *Herald* and Petrocan. We knew we'd take s—t for it, but better that than giving in to those guys.'"

Eddie LaBorde, 73, president of LaBorde Petroleums Ltd., and a founding member of the Petroleum Club, told *Alberta Report* that the *Herald* hurt the cause it had hoped to champion. Said the magazine: "He cites a speech delivered a few days before the vote by the newspaper's publisher, J. Patrick O'Callaghan, as a turning point in the debate."

LaBorde was quoted by *Alberta Report* as saying: "A lot of people resented a johnny-come-lately telling us what to do. Three people told me they had planned to vote to let women be members until that point." He added that many women convinced their husbands to vote against the proposal. "There's some very aggressive women in this town,' he said. "A lot of wives are damn glad their husbands won't be hobnobbing with women in that kind of setting."

*Alberta Report* also quoted another club member "who, not wishing to engage in a public battle with the *Herald*, wishes to remain anonymous." This timid soul told *Alberta*

*Report*: "O'Callaghan doesn't understand the oilpatch and the business community here. He takes a progressive view of everything. We aren't dinosaurs, like they're calling us now, but we like our traditions."

In a news story on the vote, the *Herald*'s Rosemary McCracken quoted me as saying "This is just a skirmish in what is shaping up to be a war." I said the club had shot itself in the foot.

The war broke out again only eight days after the vote. This took the form of another letter to the battle-weary Barkwell. Pointing to several major companies — Petro-Canada, Nova and Husky among them — pulling their memberships and the "House of Commons becoming a sounding chamber echoing the now common public belief that the Petroleum Club is archaic, a relic of 19th-century male chauvinism," I said the momentum for change was actually gathering speed.

The vote was no more than a stalling tactic, I claimed. There would be no peace within the club until the true democratic principle of requiring a simple majority of members to approve or defeat a motion was applied and, under the rules, that could only be done at the annual meeting.

"I have chosen to remain a member of the club, not because I approve of its unisex philosophy, but because when it is a matter in which principle is more important than personality, I believe it is imperative to stay to work for change from within."

I then urged Barkwell to take the defeated resolution to the next annual general meeting to seek a straight majority. I sent copies of my letter to the presidents or chairmen of 24 major oil companies. This produced a number of phone calls, and a letter from Bob Blair, chairman of Nova. He was disappointed that the board had taken no position of leadership on the issue, preferring to remain silent at the extraordinary general meeting.

Blair wrote: "Personally, I don't buy the proposition that this was a private club matter. The Petroleum Club is, I believe, supported overwhelmingly by expenses of petroleum companies, which are shareholder-owned. By the club's name and the impression which it creates of being a forum for industry meetings, I think it is hardly any more private than the Canadian Gas Association or the Canadian Petroleum Association or numerous other organizations which are supported by petroleum industry expense coverage."

Barkwell, whose time as president was running out, did not feel it was fair to commit a new board to my proposal for still another vote only six months after the Nov. 17, 1986, failure. So I turned my attention to his successor, Bill Siebens.

Siebens even took me to lunch — at the Petroleum Club, naturally — charmed me in his own blunderbuss fashion, metaphorically patted me on the head and sent me on my way with an admonition to be a good boy. Siebens was an interesting study in rampant male chauvinism. He came from a family which had quietly distributed millions of dollars to Calgary charities. The family hated publicity. Its vehicle for earning the wealth that allowed such munificence was Candor Investments. But Bill Siebens himself had a finger in a lot of energy and development pies and, at one time or another, he was a director of Canadian Roxy Petroleum, Markborough Properties, Petro-Canada and Sovereign Oil and Gas, the British company. He had also been actively involved with the right-wing think-tank, the Fraser Institute.

Given this background, and his own overpowering personality, it wasn't difficult to understand why I felt my

Petroleum Club crusade would go nowhere during his term as president. But nevertheless, I tried.

On Aug. 11, 1987, I wrote to Siebens to say that I thought enough time had elapsed to dust off the Barkwell proposal and try again. A number of attitudes had changed since then, I said, although neither he nor I needed to mention that he was not among those whose attitudes had become more progressive. Only recently, I told him, the Canada Club, a male-only bastion in England for 177 years, had called a special meeting to discuss the same issue. The Canada Club met four times a year for dinner in the gilded surroundings of the venerable Savoy Hotel in London. Dinners were traditionally hosted by the Canadian high commissioner, but when Roy McMurtry took over the job in 1986, he flatly refused to join the club because of its refusal to allow women to become members. He also ordered his staff to withdraw from membership, and he saw to it that no visiting Canadian cabinet minister would address any dinner at the club. Jean Wadds, McMurtry's predecessor as high commissioner, had been allowed to chair the dinners, but she had to go to the ridiculous extreme of having herself declared "an honorary man."

In my letter to Siebens, I said: "If I prove to be a two-time loser (in a vote to admit women as members), then I think the reasonable thing for me to do would be to proffer my resignation as a member of the club. That offer is made with no animosity intended ... but simply as a matter of principle."

Nothing was heard from Siebens, so on Sept. 14, I wrote again asking for an indication of the status of my letter.

The silence was so deep that you could have heard a pin drop to the bottom of an exploration well. It was obvious I was only going through the motions, trying to wait out

Siebens' one-year term as president. Nevertheless, I had one more shot at him by mail.

In a letter dated March 18, 1988, I told him I saw "no sign of any change of mood, no weakening of the rock-ribbed resistance to modernization and equality between the sexes." I repeated my offer to resign, if that would help.

Still nothing from him. Finally, on May 19, I tracked him down by phone.

"What," I asked him, "does the board intend to do about my letter offering my resignation if nothing is done about admitting female members?"

In response, I listened to the usual redneck reactionary lecture from Siebens, pointing out that the club had been men-only for 40 years. It had received only two letters concerning the 1986 vote rejecting women members, he said. Both of them were from me.

Under the circumstances, I said, I would exercise my option and resign.

"Now hold on!" he roared. "Don't be so impatient. You goddamn Irish are all alike. I haven't finished with you yet!"

He said his term expired at the end of the month. The board felt that it had to let two years pass before attempting another vote and, he told me, it was his understanding that the new board was planning to take another run at seeking approval for women members by November.

Then he added: "Frankly, I don't give a damn whether you resign or not, but if only we can get certain companies and editors (meaning me, I suppose) not to kick up a fuss in the meantime, I think we'll see it pass."

I made it plain to him that if he was simply trying to sell me a bill of goods to shut me up, I would resign noisily and publicly. In all fairness to Bill, that was a relatively amiable discussion by our standards.

And that left me a new target to zero in on, the successor to Siebens. Tony Vanden Brink was president and chief operating officer of Trimac, a director of Banister Continental and of Bantrel Group of engineers, Cactus International, Mark Resources, Triton Canada Resources, Western Rock Bit and, for a change of pace, the Salvation Army.

I waited until June 21, 1988, to make my standard pitch to him. I gave him the gist of my conversation with Siebens and mentioned the promise that the new board might be undertaking a fresh initiative. I told him I would like to have lunch with him, and I sent him a clipping from the *Christian Science Monitor* reporting a decision by the U.S. Supreme Court to uphold a New York City law barring discrimination against women and minorities by private clubs with more than 400 members. While that American decision had nothing to do with Canadian clubs, surely the Petroleum Club should now be ready to end what had become a national embarrassment. I said I would be happy to step out of the picture if he and his board were ready to act.

Vanden Brink took me up on the lunch suggestion and told me he was totally committed to the cause. He outlined his game plan. He said the 1986 board had not endorsed its own recommendation and that had hurt, a point made to me earlier by Bob Blair. He intended to meet individually not only with his board and executive, but also with some of the hard line reactionary members. To appease them, he would set aside the McMurray Room for men only. And, when I raised it with him, he also had in mind reserving a room for women.

The quiet-spoken Vanden Brink, with his voice giving away his Dutch origins, had fled from the Indonesian territories Holland had lost in the Second World War. His determination impressed me.

He said he had some important supporters spotted on the key committees, and his reading of both the board and the executive was that he would get their unanimous support in a presentation to the membership. With no disrespect intended, I told him he had more faith in his persuasive powers than I could have — it would be a miracle if he could get Bill Siebens to cross over to the side of the angels. But that is exactly what he did.

So, in 1989, the Petroleum Club, one of the last holdouts of male chauvinism, opened its doors to women members. But I wasn't there to see it. Having retired as publisher of the *Herald* at the end of 1988, and given my membership share back to the newspaper, I was in Toronto when Tony Vanden Brink worked his miracle.

In the end, Catherine Ford did something Pat Carney never could: she walked into the Petroleum Club as a member and took a guest with her for lunch.

They will never put up a plaque in my name at the Petroleum Club, but the least they could do to honour my memory would be to put up an eight-by-ten photograph of me above the men's urinals. I leave the rest to the graffiti artists.

# CHAPTER 29

Free trade gave John Turner the opportunity in the Nov. 21, 1988, election to wrap himself in the flag as the defender of all our sovereign virtues. Those baby-blue eyes flashing, his theme was Canada Is Not For Sale. The Tories, by contrast — according to him — formed the fifth column in our midst whose sole aim was to hand us over, body, soul and culture, to the rapacious Americans.

Two months before the election, Brian Mulroney found himself running behind NDP leader Ed Broadbent in the polls. But free trade produced an election anomaly — a government with a solid issue was opposed by two parties, united only in their distaste for free trade, running two separate campaigns against it. Such a split of the Liberal and NDP votes could work only to the advantage of the Tories.

Amid all the hysteria, Mulroney found time to tell me that Beland Honderich, the venerable publisher of the *Toronto Star*, "has definitely lost his marbles" for the *Star*'s one-sided coverage of free trade. And Don McGillivray, who wouldn't hurt a fly if you took away his computer, was a "malicious old bastard." As for Claire Hoy, who was freelancing his views during the election, "the man's an asshole," Mulroney said. Mulroney was still fuming over Hoy's book, *Friends in High Places*, and suspected that the source of much of Hoy's racier material for it was Gillian Cosgrove. She was the wife of Raymond Heard, John Turner's press secretary.

Mulroney had always been an easy target for the gunslingers of the National Press Gallery. Where Joe Clark was ridiculed, Mulroney was despised. Mulroney was given to rhetorical excess, and his later "rolling the dice" interview in the *Globe and Mail* on the Meech Lake discussions with the premiers[93] showed how hard it was for him to kick the habit. In his better aspect of extravagant flourish, he could paint drab daisies to look like orchids when the humour was on him; at his worst, it was the bending of the truth that often grated more than the facing of unpalatable circumstance.

Turner's do-or-die election effort was noted in the last editorial I ever wrote for the *Herald*. Carrying the headline Free Trade Can Free The West, it started on the front page of the Nov. 18 issue, and turned to fill the entire column of regular editorial space on Page A4.

Saying that Turner was a one-issue candidate in this "nastiest of all federal elections," I wrote: "If Turner wins, free trade is in the grave with its toes turned up and the Americans will not attempt to resurrect it."

Time will show that Mulroney's free trade initiative "was one of the most courageous political courses ever undertaken by a Canadian prime minister," said the editorial.

My editorial swan song caused a great deal of outrage amongst readers. *Herald* ombudsman Jim Stott said that his phone rang continuously and his callers ranged from the civil and civilized who wanted a debate, to the near-hysterical and venomous who heaped personal abuse and four-letter words on him. The main switchboard at the *Herald* was clogged for two days, and personnel manning phones in the newsroom and the community relations department were also swamped with calls.

According to Stott, two themes emerged in conversations he had with callers. One was that the newspaper was unfairly manipulating public opinion by running the editorial on the front page and, by doing so, was warping the conduct of the free trade debate. The other theme was the frequently expressed opinion that the *Herald*'s coverage of the election campaign was biased in favour of the free trade deal and the Tories. One caller demanded that the paper run another Page 1 editorial the next day condemning the free trade agreement "so that coverage would be balanced."

Perhaps we should have referred this caller to Beland Honderich and the *Toronto Star*. Canada's largest-circulation newspaper ran its main election editorial on Page 1 on Nov. 16 — condemning free trade.

No doubt, Mulroney was more than happy with the *Herald*'s consistent stance on free trade, but his views on the manner in which the *Journal*, just 322 kilometres north of Calgary, comported itself during the election campaign, were less than flattering.

The day after the election, still jubilant over retaining an overall majority, Mulroney phoned me at my office and mentioned a meeting he had had with the *Journal*'s ivory-tower thinkers during the campaign. (This was a year after coming to the conclusion that the *Journal*'s editorial board were all "cute little NDP types.") After he got back to Ottawa from his pre-election meeting with the *Journal* board, he said, Mila asked him "How did it go?" The only word he could find to describe to her his feeling for the meeting was *snottiness*.

I pointed out that the *Journal* was the only western paper that did not support free trade. I wondered if it had lost its sense of history, its understanding of Alberta's beliefs, hopes and expectations.

"No, Patrick," he answered. "It did not lose its sense of history. It lost its roots." He used a French expression loosely translated as "sense of attachment" to explain what papers like *La Presse* meant to Quebec, and said Alberta's population had not changed since my days as publisher in Edmonton, but the *Journal* had. It had lost that sense of attachment to its own readership. "All I can say about the *Journal*," he added, "is that has become a second-rate *Toronto Star*." In his book, there was no bigger insult for a newspaper.

On analyzing the election, he noted that the Tories had lost some votes in British Columbia to both the NDP and the Reform Party. He asked me: "Do you know what our biggest problem was in B.C.?"

Without hesitation, I answered: "Vander Zalm. " (Then premier of British Columbia and supposedly a backer of the Tories on free trade, Bill Vander Zalm all but single-handedly wiped out his own party, Social Credit, once the dominant force in B.C. politics.)

"You're absolutely right," Mulroney replied.

Vander Zalm apart, Mulroney's private analysis of the election may have been somewhat self-serving, but it lacked the edge of boastfulness. He read me a congratulatory message from Ireland's *an taoiseach* (prime minister). Charles Haughey said that Canada had advanced the cause of western decency in foreign affairs. The message ended by saying that Mulroney now had a legitimate excuse to sing *When Irish Eyes Are Smiling* to his Baie Comeau supporters. (Frankly, there is never a legitimate excuse for an Irishman to sing that song — it is of Tin Pan Alley heritage, without a drop of Dublin or Cork in its veins![94])

Mulroney said his dilemma during the election was that there were really two campaigns. The first was up to the TV debates featuring the party leaders. "We clearly won that," he said, "but we had to win the second campaign." He was hurt by the public perception that Turner came out on top in the English-language portion of the debates. Quebec Premier Robert Bourassa had told the prime minister that there were really two debates in one package: Mulroney won his clash with Turner, but in a debate of public expectations, pitting the Turner of 1984 against the Turner of 1988, Turner obviously acquitted himself much better. Hence the perception that Turner was the ultimate debating champion.

"We were perplexed by the monstrous fabrications by Turner on free trade," Mulroney said. "They talk about my lack of credibility, but Turner doesn't have any at all. Because of the TV debate, it gave us the opportunity to switch our strategy, to go head to head with Turner on his weakness, his own lack of credibility. Because of the way he manipulated a confused electorate on free trade, he became a bridge for the uncertain and we had to overcome that, to demolish his bridge. That we did."

# CHAPTER 30

"Are you two an item?"

The speaker was Conrad Black and the occasion was the 1988 Canadian Press (CP) annual dinner at the Westin Hotel in Toronto. The remark was addressed to Joan Abeles. As CP board chairman, I was host of the black-tie dinner, and Joan was my head-table guest.

Yes, she told Black, we were very much an item. And we remained that way; we were married on Valentine's Day in 1989.

The erudite and courtly Conrad Black was an entertaining conversational companion for the evening. That night, amongst other things, the three of us discussed not only Canadian newspaper affairs but British naval battles. Black is a military history buff.

We got on to the subject of the loss of the British battle cruiser, HMS *Repulse*, sister ship of the *Renown*. The British fleet in the Far East had been beefed up to withstand the Japanese advance on Singapore in 1942. One of Britain's newest and biggest battleships, the 32,259-tonne *Prince of Wales*, was ordered to Singapore, along with the *Repulse* and the aircraft carrier *Indomitable*. The fleet in the Far East was commanded by Admiral Thomas (Tom Thumb) Phillips, who came from Upton-on-Severn, only a few kilometres from Malvern, where I got my first newspaper job. Phillips, a tiny man, had an old-time British career naval officer's contempt for those trained to make war from the air. When he and his fleet of heavyweights set sail from Singapore to attack the Japanese invaders north of the British colony, he had to do so without the *Indomitable*, which had run aground off Jamaica en route to Singapore. Phillips scoffed at the loss of *Indomitable*'s air umbrella. "Bombers are no match for battleships," he said. On the morning of Dec. 10, 1942, about 80 Japanese bombers attacked the *Prince of Wales* out of a cloudless sky. Two torpedoes tore her stern apart. Then the *Repulse*, after weaving and dodging to avoid nearly 20 torpedoes, was mortally wounded by four that ripped her open. Although more than 2,000 men were rescued before the two ships capsized, Capt. John Leach refused to leave the *Prince of Wales* and was among the 840 sailors who died. Admiral Phillips went down with the *Repulse*, although its commander, Captain William Tennant, was saved after his officers manhandled him into joining the evacuation. The foolhardiness of Phillips — whose disdain for air power made his armada sitting ducks for the Japanese — cost the British control of the seas all the way from Africa, eastwards to America, through the Indian Ocean and the Pacific, as Britain's Chief of the Imperial General Staff, Sir Alan Brooke, sadly deduced.

But none of that stopped Conrad Black from keeping a soft spot in his heart for a British cruiser. He told me he had gone home from his office in Toronto early one day, to his house on the Bridle Path, not feeling too well. However, when his spirits began to pick up, he went for a walk and passed a store where a model of either the *Repulse* or the *Renown* — I can't remember which — caught his eye. He went into the shop and bought it, without at first realizing that he had no cash, cheque book or credit card with him to pay for it.

Recognizing his dilemma, the shopkeeper, who knew him, said: "Mr. Black, I think I can trust you to pay me when you come into some funds."

So one of Canada's richest men, a restless newspaper tycoon of the new breed, walked out, proud as punch, with a large model of a battle cruiser tucked under his arm.

That's not quite the image one normally has of Black. The side best known to the newspaper industry emerged when he got up to give his rapid-fire address at the CP dinner, attacking the dailies for their incompetence and their legion of failings. He strings words together with the insouciance of a master of the English language, and I entertained myself reading the speech, word for word, over his shoulder, rather than listening to it, as he turned the pages on the podium alongside me.

However, occasionally glimpsing the faces of the audience, I got the impression that most of them were two or three paragraphs behind his delivery, still trying to get the hang of the big words so rich in resonant splendour. His sentences are framed in a baroque eloquence that is dictionaries removed from the clipped journalese of the industry he went on to embrace as both writer and as press baron. Speaking of the media, he has been known to castigate the working press in general as "ignorant, lazy, opinionated, intellectually dishonest and inadequately supervised . . . a very degenerate group whose mental stability . . . is more open to question than that of any other comparable group in society."

It is small wonder, then, that when he sat down to somewhat lukewarm applause, he needed to ask me: "Do you think I came on a little too strong?"

I shrugged and said: "A little, perhaps, but unlike the last two CP dinners, nobody fell asleep during your speech."

At the time, everybody was intrigued by the *Financial Post*'s move into the daily field under the initiative of the *Toronto Sun*'s Doug Creighton. Black was a minority shareholder in the venture. Pointing out that the *Financial Post* seemed to be on a collision course with the *Globe and Mail*'s highly respected Report on Business (ROB), I told Black: "I can't understand the audience you are trying to reach with a tabloid."

"Neither can I," he replied. "I leave that sort of thing to Creighton."

Trusting soul! However, Black seemed happy enough to have somebody take a run at the *Globe and Mail* because it had just fired him as a columnist. In his last column for the *Globe*'s ROB magazine, he didn't quite express it that way. What he said was that the *Globe* had determined that his status as a shareholder of the rival *Financial Post* deemed him unsuitable as a columnist for the ROB magazine.

That might be a somewhat negative view by the *Globe* of a man so influential in the print business. As history has a tendency to repeat itself, somebody should have warned the *Globe* to start listening for footsteps. The last time a magazine — Britain's *Spectator* — said unkind things about Black, he put down about $6 million to add it to his growing media empire. But before doing so, Black treated the magazine to one of his magnificent letters of contemptuous ridicule.

Talking of the man who had penned a somewhat unflattering article about him in the magazine, Black described the writer as a "familiar and somewhat pitiful figure." He then went on: "Those who would retain his services should confine him to subjects better suited than this one was to his sniggering, puerile, defamatory and cruelly limited talents."

By this time, Black was clearly shifting careers from commerce in general to newspaper publishing in particular, so getting a pink slip from the *Globe* was hardly a matter of impending poverty for him. Indeed, by the time he was 35, Black had made one fortune, inherited another, taken control of Argus Corp. and written a lengthy, but major, book on Maurice Duplessis, former premier of Quebec.

Starting with the *Sherbrooke Daily Record*, he put together a string of dailies under the banner of the Sterling Newspaper Group. Journalists sniffed that Sterling pioneered the two-person newsroom, but Black moved on from the slightly comic-opera Sterling to the stuffily sublime *Daily Telegraph*, a quality British daily that at the time appeared to be mired and sinking fast in the bloody-minded Luddite bogs of archaic British craft unions. Although he began spending more time in England, moving into the Margaret Thatcher dinner circuit, Black hopscotched backwards and forwards across the Atlantic to accumulate more than 50 North American small dailies under the Hollinger label.

From that point, he changed direction once again, this time descending upon the hapless Australians before they knew what had hit them. After a seven-month financial and political tug-of-war with Tony O'Reilly, Ireland's legendary rugby hero and chairman of Heinz, the canned food empire, Black's Tourang consortium successfully bid more than $1.32 billion (Canadian) for the John Fairfax newspaper group. Under complex Australian restrictions on foreign ownership of media, Black's share of the deal was only 15 per cent voting equity — through the *Daily Telegraph* — with 80 per cent held by Australian institutions and five per cent by the U.S. investment firm Hellman and Friedman. But there was never any doubt that Black dominated the consortium. Only a week before Tourang's bid was accepted by the receiver for John Fairfax in December 1991, the O'Reilly group appeared to have won the day, but Black feverishly reconstructed the Tourang bid with only hours to spare before the deadline for closure. A third bidder, the Melbourne-based Australian Independent Newspapers, was never seriously in the hunt.

The key papers acquired by Tourang were the *Sydney Morning Herald*, *The Age* in Melbourne and the *Australian Financial Review*. All of a sudden, with Sherbrooke only a memory, Black was in the international top three of newspaper owners, along with Thomson and Rupert Murdoch. Ironically, with Robert Maxwell dead and his memory quickly defiled[95], the international scene was dominated by three "colonials" — Black and Thomson and Murdoch, an Australian.

Black once denied in a magazine article that he was a professional renegade, but he has certainly shown a willingness to wander outside the boundaries of conventional thought and action. While most Anglo-Canadian newspaper groups had shied away from francophone ownership, Black and his partners (Peter White — when he was not working the patronage beat for Prime Minister Mulroney — and David Radler) had acquired the Unimedia group, owners of three French-language dailies, including *Le Soleil*, and 20 Quebec-based weeklies. When Jacques Francoeur had wanted to sell Unimedia, he first approached Southam. But, as with the earlier sale of the *Peterborough Examiner* to Thomson, and the *Montreal Star* to FP, Southam could not make up its mind quickly enough and the frustrated Francoeur went to Black instead.

On the question of Southam, Black denied to me at the CP dinner that he was the mysterious bidder for Southam shares in the takeover rumours and confusion following the death of Gordon Fisher. At that time, St. Clair Balfour was already 75 and barred by an age ceiling from returning even as interim chairman or president. However, he was still the dominant figure behind the scenes when the board was desperately trying to find someone with Southam blood in his veins to run the company. "I phoned Clair Balfour," Black told me, "and said, 'Clair, if I want to take a run at Southam, you will be the first to know, and it won't be done through the back door.'"

Nevertheless, Black had accumulated a fair-sized block of Southam shares and it was assumed that, by May of 1990, when the five-year hands-off deal with Torstar was due to expire, Black would have been in a bidding contest with Torstar for the billion-dollar Southam company. However, at the end of 1989, Black surprised everybody by disposing of all his Southam shares.

But Black has more colours than a chameleon in a striped-paint factory. And he is not above playing poker for big stakes when it comes to empire-building. He made a handsome profit out of the 1989 sales of Southam stock at a time when it was obvious Southam was protected from any outsider with ambitions of taking over the company. When the five-year freeze — that initially was supposed to be for 10 years — finally expired, Black didn't use either the front door or the back door to make his move on Southam. He deduced correctly that Torstar was disillusioned with Southam and its diminished status in the newspaper field, and he made Torstar an offer for its Southam shares that it couldn't resist.

Then into the picture came Paul Desmarais of Power Corporation of Canada, owners of *La Presse*. Between them, Black and Desmarais ended up with nearly 40 per cent of Southam, enough to exercise joint control, should they so desire it. Or, alternatively, each could act as a restraining influence on the other.

As an investment manager once said of Black: "He just believes he can pit his own brilliance against anybody." I'm not sure that was meant as a compliment when Stephen Jarislowsky, later a Southam director, said it, but it rings true enough.

When Robert Maxwell was discovered dead in the Atlantic Ocean off the Canary Islands in 1991 after disappearing from his yacht, the inability of the *Daily News* in New York to shake loose of the restrictive unions that had prevented its previous owners from turning a profit on what was once the most-read tabloid in the U.S., was one of the major problems he left behind. The sale of the *Daily News* was one of the only options left to the impoverished daily; the other was to shut it down permanently.

Black was the front-runner in the New York bidding war, but he made it clear that while he was prepared to spend millions of dollars on a new plant and putting fresh cash into a pension fund for the unions, he would not proceed with the offer unless he could trim the labour force to manageable proportions. He never got those assurances, so he picked up his cards and walked away from the table with his gambling stake intact. It was estimated that more than $10 million a year was being paid in wages and benefits to 167 printers for work made unnecessary by technological advances.

Mortimer Zuckerman, owner of the *U.S. News and World Report*, thought he knew how to handle the obdurate unions, and got court permission to proceed with the purchase, but then ran afoul of a judge sympathetic to the printers. U.S. Bankruptcy Judge Tina Brozman had ruled that Zuckerman could reject an 18-year contract that guaranteed lifetime jobs to printers even when their work had been replaced by computerized equipment. However, U.S. District Judge Lawrence McKenna overruled her and said Zuckerman could resume negotiations with the printers' union so that buyouts might be arranged to clear the way for the sale. But the union insisted it would have none of that, and Conrad Black, now out of the picture, was probably grinning from ear to ear in one of his many corporate headquarters around the world.

Nevertheless, by inserting himself into the Southam picture, Black was about to see a *Daily News*-type nightmare unfold in one of Southam's prime markets, Vancouver. There, the biggest obstacle to Southam's return to adequate profitability was simply a repeat of the *Daily News* scenario. The 165 printers who once set the type for the *Vancouver Sun* and the *Province* got paid more than $1,000 for a four-day work week, plus all the generous benefits their union had winkled out of Southam over the years. They had a guarantee of lifetime employment as printers, and there was no retirement age. They were there until death do us part, a permanent impediment to a happy marriage with Southam.

Nobody would argue with Harry Funk, president of their union — Local 226 of the Communication Workers of America — when he said: "It is probably the best guarantee there is in North America." It was this, and other rich collective agreements Southam surrendered to the unions in the past, that made Pacific Press the biggest underachiever in the company. Pacific Press dragged down the rest of Southam.

That may have been a bitter pill for Black to swallow if he wanted Southam to build up its profits. When he took over the *Daily Telegraph* in Britain — a paper whose history dates back to the Crimean War — he gradually trimmed its staff from 4,000 to about 1,600. It is not likely that he would tolerate for long the featherbedding in Vancouver.

Doug Creighton may well have been the most influential figure in the Canadian newspaper industry in the past two decades, but with his downfall and the sudden emergence of Conrad Black as a self-appointed potential saviour of suffering Southam, the rest of the century is

Black's to dominate. The newspaper business is utterly altered for all time, but does Southam fit snugly into all this?

# CHAPTER 31

It couldn't have been more Jewish — a meeting of the Canadian Jewish Congress (CJC) at the Samuel Bronfman Centre in Montreal.

It was Sept. 10, 1989, a beautiful fall Sunday evening, and Joan and I were enjoying the sunshine outside the centre, waiting for our cab to arrive after I'd spoken to CJC delegates from all across Canada. At last, the taxi pulled up and the driver smiled sweetly at us. He was young, boyishly handsome, soft-spoken, and well-mannered. And he was wearing a flowing white *djellaba*, topped with a Bedouin *kaffiyeh*. If we looked a little startled, then I wonder how he felt being summoned to a Jewish centre to pick up somebody with the unlikely name for that neighbourhood, of O'Callaghan.

"You don't look Jewish," my wife told me.

But there have been times, given the Middle East policy of Joe Clark, when I have certainly felt Jewish, but with the added outrage only an Irishman, an unadulterated Gael, can muster.

That outrage was given extra impetus in December 1987, when the intifada in all its fury burst on to our front pages. What is significant, other than the awful toll of life and limb that resulted from the violence in the occupied territories of the West Bank and the Gaza Strip, was the hint of a disagreement between Prime Minister Mulroney and External Affairs Minister Joe Clark, on Canada's policy toward Israel. While External Affairs had deplored the harsh response of Israeli troops to stone-throwing young Arabs,

Mulroney took the view that the response was no more and no less than what was required to keep peace, order and good government.

Mulroney said he did not think the use of ammunition, resulting in at least 22 deaths in the initial stages of the intifada, violated the human rights of the Palestinians. That statement raised a few eyebrows, and not just in Clark's department.

Mulroney, for all his shoot-from-the-lip style, might have been closer to reality than those who mourned the Palestinian deaths. He had accepted what the Arab world — with the possible exception of Egypt — had not: Israel was here to stay and would defend to the last drop of Israeli blood its right to exist.

If there was only a public hint that Mulroney and Clark spoke with different voices in the Middle East, then there were several other occasions when the prime minister appeared to be yanking on his minister's chain. Even after the Gulf War, when Palestinians cheered as Scud missiles landed in Israel, Clark talked in terms of a "window" opening on the possibility of an Arab-Israeli settlement. "There's no better time to start talking with the Palestinians," said Clark. In politics, timing is everything, and Clark so often appeared to be in the wrong place at the wrong time. In his own stubborn fashion, Clark refused to give up on having Yasser Arafat and the Palestine Liberation Organization (PLO) as the spokesmen for the Palestinians wanting land for their own state in return for a lasting peace with Israel. Of the man who later shared a Nobel Peace Prize, Mulroney told the Commons that Arafat had "zero credibility."

Within the context of its times, Israel's policy on its occupied territories may not have fitted within the genteel, lace-curtain attitudes of Canada, but it had no choice but to thumb its nose at world opinion. In that harsh period of a 1980s' reality that Clark never quite understood, many Canadian Jews were unhappy over various pronouncements made by Clark, especially some ill-tempered comments he addressed to members of the Canada-Israel Committee at its national conference in Ottawa in 1988. On that occasion, he was booed, and many walked out because they felt he was unsympathetic to Israel when he took direct aim at what he alleged were human-rights violations by Israel against Palestinians in the West Bank. He followed up this attack by putting forth a policy that would have allowed low-level contacts with the PLO.

Joan, like many others, put her feelings about Clark into a letter to the prime minister on March 15, 1988. She said any role Canada undertook to play in the Middle East should start from the basic premise that Israel's survival was paramount.

"Canada should provide leadership, built on moral principle and a more knowledgeable appreciation of history," her letter read. Clark's stern lecture to Israel had fuelled to greater ferocity the anti-Semitic fires that still smoulder in parts of Canada. "Mr. Clark is ill-informed, unfit to represent Canada in a balancing position on the world scene. What he said ... has done serious damage to the Canadian Jewish community whose roots are firmly planted on Canadian soil," she wrote.

Born in Canada of Czechoslovak and Austrian Jews who fled from Europe just before Nazi Germany closed down the frontiers on the free world in 1939, Joan ended her letter this way: "We are Canadians first and foremost, not Jews, not Israelis, but we cannot forsake our race while acknowledging Canada as our home, a place where we hoped we would be eternally welcome."

(When Paul Abeles, Joan's father, was dying in Toronto in November 1989, he said to me: "Pat, you and I are both lucky. We were allowed to choose the country in which we wanted to live and we chose the best country in the world." This, from a man who arrived here with only the proverbial five dollars in his pocket and who felt that the greatest accomplishment of his long life was to bring his parents with him so that, in the fullness of time, they could die in dignity in their own beds in a free country, instead of in sorrow and shame in the unhappy land they had left behind.)

On April 27, 1988, Geoff Norquay, special advisor, policy and planning, in the prime minister's office, wrote to Joan, thanking her for expressing her concerns over recent statements by Clark on Israel. He enclosed a copy of a letter the prime minister had written on March 22 to Sydney Spivak, national chairman of the Canada-Israel Committee, reaffirming Canada's policy on the Middle East.

Spivak was told: "Canadian policy toward Israel is clear, consistent and unchanged. Israel is our friend. We believe that Israel has a right to exist in peace, to be recognized by its neighbours and to be secure. This is an unshakeable commitment."

The letter said that history provided ample evidence of the unacceptable use of terror against the Israeli people. "Throughout this too often tragic history, Canada has stood second to none in its support for Israel in its struggle to survive and prosper."

Norquay's reply to Joan — along with the copy of the prime minister's letter to Spivak — had not been received when, on April 28, 1988, the Canadian Daily Newspaper Publishers Association put on a luncheon with Mulroney as the guest speaker. I had to introduce him to a full house at a

Toronto hotel, and over lunch Joan and I had a spirited discussion with him on Israel.

"Our policy is firm and unshakeable support for Israel's right to exist," he told us, echoing the words of his letter. In that regard, Mulroney never wavered, but Clark often gave the appearance of being a slow learner.

When I spoke to the CJC in Montreal on Sept. 10, 1989, I sent Mulroney a copy of my speech, a courtesy I also extended to Clark. In a covering letter, I rather peevishly mentioned to Mulroney that I had written to Clark on April 25 to mention my personal concerns about Canada's Middle East policy and had not received so much as an acknowledgment.

Three days after writing to Mulroney, he phoned me at home in Toronto and chuckled: "You didn't have to wait from April 25 for a reply from me."

Saying that his recent invitation to Israeli President Chaim Herzog to visit Ottawa was the first time since Israel was founded that its head of state had been officially asked to visit Canada, Mulroney added: "I had to override the Establishment to bring him here."

Getting on to the subject of External Affairs, Mulroney said: "I've had a tough time with them. Not fist fights. There is a strange subculture over there. They nearly croaked when I invited the president of Israel.... People forget. A lot of people don't understand we are talking about a tiny democracy that is being ravaged. I told Herzog, 'If you are non-Jewish, you have to be Irish to understand Israel.'"

Mulroney said his position had always been that "I have the right to open my mouth and tell my friends, George Bush and Margaret Thatcher, what I think about issues concerning Canada. But I don't feel I have the right to tell Israel about national security considerations. It is their country. Our position at the United Nations has not changed."

He agreed that it was the Clark speech that "scared the Jewish community. I've been trying to rebuild things. I've got good relations with the Jewish community. The Jewish community had tears in its eyes when Herzog came and they saw the flag of the state of Israel fluttering alongside Canada's Maple Leaf on Parliament Hill."

I told him the impression I got from talking to members of the Jewish community was that they remained deeply suspicious of External Affairs. Mulroney replied: "They (Jewish leaders) tell me: 'We trust the government, but we don't trust External.'"

I reminded Mulroney of our conversation at the CDNPA luncheon when he said that Canada's policy was one of firm and unshakeable support for Israel's right to exist.

"Nothing has changed, Patrick," he replied.

And nothing ever changed very much in Clark's attitude to Middle East policy either. His departure from External — the only job he asked for in 1984, according to Mulroney — was not without joy in the Jewish community.

Clark had always had the full backing of External, the former elite of Canada's civil service, for his policy of supporting the Arab desire to force Israel into negotiating with the PLO. In private, Mulroney seethed over it. From time to time, the prime minister tried to mitigate the damage by seeking out Jewish leaders in Canada to reassure them that Ottawa did not intend to abandon the stance of "firm and unshakeable support for Israel's right to exist."

A senior Arab diplomat was once asked what he told his government at home about seemingly contradictory statements about Canada's Middle East policy.

Said the diplomat: "I send the comments of Mr. Mulroney. Then I send the comments of Mr. Clark. And then I send another cable and tell them to figure it out for themselves."

When Canada's history is examined, it is not surprising why so many Jewish people have had reservations about Canada's attitude toward Israel. More than half a century ago, Canada turned away a boatload of Jewish refugees trying to find sanctuary from the coming Holocaust[96]. Since the Second World War, successive governments had steadfastly refused to investigate or prosecute Nazi criminals thriving under Canadian freedom. (As late as 1995, Justice Minister Alan Rock announced the government was going to move to expel a number of suspected Nazis who had lied about their pasts in order to obtain Canadian citizenship. His department had a list of at least 12 of these people.)

Because of Canada's hazy approach to possible Nazi sympathizers and war criminals, Simon Wiesenthal[97] always refused to set foot in Canada.

Some years ago, Canada set up a commission of inquiry, headed by Justice Jules Dechênes[98], to examine evidence suggesting there were still many murderous Nazis living out their lives happily in Canada. Only four or five minor prosecutions ensued, and that despite the identification of dozens of these criminals.

Mulroney explained it to me this way: "(Pierre)Trudeau was minister of justice and prime minister for 20 years and had full personal knowledge of all this (the revelations that former Nazis were still at large in Canada) and he did nothing about it. When I got the information, I set up a royal commission immediately. I did it, despite having a large Ukrainian caucus to contend with and a Ukrainian justice minister (Ramon Hnatyshyn)."[99]

The Dechênes Commission apart, there is good reason for many Jewish people, a great number of whom are either Holocaust survivors or the family of Holocaust victims, to wonder if there isn't still a latent strain of anti-Semitism in the makeup of this nation. They look at such people as Ernst Zündel and Jim Keegstra and Malcolm Ross, hatemongers and peddlers of the myth that the Holocaust never took place.

Not far from Keegstra's Eckville, in the lonely forested area of Caroline, Alta., lived Terry Long, who attracted some attention with anti-Semitic recorded phone messages. He claimed an association with the Aryan Nations, a dangerous outlaw group of American racists. He was a brooding and not very bright woodsman, but he and his followers bear watching because of their devilish concoction of racial hatred and fraudulent Christian fundamentalism.[100]

Another twisted fugitive from reality was an Ron Gostick, Welsh-born to Canadian parents and Alberta-raised, who returned to his roots in 1989. He moved the incongruously named Canadian League of Rights (CLR) from Flesherton, Ont., right into the heart of Joe Clark country — High River. Gostick made a living out of peddling racist trash for almost half a century. His group was linked to anti-Semetic U.S. organizations. It offered assistance to speakers who denied the Holocaust took place. It supplied Keegstra, the poisoner of child minds, with material for use in his classroom diatribes on the so-called Jewish plot to take over the world.

Gostick's anti-Semitism sprang from a deep well. He was a throwback to William Aberhart and the original bigots of Alberta's Social Credit movement of the 1930s. His mother, a one-time secretary to Aberhart, was a Social Credit MLA. Not only did Gostick get his twisted view of life at his mother's knee, but Aberhart was his principal at Crescent Heights School in Calgary.

Gostick said he moved his printing shop to High River to be in the vanguard of the "constitutional revolution" he expected to hit the West in the coming decade. He published a weekly newspaper called *On Target*, and a monthly publication called the *Canadian Intelligence Service* – an oxymoron if I ever heard one.

Gostick may be a sick joke, left over from a tide of anti-Semitism that has long since receded from Alberta, but he and his kind still represent a danger to democracy.[101]

***

Joan and I were in Bordeaux in the spring of 1990, attending the wide assembly of the International Press Institute. On one of the panels, two mayors, Catherine Trautmann of Strasbourg and Michel Noir of Lyons, joined forces in condemning Jean-Marie Le Pen, the leader of an ultra-right-wing movement that was showing surprisingly strong popular appeal in France. This panel discussion was held a couple of days before the desecration and violation of 34 graves in Carpentras cemetery, the oldest Jewish graveyard in France. Le Pen's anti-Semitic rhetoric was blamed for igniting this outrage. The issue of Le Pen's anti-Semitism had not been resolved, Trautmann said. This nationalist, Nazi-type ideology had not been defused. Le Pen was a racist, a "democratic political monster," she said.

On the day Joan and I left Paris for home, close to 100,000 men and women, including President François Mitterand, took to the streets of the French capital to show their disgust over the Carpentras affair.

There is no room in a civilized society for another Carpentras. But the fires of anti-Semitism have not gone out, and as long as they smoulder and smoke somewhere in the world, the Holocaust must not be forgotten.

# CHAPTER 32

I once got a letter addressed to me as the First President of the Republic of Canada West. The letter said: "Dear Mr. President, I expect you to straighten out that patently absurd nonsense with Quebec. You should not give consideration to their plea to join our republic."

But before I could get used to that presidential aura, I got a letter from a Louisville pastor that said quite simply: "I pray for the day when men of your calibre are no longer in authority or a place of public influence."

So there you have it, and the public at large has still not decided what role a publisher and his/her newspaper must play.

Stripped of its lofty aspirations and its noble intent, the newspaper is basically a creature of free enterprise dedicated to maximizing profits for its shareholders.

However, there is one vital difference between a newspaper and all other commercial undertakings. Newspapers — jealously guarding the freedom of speech they have enjoyed since the late 17th century when they said goodbye to the British Restoration monarchs and their attempts at state censorship — have made themselves totally independent of government.

Unlike broadcasting, the newspaper needs no licence to operate. Because it values this freedom — the freedom that is no more and no less the guaranteed right of every individual Canadian citizen — the newspaper fights with its full arsenal of editorial bombast against any encroachment by government into how it conducts its affairs. Because they have an almost obsessive disdain for government of any ilk, newspapers, financially ailing or otherwise, have spurned attempts by government to fund them, as was attempted through the aborted Newspaper Act that followed the report of the Kent Commission. Such rejections of sugar-coated lollipops have never stopped governments from challenging independence of the press. Within living memory, there have been two major public inquiries into the role the press plays in our lives — Keith Davey's Special Senate Committee on the Mass Media and the Royal Commission on Newspaper chaired by Tom Kent.

A newspaper has to live with its own conscience, not the dictates of politicians. Governments are not alone in failing to understand that logic.

Every special-interest group wrapped in the self-righteousness of its own beliefs is firmly convinced it has, or should have, special access to the news columns of any newspaper.

The cozy relationship between politicians and the press was evident in the days when Canada's newspapers were struggling to form their own identities. The time when political parties owned their own newspapers is now happily behind us, much to the dismay of many politicians of all stripes who feel that, as a public service, newspapers should give unvarnished news of government programs and policies. Those who advocate that view have carelessly forgotten how dictatorships imposed their wills when there was nobody to challenge the truth or accuracy of what was being forced upon captive peoples.

In the process, it is fair to conclude the press has lost all respect for our democratic institution of Parliament. It was that lack of respect that finally forced the departure of Brian Mulroney and brought the Tory party to its knees. While examples of what caused that disrespect are boundless, one should suffice to make a point: the leak of the 1989 federal budget. The document, allegedly stolen, fell into the hands of a television reporter. It is obvious the government was aware that there was more than one leak. Such a leak could have led to fortunes being made if it had been exploited by those who know the stock market, or if the document had fallen into the hands of those without business ethics or morals.

Day after day, the House of Commons was misled by the government, which was never prepared to admit what it really knew. Half-truth was piled upon half-truth, innuendo upon rumour. Character assassination was the daily order of business in the Commons. Nobody came out of it with dignity, and the sad fact is that somewhere we have lost the honour, decency and truth that should be the hallmarks of government of the people by the people.

Along with politicians and special-interest groups, business is another segment of society that seems to be permanently disgruntled with the press. One of Canada's leading businessmen, Sen. Trevor Eyton[102], firmly believes business gets unfair press. In 1989, when I was spending a year at Ryerson University's School of Journalism, I persuaded Eyton to explain his views to a class of my students. By and large, Eyton said, newspaper stories on business matters are timely and accurate, but they lack balance, research and analysis. The inference to be drawn by his audience of skeptical students, it seemed, was that through ignorance of complex subjects, lack of timely research, bias or prejudice, the press does not treat business fairly.

Chief executive officers are secretive by nature. They fear that anything they say might be used against them by a competitor, or by their customers, or by a consumers' association, government or human rights organization, or by all those myriad of Crown-appointed do-gooders and watchdogs who start with the premise that the very business of earning a profit might be somewhat immoral or heartless, to say the least. They can't understand why newspapers don't mind their own business, while forgetting that a newspaper's first obligation is to all its readers, not to the shareholders of a particular company.

A newspaper is in the information business. It exists because men and women have a certain curiosity about what is happening in the world and, for a few cents a day, some of that curiosity is rewarded with facts and comment. A newspaper is not an arm of government. It is not a propaganda platform for politicians, or a booster club for overpaid baseball stars. It has no mandate to force-feed the reader, no matter how silver the spoon employed for those otherwise unwilling to eat. It will try to encourage its readers to be more involved in the world around them and in the issues that exercise the conscience and well-being of that world, but it cannot splash water from its trough into the mouth of a reluctant horse.

An example of the distrust both politicians and businessmen hold for the press, and the press's matching distrust of politicians and businessmen, was clearly the root from which sprang the Canadian Journalism Foundation.

With funding from the Jackman Foundation and the Southam Foundation, the Niagara Institute initiated a study of the media after a series of in-camera interviews that took place across the country, but mostly in Central Canada, in the spring of 1988. (By way of explanation, the Southam Foundation was a Southam family service that was totally independent of the Southam Newspaper Group.)

The original list of participants included: Trevor Eyton; Bill Dimma, then deputy chairman of Royal LePage; John

Fisher, president of Southam Inc; Dennis Patterson, government leader in the Northwest Territories; Harry Rogers, deputy minister in the department of regional industrial expansion in Ottawa; Bob Fleming, president of Robert Fleming International Research Inc; Eric Jackman, chairman of the Jackman Foundation; Paddy Sherman, president of the Southam Newspaper Group; Arnold Edinborough, author, editor and journalist; Hugh Winsor of the *Globe and Mail*; Elly Alboim, Ottawa bureau chief for CBC; Peter Desbarats, dean of the graduate school of journalism at the University of Western Ontario; and Bill Wilton, director of the Niagara Institute.

Others who came and went at various times included: Mickey Cohen, once a powerful Ottawa mandarin and later president of Molson Breweries; John Honderich, editor and later publisher of the *Toronto Star*; Neville Nankivell, publisher of the *Financial Post*; Bob Lewis of *Maclean*'s magazine; and Stephen Bindman of Southam News and then president of the Centre for Investigative Journalism.

I attended most of the meetings, delegated by Sherman to take the places of John Fisher and Sherman himself. From the start, I was recognized as the token dissident, a necessary evil, given the Southam Foundation's initial financial help. The views I expressed were my own, not necessarily those of Southam.

Following the seminar of June 1988, the Niagara Institute produced a working paper, dated July 7. That report raised concerns about the media's balance, accuracy, professionalism, ethics, agenda-setting, scarce resources and accountability. None of this was surprising, given that the people interviewed or taking part in the first seminar were, by and large, involved in industry and government, two sectors of society that are generally suspicious of the media. They could not understand why the media is not a booster of business and the institutions that supposedly serve this democratic society. The undertone of the working paper was that these cynical critics wanted a tamed and subservient media. In the circumstances, the whole exercise was based on an impossible supposition.

While the initiative was originally undertaken by the Niagara Institute, it soon became evident that one of the prime movers was Eric Jackman (brother of Hal Jackman, Ontario's lieutenant governor from 1991 to 1997), who was convinced the media had done a lousy job in its coverage of government and business. The Southam Foundation bowed out, leaving most of the funding to the Jackman Foundation. Brascan, through the influence of Eyton, also provided financial assistance.

One of the more vocal critics of the media — and it soon became obvious that when the group talked about the "media," what it really had in mind was the newspaper business — was Eyton. Another constant and persistent critic of the newspapers proved to be Alboim. Because of his carping comments, he proved to be the darling of the Jackman-Eyton set, and he figured prominently in the subsequent committees that were set up.

By 1989, from all of this hot air, emerged an organization called the Canadian Journalism Foundation/La Fondation pour le Journalisme Canadien. Knowlton Nash[103] became its first chairman, and an interim working budget of $100,000 was approved. The Jackman Foundation undertook to provide that sum, on the understanding that further funding of about $500,000 would have to be solicited. A nominating committee was formed to search for an executive director and to prepare a list of candidates for the board of governors.

At one meeting, in response to the foundation's summary of activities, I remarked rather caustically that all it had established was that the foundation's movers and shakers formed an elitist special-interest group, drawn mainly from the ranks of business and government, and was by no means representative of the general audience newspapers were supposed to serve.

The foundation came forward with three main proposals: professional development in the media; media awards; and media research.

The foundation wanted to find some Canadian equivalent of the American Pulitzer prize, but began to step on the toes of such long-established organizations as the National Newspaper Awards (NNA) and the Michener Awards. My concerns grew as the foundation talked of some joint print-broadcast award that would take the place of both the NNA and the broadcast equivalent. I did not feel print and broadcast could co-exist in this fashion. The foundation was rebuffed when it made a pitch to the Michener organizers to take over that prestigious award, whose "godfather" was Roland Michener, the late governor general. I had opposed the proposal to try and sell the Michener on the advantages of a joint award — this was hardly surprising as I had been a director of the Michener almost since its inception.

My biggest beef with the three main proposals drawn up by the Canadian Journalism Foundation was the consideration being given to a media research centre to be based at the University of Western Ontario (UWO) under the control of Peter Desbarats. I pointed out that this was the same watchdog agency proposed by the Kent Commission and rejected in total by the newspaper industry. The Desbarats equivalent had been funded with $500,000 from the Liberal government just days before it fell in 1984. That grant of $500,000 had come after a sales pitch done on Ottawa by Desbarats, the architect through the Kent Commission, for an agency to "monitor and report on the social responsibility function of Canada's mass media." Desbarats had got the UWO to match the government's $500,000 but that mass media centre, despite its $1-million inheritance is virtually dormant. That Kent Commission agency had been soundly booted out the front door and here it was being ushered in once again via the back door by Desbarats. That word *monitoring* was really a euphemism for finding a method of bringing newspapers under control of the Establishment.

As for the proposal for professional development, it was too nebulous to take seriously. One proposal along these lines put forward by Elly Alboim was priced at $10 million by Mickey Cohen and seemed to be a Canadian version of the American Press Institute (API) at Reston, Va.

Both the monitoring agency and the Canadian version of API had been discussed at earlier meetings in Niagara-on-the-Lake and, I thought, ruled out. Somebody behind the scenes was obviously trying to resurrect both.

A working group was appointed for plotting future strategies, and this was to consist of Stephen Bindman, Eric Jackman, Elly Alboim as chairman, and Peter Desbarats. But Desbarats withdrew his name after my remarks linking his pitch for funding for a monitoring agency to his connections with the Kent Commission. He was replaced on the working group by Stuart Adam of Carleton's School of Journalism. Adam had tried to breathe life into the UWO monitoring agency.

My last official contact with the foundation was at the Dec. 7 meeting of the Media Advisory Committee. The Canadian Journalism Foundation appeared to be getting along fine without me. From the start, I was not on the same wavelength because I believe a free press should steer clear of all those who want to bring it under the Establishment's heel. I don't want to see such freedom nibbled to death by self-interest groups who loudly proclaim in sanctimonious tones that they have the newspaper's best interests at heart.

In one letter, Bill Wilton, director of the Niagara Institute, declared that what the group wanted was a newspaper that would "render credibility to Canada's major institutions." That is a thinly veiled code to describe a newspaper that is under the control of an institution with all vitality sucked out of it. If "Canada's major institutions" have fallen into disrepute, as Wilton seemed to suggest, it is not because of an overly cynical press, but because of the actions of those major institutions that deserve such condemnation.

The erratically brilliant writer Dorothy Parker[104] was once thrown out of San Simeon, home of William Randolph Hearst[105], because she had violated one of Hearst's rules that there should be no love-making between unmarried couples. As she left, with thoughts of Marion Davies, Hearst's film-star mistress, in mind, she wrote these lines in the San Simeon visitors' book:

*Upon my honor,*
*I saw a Madonna*
*Standing in a niche,*
*Above the door*
*Of the famous whore*
*Of a prominent son of a bitch.*

Perhaps when politicians and business tycoons stop referring to publishers and editors of newspapers as "sons of bitches," then we will know we are doing something wrong.

# CHAPTER 33

The Thomsonization of Southam, distressingly inevitable though it was, spelled the end of more than a century of localized autonomy for the publishers under generally benevolent and gentlemanly family guidance from Toronto.

Seven years after that process began, for the first time in 115 years, the board went outside the family circle in the spring of 1992 to find its new president. When John Fisher, great-grandson of founder William Southam, decided it was time for him to go, there was no other Southam in sight considered worthy of carrying on the family tradition. The board turned to William Ardell, a man with no Southam family ties through blood or marriage, and no newspaper experience.

Confusion caused by a combination of disturbing circumstances arising from the untimely death of Gordon Fisher from liver cancer in 1985 was the spark that caused the massive changes in Southam's publishing tradition. At that time, St. Clair Balfour, former president of Southam and the son of a granddaughter of founder William Southam, had already stepped down as chairman on reaching the age limit of 75. No logical successor had been groomed to replace his cousin, Gordon Fisher, as president or as chairman. All of a sudden, Southam was seen as leaderless and a prime target for takeover. The investment sharks began to gather, urged on to a blood lust by the industry analysts who said Southam was under-performing as a company.

The frantic search for a suitable person to take over the helm was left in the hands of a committee headed by Hugh Hallward, Gordon Fisher's brother-in-law. This committee sent a letter to the officers of Southam, Southam Communications, Southam Printing, Coles Book Stores and Dittler Brothers (an American company then owned by Southam) asking for suggested candidates. It also urged those receiving the letter to volunteer their own names, if they wished. This notion was not so much democratically inspired as intended to soothe a few giant-sized egos, in and out of the publisher ranks.

In a letter to Hallward dated Aug. 19, 1985, I ruled myself out. "I have no illusions on that score," I said. "My feeling is that if your search committee came up with a 'short' list of 1,000 names, mine would be 1,001 on your list. Put it down to the realities of frustration, or the frustrations of reality; it makes no difference."

In the end, the search committee found what it was looking for right under its own nose. Gordon Fisher's older brother, John. He was installed as president of Southam Inc. He had been running a small newsprint company in New Brunswick, but was steeped by osmosis in the family newspaper tradition and philosophy.

In the meantime, Balfour was acting as ringmaster, rounding up the family shareholders to show a totally united front for perhaps the first time in the 20th century. It was Balfour who orchestrated the new family alliance, and it was Balfour who scared off the sharks when he and Beland Honderich worked out the terms of a Torstar-Southam arrangement that gave Southam a 30 per cent interest in Torstar and Torstar 20 per cent of Southam in return. There was a five-year freeze on the partners disposing of their shares; thus, a hostile takeover of Southam was avoided.

John Fisher took over in the most difficult of times, and his own personal goal was to safeguard the family's interests. Nobody made it easy for him, but he had a pretty gritty nature to go with a well-developed sense of family pride. The writing was on the wall even before he arrived, and it could best be summed up by the statements expressed at a meeting of shareholders that had been called to make certain changes in the bylaws intended to act as a shark repellent against takeover.

One of Canada's leading professional money managers, Stephen Jarislowsky, who represented 982,665 shares — and that was before a four-for-one split — put it this way: "Why are we here? We are here because our stock price is so low as to attract attention from people outside. We are here because our earnings haven't been good enough in terms of what they could be, and our properties are more valuable than what they earn. Otherwise, if that wasn't the case, nobody would be interested to make a takeover bid because the shares would sell too high. What was the response of the board to this situation? Well, they indicate first that all the newspapers we have continue to operate on the type of basis which they are operating, namely, free press, free editors, free publishers. I share that, as long as they earn enough money."

One who got that message loud and clear was Balfour. In a letter dated Nov. 22, 1985, commending me on a speech that I made to all 700 *Herald* employees to explain what was happening with the company, he added: "I'm glad you quoted Jarislowsky — he's dead right. We have a responsibility to our readers, our customers, our employees and our shareholders. There are instances where we have spent money unnecessarily in pursuit of quality, ignoring the law of diminishing returns on that investment."

Those weren't exactly my sentiments. My feelings could best be summed up in the words of Abe Rosenthal, famous executive editor of the *New York Times.* Asked how the *Times* coped with an economic crunch in the 1970s that threatened its very existence, Rosenthal said: "There are two ways the *Times* could have gone, like a lot of other businesses that face the same problem. It could have put more water in the soup or more tomatoes in the soup. And the business decision at the *Times* was to put a lot more tomatoes in the soup."

Over the years, by putting more tomatoes in the soup, I had managed to make more money for Southam shareholders than any other publisher up to that time. And I had done so in two competitive cities, Edmonton and Calgary, without yielding an inch to either of the *Sun* tabloids. For instance, in 1985, when all these storm warnings were being hoisted, the *Calgary Sun* had gained only 157,700 lines of advertising over the previous year, while the *Herald* added 1,250,000 more lines.

By January 1986, John Fisher was getting a feel for the company, and his first major move was to set up a separate division for the newspapers. The choice of Paddy Sherman, publisher of the *Ottawa Citizen*, as president of the Southam Newspaper Group, was one I welcomed initially because Sherman was a tough, outstanding journalist and I did not want to see the newspapers fall into the hands of anyone with no track record in journalism. With Sherman, I reasoned, the newspapers would have their own champion at head office, where there was nobody with newspaper-working experience. He would understand the concerns of the publishers and editors, something Ardell clearly did not. Despite his many years running the *Province*, Southam's perpetual bath of red ink, Sherman had breathed journalistic life into the *Citizen* in

Ottawa while providing shareholders with more than a decent return for their investment.

I have always respected Sherman's editorial talents, although he rarely socialized with fellow scribblers and publishers. My fond wish — as expressed in a letter to him dated Jan. 30, 1986 — that Southam would finally face up to the reality of having newspapers run by newspaper people without undue head office interference, was not fulfilled.

Fisher, in order to appease the family, the analysts and the Jarislowsky money men, decided to batten down the hatches. He set a goal for the newspapers of 15 per cent return on revenue. Sherman, with David Perks — later publisher of the *Montreal Gazette* — as his accounting hatchet man, tightened the screws. Costs were slashed and news space drastically reduced even as Sherman decreed that "quality" journalism remained the Southam goal. Jobs were eliminated, and a doleful procession of the unwanted, amounting to thousands, was shown the door through a combination of attrition, early retirement and outright layoffs. Old Mother Southam was cutting the apron strings that many long-term employees had clung to so tenaciously and faithfully over the years.

After a century of virtual autonomy — at least with the editorial product — the newspapers were now firmly under head office direction, with the power and the initiatives of the publishers miserably curtailed. Individualism was banned, replaced by group think and centralized task forces that sprouted like summer weeds in the greenest of lawns.

The days of adding tomatoes to the soup were over, and many of the newspapers took on the appearance of a bowl of thin gruel.

But that 15 per cent goal seemed as far away as ever. Indeed, in the first six months of 1988 Southam newspapers achieved only a 12.6 per cent return on revenue before tax. This is how Southam stacked up against other major North American companies in the same period:

- Thomson, 31.4 per cent;
- Dow Jones (*Wall Street Journal*), 23.9 per cent;
- *Washington Post*, 20.1 per cent;
- Affiliated (*Boston Globe* etc.), 16.8 per cent;
- Gannett, 15.1 per cent;
- *New York Times*, 14.9 per cent;
- Times Mirror, 14.4 per cent;
- Southam, 12.6 per cent;
- Knight Ridder, 12.3 per cent;
- *Toronto Sun* Group, 10.8 per cent.

Percentages, of course, can be deceiving. What might be more relevant is the amount of money each newspaper contributed to the Southam pot. For instance, in 1983, my first full year in Calgary, the *Herald* had a return of 19.7 per cent on revenues of $71,228,000. in my second year, we hit 23.3 per cent on revenues of $71,012,595. And in my third year, we dropped to 18.28 per cent, but revenues were at their highest, $73,359,000. What is far more significant, we did all that without in any way weakening the editorial product.

However, my philosophy of quality being the key to profits did not meet with favour with the new regime, driven as it was by bottom-line interests pure and simple.

It would be unfair to say Sherman surrendered his editorial soul when he went to head office. In fact, nobody could have done that difficult job better, given that the Southam tradition of editorial excellence was being sacrificed, presumably to save the company. But none of it sat too comfortably with me. There was a fundamental disagreement between Sherman and myself on the policy that should be followed in a competitive city. I felt somewhat vindicated by comparing the results obtained by Edmonton (after I had left there) and Calgary. The *Journal* followed head office's directions to the letter and slashed away madly at its costs. Its bottom line improved considerably in the short term, but then the rot set in along with the decline in quality. Both advertising and circulation took a steep nose-dive, and the *Edmonton Sun* was the beneficiary. In Calgary, I refused numerous head office entreaties and directives to follow the *Journal*'s lead and, as a result, profits remained high and the *Herald* kept the *Calgary Sun* from making absolutely any headway.

All that really proved, as I told Sherman in one of our bitter exchanges, is that the *Herald* remained on a solid foundation and the *Journal* now rested on shifting sands. "My heart bleeds for the *Journal*," I wrote to Sherman on Jan. 12, 1988, "because I know what it once was.... What a tragedy that our company suffers from accountant's tunnel vision."

Our relationship continued to deteriorate and Sherman, no slouch himself in the art of vitriolic letter-writing, had this to say to me in one missive: "I must say that I found your letter arrogant, patronizing and insulting.... But once you get involved in a defensive diatribe, there are times when your brain seems to stop working and all that comes out is smoke. Pity. Because underneath it all, you really do know better."

My objections to having publishers turned into eunuchs and "ripping the heart out of the product" brought a reply from Sherman that he recognized a proud wake for an ancient status quo when he read one.

By the end of August, wearying of my lonely rearguard action, I had given up any thoughts I might have had about soldiering on in Calgary for another two years until normal retirement age. I told Sherman: "In more than 20 years of serving Southam to the best of my capability and energy, I have never been so disillusioned. Southam can't live in the past, I know, but it shouldn't throw away all that carefully nurtured past for present gains that translate only into future losses."

Sherman was relieved that I wanted to go. He knew I wanted to be in Toronto because I was getting married there on Feb. 14, 1989, and Joan and I intended to make our home in Central Canada. He made the transition easy for me by setting up a position as Southam Travelling Professor of Journalism, attached to Ryerson University, with salary, all costs and expenses covered by Southam. At the end of 1988, I retired as publisher of the *Herald.* I had spent 48 years in active journalism.

Sherman and I, although we differed and squabbled over the philosophy and the economics of newspapers in a recessionary world, both had the best interests of Southam at heart, one supposes, but we approached those interests from different directions. He always adapted to the rules of the corporate game, but that should not be an excuse for questioning the motivation behind his style in the presidential exercise of power.

But everything comes full circle. When he retired as Southam Newspaper Group president at 62, as planned, he fully expected to remain on the Southam Inc. board and the board of Pacific Press at least until reaching the official retirement age of 65. But Fisher's replacement by Ardell changed a lot of things, and Southam devised a somewhat petty strategy to get Sherman fully out of the picture. At its 1992 annual meeting, Southam reduced the size of the board by one, and Sherman was the odd man out, the last working newspaperman on the board. (The change in direction became more evident when it is remembered that Jarislowsky, the money man, became a director of Southam.) To cap Sherman's exit, Pacific Press lost its own board in the process.

I remember the words of George Crawford, a Calgary lawyer, when he was appointed by the Southam board as interim chairman of the company on the death of Gordon Fisher in 1985. Crawford told a *Calgary Herald* reporter: "We are not about to sacrifice the quality of any of our newspapers for the purpose of increasing profitability." The publishers, he added, would continue to manage their operations largely independent of Toronto head office.

I believed you, George. Oh, yes, I believed! But something got lost in the translation.

# CHAPTER 34

One of the last impressions I took with me into retirement is that scope for exercising individuality in the running of a newspaper is not what it was when Beland Honderich was publishing the *Toronto Star* from 1966 to 1988. Honderich told a Carleton University audience after his retirement: "The role of a newspaper is to engage in the full and frank dissemination of news and opinion from the perspective of its values and particular view of society. It should report the news fairly and accurately, reflect all pertinent facts and opinions and not only what the official establishment thinks and says."

And Gordon Fisher, in rewriting a statement of corporate policy for Southam in 1972 said: "There are no rigid rules for producing a 'Southam' newspaper. Diversity and innovation are encouraged."

Contrast that with the view of Southam president William Ardell in announcing a change of direction for his group's 17 dailies in February 1995. "Southam is really going back to the basics of good newspapering" he said.

In the wake of downsizing that cost more than 1,500 their jobs in the company, Ardell said it didn't make much sense for the newspapers to remain as independent as in the past without taking advantage of a lot of the opportunities that exist within an organization of Southam's size.

"The publishers have come from a background of fierce independence and autonomy, and that certainly worked for 100-plus years," he told the *Globe and Mail*, "but we are now living in a world of rapidly moving information."

To compensate for that loss of independence and to save them a little face with the public in the communities they served, the publishers of the larger Southam dailies were upgraded on their mastheads from "vice-president and publisher" to "president and publisher." It was never explained what they were president of, because the newspapers were overwhelmingly under central control, and the publishers were certainly not presidents of Southam, unless Ardell wanted to split his authority with them. At least, as "vice-presidents," they were technically vice-presidents of the Southam Newspaper Group (SNG). However, SNG is now just a memory.

To further its centralization process, Southam appointed a vice-president of editorial at the corporate level. Publishers, who once reported directly to the chairman, president and board of Southam Inc., now came in at the lower end of the scale, reporting to a vice-president who could more carefully screen the editorial decisions that were once the sole prerogative of the publisher on his own turf. Major newsroom appointments had to go through this editorial vice-president, and this meant that instead of grooming someone for a specific executive position, the publishers could now have someone from another Southam newspaper — or from outside the company altogether — pushed by head office into senior positions; all that was left for publishers to do was rubber-stamp the appointments. The new executive was supposed to encourage such things as tighter editing, training and the development of special sections to be distributed throughout the chain. While maintaining that responsibility for serving local communities would remain with the publishers and their staff, Ardell said he wanted to seize opportunities afforded by having such a chain, such as developing national columnists or joint editorial efforts.

The last "national columnist," so designated by Southam, was Charles Lynch, operating from Ottawa. But apart from Charlie's quirky comments on federal politics, it became necessary for a number of Southam dailies to put their own correspondents in Ottawa to provide coverage of local interest that Charlie could not possibly be expected to provide. It is difficult to imagine such a thing as a "national" columnist, given the nature of the company with interests as varied as the regions themselves. Apart from the morale-lowering impact of having a "national" columnist thrust upon each newspaper, the obvious inference to be drawn from such a move is that a head office viewpoint can now take the place of the purely local commentary that is so important in trying to convince the public that editorial decisions on controversial topics are made locally.

Ardell himself did not agree that there was a risk inherent in having a "national" opinion forced upon a local paper. "There's a fountain of things that can be written about that would have national interest," he said. "We've never pooled that talent and it is extraordinary."

"Pooling of talent" has a tantalizing ring to it, but the danger is far greater than the benefits that might be gained from it. There are far too many issues of a controversial nature that mark the differences between regions; there is no national unifying factor. In the energy and constitutional wars that left Alberta isolated from mainstream thinking, the prospect of having only one point of view go out to all the Southam papers was just too painful to contemplate, even in retrospect. The *Edmonton Journal* and *Calgary Herald* under my direction took a strong Alberta position that flew in the face not only of most of the rest of the Southam group, but of the board itself. But now there was a new mechanism in place that would homogenize Southam viewpoints on all major issues. How long before a single point of view would be peddled from head office, with the board itself dictating the stance that should be taken? This has yet to happen, but the future has a habit of swallowing up noble intentions.

One of the early casualties of this new centralized approach to editorial commentary was Catherine Ford. She was moved out of her position as editor of the *Calgary Herald*'s editorial page and forced to resurface as a national columnist. The result was inevitable: in writing a column for all Southam dailies, she was forced to make it appealing to all of them by reaching positions that were compromises. She could no longer fire all her verbal guns at a single target, and this reduced the concentrated impact she would have made by confining herself to an Alberta readership. It meant that some column ideas would have to be discarded because newspapers from other parts of the country did not share an Alberta point of view, or did not understand the subject under discussion. How many readers outside of the Prairie provinces know or care what the Crow's Nest Rate[106] is about? It was not in Catherine's nature to seek a common root for all the Southam dailies. Catherine herself does not suggest she was pushed out of her editor's job because her views were too extreme, but the suspicion remains.

When Cam Cole of the *Edmonton Journal* was appointed a national sports columnist, the dismay in the *Herald*'s sports department was palpable. Edmonton and Calgary are only 322 kilometres apart. Both cities have NHL teams; both have CFL teams. There is tremendous rivalry between the two cities. Both newspapers have excellent sports departments with first-class columnists. What is paramount in the minds of readers of the *Herald* has less interest to the readers in the northern city. When the NHL's Calgary Flames meet the Edmonton Oilers, the intensity is enough to melt the ice, but the clash of these generally talented teams must be seen through different eyes. This meant that instead of a pooling of talent, as suggested by Ardell, there could be an overflow in the coverage, with neither the *Herald* nor the *Journal* satisfied with the end result. A "national" point of view introduced into the mix, with no local feeling or interest. This is no reflection on the talents of Cam Cole, a highly respected sports journalist, but instead of serving the audience the *Journal* already delivered for him, he was bound to fall between the stools of Edmonton and Calgary, pleasing no one.

"Trying to run 17 papers is sort of like trying to herd cats," Len Kubas, a respected newspaper consultant, once said. That certainly applies to the editorial end of the business, where the cats can be as fiercely independent and quarrelsome as wild Kilkenny felines, but there is more scope in other areas of the newspaper to bring about a co-operative approach to such things as advertising, circulation, accounting, computerization and technology. In those areas, Southam made great strides and was achieving efficiencies that helped the company double its profits in the 1994 calendar year. This was done despite slippage in advertising linage.

Obviously, Southam must have been doing something right, and perhaps this helps to explain why the board rewarded Ardell with a 23 per cent increase in salary to $765,197 in 1995, up from $620,000 in the previous year. His basic salary was $460,000 while he took home a performance bonus of $230,000, half of his salary, up from $200,000 the year before.

Ardell had made numerous attempts to restructure the company, especially at the head-office level, and this tended to leave the impression that he was always looking over his shoulder to reduce the risk of challenge to his authority. Soon after taking over as president, he ended the existence of SNG as a separate operating company. In the resulting shuffle, Russell Mills, who had succeeded Paddy Sherman as president of SNG, returned to the *Ottawa Citizen* as publisher. Ardell's explanation was that the old SNG structure was too unwieldy. "Russ and I talked of the danger of tripping over each other, and he said his real preference was to return to being a publisher," Ardell said.

As part of the restructuring, the newspapers were broken into two groups, with each run by newly appointed chief operating officers, who would report directly to Ardell. In this way, he said, he saw his role as being "intimately involved with strategy and direction, while the COOs would be responsible for the implementation of annual operating plans."

This reorganization meant setting up a Metro Market newspapers group, consisting of Southam's seven biggest dailies. To assist in this further intrusion into the role of the hands-on publishers, Ardell brought in Jim Armitage, president and associate publisher of the *London Free Press*, as COO of this group.

Armitage was a former management consultant, seen by many as an aggressive innovator. He startled many of the old *Free Press* regulars by turning the *Free Press* into a copycat of *USA Today*, with pint-sized stories and lots of small colour pictures. This radical redesign was a departure from the usual format of a staid daily and was intended to stop the slide in circulation. It was a change that did not appeal to London's somewhat old-fashioned readership. They liked things the way they were.

When Armitage joined Southam, there were whispers that this indicated Southam was interested in buying the *Free Press*. Southam once owned 25 per cent of the *Free Press*, but sold it back to Walter Blackburn on an amicable basis when Blackburn wanted to put a totally home-brew label on what was once an independent without outside involvement. He undertook to give Southam first refusal rights if he ever decided to sell out. When Walter died, his daughter, Martha White, took over the paper and revelled in her new-found prestige. However, the death of Martha at the age of 47 led to further public pondering over the future of the *Free Press*. Instead of offering it for sale, the family set up a new organization protecting it from predators. Therefore, the likeliest reason for Armitage's quick exit from London was not to bring the *Free Press* with him to Southam, but an acknowledgment of his personal frustration at being squeezed out altogether in London.

What Ardell overlooked in bringing Armitage on board at Southam was that, given the personality of each of them, there was bound to be the danger of a clash, something Ardell said he had wanted to avoid by sending Russ Mills back to the *Ottawa Citizen*. Armitage, quiet-spoken but unworried about stepping on the toes of the publishers, gradually began pushing his nose into areas of authority that Ardell did not want to concede to him. In effect, Armitage was too good, too hard-driving, too ambitious, perhaps too insensitive for the job he had been hired to do. The result was never in doubt: by the beginning of 1995 Armitage was gone with a handsome severance package that encouraged him not to wash any dirty linen in public. No explanation for his departure, other than the standard "pursuing new opportunities," was ever given. As salary, Armitage had been paid a total of $376,152 in 1994, down from $394,200 in 1993.

After Armitage's departure, the Metro Market Newspapers reported to Ardell, so he tightened his grip on what he saw as a necessity for getting the new-look Southam dailies into a more subservient grouping. It was doubtful if Ardell would ever again allow anyone to dog his footsteps.

The Southam company came back into play as a potential takeover target in April 1995, when shareholders voted to end its poison-pill scheme. The two likeliest bidders who might take advantage of this burgeoning possibility were obviously Conrad Black or Paul Desmarais, co-chairman of Southam. The shareholders' rights plan had been set up in 1990 to make a hostile takeover difficult. By the time it was killed, Desmarais's Power Corporation of Canada owned 21.4 per cent of Southam, and Desmarais greeted the ending of the poison-pill arrangement by saying "there are possibilities we'll increase our interest." Black's Hollinger Inc. then owned 19.4 per cent, and Black declared, "I think it's a buy."

"We're not talking about control," Mr. Desmarais said. "We have a very significant investment in the company and so does Mr. Black, and we want to make sure the investment goes well for our shareholders." That was a sentiment echoed by Black, but the air crackled in anticipation of what might happen.

Apparently standing in the way of any possible hurried expansion of Black's holdings in Southam was a rather messy newspaper war he was waging with Rupert Murdoch in Britain. As the proprietor of the *Daily Telegraph*, the best-selling of the British "quality" broadsheets, Black saw his revenues begin a rapid slide when Murdoch lowered the price of his *Times of London* first to 30 pence (65 cents) from 45 pence in September 1993, and then to 20 pence when Black cut the *Daily Telegraph* to 30 pence from 48 pence. Murdoch's strategy raised the circulation of the *Times* from 350,000 to 664,000. In the early days of the price war, the *Telegraph* had dipped below the one-million mark, but it rebounded to 1,073,000 when price adjustments were made.

But all this hit the *Telegraph*'s profits hard and the shareholders began to show their displeasure. In any newspaper battle over prices, there can be no winner if both combatants are prepared to carry the financial burden that a do-or-die strife demands. In this particular instance, Murdoch had revenue from his global empire to fall back on, while Black was stretched closer to the limits.

With the deeper pockets, Murdoch seemed happy to continue the scorched-earth struggle. In doing so, he was probably aware of one of the titanic circulation battles of all time in the 1890s between William Randolph Hearst's *New York Journal* and Joseph Pulitzer's *World*. When someone remarked to Hearst's mother that it was costing her son about a million dollars a year, Mrs. Hearst said: "Is it? Then he will only last about 30 years."

If Murdoch could reach that deep into his pockets, then Black would have to match him dollar for dollar. This he did, and to media watchers' surprise it was Murdoch who blinked first. At the end of June 1995, Black declared himself triumphant and raised the price of the *Daily Telegraph* by five cents to 25 cents. "We faced an absolutely fanatical onslaught and saw it off," Black declared. By then, the *Telegraph* had maintained and even improved its circulation slightly to 1,073,463.

Given all the vicious circulation battles in London, Black appeared less inclined in 1995 to try to increase his stake in Southam. Presumably, Desmarais was prepared to stand on the sidelines and wait for events to unfold. No matter how things appeared on the surface, the two titans of Canada's newspaper industry were unlikely to declare eternal friendship when the opportunities for expansion beckoned separately to them both. In London, Black had had the uneasy position of waiting for Murdoch to bend. In Canada, perhaps both Desmarais and Black were keeping a weather eye on each other.

At a time when Thomson was getting out of the newspaper business, Southam was travelling in the opposite direction, stripping itself of its non-newspaper properties in order to get back to the basics of newspapering. But the fragile alliance between Desmarais and Black meant that the future of Southam remained in doubt. Basic newspapering and increased profits can only be achieved by ensuring all the dailies are functioning at the highest level.

In scaling down its newspaper holdings, Thomson was obviously aware that in the days before television, newspaper proprietorship provided the key to the vault for those willing to satisfy the public's hunger for information. Those days, Thomson might have suggested, were over. If they were, then Southam's crystal ball might have been clouding over, unless Black saw a different vision than everyone else in the newspaper business[107].

# CHAPTER 35

Coming from a former chairman, it was probably close to heresy to ask the question, but did the newspaper industry need the Canadian Daily Newspaper Publishers Association (CDNPA)?

By the same token, what role was there for The Canadian Press (CP) as a newspapering organization?

Questions along those lines were given impetus by word that the presidents of both CDNPA and CP had decided to retire.

Keith Kincaid, president of CP for 17 years, surprised few people in the industry when he announced at the end of May 1995 that he had advised the CP board of his intention to end his 38-year service with the wire service at the end of the year. At the age of 60, still in robust health, Kincaid decided he'd had enough.

Notice that John Foy would "reach retirement" in April 1996, rated one line in the CDNPA's 20-page annual report for 1995. At the same time, CDNPA chairman Kevin Peterson wrote: "It is time for the association to contemplate what its future looks like and what kind of president is required for that future."

Peterson said: "At its April meeting, the board agreed that this is an appropriate time to take a look at the overall structure of newspaper industry associations and what would best serve our interests in the near future. CDNPA will be approaching the Newspaper Marketing Board (NMB) to seek co-operation in a study that will examine whether current industry structures are appropriate or whether they need to be altered. As part of that report, we will also ask what kind of leadership is required for whatever structures we choose to adopt."

All of which was long overdue. In a sense, a merger between CDNPA and NMB was no different than the merger that took place in 1991 between the American Newspaper Publishers Association and the Newspaper Advertising Bureau. The Americans, more than 10 times bigger than Canada's newspaper industry, recognized the economies in scale that could be accomplished in such a merger. We were a bit slower on the uptake.

In a membership survey done for CDNPA by the Boston consultants Chris Urban and Associates and dated March 30, 1989, CDNPA was criticized by various publishers as being reactive rather than proactive. This comment from the report was fairly typical: "As the years progress, you sit back and ask, 'What is it really giving me for the years I'm putting in?' It's really an old boys' club."

Another publisher (all such comments were anonymous in the report) said: "I think there's a need for an enormous amount of change, and there's really no person, vehicle or organization that's really leading it.... Good, aggressive, innovative people don't operate well in that milieu."

Another publisher quoted by Urban said: "What CDNPA is to me is a general meeting once a year, the wives come, we have these long meetings; it seems to me that there are a lot of cobwebs on the wall."

Still another commented: "They're about the best-kept secret in the world. We are an industry which could take a leadership position and we rarely do."

The major flaw in Urban's report was that it did not address the future of CDNPA. Urban was never asked to determine if CDNPA had any sort of role to play in these rapidly changing times in the newspaper industry. Task forces were set up to plot the revitalization of CDNPA but all such good intentions to pump some life into CDNPA were lost in a bog of obfuscation, the usual treatment at CDNPA head office for anything that might question the organization's own dull past or need for change. Six or seven years after Chris Urban completed her study, CDNPA settled back into its interrupted slumber with no one having the faintest idea of what it was supposed to be or do. In the face of the old stonewall treatment, the Urban report was quietly and discreetly shelved.

According to its own profile, as printed in 1994, CDNPA was a non-profit organization, representing more than 80 daily newspapers (English and French) with circulations ranging from less than 5,000 to more than 500,000 per day. Membership represented 87 per cent of all dailies in Canada.

Founded in 1919[108] as a clearing house for general business information among newspapers, CDNPA was involved from the start in lobbying the federal government on newspaper matters, and dealt with national advertisers and agencies. It had grown to encompass five divisions — advertising, circulation, editorial, marketing services, and operations. But how well were those key areas of the newspaper being served?

The two most traumatic events in the life of CDNPA were the Keith Davey Special Senate Commission on the Mass Media (set up on March 18, 1969) and Tom Kent's Royal Commission on Newspapers, which issued its final report on July 1, 1981.

The meddling mischief of the Davey Commission so spooked CDNPA that, in order to avoid the possibility of government intervention, it dropped like a hot potato the major role it had once played in soliciting advertising for its members. This action was taken when the Davey Committee declared there was an apparent conflict of interest between news and advertising contained in such an operation. As a result, small newspapers and the single-ownership independents were left with no national advertising sales body. To fill that gap, various advertising organizations sprang into being. Through the initiative of Beland Honderich and Southam, the Metro Market group was set up; it was to some extent "elitist" in that it restricted membership to the major market newspapers and excluded all Thomson dailies. The Thomson response was to spearhead something called ABCDN — the initials, so far as I can tell, stood for Advertising Bureau for Canadian Daily Newspapers. Gradually ABCDN drowned in its own alphabet soup, and other selling groups such as the Newspaper Marketing Bureau came on the scene. In addition, the major groups — Southam, Thomson, Torstar and the *Toronto Sun* — also developed their own highly proficient selling arms for their own newspapers.

All that was left of CDNPA's high-flying advertising force of the early 1960s was a statistical linage service for member newspapers.

Throughout the nightmare of the Kent years, the official voices of the biggest newspaper groups — Southam and Thomson —were effectively silenced when the two groups were charged with collusion in the closing of the *Winnipeg Tribune* and the *Ottawa Journal.* So the defence of the free press came not from the major newspaper owners, but from the "hired hands."

In a letter to me when all the Kent dust had settled, Gordon Fisher said: "It is a good time to recognize and acknowledge the wonderful contribution that you made as chairman of CDNPA in fighting the industry's fight. It was always clear to me that it was highly desirable that the industry's principal spokesman on this issue should be a publisher rather than a corporate chief executive officer. That the publisher in question should have been from Southam and chairman of the industry association was doubly fortunate."

The only purpose in quoting that letter at this time is to make a point: the war against Kent and the Trudeau government's assault on a free press was waged by individual publishers — others besides me, of course — and not by CDNPA management. In matters involving industry associations and their brushes with government, the rules are quite simple: the board gives direction, and the ammunition needed for the fray is provided by paid management. In the case of the Kent commission, CDNPA head office was missing in action. It reported faithfully, of course, to its members — after the battle had been waged and won by the publishers themselves. All the initiatives taken, letters written, the speeches made, the delegations to Ottawa, the articles published, the interviews given, were by publishers from the newspapers, sometimes acting in concert but generally alone.

From the start of its existence, according to CDNPA's own profile, "it undertook discussions with the federal government and dealt with national advertisers and agencies." Originally, that mandate was scrupulously followed, but in looking at the history of CDNPA it was clear it had lost its way in both regards — as a lobbyist of government and as a major contributor to the newspapers' advertising relationship. Its crystal ball was clouded; instead of anticipating change, it reacted to it.

The CDNPA board was on the right track in 1995 when it began exploring the possibility of some form of association or merger with the NMB. Such a merger was long overdue.

The sensitivity toward the independence of the news-gathering part of the industry precluded CDNPA from getting too actively involved in editorial. In this area, CDNPA best served by remembering its own definition of itself as a clearing house for information. If those who run the newsrooms of the nation want to talk on the philosophy or practical purposes of newsgathering, they had the Canadian Managing Editors Conference as the forum in which to do it. And CP was of far more significance than CDNPA for editorial people and publishers. CDNPA, however, did get involved in some training seminars, usually with the support of Ryerson or other schools of journalism.

The circulation managers had their own association and generally didn't have much involvement with, or support from, CDNPA. However, in recognizing that declining readership was the major problem facing the industry, most of Canada's dailies missed a golden opportunity to reach new audiences through their Newspaper in Education (NIE) programs. The NIE program wilted almost into disuse at a time when it was never needed more. Thomson showed its lack of faith in CDNPA's NIE programs by bringing in its own co-ordinator/consultant from the United States.

In the key area of human resources, the groups and the major newspapers generally went their own way and did not look to CDNPA for guidance.

In going through all the major facets of the newspaper industry — advertising, editorial, circulation, marketing, human resources, production, administration, communications, industrial relations, forward planning — it was fairly obvious CDNPA had lost all relevancy. In most of those areas, CDNPA did no more than duplicate services already provided to newspapers by their ownership groups.

CDNPA was a noted paper shuffler. The paper flowed out of Toronto straight into wastebaskets and recycling bins at most Canadian newspapers.

*Globe and Mail* columnist Terence Corcoran spoke in contemptuous terms of CDNPA in his column of May 3, 1995. "Canada's newspaper publishers, it must be remembered," he wrote, "collectively have a shaky reputation in matters that relate to their own affairs. Possibly the CDNPA's most famous self-embarrassment came during the GST (goods and services tax) debate. Every industry had a special reason to be excluded from the tax, but nobody matched the CDNPA for sheer self-indulgent overreach. Armed with a commissioned brief from a high-powered constitutional lawyer, the CDNPA claimed that if the tax were applied to newspapers, it would represent a threat to freedom of the press. Today, five years after the tax was introduced, the CDNPA for some reason has never followed up that opinion with a GST court challenge."

The contrast between CDNPA and CP was all the more striking despite the fact that these were tough times financially for CP. Keith Kincaid, a dynamic technocrat, guided the news-gathering organization through rough waters with a sure touch. Its total budget was more than $50 million. He remained optimistic about the future of CP, pointing out that it was well positioned as communications technology evolved because news agencies disseminate information almost instantly. "Newspapers have got a very good future if they can properly identify their market and have the right business plan in place," Kincaid told the 1995 annual meeting of CP.

Founded in 1917 as a service in English to daily newspapers across Canada, The Canadian Press added a full service in French in 1951 through La Presse Canadienne. CP first provided news for English-language broadcast in 1933 and for French-language broadcast in 1945. Fifty years later, through its wholly owned Broadcast News, it provided audio and print service to more than 600 radio and television stations and cable TV systems, delivered by satellite. CP's picture service began in 1948 and went on to deliver nearly 1,000 colour and black-and-white photos a week, in condensed digital form, from Canada and abroad via satellite network.

CP has editorial bureaus in more than 14 major cities in Canada. It has full-time bureaus in Washington and London. Its overseas news is complemented by reports from The Associated Press and Reuters. It employs more than 460 people.

Reporters and editors write and edit on video display terminals (this was in 1995). Portable terminals enable reporters to feed stories to the system from remote locations. Individual newspapers send their stories to CP electronically for editing and transmission elsewhere. News wires, distributed by satellite, are tailored to the needs of the newspapers and broadcasters. Large newspapers receive about 300 columns of news a day from CP along with 120 photos. CP also provides columns of agate (small type) material for stocks and sports pages, editorial material to be used in advertising supplements and other services requested by its member newspapers and client broadcasters.

The Kincaid years were years of growth, always keeping up to date with new technology and changing trends. CP was a service respected worldwide. Its strong point, of course, was its blanket coverage of Canada. This meant that wherever there was a CP paper, there would be a source for news to go to the smallest and largest of Canada's newspapers.

However, times were changing. With Southam setting up its own news transmission service, it was in a position to provide a rapid exchange of Southam specials and exclusives. There was a growing desire on the part of Southam to put its own "national" or "Southam" stamp on all its papers. While this was bound to have a negative effect on the local autonomy of the Southam dailies, it also represented a challenge to CP's dominance in the field. CP had weathered such challenges before. When Doug Creighton was at his boldest, willing to take on the world, he poured money into United Press Canada (UPC) in the hope it would bring CP to its knees, but in the end his *Toronto Sun* organization had to acknowledge UPC could not compete with CP. However, the Southam approach was somewhat different to that of UPC. It had the corporate funds to sustain it. No matter how good Southam News was, it could not replace CP. It always had to be a complementary and exclusive speciality analytical service.

The Davey report described the Southam service as the "Cadillac of the news service business." Even Tom Kent had kind things to say about it. When he and I debated the Kent Commission at the University of Calgary, he compared Southam and Thomson in this way: "Southam is still largely a newspaper company and it spends, on Southam News Service and the like, millions of dollars a year that make for better quality papers but which it could not spend if it were a Thomson-type conglomerate, more interested in generating cash for further acquisitions to the corporate empire." If Southam is the Cadillac, then CP is the sturdy working wagon. There was no doubt of it, but CP and Southam had to share the same thoroughfare.

However, the impact of Southam at a time when CP's members were reluctant to increase funding for the premier news service put a tight grip on the growth of CP. It took a deft balancing act by Kincaid to keep CP not only solvent but efficient.

Although CP did not come on the scene until 1917, it should be remembered that wire services in general had been around a lot longer than that. The necessity for some means of speeding up getting news from the battle fronts was painfully obvious because handwritten "dispatches from the front" could take weeks to reach the newspapers. The reporter with the army abroad was on the spot, watching the guns roar and dying men scream in agony as history was written in blood. He had no telegraph service to help him. In its Nov. 14, 1854 edition, the *Times of London* carried a graphic account of the futile charge of the Light Brigade from the man whom many regard as the first professional war correspondent, William Howard Russell. Other than that, reporting of wars and battles was more likely to come from letters sent from the front by junior officers. The accuracy of such reports was questionable. One such correspondent, soon after war with Russia broke out in the Crimea, kept a journal of the siege of Constantinople but did not bother to send any word of it back to the newspaper until the siege was over.

After the British Education Act of 1870 made it compulsory for every child to be taught to read, the newspaper audience grew rapidly as the number of British newspapers doubled between 1880 and 1900. With the growing use of the telegraph came also the founding of a news agency, The Associated Press (AP), and an AP correspondent showed up with Custer at Little Big Horn. The founder of Reuters chose carrier pigeons to report on the siege of Paris in 1870.

The British newspapers set up their own co-operative service, Press Association, pooling their money and resources to get a full flow of copy from all corners of the British Isles. Britain took over the Reuter service for its international coverage. The United States, having pioneered the way with The Associated Press, had a rich and growing market for its own news. The United Press (UP) followed. France had Agence France-Presse (AFP).

The agencies have proliferated, with various major newspapers setting up their own services. Southam News Service began as a service to Southam papers only but then went on to sell its wares to any newspaper willing to pay for them. However, the major benefit of a co-operative like CP is that, through its members it covers most of the Canadian landscape, something no individual newspaper could afford.

To put all of that in perspective, the wire services provide millions of words daily from which their clients can pick and choose their own requirements. These words pour into newsrooms mainly by satellite these days, but there was a time when CP provided its material on a tape that was then fed into the Linotype machines to produce molten lead slugs. These "high-speed" Linotypes could handle all of seven lines a minute, flat out.

Under Kincaid's driving force, the news that filled Canadian dailies arrived via a highly sophisticated delivery system.

Comparing CP with CDNPA, it was evident the difference between the two major organizations stemmed from leadership patterns, in the one case always ahead of events and in the other sadly lacking. CP always kept abreast of the industry's needs, more often anticipating necessary change before its own members recognized the need. CDNPA, on the other hand, moved to the pace of its own death march, ponderous and outdated. The irony was that the boards of both organizations were drawn from the same pool of publishers.

While CP and CDNPA commanded most attention in the newspaper field, there were several other organizations which had the industry's interests at heart. For the most part, these were "trade" organizations catering to the special needs of their members.

On the international scene, there are a number of reputable organizations to which Canadians have belonged. By far the most influential is the International Press Institute (IPI), whose primary goals are safeguarding freedom of the press, and promoting the free exchange of news. The goals are noble, but freedom is not easily come by. In a 1995 *IPI Report*, the cover story was headed They Shoot Journalists, Don't They? In its Death Watch column, *IPI Report* listed 16 journalists who had been murdered or assassinated in the first quarter of 1995.

In more affluent times, it was considered appropriate for newspaper proprietors, as well as leading publishers and editors, to belong to IPI. As a former chairman of the Canadian section of IPI, I attended annual conferences in such places as Buenos Aires, Vienna, Istanbul, Bordeaux, Berlin and Kyoto. Well, that's one way to see the world! The speakers at these conferences were always top-drawer — often heads of state. In Buenos Aires, we got the presidents of three South American states for the price of one to fill one program. Other speakers included: Nelson Mandela, before the dismantling of the apartheid state of South Africa; South African social rights activist Bishop Desmond Tutu; West German Chancellor Willy Brandt; Nobel Prize-winning playwright and poet Wole Soyinka of Nigeria; Irish politician and writer Conor Cruise O'Brien; and French President François Mitterand.

All the world's problems seemed to get an airing at one time or another, although some of the solutions were outside the mainstream. On a panel on the environment, Maj.-Gen. Eustace D'Souza of India suggested the use of the armed forces (800,000 in India, not counting the elephants) to fight the battle of conservation through nature-oriented crash courses and awareness camps. Every officer-cadet in India would have to plant two trees and look after them for a year, he said. (Perhaps a rose petal in the barrels of 800,000 rifles might have been just as effective — such actions seem to work wonders for the disposition of the military, don't they?)

IPI was expensive as well as reputable, and the downsizing common to all newspapers in Canada was reflected in the dwindling numbers of Canadians still attached to IPI. The ritzy times were over!

# CHAPTER 36

The trouble with newspapers is that journalists don't communicate with the public any more. They talk only to Heaven. There is no guarantee, of course, that Heaven listens and there is even less indication that Heaven has ever placed a collect call to a journalist, or even slipped a plain brown envelope into a reporter's mailbox.

Newspapers were once the benchmarks for understanding a world that moved at its own pace of deadlines, righteousness, calculated taste and certainty of purpose. The television habit has reduced all news-gathering and commentary to 30 seconds of applied, implied and inferred understanding, the pretty faces and blow-dried hair more compelling information-spreaders than mere words set out soberly on a page of mouldering newsprint by a writer whose only contact with the public is a byline.

Has the newspaper lost its power to influence the public? It has always been an honourable tradition of the press to swim against the mainstream. Has its lack of sting in rabble-rousing made it less feared than in those days when those who ran public institutions trembled in its spotlight? Have the primping matadors of print pranced their way out of the public's grace and favour? Perhaps the things that journalists go to battle for are no longer the sort of things that move the passions of the general public.

Back in March 1908, when those who ran, edited or wrote for newspapers were creatures of flesh and blood, albeit not telegenic mouthpieces, Calgary city council voted on a resolution calling the owners and editor of the *Calgary*

*Herald* "vile traducers and cowardly, base and malicious propagators of falsehoods." The resolution was defeated by only one vote, 6-5, but one alderman was absent.

The newspaper business then was in its vibrant phase of devil-may-care immaturity, with many of its characters the forefathers of the Bob Edwards school of journalism. (Edwards, publisher of the *Calgary Eye Opener*, was known for using humour and satire to promote social causes.)

Rousing strong emotions and reaction has always been the theme of lusty newspapers in their necessity to establish a link with their readers. What's the use of filling a newspaper's commentary space with words that have no impact? Newspapers were born to be free and independent and cynical and critical. Candour has no boundaries except those of taste and honesty. Even sin ceases to be fun if the sermon that condemns it makes the sinner yawn.

In chasing after unpopular causes, we may be out of step with our readers. But the corollary of that means we may be ripping the heart and soul out of journalism by making newspapers mere purveyors of facts and information, missing the point that the public wants to be entertained, antagonized and amused, as well as informed.

We have discovered that it is the whiff of scandal that stirs the public's blood, not the wrangles over reinventing the United Nations or — Heaven help us! — feeding the world's starving millions. We can't even summon up a sigh over the latest barrier thrown up by the First Nations to close some lonely road in the far north of British Columbia. Our alarm bells have a muffled sound.

Who sets the agenda for determining what is in the interests of the readers, or in the interests of those newspapers and journalists who pursue a social policy that does not conform to the public's current motivations? Only a few days after Mike Harris won a majority in the spring provincial election of 1995 in Ontario, the *Toronto Star* was already running features on its front page with such headings as People On Welfare Face Harris' Ontario. As is usual with this form of journalism, the first paragraph set the tone with a poignant story of the "single mom" who is "scared to death of Mike Harris and his plan to cut social assistance by 20 per cent." The *Star* set itself up as the defender of the poor, the downtrodden and the helpless; that may be righteous and noble, but did it conform with the trend set by Mike Harris and accepted by the public through the ballot box as the hard-nosed response to soaring welfare bills? While the *Star*'s stable of columnists veered to the left, its readers preferred to follow Harris in a rightward direction. Who's out of step with whom? Perhaps the dogged determination of the newspaper to follow its own star is one of the reasons the public feels the journalist is arrogant and praying over its head.

By the same token, quality journalism should not be tedious journalism; even as it faces an uncertain future, facing horrendous increases in newsprint costs, the newspaper must always search for that spark that ignites the public's interest. There are many approaches to such a goal.

The *Globe and Mail* for instance, boasts of its foreign coverage. In a backgrounder to changes it was making "to keep pace with the needs of its readers" it said on Feb. 4, 1995, that it would give regular reports drawn from its extensive network of foreign correspondents and independent sources. Its schedule ran thus:

- Mondays: Africa;
- Tuesdays: Latin America;
- Wednesdays: Europe;
- Thursdays: Asia;
- Fridays: the Middle East.

All of which was to be supplemented by the *Globe*'s extensive news and feature coverage from bureaus in the United States, Europe, Russia, China, Latin America, the Middle East and India. Take your pick. Is that what the public wants?

If that is a little high-flown for your tastes, then take some relief from features such as Middle Kingdom, Collected Wisdom, the Entrepreneur's Page, the Change Page, Climate of Ideas, and Facts & Arguments Page, not to mention — using the *Globe*'s own words — the unpredictable daily offering of essays by Canadians from every walk of life about every kind of living.

At least give the *Globe* credit for recognizing that after 150 years it, too, has to change. But is that the sort of change its readers want?

If the industry is in crisis, it is because television is gaining at the expense of newspapers as the most credible source of information, according to pollster Michael Adams, president of Environics Research group. Adams said back in 1992 that about three-quarters of Canadians now turn to television as their primary source of national and international news. "In another 20 years, TV will be the prime source of information for virtually everyone in our society," he said.

Adams was not saying anything profound that had not already been taken to heart by the newspaper industry. There were some publishers who had already redefined the role of the daily paper. Some believed the newspaper should no longer try to deliver news but rather supplement television by adding depth and meaning to the meagre headline stuff seen on television the night before. "Readers already know the facts. Your job is to provide meaning, context and analysis," Adams said. For those whose eyes bulged with lascivious interest over the horrors revealed in the Bernardo-Homolka trials[109], the newspapers filled page after page with sexual perversion carried to a media extreme. Was that a demonstration of the newspaper's fall from grace, or, more likely, a case of giving the public what it wants, something television could not supply?

It is hard for a newspaper to be boringly self-righteous when its readers want all the unvarnished facts set out in full detail. Some would see it as a trend toward outrageous British tabloid journalism, drifting away from the soup-can-label journalism of *USA Today*. Newspapers are now customer-driven, involving the reader in reinventing the newspaper. The first obstacle that had to be overcome in this search for a new identity was appearance. In their continuing combat with television, the newspapers were handicapped by outmoded printing presses. In the search for a formula for survival into the next century we have ended the era of black-and-white journalism through computerized technology, bursting into splendid colour on almost every page. It took millions of dollars to put colour into their lives, but that was a necessary cost of staying in business.

Following the desires of their readers, the newspapers have begun producing a whole range of service features — news-you-can-use topics such as personal finance, entertainment guides, consumer advice and phone numbers to call for instant information.

But some traditional aspects of the newspaper remain the same. The front page, for instance, is still its display case. The way the front page has retained its character, despite changes of style, helps to explain the evolution of today's bright and eye-catching information sheets. For instance, back in the 1950s, when he was publisher of the *Winnipeg Free Press*, Brig. Richard Malone believed in cramming the front page with news stories. By one random count, on a not-untypical day, the *Free Press* started 27 stories on the front page. Putting a gallon of news into a pint pot of a front page was achieved by carrying as many stories as possible under modest single-column headings. Malone's theory was that the average reader wanted a quick, not necessarily detailed, look at the day's main events. The resulting confusion was that stories ran to only two or three sentences on the front and were then turned to an inside page, often in the middle of sentences; thus the poor reader was forced to keep turning the pages to arrive at a comprehensive whole for each story. While the theory of maximum stories was carried to an unmanageable extreme under the Malone system, it really served to emphasize the importance of the front page, acting as it does as the shop window to a store of fascinating and often tantalizing glimpses of life and history in the making.

Today's front page has gained new importance, because it can concentrate on no more than four or five stories, bolstered by splashy colour graphics. The reader misses nothing, being steered to the other top-of-the-day news items by guideposts carried on the front or second page.

Another tradition of newspapers that has been preserved is that of its coverage of local and community events. Often, this means the main news section of the paper is crammed with crime, devastating fires, accidents, drug wars, heartbreaking stories of human suffering, etc. This is real life on the streets, in your neighbourhood, something beyond the means of television to cover in detail.

The custom of editorial writing remains an honourable one. The primary purpose of an editorial is to give guidance, leadership and understanding to readers who might otherwise be perplexed and confused by complex issues affecting their lives. An editorial is a special point of view that is not so much the opinion of the person who wrote it, but the distillation of the collective wisdom of the editorial board. It is the newspaper equivalent of drawing a line in the sand. Not that everybody holds such faith in editorials. At the 1989 National Newspaper Awards dinner, Pierre Péladeau, owner of three tabloids in the province of Quebec and one more in Manitoba, bluntly told an audience gathered to honour journalism's elite that his mass circulation dailies in Montreal and Quebec carried no editorials because he preferred to sell the space to advertising! I would like to think he was joking. Unfortunately, he was not.

Today's new printing equipment allows a newspaper to break itself down into different sections, catering to special interests of the readers — sports, cars, fashions, entertainment, business, food, classified, computer technology, etc. If readers want it, the newspaper will supply it. Weekend editions of most metropolitan dailies are replete with investigative journalism, obviously with no holds barred. Newspapers have moved beyond being the mere recorder, the sideline observer. They are now turning over every stone, trying to keep the rascals honest, so to speak.

But how relevant is the newspaper to the community it serves? And why does it not get the respect it thinks it deserves?

Kathleen Hall Jamieson, communications scholar and former dean of the Annenberg School for Communication at the University of Pennsylvania, told the *New York Times* in 1984: "Journalists are now creating the coverage that is going to lead to their own destruction. If you cover the world cynically and assume that everybody is Machiavellian and motivated by their own self-interest, you invite your readers and viewers to reject journalism as a mode of communication because it must be cynical, too."

In a *Toronto Star* article on June 10, 1995, media critic Antonia Zerbisias wrote: "In just two decades, reporters have tumbled from crusading heroes who brought down the bad guys to cynical hypesters who make media heroes of some bad guys (O.J. Simpson[110])."

In a forum at Toronto's St. Lawrence Centre, there was audience applause every time somebody attacked journalists. "Reporters have become too self-important, too pompous," said one man, before enthusiastic applause drowned him out. "News has given up the search for truth, news is agenda-driven," he finally added.

If the public is more cynical than media, Zerbisias asked, is it because journalists do hatchet jobs on politicians or because they are out of touch with the public? "The point is that many of us in the media are out of sync with reality," she concluded.

One who shared that opinion with her was Ralph Klein, premier of Alberta. Speaking to the annual Canadian Press dinner in Toronto in May 1995, Klein drew a parallel between public perception of newspapers and politicians. Both were once among the most respected groups in Canadian society. Both had fallen out of favour with the public. In the case of newspapers, there was a whole host of ways for the public to get information, and get it faster, more focused and more tailored to its needs. "From their home computers with access to the Internet to their 500-channel television dish, they get their information the way they want it, when they want it and how they want it."

As for politicians — in Alberta, at least — they responded to public demands to cut government spending. As a result, a public opinion poll pegged Klein's government at a 73 per cent approval rating despite the editorial disapproval of its policies by the two major Southam dailies in the province (the *Calgary Herald* and the *Edmonton Journal*).

"In other words, we were making government relevant again," said Klein, while newspapers, with all their hand-wringing, were missing the point. "My candid opinion is that a new generation of Canadians are looking for a new generation of elected officials and a new generation of news coverage. And it is also my candid opinion that I am succeeding better than you in meeting that challenge."

Klein maintained that newspapers are hung up on victim-of-the-week journalism, putting forward a bleeding-hearts point of view out of line with the wishes of the public. As an example of that attitude of the press, he cited the case of the *Edmonton Journal*, which, in advance of an Alberta budget, had prepared a document for its reporters suggesting how they might put budget items into context. At the head of the list was the proposal to put forth the case for those who would be "victimized" by certain budget cuts. To that extent, Klein was stretching the elastic to breaking point, because the document he referred to was simply a means of identifying possible areas for coverage.

All of which drew a somewhat angry response from Kevin Peterson, the CDNPA chairman who was to thank Klein for his speech. In defence of fellow publisher Linda Hughes, Peterson said it was wrong to characterize such stories as victims of the week. "Their stories must be told," said Peterson. "Minority voices … we might not agree with them, but it's part of our job to give them a voice."

Klein merely grinned. He had made his point. Once again, the newspapers were demonstrating how thin-skinned they were in the face of public criticism. By contrast, politicians and prominent figures in the public eye had no such means of establishing their own case in reply. Peterson's gallantry on behalf of a colleague apart, his response simply touched a raw nerve.

At the time, the *Herald* was running a series of "special reports," all of them aimed at the actions of a "cruel" provincial government in cutting back financial support for medical services. Labelled Taking The Pulse — Health-Care Revolution, each day, for 10 days, the series spread itself across page after page with *Herald* writers from all corners giving it their all. And, as Klein pointed out to his Toronto audience, the actions of his government had the support of more than 70 per cent of Albertans. In throwing itself down in front of such a juggernaut, was the *Herald* perpetuating a brave and idealistic way of standing up for truth and justice, or was it totally ignoring the public's own point of view? Is this what the public perceives as journalistic arrogance or mistaken chivalry?

Despite public cynicism, the newspaper is not about to become a "sunset industry." Its challenges are enormous. Many believe that the growth of online services will create new competition for advertising. As that threat grows, newspapers are looking into implementing online services of their own. Already, according to a survey by the American Opinion Research of Princeton, N.J., more than 60 per cent of American newsrooms were using online services as information sources.

The biggest challenge of all, of course, is determining what the public expects from its newspapers. And then delivering it.

In the 1960s, the editor of the *Longford News*, a tiny Irish weekly, told his subscribers: "As youse well know, our circulation has dropped from its highest all-time record of 273 to a bare 150 ... all of whom want to know what sort of trouble the neighbours are in. Well, they won't read it in the *News* — because we've got away from all that." The editor had put his finger on the cause and effect of his own circulation problem, but he wasn't prepared to do anything about it. The same problem of unctuous self-righteousness, of giving the public what the journalist thinks it should have, with or without the reader's blessing, may well be plaguing today's newspapers. The insufferable high-mindedness of today's spoon-fed graduates of our schools of journalism may well have taken all the myth and romance out of the newspaper business. They are out of touch with the public, forcing their own ideological extremes on to those who want information without too many strings attached.

The old Longford editor once ruminated over the possibility of his own flashy funeral. Writing about an afterlife interview at the Pearly Gates, he said: "Somehow, we feel that Peter will tell us to get up and get measured for a halo, but that we won't be happy in heaven. There will not be anybody there we know."

I know that feeling.

We have come a long way, indeed, from the stereotypical image of a reporter as a man with hat pushed to the back of his head, given to strong drink and even stronger language, more noted for his bad manners and cynicism and his way with the ladies than for his literary talents. Indeed, he was often seen as the hod carrier of journalism, providing the bricks and mortar on which the newspaper was built. Perhaps, for all his faults, he was closer to the souls of the people than today's scavengers in the dustbins of history. Sad, perhaps, but true.

# POSTSCRIPT

Somebody told me that the *Edmonton Journal* newsroom had a wake when they learned I was being moved to Calgary in 1982.

That bothered me, because in Irish terms a wake is a matter of celebration, not of sorrow, a means of speeding the parting guest. There is always one drunk fewer at an Irish wake than at an Irish wedding, and he only recently lost his taste for the stuff — with his dying breath.

If the stuff that has left me enthralled and stimulated by its taste all these years is the sheer joy of being a newspaperman, then I don't want to be the corpse at anybody's wake.

In the swirl of shifting light and dancing images of fading memory, most of us pass like shadows, but — for me, at least — the regrets are few. The days that are no more were never dull.

A generations-distant ancestor, John Cornelius O'Callaghan, wrote a book entitled *Gleanings from the Writing Desk of a Literary Agitator*. I could have used that title!

But it was the poet William Butler Yeats, not an O'Callaghan, who had carved on his tombstone in the lonely Protestant cemetery in Drumcliff, this epitaph: *Cast a cold eye on life, on death.*

What a send-off for a newspaperman!

# NOTES

The following are capsule descriptions of some of the persons, places, events or things referred to by the author in his manuscript. The notes, with information drawn from various websites, are intended to be a guide for readers unfamiliar with the references. Links to website sources follow each note.

## INTRODUCTION

**1.** William Southam (1843-1932) started Southam Ltd. in 1903 with himself as president and five of his sons — Wilson Mills Southam, Frederick Neil Southam, Richard Southam, Harry Stevenson Southam and William James Southam — as directors. The sixth and youngest son, Gordon, became a major with Canadian Field Artillery, 8th Brigade, during the First World War and was killed in the Battle of the Somme in France on Oct. 15, 1916. Southam had one daughter, Ethel May Southam Balfour.

**Sources:** https://en.wikipedia.org/wiki/William_Southam;

http://www.biographi.ca/en/bio/southam_william_16E.html.

## CHAPTER 1

**2.** In 1938, the Pulitzer jury awarded the *Edmonton Journal* a special bronze plaque "for its editorial leadership in defence of the freedom of the press in the province of Alberta, Canada." The Aberhart government's Accurate News and Information Act, declared unconstitutional by the Supreme Court of Canada, would have forced newspapers to print government rebuttals to stories the provincial cabinet deemed "inaccurate." For more, see Chapter 6.

**Sources:** http://www.pulitzer.org/awards/1938; http://www.thecanadianencyclopedia.ca/en/article/alberta-press-act-reference-1938/; https://en.wikipedia.org/wiki/Accurate_News_and_Information_Act.

**3.** William Maxwell (Max) Aitken (1879-1964), Lord Beaverbrook, was a Canadian-born newspaper tycoon, businessman, British politician and writer, and is regarded by some historians as the first baron of Fleet Street. He joined the Royal Securities Corp. as manager in 1903 and within five years was a millionaire. In 1910, he pursued business and political interests by moving to London, England. Knighted in 1911, he was minister of information under Prime Minister David Lloyd George in 1918. After the First World War, he established a newspaper empire, buying the *Daily Express* and the *Evening Standard*, and creating the *Sunday Express*. He served in Winston Churchill's wartime cabinet as minister of aircraft production. He left politics in 1945 to oversee his newspaper empire and write memoirs and biographies. Aitken also became a benefactor of the University of New Brunswick, the city of Fredericton and the province of New Brunswick. His name survives in various buildings such as the Beaverbrook Art Gallery and the Lord Beaverbrook Hotel.

**Sources:** http://www.thecanadianencyclopedia.ca/en/article/max-aitken-lord-beaverbrook/; https://en.wikipedia.org/wiki/Max_Aitken,_1st_Baron_Beaverbrook.

## CHAPTER 2

**4.** Jack Horner (1927-2004), a rancher, was elected as a Conservative MP in 1958 and was a staunch supporter of Tory leader John Diefenbaker. Considered an advocate of farmers' and ranchers' rights, he made an unsuccessful bid for the Progressive Conservative Party leadership in 1976, which was won by Joe Clark. In 1977, he crossed the floor to join Pierre Trudeau's Liberals as minister without portfolio and later minister of industry, trade and commerce. Horner was defeated in the 1979 federal election. He was later chairman of Canadian National Railways and administrator of the Western Grain Transportation Agency.

**Sources:**
http://www.thecanadianencyclopedia.ca/en/article/jack-horner/;
https://en.wikipedia.org/wiki/Jack_Horner_%28politician%29.

**5.** The current owner of the *Red Deer Advocate*, Black Press Ltd. of Victoria, B.C., acquired the newspaper in 1996.

**Source:** http://www.reddeer.ca/about-red-deer/history/history-of-red-deer/centennials-and-anniversaries/red-deer-advocate/.

**6.** Jerome K. Jerome (1859-1927) was an English writer and humourist, best known for his comic account of a boating trip, *Three Men in a Boat.*

**Sources:** http://www.online-literature.com/jerome/;
https://en.wikipedia.org/wiki/Jerome_K._Jerome.

## CHAPTER 3

**7.** Don Getty (born in 1933), a former quarterback with the Edmonton Eskimos of the Canadian Football League, served as energy minister and federal and intergovernmental affairs minister under Peter Lougheed. He later served as Alberta's premier, from 1985 to 1992.

**Sources:**
http://www.assembly.ab.ca/lao/library/premiers/Getty.htm;

https://en.wikipedia.org/wiki/Don_Getty.

**8.** George Gobel (1919-1991) was an American comedian and actor who starred in his own weekly TV series, *The George Gobel Show*, from 1954 to 1960.

**Sources:** https://en.wikipedia.org/wiki/George_Gobel; http://www.imdb.com/name/nm0323597/.

**9.** After working for the Reuters news agency and the CBC, Charles Lynch (1919-1994) joined Southam News in 1958 and was appointed its chief in 1960. For 20 years, he wrote a five-times-a-week column for Southam News. From 1970 to 1974, while still working for Southam, he co-hosted CBC's TV program *Encounter*, which featured major Canadian political figures as guests. Lynch served as president of the Parliamentary Press Gallery in 1976, and was inducted into the Canadian News Hall of Fame in 1981. He retired in 1984 and became a freelance writer.

**Sources:**
http://www.thecanadianencyclopedia.ca/en/article/charles-burchill-lynch/;
https://en.wikipedia.org/wiki/Charles_Lynch_%28journalist%29.

**10.** Bryce Mackasey (1921-1999), a federal MP who represented the Quebec ridings of Verdun and Lincoln, held a number of cabinet portfolios, including Labour, Manpower and Immigration, Secretary of State, Postmaster General and Consumer and Corporate Affairs. He also was chairman of Air Canada and a member of Quebec's national assembly for

Notre-Dame-de-Grâce from 1976 to 1978. When Prime Minister John Turner appointed him ambassador to Portugal in 1884, Conservative leader Brian Mulroney, then leader of the Opposition, quipped, "There's no whore like an old whore." When he became prime minister, Mulroney cancelled the appointment and named another Liberal, former Speaker of the House Lloyd Francis, to the position.

**Sources:** https://en.wikipedia.org/wiki/Bryce_Mackasey; http://www.parl.gc.ca/ParlInfo/Files/Parliamentarian.aspx?Item=356b3da2-aff0-4859-9541-4fdcbaad2a58&Language=E; http://www.parli.ca/whore-like-old-whore/.

**11.** Charles Haughey (1925-2006), then Ireland's minister of finance, and Neil Blaney (1922-1995), then minister for agriculture and fisheries, were dismissed from the Irish cabinet of Jack Lynch for their alleged involvement in a plot to smuggle arms to the Irish Republican Army in Northern Ireland. At what became known in Ireland as the Arms Trial in 1970, charges against Blaney were dropped, and Haughey and three other alleged conspirators were acquitted.

**Sources:** https://en.wikipedia.org/wiki/Arms_Crisis; http://www.independent.ie/opinion/analysis/the-idiots-guide-to-the-arms-trial-26248478.html.

## CHAPTER 4

**12.** When the *Toronto Sun* started up over the Halloween weekend of 1971, it rented space at the Eclipse Building at King and John streets in what is now Toronto's Entertainment District. *Sun* columnist Paul Rimstead wrote at the time: "From the outside, it does not look so hot. And, frankly, it is even worse on the inside. But it is the home of the *Sun*, right next door to Farb's Car Wash and across the street from the King's Plate Open Kitchen, where you can buy a beef steak pie for 50 cents."

**Source:**
http://www.canoe.ca/TorSunHistory/30th_rimmer.html.

**13.** Damon Runyon (1884-1946) was an American journalist, short story writer and humourist. He was best known for his short stories of Broadway before the Second World War. His stories featured gamblers, hustlers, actors and gangsters, and were written in a unique slang. A number of his stories were made into movies, most notably the Oscar-nominated musical *Guys and Dolls*, which was also a Tony Award-winning Broadway musical.

**Sources:** https://en.wikipedia.org/wiki/Damon_Runyon; http://www.literalmedia.com/index.php?option=com_content&view=article&id=44&Itemid=71; http://www.newyorker.com/magazine/2009/03/02/talk-it-up.

## CHAPTER 5

**14.** Southam Inc.'s head office was located at 150 Bloor St. W., Suite 900, Toronto, Ont.

**Source:** http://www.fundinguniverse.com/company-histories/southam-inc-history/.

**15.** Donald Macdonald (born in 1932) became part of Pierre Trudeau's cabinet in 1968 and served as president of the Privy Council, minister of defence, minister of energy, mines and resources, and minister of finance. As finance minister, he introduced wage and price controls. In 1982, Trudeau appointed Macdonald chairman of the Royal Commission on the Economic Union and Development Prospects in Canada. It recommended that Canada enter into a free-trade agreement with the United States, which was pursued by Prime Minister Brian Mulroney. Macdonald served as high commissioner to the United Kingdom from 1988 to 1991.

**Sources:**
http://www.thecanadianencyclopedia.ca/en/article/donald-stovel-macdonald/;
https://en.wikipedia.org/wiki/Donald_Stovel_Macdonald

## CHAPTER 6

**16.** The World Hockey Assocation's 1979 All-Star Game featured a three-game series between the league all-stars and Dynamo Moscow at Edmonton's Northland Coliseum. The line of Wayne Gretzky, Gordie Howe and Mark Howe scored seven points in the first game and three in the second match, but none in the third. The WHA squad won all three games by scores of 4-2, 4-2 and 4-3.

**Source:**
https://en.wikipedia.org/wiki/1978%E2%80%9379_WHA_season.

## CHAPTER 7

**17.** Ted Byfield (born in 1929) launched the *Saint John's Edmonton Report*, a weekly magazine, in 1973 and a sister publication in Calgary in 1977. The two were merged to become *Alberta Report* in 1979. The magazine was later published in three separate editions — *Alberta Report, BC Report* and *Western Report*. In 1999, those were merged into *The Report*, later known as the *Citizens Centre Report*. The magazine struggled financially and was closed in 2003.

**Sources:**
http://www.thecanadianencyclopedia.ca/en/article/ted-byfield-profile/;
https://en.wikipedia.org/wiki/Alberta_Report.

**18.** Puck is the name of a mischievous sprite or goblin believed, especially in the 16th and 17th centuries, to haunt the English countryside. Puck is also a character in William Shakespeare's play *A Midsummer Night's Dream.*

**Sources:** *The Canadian Oxford Dictionary*; William Shakespeare's *A Midsummer Night's Dream.*

## CHAPTER 8

**19.** Based in Edmonton, Felix (Fil) Fraser (born in 1932) is an author, columnist, radio personality, TV program director, radio, television and feature film producer, and adjunct professor of communications studies at Athabasca University. Fraser worked for radio stations in Toronto, Timmins, Barrie and Montreal. He founded and published the *Regina Weekly Mirror* before moving to Edmonton in 1965. He has served as chief commissioner of the Alberta Human Rights Commission, CEO of Vision TV and program director at Metropolitan Edmonton Educational Television Association, Canada's first on-air educational television station.

**Sources:** http://www.filfraser.ca/?page_id=2; https://en.wikipedia.org/wiki/Fil_Fraser

**20.** The Anti-Inflation Board was established in 1975 to administer the federal government's wage-and-price-control program. In the first year of the program, wage increases were limited to 10 per cent in the first year, eight per cent in the second year and six per cent in the third year. The board could recommend reductions in consumer prices, wage rollbacks and customer rebates. The program was phased out in 1978, but the board did not cease all operations until 1979.

**Sources:**
http://www.thecanadianencyclopedia.ca/en/article/anti-inflation-board/;
http://www.canadahistory.com/sections/eras/trudeau/wage_&_price_controls.htm

## CHAPTER 9

**21.** A 1957 fire at the Windscale nuclear reactor and plutonium production plant in northwest England is considered to be the United Kingdom's worst nuclear power accident. The fire left about 10 tonnes of radioactive fuel melted in the reactor core and caused the release of radioactive iodine into the atmosphere. According to a BBC News report, an estimated 240 cases of thyroid cancer were caused by the radioactive leak, and all milk produced within 800 square kilometres of the site was destroyed for a month after the fire. Following the fire, the reactor's two pile chimneys were sealed, contaminated filters removed and air inlet ducts isolated. Work on cleaning up and decommissioning one chimney began in 2013. (The other chimney stack was taken down in 2001.)

**Sources:** https://en.wikipedia.org/wiki/Windscale_fire;
http://www.britannica.com/event/Windscale-fire;
http://www.bbc.com/news/uk-england-cumbria-29803990
http://www.counterspill.org/article/windscale-fire-disaster-brief-history;
http://www.neimagazine.com/features/featurewindscale-chimney-decommissioning-transforming-the-sellafield-skyline-4254702/.

## CHAPTER 10

**22.** Mandatory Palestine (also called British Palestine or simply Palestine), under British administration from 1920 to 1948, was created out of part of the former Ottoman Empire by a League of Nations mandate after the First World War. Following the Second World War, thousands of Jewish refugees wanted to emigrate to Palestine, but Britain had an immigrant quota in place. Jews organized flotillas to enter Palestine, while the Royal Navy enforced a blockade to reroute them to camps in Cyprus or their ports of origin. After Britain announced it would terminate the mandate, David Ben-Gurion declared the establishment of the State of Israel on May 14, 1948. Under the terms of a 1949 ceasefire agreement to end an Arab-Israeli war, Mandatory Palestine was partitioned into Israel; the West Bank, annexed by the Jordanian Kingdom; and the Arab All-Palestine Government in the Gaza Strip, under the military occupation of Egypt.

**Sources:** http://time.com/3445003/mandatory-palestine/; http://www.jewishvirtuallibrary.org/jsource/History/mandate3.html; http://www.merip.org/primer-palestine-israel-arab-israeli-conflict-new; https://en.wikipedia.org/wiki/Mandatory_Palestine; http://www.jewishvirtuallibrary.org/jsource/History/mandate.html; https://en.wikipedia.org/wiki/SS_Exodus.

**23.** Roy Farran (1921-2006) of the Special Air Service was one of the Second World War's most decorated officers, earning a Distinguished Service Order, three Military Crosses, a Croix de Guerre and the American Legion of Merit. In 1947, he was assigned to the British section of the Palestine Police to head an undercover unit. He was court-martialled for the murder of an unarmed 16-year-old member of the Lehi, an underground Jewish organization. Farran was acquitted for lack of evidence. But when he was in Scotland shortly before the first anniversary of the teen's disappearance, Farran's youngest brother, Rex, was killed by a letter bomb sent to the family home near Wolverhampton on May 3, 1948, less than two weeks before Israel declared its statehood. Lehi claimed responsibility, but admitted Rex Farran had been killed by mistake.

**Sources:** https://en.wikipedia.org/wiki/Roy_Farran;

http://www.telegraph.co.uk/news/obituaries/1520303/Major-Roy-Farran.html;
http://www.cjnews.com/columnists/roy-farran-affair.

**24.** Borstal refers to youth detention centres and reformatories in the United Kingdom and British Commonwealth. The first of these was established at Borstal Prison in the English village of Borstal, near Rochester, Kent, in 1902. Irish writer Brendan Behan wrote of his experiences in the English Borstal system in his autobiography *Borstal Boy*.

**Sources:** https://en.wikipedia.org/wiki/Borstal;
http://www.thefreedictionary.com/borstal;
https://en.wikipedia.org/wiki/Borstal_Boy.

## CHAPTER 11

**25.** Grant Notley (1939-1984) served as an Alberta MLA for Spirit River-Fairview from 1971 to 1984, and as Alberta NDP leader from 1968 to 1984. For 11 years, he was Alberta's only NDP MLA. Following a 1982 byelection, he was joined by a second NDP MLA and became the leader of the Opposition. Notley and five other passengers were killed in a plane crash near Slave Lake in 1984. His daughter, Rachel Notley, won the Alberta NDP leadership in 2014 and was elected premier of Alberta in 2015.

**Sources:**
http://www.thecanadianencyclopedia.ca/en/article/walter-grant-notley/;
https://en.wikipedia.org/wiki/Grant_Notley.

**26.** Robert (Bob) Bogle (born in 1943) served as an Alberta MLA from 1975 to 1993. Under Premier Peter Lougheed, he served as minister without portfolio responsible for native affairs, minister of social services and community health, and minister of utilities and telecommunications. Following Ralph

Klein's election as premier, he was made the Tory caucus chairman and party whip, as well as serving on the cabinet's priorities committee.

**Source:** https://en.wikipedia.org/wiki/Robert_Bogle.

## CHAPTER 12

**27.** Cornelius (Chevy) Chase (born in 1943) is an American comedian, actor and writer. He rose to fame as a member of the original cast of *Saturday Night Live* (*SNL*) in 1975 and subsequently went on to star in movies such as as *Caddyshack*, *National Lampoon's Vacation* and *Three Amigos*. While on *SNL*, he became known for performing pratfalls.

**Sources:** https://en.wikipedia.org/wiki/Chevy_Chase; http://www.imdb.com/name/nm0000331/.

**28.** Allan MacEachen (born in 1921) is a retired Nova Scotia MP and senator. Under prime ministers Lester Pearson, Pierre Trudeau and John Turner, he held the cabinet portfolios of Labour, National Health and Welfare, Manpower and Immigration, president of the Privy Council, External Affairs and Finance. Under Trudeau, he was also Canada's first deputy prime minister, from 1977 to 1979 and from 1980 to 1984. From 1984 to 1991, he served as leader of the Opposition in the Senate. He retired from the Senate in 1996.

**Sources:**
http://www.thecanadianencyclopedia.ca/en/article/allan-joseph-maceachen/;

https://en.wikipedia.org/wiki/Allan_MacEachen.

**29.** Baseball manager Charles (Casey) Stengel (1890-1975), nicknamed The Old Professor, led the New York Yankees to consecutive World Series titles from 1949 to 1953, and two more World Series championships in 1956 and 1958. He was talked out of retirement to manage the expansion New York Mets from 1962 to 1965. *Can't Anybody Here Play This Game?* is the title of a book by columnist Jimmy Breslin about the bumbling Mets' first season. The title is said to have come from a remark made by Stengel expressing frustration with his club's ineptitude.

**Sources:** http://www.caseystengel.com/index.php; http://baseballhall.org/hof/stengel-casey; https://en.wikipedia.org/wiki/Casey_Stengel.

**30.** Harrington Lake (also known as Lac Mousseau) is the official summer residence of the prime minister of Canada and an all-season retreat in Gatineau Park in Quebec.

**Source:** http://www.ncc-ccn.gc.ca/places-to-visit/official-residences/harrington-lake-lac-mousseau.

## CHAPTER 13

**31.** Bob Bierman (1921-2008) was primarily a freelancer whose editorial cartoons appeared in the *Victoria Daily Times*, the *Victoria Times Colonist* and *Monday* magazine.

**Sources:**
http://www.comicsreporter.com/index.php/bob_bierman_1921_2008/;
https://groups.google.com/forum/#!topic/alt.obituaries/kxIpVA1jjYY;
http://www.canada.com/victoriatimescolonist/news/story.html?id=49dd4a09-db4c-4294-9673-5766c1335115.

**32.** "If you can't stand the heat, get out of the kitchen," was a favourite saying of Harry S. Truman (1884-1972), who was U.S. president from 1945 to 1953.

**Sources:** http://www.phrases.org.uk/meanings/get-out-of-the-kitchen.html;
https://en.wikipedia.org/wiki/Harry_S._Truman.

**33.** Notable editorial cartoonists mentioned here, and some of the publications they have worked for, include: Vance Rodewalt (born in 1946), the *Calgary Herald*; Terry Mosher (born in 1942), who goes by the pen name Aislin, the *Montreal Gazette*; John Yardley-Jones (born in 1930), the *Edmonton Sun* and *Edmonton Journal*; Edd Uluschak, the *Edmonton Journal*; Duncan Macpherson (1924-1993), the *Toronto Star*; and Roy Peterson (1936-2013), the *Vancouver Sun.*

**Sources:**
http://www.thecanadianencyclopedia.ca/en/article/vance-ronald-rodewalt/;
https://en.wikipedia.org/wiki/Terry_Mosher;
http://www.thecanadianencyclopedia.ca/en/article/terry-mosher/;
http://www.yardleyjones.com/about.php;
http://edocs.lib.sfu.ca/projects/Cartoons/bio-uluschak.htm;
http://www.thecanadianencyclopedia.ca/en/article/political-cartoons/;
http://www.thecanadianencyclopedia.ca/en/article/duncan-ian-macpherson/
https://en.wikipedia.org/wiki/Roy_Peterson.

**34.** Television cameras caught Robert Stanfield (1914-2003), a former Nova Scotia premier, eating a banana during the 1967 federal Conservative leadership convention.

**Sources:** https://en.wikipedia.org/wiki/Robert_Stanfield;

http://www.cbc.ca/archives/entry/robert-stanfield-wins-pc-leadership.

## CHAPTER 15

**35.** Ron Ghitter (born in 1922) was an Alberta MLA for Calgary-Buffalo from 1971 to 1979. In 1983, he chaired the Committee of Tolerance and Understanding, established to review the province's school system and curriculum, and recommend how to achieve greater tolerance and respect for human rights. In 1985, he made an unsuccessful bid for leadership of Alberta's Conservatives, losing to Don Getty. Ghitter was appointed to the Senate in 1993, and from 1996 to 1999 chaired the Senate Standing Committee of Energy, the Environment and Natural Resources. He resigned from the Senate in 2000.

**Source:** https://en.wikipedia.org/wiki/Ron_Ghitter

**36.** Roy McMurtry (born in 1932) served in the cabinet of Ontario Premier Bill Davis as attorney general and solicitor general between 1975 and 1985. From 1985 to 1988, he was Canada's high commissioner to the United Kingdom, and from 1989 to 1990, he was commissioner and CEO of the Canadian Football League. He was appointed associate chief justice of the Superior Court (Trial Division) in 1991 and became chief justice of that court in 1994. McMurtry became chief justice of Ontario in 1996 and retired in 2007.

**Sources:** https://en.wikipedia.org/wiki/Roy_McMurtry; http://news.ontario.ca/mcscs/en/2010/09/the-honourable-r-roy-mcmurtry-qc---biography.html

**37.** The Alberta Heritage Savings Trust Fund was established in 1976 by Premier Peter Lougheed to set aside non-renewable resource revenue as savings for the future. According to the Alberta Treasury Board and Finance Ministry, as of June 30, 2015, the fund's fair value was $17.7 billion. Since its inception, the fund — with a portfolio of investments in private and public companies, bonds, real estate, infrastructure and equities — has generated about $36.5 billion in investment income that has been transferred to the province's general revenue.

**Source:**
http://www.finance.alberta.ca/business/ahstf/faqs.html.

**38.** In 1938, British Prime Minister Neville Chamberlain (1869-1940) signed the Munich Agreement, permitting Nazi Germany to annex the Sudetenland region of Czechoslovakia, and said the pact represented "peace for our time." But the following year, the Nazi invasion of Poland marked the beginning of the Second World War.

**Sources:** https://en.wikipedia.org/wiki/Peace_for_our_time; http://news.bbc.co.uk/onthisday/hi/dates/stories/september/30/newsid_3115000/3115476.stm.

**39.** Edmund (Ed) Clark (born in 1947) was a deputy minister in the Trudeau government who won an outstanding civil servant award in 1982. After being fired by Prime Minister Brian Mulroney, he landed in the private sector with the Toronto office of investment bank Merrill Lynch in 1985. He moved on to Morgan Financial Corp. and Canada Trust Financial Services Inc. Canada Trust was purchased by Toronto-Dominion Bank in 2000, and Clark became president and CEO of TD Bank Group, retiring from the post in 2014.

**Sources:** https://en.wikipedia.org/wiki/W._Edmund_Clark; http://www.theglobeandmail.com/report-on-business/how-tds-red-ed-clark-became-a-force-in-canada/article10713002/; http://business.financialpost.com/news/fp-street/how-ed-clark-transformed-td-into-a-behemoth.

**40.** Ian Stewart (died in 2014) was an economic policy maker in the federal public service, serving in a number of senior positions. After teaching at Queen's University and Dartmouth College, he joined the Bank of Canada in 1966 and moved to the Treasury Board Secretariat in 1972. He subsequently served as assistant secretary to the cabinet committee on economic policy and as an economic advisor to the Privy Council Office, deputy minister of Energy, Mines and Resources, and deputy minister of Finance.

**Source:** https://www.google.com/search?q=ian+stewart&ie=utf-8&oe=utf-8#q=ian+stewart+canada.

**41.** Businessman and lawyer Marshall (Mickey) Cohen (born in 1935) was president and CEO of the Molson Companies Ltd. from 1988 to 1996. He served in the federal government for 15 years, including appointments as deputy minister of Industry, Trade and Commerce, Energy, Mines and Resources, and Finance.

**Source:** https://en.wikipedia.org/wiki/Marshall_A._Cohen.

**42.** Britain's 11-member, all-party Foreign Affairs Committee (known as the Kershaw Committee, chaired by Anthony Kershaw) said the British Parliament had the duty "to exercise its best judgment" in deciding whether a requested constitutional amendment would affect Canada's federal structure and whether it reflected the wishes of the people.

Source: https://news.google.com/newspapers?nid=2519&dat=19810131&id=ke9dAAAAIBAJ&sjid=aF8NAAAAIBAJ&pg=5490,4415160&hl=en.

**43.** Jim Keegstra (1934-2014) was a former high school teacher in Eckville, Alta., who was charged and convicted of hate speech in 1984 for telling students the Holocaust was a fraud and for promoting anti-Semitic views. The Alberta Court of Appeal overturned his conviction, but it was upheld by the Supreme Court of Canada in 1990. In 1992, Keegstra was convicted in a retrial and fined $3,000.

**Sources:** https://en.wikipedia.org/wiki/James_Keegstra;

http://www.thecanadianencyclopedia.ca/en/article/keegstra-case/;
http://www.theglobeandmail.com/news/national/holocaust-denier-and-former-alberta-teacher-jim-keegstra-dead-at-the-age-of-80/article19155171/;
http://www.cbc.ca/news/canada/edmonton/jim-keegstra-notorious-canadian-holocaust-denier-dead-at-80-1.2674372.

**44.** Ernst Zündel (born in 1939) is a German publisher known for promoting Holocaust denial. He has been jailed in Canada, where he lived from 1958 to 2000, for publishing material "likely to incite hatred" and on charges of being a threat to national security; in the United States for overstaying his visa; and in Germany for "inciting racial hatred."

**Sources:**
https://en.wikipedia.org/wiki/Ernst_Z%C3%BCndel;
http://archive.adl.org/learn/ext_us/zundel.html?LEARN_Cat=Extremism&LEARN_SubCat=Extremism_in_America&xpicked=2&item=zundel.

**45.** Malcolm Ross (born in 1946) is a former New Brunswick school teacher who achieved notoriety for his writings, declaring that the Holocaust was a hoax and expressing anti-Semitic and anti-abortion views.

**Sources:**
https://en.wikipedia.org/wiki/Malcolm_Ross_%28school_teacher%29;
http://self.gutenberg.org/articles/malcolm_ross_%28school_teacher%29.

**46.** A police officer in Hungary during the Second World War, Imre Finta (1911-2003) — a restaurant owner and caterer in Toronto who became a Canadian citizen in 1956 — was accused of manslaughter, kidnapping, unlawful confinement and robbery for allegedly assisting the Nazis in the forced deportation of 8,617 Jews. Finta claimed he was only responsible for transporting Jews. He was charged in 1987 and acquitted in 1990. The acquittal was upheld by the Ontario Court of Appeal in 1992 and by the Supreme Court of Canada in 1994.

**Sources:** https://en.wikipedia.org/wiki/Imre_Finta; http://www.thecanadianencyclopedia.ca/en/article/war-crimes/.

## CHAPTER 16

**47.** The price of oil rose above those levels after the death of the author. According to inflationdata.com, the nominal (not adjusted for inflation) per-barrel price of oil in U.S. dollars (average annual prices, but not showing absolute peak prices) was $3.39 in 1970, $37.42 in 1980, $23.19 in 1990, $27.39 in 2000, $50.04 in 2005, $71.21 in 2010, $91.17 in 2013 and $85.60 in 2014.

**Source:**
http://inflationdata.com/inflation/inflation_rate/historical_oil_prices_table.asp.

**48.** In 1864, during the American Civil War, Maj. Gen. William Tecumseh Sherman of the Union Army led a month-long campaign behind enemy lines from Atlanta to Savannah known as Sherman's March to the Sea.

**Sources:**
https://en.wikipedia.org/wiki/Sherman's_March_to_the_Sea;
http://www.historynet.com/shermans-march-to-the-sea.

## CHAPTER 17

**49.** The Kent Commission was the popular name for what was formally the Royal Commission on Newspapers, created in 1980 and chaired by Tom Kent (1922-2011), a journalist, public servant and expert on public policy.

**Sources:**
http://www.thecanadianencyclopedia.ca/en/article/newspapers/;
http://www.thecanadianencyclopedia.ca/en/article/thomas-worrall-kent/;
https://en.wikipedia.org/wiki/Royal_Commission_on_Newspapers.

**50.** Michael Pitfield (born in 1937) joined the public service in 1959. He served as secretary to the cabinet and clerk of the Privy Council from 1975 to 1979 and again from 1980 to 1982. Pitfield was appointed to the Senate in 1982 and retired in 2010.

**Sources:**
http://www.thecanadianencyclopedia.ca/en/article/peter-michael-pitfield/;
https://en.wikipedia.org/wiki/Michael_Pitfield.

**51.** Josef Goebbels (1897-1945) was the Nazi minister of propaganda from 1933 to 1945.

**Sources:** https://en.wikipedia.org/wiki/Joseph_Goebbels; http://www.jewishvirtuallibrary.org/jsource/Holocaust/goebbels.html.

**52.** Winston's started when Hungarian émigrés Oscar and Cornelia Berceller purchased a diner at 120 King St. W. around 1940 and named it after British Prime Minister Winston Churchill. Its clientele — many with ties to the theatre — grew as the menu was expanded and the premises were renovated. In 1966, John Arena, food manager of the Rosedale Golf Club, bought the nearly bankrupt restaurant for $2. He transformed it into a lunch spot for Toronto's business elite and later relocated it to 104 Adelaide St. W. By the early 1980s, Winston's was the known as *the* dining establishment for power brokers and the business elite. Winston's reputation and fortunes declined after it was sold in 1989. Winston's Adelaide Street site was ultimately bulldozed.

**Sources:**
http://torontoist.com/2011/08/historicist_winstonswhere_celebrities_meet_to_eat/;
http://www.thestar.com/news/insight/2009/09/05/when_lunch_was_a_boozy_affair_on_the_bosss_tab.html.

**53.** Perrin Beatty (born in 1950) held a number of cabinet posts under Progressive Conservative prime ministers, including: minister of state for the Treasury Board under Joe Clark; minister of national revenue, minister responsible for Canada Post, solicitor general, minister of defence, minister of national health and welfare, and minister of communications under Brian Mulroney; and secretary of state for external affairs under Kim Campbell. He was president and CEO of the Canadian Broadcasting Corp. from 1995 to 1999, of the Canadian Manufacturers and Exporters from 1999 to 2007 and of the Canadian Chamber of Commerce from 2007 to today (2015).

**Sources:**
http://www.thecanadianencyclopedia.ca/en/article/henry-perrin-beatty/
https://en.wikipedia.org/wiki/Perrin_Beatty;
http://www.bloomberg.com/research/stocks/private/person.asp?personId=36409902&privcapId=22687016.

## CHAPTER 18

**54.** Samuel Butler (1835-1902) was an English author, best known for the Utopian satire *Erowhon* and the semi-autobiographical novel *The Way of All Flesh.*

**Sources:**
https://en.wikipedia.org/wiki/Samuel_Butler_%28novelist%29;
http://www.online-literature.com/samuel-butler/.

**55.** In 1987, Prime Minister Brian Mulroney introduced the Meech Lake Accord, an agreement between the federal and provincial governments to amend the Constitution by strengthening provincial powers and recognizing Quebec as a "distinct society." Over the next three years, political support for the accord fell apart, and it was not enacted. In 1992, the Mulroney government and the premiers brought forward a package of constitutional amendments known as the Charlottetown Accord. The accord, which would have decentralized a number of federal powers to the provinces, was rejected by Canadian voters in a national referendum.

**Sources:**
http://www.thecanadianencyclopedia.ca/en/article/meech-lake-accord/;
http://www.histori.ca/peace/page.do?pageID=260;
https://en.wikipedia.org/wiki/Meech_Lake_Accord;
http://www.thecanadianencyclopedia.ca/en/article/the-charlottetown-accord/;
https://en.wikipedia.org/wiki/Charlottetown_Accord.

## CHAPTER 19

**56.** Damocles was a 4th-century BC courtier who, having extolled the greatness of Dionysius, the tyrant of Syracuse, agreed to take the ruler's seat at a banquet. He then saw a sword suspended over his head by a single hair, showing him how precarious Dionysius's fortunes really were.

**Sources:** https://en.wikipedia.org/wiki/Damocles;
http://ancienthistory.about.com/od/ciceroworkslatin/f/DamoclesSword.htm.

## CHAPTER 20

**57.** In 1982 Ralph Klein (1942-2013), then Calgary's mayor, described people moving to the city from eastern Canada looking for work "bums" and "creeps." He urged police to "kick ass" and get unwanted newcomers out of town. "You're welcome to stay here a couple of weeks at government expense, but if you can't make it after that particular time, then don't go out and rob our banks ... get the hell out of town," Klein told CBC News at the time. Many Calgarians, worried about rising crime and homeless rates, supported him. Klein was Calgary's mayor from 1980 to 1989, and went on to become Alberta's premier from 1992 to 2006.

**Sources:** http://www.cbc.ca/news/canada/calgary/5-memorable-ralph-klein-moments-1.1347249; https://en.wikipedia.org/wiki/Ralph_Klein

**58.** The Mackenzie Valley Pipeline Inquiry, also known as the Berger Commission after its head, Justice Thomas Berger, was established by the federal government in1974 to investigate the social, environmental, and economic impact of a proposed gas pipeline that would run through the Yukon and the Mackenzie River Valley of the Northwest Territories; the proposed project became known as the Mackenzie Valley Pipeline. The commission recommended that no pipeline be built through the northern Yukon and that a pipeline through the Mackenzie Valley should be delayed for 10 years.

**Sources:**
http://www.thecanadianencyclopedia.ca/en/article/mackenzie-valley-pipeline/;
https://en.wikipedia.org/wiki/Mackenzie_Valley_Pipeline_Inquiry.

**59.** Li Ka-shing (born in 1928) is a Hong Kong business magnate, investor and philanthropist. In 2015, he was ranked

17th among world billionaires, with a net worth of $26.1 billion, by *Forbes* magazine, which also said he's the richest person in Hong Kong.

**Sources:** http://www.forbes.com/profile/li-ka-shing/; https://en.wikipedia.org/wiki/Li_Ka-shing.

## CHAPTER 21

**60.** Junius was the pseudonym of a writer (identity unknown) who wrote a series of letters, from 1769 to 1772, to the *Public Advertiser*, a London newspaper. Junius discussed elections, freedom of the press, civil liberties and constitutional rights. He also made claims of corruption and nepotism against government officials and was critical of King George III. For years, the *Globe and Mail*'s editorial page has carried this injunction from Junius: "The subject who is truly loyal to the chief magistrate will neither advise nor submit to arbitrary measures."

**Sources:** https://en.wikipedia.org/wiki/Junius; http://speakesto.blogspot.ca/2010/07/1867-in-canada-and-estonia.html; http://www.theglobeandmail.com/globe-debate/editorials/qa-the-new-globe-and-mail/article4327768/?page=all

**61.** During the run-up to the 1983 Conservative leadership convention, both the Joe Clark and Brian Mulroney camps were vying for delegates from Quebec. As there were no age limits for party membership, children as young as nine were reportedly being recruited by the Clark and Mulroney camps to vote for delegates to the convention. And a CBC TV report showed a bus full of apparently intoxicated men from a homeless shelter travelling to Montreal to vote for Mulroney.

**Sources:**
https://en.wikipedia.org/wiki/Progressive_Conservative_leadership_election,_1983#CITEREFMartin.2C_Gregg.2C_Perlin.

(The Wikipedia entry cites the book Contenders: The Tory Quest for Power , by Patrick Martin, Allan Gregg and George Perlin, as a source.)

## CHAPTER 22

**62.** In 1985, the CBC program *the fifth estate* reported that tuna, sold under the names StarKist, Ocean Maid and Bye-the-Sea and produced at the StarKist Canada plant in St. Andrews, N.B., had been released for sale to consumers, even though government inspectors had said it had spoiled so badly that it wasn't fit to be used as cat food. Fisheries and Oceans Minister John Fraser ordered its release, saying an independent test had shown it was edible. However, the lab conducting the test said its testing was not complete when Fraser made his decision. Fraser told Parliament that the tuna posed "no health hazard whatsoever," and that he wanted to give the company "the benefit of the doubt." According to some reports, New Brunswick Premier Richard Hatfield feared that the plant would close and 400 jobs would be lost. (StarKist pulled out of Canada in 1991.) Prime Minister Brian Mulroney ordered the tuna recalled and Fraser resigned. In 1986, he became Speaker of the House of Commons and held the position until his retirement in 1993.

**Sources:**
http://www.cbc.ca/news2/background/cdngovernment/scandals.html;
http://articles.chicagotribune.com/1985-09-24/news/8503040941_1_star-kist-canada-tuna-fisheries-minister-john-fraser;

https://en.wikipedia.org/wiki/Tunagate.

**63.** Suzanne Blais-Grenier, a Quebec Tory MP, was named environment minister when Brian Mulroney came to power in 1984. She was criticized by environmentalists for various program cuts and by Opposition MPs for her travel expenses. In 1985, she was demoted to minister of state for transport. Late that year, she resigned from the cabinet to protest the government's refusal to prevent the closure of a Montreal oil refinery. In 1988, she was expelled from the Tory caucus for refusing to withdraw allegations of kickbacks involving the Quebec wing of the party. She ran as an independent candidate in the November 1988 general election, but was defeated.

**Sources:** https://en.wikipedia.org/wiki/Suzanne_Blais-Grenier; http://www.parl.gc.ca/parlinfo/Files/Parliamentarian.aspx?Item=eb8e4bca-eafc-4b10-8e77-8437fc727c9e&Language=E&Section=ALL

**64.** Lloyd Axworthy (born in 1939) enjoyed a 27-year career as a politician, as a member of the Manitoba legislature from 1973 to 1979 and as a Liberal MP from Winnipeg from 1979 to 2000. Under Prime Minister Pierre Trudeau, he served as minister of employment and immigration, minister responsible for the Status of Women and minister of transport. As a member of the Opposition, he was a prominent critic of Canada's trade negotiations with the United States, as well as serving as the Liberal critic for regional and industrial expansion, the Wheat Board and external affairs. In Prime Minister Jean Chrétien's cabinet, he served as minister of human resources development and minister of external affairs.

**Sources:**
http://www.thecanadianencyclopedia.ca/en/article/lloyd-axworthy/;
https://en.wikipedia.org/wiki/Lloyd_Axworthy.

## CHAPTER 23

**65.** The Triple-E Senate (elected, equal, effective) is a proposal for a Senate that would have more effective powers than the existing Senate and which would consist of elected members equally representing the provinces.

**Sources:** https://en.wikipedia.org/wiki/Triple-E_Senate;
http://mapleleafweb.com/features/senate-reform-canada.

## CHAPTER 24

**66.** Barry Fitzgerald (1888-1961) was an Irish stage, film and television actor who won a Best Supporting Actor Oscar for portraying a Catholic parish priest in the 1944 film *Going My Way*. He is also remembered for playing an Irish village horse-drawn cab driver, bookie and matchmaker in the 1952 movie *The Quiet Man*.

**Sources:** https://en.wikipedia.org/wiki/Barry_Fitzgerald;
http://www.imdb.com/name/nm0280178/bio?ref_=nm_ov_bio_sm.

**67.** A Papal Nuncio is an ecclesiastical diplomat, an envoy of the Vatican to a state or international organization. He also serves as a liaison between the Catholic Church in that country and the Vatican.

**Sources:** https://en.wikipedia.org/wiki/Nuncio;
http://www.newadvent.org/cathen/11160a.htm.

**68.** Bob Edwards (1860-1922), publisher of the *Calgary Eye Opener*, used humour and satire in reporting on local scandals and in working for political change. The causes he championed included giving women the right to vote, Senate reform, and revealing scams by fraudulent real estate developers. Edwards, who battled severe alcoholism, supported the introduction of prohibition in Alberta in 1916.

**Sources:**
http://www.thecanadianencyclopedia.ca/en/article/bob-edwards/;
http://plainshumanities.unl.edu/encyclopedia/doc/egp.med.017;
http://www.albertachampions.org/champions-bob_edwards.htm#.Ve9JOJc3mRM.

**69.** *Cagney and Lacey*, which aired on CBS from 1982 to 1988, centred around two female New York City police detectives. Sharon Gless played Christine Cagney, a single woman, while Tyne Daly played Mary Beth Lacey, a married working mother. For six consecutive years, one of the show's two stars won TV's Emmy Award for best lead actress in a drama. (Daly won four times, while Gless won twice.)

**Source:** https://en.wikipedia.org/wiki/Cagney_%26_Lacey.

## CHAPTER 25

**70.** Dalton Camp (1920-2002) was president of the Progressive Conservative Party of Canada from 1964 to 1969, during which time he was instrumental in bringing about a leadership review that dethroned John Diefenbaker. He worked on a number of leadership campaigns, including those of Robert Stanfield and Brian Mulroney. He was a senior advisor to Mulroney from 1986 to 1989, including consulting on the 1988 election campaign when Mulroney was pressing for a free trade deal with the United States. During the 1980s and 1990s, he was a regular political commentator on the CBC program *Morningside*, and his columns appeared in the *Toronto Star*, *Toronto Sun* and *Saint John Telegraph Journal.*

**Sources:** https://www.friends.ca/DCA/biography; http://www.thecanadianencyclopedia.ca/en/article/dalton-camp/; https://en.wikipedia.org/wiki/Dalton_Camp.

**71.** *The Shirley Show* was a daily afternoon talk show, which ran from 1989 to 1995 on the CTV network. It was hosted by Shirley Solomon.

**Source:** https://en.wikipedia.org/wiki/Shirley_Solomon.

**72.** Jimmy Hoffa (born in 1913, disappeared in 1975) was an American union leader with ties to organized crime. He was president of the International Brotherhood of Teamsters from 1958 to 1971. Hoffa served four years in prison for jury tampering, mail fraud and bribery. In 1971, he was pardoned by President Richard Nixon and resigned from the Teamsters' presidency as part of a release agreement. Hoffa was last seen outside a suburban Detroit restaurant in 1975, and is widely believed to have been murdered. He was declared legally dead in 1982.

**Sources:** https://en.wikipedia.org/wiki/Jimmy_Hoffa; http://content.time.com/time/specials/packages/article/0,28804,1846670_1846800_1846821,00.html; http://www.biography.com/people/jimmy-hoffa-9341063.

**73.** The Wash is a bay and estuary on the east coast of England, where Norfolk meets Lincolnshire, and is fed by the Witham, Welland, Nene and Great Ouse rivers. In 1216, King John's baggage train, which was said to have contained all of the royal treasures, including the crown jewels, was lost amid rising waters of an incoming tide and quicksand.

**Sources:** http://unmyst3.blogspot.ca/2009/07/king-johns-lost-treasure.html; https://en.wikipedia.org/wiki/The_Wash.

**74.** The Reichmann family, the force behind Olympia & York Developments Ltd., sued Toronto *Life* magazine and writer Elaine Dewar for $102 million over a 1988 article about the family's business dealings in Europe and Africa during the Second World War. After three years, there was an out-of-court settlement, and the magazine published an apology to the Reichmanns.

**Sources:** http://www.julianporterqc.com/press/defenders-of-the-pen;
http://rrj.ca/anatomy-of-a-libel/.

**75.** A 1992 *Washington Post* article on libel chill in Canada reported that Ron Beese, then president of Macmillan of Canada, said Macmillan would not publish a book about Hees International Bancorp. Inc., the Bronfman holding company, after receiving a letter from Hees president William L'Heureux complaining that the planned book —the manuscript had not been submitted — by *Globe and Mail* business reporter Kimberley Noble would be "actionable" if published. Beese said that because Macmillan did not have the financial resources to defend itself against possible legal action, he had cancelled Noble's contract.

**Source:**
http://www.washingtonpost.com/archive/lifestyle/1992/03/24/libel-chill-in-canada/c347d7b3-4382-4c00-ac17-b5aacfd2c3b9/.

**76.** J.R. Ewing, played by Larry Hagman, was a villainous character on the CBS TV series *Dallas*, which aired from 1978 to 1991. He was a ruthless oil tycoon, who was philandering, manipulative, amoral, egocentric and engaged in subterfuge.

**Source:** https://en.wikipedia.org/wiki/J._R._Ewing.

**77.** Colin Thatcher (born in 1938) maintained his innocence throughout his trials and appeals. He served 22 years of a 25-

year prison sentence and was paroled in 2006. He has written a book about his case, *Final Appeal: Anatomy of a Frame*, published by ECW Press in 2009.

**Sources:**
http://www.thecanadianencyclopedia.ca/en/article/wilbert-colin-thatcher/;
https://en.wikipedia.org/wiki/Colin_Thatcher.

## CHAPTER 26

**78.** Alexandre-Pierre Georges (Sacha) Guitry (1885-1957) was a French actor, director, screenwriter and playwright. His films include *Confessions of a Cheat*, *Pearls of the Crown*, *La Poison*, *Royal Affairs in Versailles* and *Napoléon*.

**Sources:** http://www.britannica.com/biography/Sacha-Guitry;
https://en.wikipedia.org/wiki/Sacha_Guitry.

**79.** R. Alan Eagleson (born in 1933), a disbarred lawyer, was a prominent figure with the Ontario Progressive Conservative Party, but is probably best known as a one-time hockey kingpin. As a player agent, he negotiated star defenceman Bobby Orr's first contract with the Boston Bruins and ultimately had 150 athlete clients. He was a key figure in arranging matches between European teams and the National Hockey League, notably the 1972 series between Team Canada, consisting of NHL all-stars, and the Soviet Union, and subsequent Canada Cup series. In the early 1990s, he was ousted as executive director of the NHL Players Association and was investigated by the FBI and the RCMP. In 1993, a Boston grand jury indicted him on charges of racketeering, fraud and embezzlement, and in 1996 the RCMP charged him with fraud and theft. In 1998, in Boston, he pleaded guilty to mail fraud and was fined $700,000; in Toronto, he pleaded guilty to fraud and embezzlement, receiving an 18-month prison sentence. Eagleson also resigned from the Hockey Hall of Fame in 1998 when star players such as Orr, Brad Park, Gordie Howe and Bobby Hull threatened to leave if he wasn't removed.

**Sources:**
http://www.thecanadianencyclopedia.ca/en/article/alan-eagleson/;
http://www.hockeycentral.co.uk/nhl/movers/R--Alan-Eagleson.php;
https://en.wikipedia.org/wiki/Alan_Eagleson.

**80.** John Rambo is a Vietnam War veteran and Special Forces soldier, a character played by Sylvester Stallone, and featured in, as of 2015, four movies, beginning with *First Blood* in 1982. *The Canadian Oxford Dictionary* defines a Rambo as "a man given to displays of physical violence or aggression; a macho man."

**Sources:**
https://en.wikipedia.org/wiki/Rambo_%28film_series%29;
http://www.imdb.com/character/ch0005265/bio.

**81.** Calgary's Mount Royal College became Mount Royal University in 2009 after the Alberta legislature passed a bill allowing two public colleges (Mount Royal in Calgary and Grant MacEwen in Edmonton) that offered degrees to call themselves universities.

**Source:**
http://www.liquisearch.com/canadian_universities/alberta.

**82.** Toronto's SkyDome was renamed the Rogers Centre in 2005.

**Source:**
http://toronto.bluejays.mlb.com/tor/ballpark/reference/index.jsp?content=history.

## CHAPTER 27

**83.** *Spycatcher: The Candid Autobiography of a Senior Intelligence* was a book published in 1987 and written by Peter Wright, a former officer and assistant director of MI5, Britain's domestic intelligence service, and co-author Paul Greengrass, who later became a film director with credits such as *The Bourne Supremacy*, *The Bourne Identity*, *United 93* and *Captain Phillips*. The British government tried unsuccessfully to ban the book in the United Kingdom, and Wright was called a traitor for disclosing security service secrets. Among Wright's allegations were that Prime Minister Harold Wilson was the target of an MI5 conspiracy and that an ex-chief of MI5, Roger Hollis, was a Soviet mole in the 1960s.

**Sources:**
http://news.bbc.co.uk/onthisday/hi/dates/stories/october/13/newsid_2532000/2532583.stm;

https://en.wikipedia.org/wiki/Spycatcher.

**84.** Truffles, housed in Toronto's Four Seasons Hotel, closed in 2009 after 37 years of operation. In its heyday, it was considered one of the city's most luxurious dining spots and garnered 14 consecutive Five Diamond awards from the Canadian Automobile Association and the American Automobile Association. Among its star chefs were Jonathan Gushue, Patrick Lin and Lynn Crawford.

**Sources:**
http://www.thestar.com/life/2009/08/28/last_call_for_truffles.html;
http://www.torontolife.com/daily-dish/restaurants-dish/2009/12/02/how-the-mighty-have-fallen-24-more-restaurant-closures/.

**85.** Michael Wilson (born in 1937) was a Bay Street investment executive when he was elected as a Tory MP in 1979. He was minister of state for international trade in Joe Clark's cabinet. He served as minister of finance in Brian Mulroney's cabinet for seven years and subsequently was minister of industry, science and technology and minister of international trade. Wilson served as Canada's ambassador to the United States from 2006 to 2009.

**Sources:**
http://www.thecanadianencyclopedia.ca/en/article/michael-holcombe-wilson/;
https://en.wikipedia.org/wiki/Michael_Wilson_%28Canadian_politician%29.

**86.** William Thorsell (born in 1945) spent 25 years as a newspaper journalist, with stints at the *Edmonton Journal* and the *Globe and Mail*. He was the *Globe*'s editor-in-chief from 1989 to 1999. A year later, he was named director and CEO of the Royal Ontario Museum (ROM) in Toronto. Thorsell retired from his ROM duties in 2010 and went on to become a senior fellow at the Munk School of Global Affairs at the University of Toronto.

**Sources:** https://en.wikipedia.org/wiki/William_Thorsell; http://munkschool.utoronto.ca/profile/william-thorsell/; http://www.rom.on.ca/en/about-us/newsroom/press-releases/william-thorsell-to-retire-in-2010-as-rom-director-ceo.

**87.** Dian Cohen (born in 1932) is an economist, journalist, broadcaster and author. She began her career as a syndicated newspaper and magazine columnist on money matters, and went on to work for both the CBC and CTV. She is the author or co-author of five books on money management, investing, social and government policy issues, as well as having been involved in a number of radio, television, video and print productions. Since 1987, she has been president of DC Productions Limited, her own communications company.

**Sources:**
http://www.uc.utoronto.ca/alumni/alumniofinfluence/dr-dian-cohen;
http://umanitoba.ca/libraries/units/archives/collections/complete_holdings/ead/html/cohen_d.shtml;
http://www.bloomberg.com/research/stocks/people/person.asp?personId=1089881&ticker=NBD:CN.

**88.** Pamela Wallin (born in 1953) is a former television journalist, with CTV as co-host of *Canada AM* and its Ottawa bureau chief, and with CBC as co-host of *Prime Time News*. In 1995, she launched a daily interview show, *Pamela Wallin Live*. Wallin was appointed to a four-year term as Canada's consul general in New York City in 2002 and appointed to the Senate in 2009. In 2013, the Senate suspended her for two years without pay over allegations that she improperly charged the Senate for personal and partisan travel.

**Sources:**
http://www.thecanadianencyclopedia.ca/en/article/pamela-wallin/;
https://en.wikipedia.org/wiki/Pamela_Wallin.

**89.** Gucci is an Italian leather and fashion goods brand. In this case, Mulroney was referring to his shoes.

**Sources:** https://en.wikipedia.org/wiki/Gucci;
http://articles.sun-sentinel.com/1987-04-19/news/8701250298_1_olympic-torch-mulroney-gucci.

**90.** Simon Reisman (1919-2008) held several senior positions in the Canadian civil service, including deputy minister of the finance and industry departments, before retiring in 1975. In

1985, Prime Minister Brian Mulroney chose Reisman to be Canada's chief negotiator in trade talks with the United States.

**Sources:**
http://www.thecanadianencyclopedia.ca/en/article/sol-simon-reisman/;
https://en.wikipedia.org/wiki/Simon_Reisman.

**91.** John Robarts (1917-1982) was the Progressive Conservative premier of Ontario from 1961 to 1971. In 1967, he chaired the Confederation of Tomorrow Conference, and from 1977 to 1979, he was the co-chairman of the Task Force on Canadian Unity.

**Sources:**
http://www.thecanadianencyclopedia.ca/en/article/john-parmenter-robarts/;
https://en.wikipedia.org/wiki/John_Robarts.

## CHAPTER 28

**92.** Petro-Canada, created as a Crown corporation in 1975, had been responsible for implementing the National Energy Program (NEP). Private oil firms argued that publicly funded competition in their industry was destructive, and angry oil men dubbed Petro-Canada's office complex in the middle of downtown Calgary "Red Square," in reference to the Soviet Kremlin.

**Sources:**
http://www.referenceforbusiness.com/history2/85/PETRO-CANADA-LIMITED.html;
https://en.wikipedia.org/wiki/Suncor_Energy_Centre.

## CHAPTER 29

**93.** From June 3 to June 9, 1990, Mulroney met with the 10 premiers in an effort to get unanimous support for the Meech Lake Accord. On June 9, a deal was announced. Then, on

June 11, Mulroney told the *Globe and Mail*: "It's like an election campaign. You've got to work backwards. You've got to pick your dates (sic) and you work backward from it.... I said (to my aides) that's the day that I'm going to roll all the dice. It's the only way to handle it." In his memoirs, Mulroney said his opponents used the remark "to beat me mercilessly for a number of days. The statement is still referred to by some of Meech's fiercest opponents as evidence of skullduggery on my part.... This damaging blunder was mine, no one else's." The accord was not ratified.

**Sources:** http://articles.latimes.com/1990-06-26/news/wr-662_1_meech-lake-accord; http://www.thestar.com/news/politics_blog/2014/03/memories_of_meech_and_dice_rolling_.html; http://probability.ca/jeff/writing/meechart.html.

**94.** The song *When Irish Eyes Are Smiling* — music by Ernest Ball, lyrics by Chauncey Olcott and George Graff Jr. — was published in the United States in 1912. Tin Pan Alley refers to both the New York City-based music publishing business of the late 19th century and early 20th century, and the genre of popular music of that era.

**Sources:**
https://en.wikipedia.org/wiki/When_Irish_Eyes_Are_Smiling;
https://en.wikipedia.org/wiki/Tin_Pan_Alley;
http://www.britannica.com/art/Tin-Pan-Alley-musical-history.

## CHAPTER 30

**95.** Czech-born Robert Maxwell (1923-1991) built up a British publishing empire that included British Printing Corp., Mirror Group Newspapers and Macmillan, Inc. Following his death, reports emerged that Maxwell had used hundreds of millions of pounds from his companies' pension funds to shore up shares of the Mirror Group to stave off bankruptcy. His sons Kevin and Ian failed to keep their father's media empire from collapsing. The pension funds were replenished, but only in part, by investment banks and the British government.

**Sources:** https://en.wikipedia.org/wiki/Robert_Maxwell; http://content.time.com/time/magazine/article/0,9171,156074,00.html; https://www.lovemoney.com/news/4133/the-five-biggest-pension-scandals.

## CHAPTER 31

**96.** In 1939, more than 900 Jewish refugees from Germany aboard the transatlantic liner *St. Louis* were denied entry to Cuba, the United States and Canada, and were forced to return to Europe. Historians estimate that a quarter of the ship's passengers later died in concentration camps.

**Sources:** http://thechronicleherald.ca/novascotia/1174272-canada-turned-away-jewish-refugees; http://www.bbc.com/news/magazine-27373131; https://en.wikipedia.org/wiki/MS_St._Louis.

**97.** Simon Wiesenthal (1908-2005) was a Holocaust survivor who became famous following the Second World War for tracking down and gathering information on fugitive Nazi war criminals. As founder and head of the Jewish Documentation Center in Vienna, he usually worked with the co-operation of the Israeli, Austrian, former West German and other governments, and ferreted out nearly 1,100 Nazi war criminals, including Adolf Eichmann, who was responsible for the mass deportation of Jews to death camps.

**Sources:**
http://www.wiesenthal.com/site/pp.asp?c=lsKWLbPJLnF&b=4441293#.VfGZxJc3mRM;
https://en.wikipedia.org/wiki/Simon_Wiesenthal.

**98.** The Commission of Inquiry on War Criminals, commonly known as the Dechênes Commission, was established in 1985 in response to accusations that Canada had become a haven for Nazi war criminals, including an allegation that the infamous Nazi doctor Joseph Mengele had entered the country. It concluded that hundreds of files concerning alleged war criminals should be closed, because the accused were dead, had never entered Canada (as was the case with Mengele) or the evidence was insufficient. But it urged further investigation of dozens of other files. In 1987, legislation was introduced to allow for the prosecution of Nazi and other war criminals found in the country.

**Sources:**
http://www.thecanadianencyclopedia.ca/en/article/war-crimes/;
http://www.parl.gc.ca/Content/LOP/researchpublications/873-e.htm
https://en.wikipedia.org/wiki/Desch%C3%AAnes_Commission.

**99.** A staff report of the Parliamentary Research Branch of the Library of Parliament on the Dechênes Commission, first published in 1987, observed: "The most emotional aspect of the hearings and public debate outside the hearings seemed to pit the Canadian Jewish community against the Canadian East European and Baltic communities. The latter were afraid that the inquiry would become a witch hunt against their members who had revolted against Soviet tyranny during the war to the point of allying themselves with the Nazis. The question of whether or not the commission should travel to the Soviet Union and other Iron Curtain countries to take evidence caused a bitter controversy throughout the late summer and early fall of 1985. Baltic and Ukrainian groups were completely opposed because, they argued, Soviet-supplied evidence could not be trusted and would be used to attack any individual or ethnic group opposed to the Soviet state. Representatives of Jewish groups argued that there was important evidence in the Soviet Union, both eyewitness and documentary, and that there was no known instance in Europe or North America of the Soviets having provided a false document or a witness who committed perjury." Dechênes decided there was no reason why evidence should not be sought or heard in Soviet Bloc countries, although he set strict conditions to be met by those nations. But, the report said, a satisfactory response was not received from the Soviet Union until June 1986, and Deschênes decided there was insufficient time left for the commission to travel.

**Source:**
http://www.parl.gc.ca/Content/LOP/researchpublications/873-e.htm.

**100.** Websites describe Terry Long as having led the Canadian branch of Aryan Nations in the 1980s and early 1990s, and staging a major rally and cross burning in Provost, Alta. After losing a lawsuit, he dropped out of public view and reportedly fled to British Columbia after a warrant was issued for his arrest for refusing to hand over an Aryan Nations membership list to a human rights tribunal.

**Sources:**
https://en.wikipedia.org/wiki/Terry_Long_%28white_supremacist%29;
http://anti-racistcanada.blogspot.ca/2012/11/terry-long-comes-out-of-seclusion.html;

http://www.jta.org/1990/09/12/archive/neo-nazis-skinheads-in-scuffle-with-jews-press-at-aryan-fest.

**101.** Ron Gostick died of cancer in 2005 at age 87. Meanwhile, Doug Christie, the lawyer who made his reputation defending Holocaust deniers and right-wing extremists, died of metastatic liver disease in 2013 at age 66.

**Sources:** https://en.wikipedia.org/wiki/Ron_Gostick; https://en.wikipedia.org/wiki/Doug_Christie_%28lawyer%29.

## CHAPTER 32

**102.** Trevor Eyton (born in 1934) is a businessman, former lawyer and retired senator. After earning a law degree from the University of Toronto Law School, he joined the law firm of Tory Tory DesLauriers and Binnington (also known as Torys LLP). He left the law firm in 1979 to become president and CEO of Brascan Ltd. (now Brookfield Asset Management Inc.), where he served for 12 years. He was a senator from 1990 to 2009, and now serves as a board member of a number of corporations.

**Sources:**
http://www.bloomberg.com/research/stocks/people/person.asp?personId=1095785&ticker=IVW:CN&previousCapId=&previousTitle=;
https://en.wikipedia.org/wiki/Trevor_Eyton.

**103.** Knowlton Nash (1927-2014) anchored CBC's flagship newscast, *The National*, from 1978 until his retirement in 1988. After serving with British United Press and working as a freelance foreign correspondent, he became the CBC's Washington correspondent when John Kennedy and Lyndon Johnson were in the White House during the 1960s. In 1968, he became head of CBC news and information programming before stepping back in front of the camera for *The National*. He also wrote books about Canadian journalism and television, including his memoirs as a foreign correspondent.

**Sources:**
http://www.thecanadianencyclopedia.ca/en/article/cyril-knowlton-nash/;
https://en.wikipedia.org/wiki/Knowlton_Nash

**104.** Dorothy Parker (1893-1967) was an American poet, short story writer, critic and satirist, renowned for her sharp wit. She was also involved in screenwriting, which garnered her two Academy Award nominations, for *A Star Is Born* (1937) and *Smash-Up: The Story of a Woman* (1947). She was later placed on a Hollywood blacklist for her involvement in left-wing politics.

**Sources:** https://en.wikipedia.org/wiki/Dorothy_Parker;
http://www.imdb.com/name/nm0662213/bio?ref_=nm_ov_bio_sm;
http://www.dorothyparker.com/dpsny.htm.

**105.** William Randolph Hearst (1863-1951) was an American newspaper publisher who built up the largest newspaper chain in the United States and was one of the country's richest and most powerful men. By 1925, Hearst had established or acquired newspapers across the United States, as well as several magazines. He also published fiction and produced motion pictures featuring actress Marion Davies, his mistress for more than 30 years. In the 1920s he built a grandiose castle on a 97,000-hectare ranch near San Simeon, Calif., and he furnished it with a vast collection of antiques and art objects. In 1935, his holdings included 28 major newspapers, 18 magazines, several radio stations, movie companies and news services. But personal extravagances and the Great Depression forced him to sell off or consolidate faltering newspapers. In 1937, he had to start selling off some of his art collection, and by 1940 he had lost control of his media empire. Hearst's life was the basis for the movie *Citizen Kane*.

**Sources:** http://www.britannica.com/biography/William-Randolph-Hearst;
https://en.wikipedia.org/wiki/William_Randolph_Hearst;
http://www.biography.com/people/william-randolph-hearst-9332973;
http://www.history.com/topics/william-randolph-hearst;
http://www.imdb.com/name/nm0372558/bio?ref_=nm_ov_bio_sm.

## CHAPTER 34

**106.** In 1897, in return for a federal subsidy to build a line through the Crow's Nest Pass at the Alberta-B.C. border in the Rockies, the Canadian Pacific Railway (CPR) signed the Crow's Nest Pass Agreement. This route reduced freight rates on grain shipped east to Great Lakes ports and on certain goods shipped west. The agreement was modified in 1925 to reduce rates on grain shipped in both directions. In 1983, the Western Grain Transportation Act allowed shipping rates to increase, but never by more than 10% of the world price for grain. In addition, further cash payments were made by the government to the CPR. Subsidies were eliminated in 1995 through the Western Grain Transition Payment Program, which provided one-time payments to farmers to assist them in moving away from subsidized shipping.

**Sources:**
http://www.thecanadianencyclopedia.ca/en/article/crows-nest-pass-agreement/;
https://en.wikipedia.org/wiki/Crow_Rate.

**107.** Southam Inc. was sold to Hollinger Inc. in 1996. Under Hollinger control, Southam made a number of acquisitions, including many of Thomson Corp.'s Canadian print media holdings. In 2000, Southam was broken up, with print media holdings sold to CanWest. In 2003, CanWest completely absorbed Southam to become CanWest News Service. In 2010, CanWest's newspaper holdings were sold off and became the Postmedia Network.

**Sources:**
http://www.thecanadianencyclopedia.ca/en/article/southam-inc/;
http://www.thecanadianencyclopedia.ca/en/article/canwest-global-communications-corporation-canwest-global/;
https://en.wikipedia.org/wiki/Postmedia_News;
http://www.thecanadianencyclopedia.ca/en/article/postmedia-network-inc/.

## CHAPTER 35

**108.** The organization, founded in 1919 as the Canadian Daily Newspapers Association, was renamed the Canadian Daily Newspaper Publishers Association (CDNPA) in 1954.

**Source:** *A History of Journalism in Canada*, W.H. Kesterton, McLelland and Stewart, 1967,
p. 167 (taken from following source);
https://books.google.ca/books?id=DJaxAwAAQBAJ&pg=PA167&lpg=PA167&dq=kesterton+canadian+daily+newspaper+publishers+association&source=bl&ots=IZ_z3bDBye&sig=Gru2Fg7Gyfc6SWzsd7t9_m_WfNQ&hl=en&sa=X&redir_esc=y#v=onepage&q=kesterton%20canadian%20daily%20newspaper%20publishers%20association&f=false.

## CHAPTER 36

**109.** In 1995, Paul Bernardo was convicted of kidnapping, raping and murdering southern Ontario teenagers, Kristen

French and Leslie Mahaffy, and sentenced to life in prison without the possibility of parole for 25 years. His wife, Karla Homolka, struck a deal with prosecutors and pleaded guilty to manslaughter in the deaths in exchange for a 12-year prison sentence. Videotapes found after the plea bargain had been struck showed Homolka to be a more active participant in the teens' deaths. Homolka was released from prison in 2005.

**Sources:** http://www.cbc.ca/news/canada/key-events-in-the-bernardo-homolka-case-1.933128;
https://en.wikipedia.org/wiki/Paul_Bernardo;
https://en.wikipedia.org/wiki/Karla_Homolka.

**110.** After a highly publicized trial in 1995, Orenthal James (O.J.) Simpson (born in 1947) — once a star National Football League running back, broadcaster and actor —was acquitted of the 1994 murders of his ex-wife, Nicole Brown Simpson, and her friend, Ronald Goldman. In 1997, a California civil court awarded a $33.5-million judgment against Simpson for their wrongful deaths. In 2007, he was arrested in Las Vegas and charged with numerous crimes, including armed robbery and kidnapping. The following year, he was sentenced to 33 years in prison, with no parole possible for at least nine years.

**Sources:** http://www.biography.com/people/oj-simpson-9484729;
http://www.britannica.com/biography/O-J-Simpson;
https://en.wikipedia.org/wiki/O._J._Simpson.

Pat's grave, Mallow, Ireland

Made in the USA
Charleston, SC
23 May 2016